THINK *before* *you* WRITE

A Textbook-Anthology for College English

by William G. Leary and James Steel Smith

CALIFORNIA STATE POLYTECHNIC COLLEGE

HARCOURT, BRACE AND COMPANY *hb* NEW YORK

Contents

II. Testing Your Inferences

REASONING INDUCTIVELY

REASONING DEDUCTIVELY

Contents   v

PART TWO: THE PROBLEM OF COMMUNICATION

I. Understanding the Relation of Language to Thinking

RECOGNIZING WORDS AS SYMBOLS

DEFINING YOUR TERMS

CONTROLLING EMOTIONAL LANGUAGE

II. Understanding the Means and Ends of Propaganda in Mass Communication

Introduction

Present-day approaches to the teaching of Freshman English are many and varied, but in the main they fit one of four general categories: straight composition, composition-reading, composition-speech, and communications. Differences in methods and emphases among these four approaches are rather striking, yet all four have at least one common objective: all are attempting to treat more realistically the language needs of the contemporary Freshman.

Certainly the struggle among the various advocates is interesting and encouraging to all who feel that improvement springs from constant experimentation and periodic re-examination of commonly accepted assumptions. But so far most, if not all, of the controversy about the relative "realism" of these different approaches has revolved around their suitability to the student; there has been too little attention paid to their suitability to the instructor.

At first glance the suggestion that the welfare of the instructor is as important as that of the student seems rash, if not, indeed, impious. Are not teachers, almost by definition, dedicated to the service of their students? Is it not their function to sublimate their own interests in behalf of the students whose formal education has been placed in their hands? Theoretically, perhaps, yes. But any honest and experienced teacher knows that this theoretical ideal is practically unattainable, if not meaningless. A teacher, stereotypes to the contrary notwithstanding, is a human being, and he does what he can. And what he can do is largely conditioned by his abilities, interests, and training.

If we must take our students as we find them (a sensible, pragmatic decision to which the vast majority of English teachers, willingly or unwillingly, subscribe) must we not, if we are to be truly "realistic," also take our teachers as we find them? And what kinds of people do we find them, by and large, to be?

Is it not fair and accurate to say that most college English teachers today are rather highly trained specialists with rather highly specialized interests? These special interests are still largely centered in literature and in language; that is to say, in literary appreciation, in literary history, in literary scholarship, and in philology. None of these special interests is shared by any great number of the general public or even that portion of the general public that finds its way into the Freshman English classroom. Yet Freshman English—one of the few subjects almost universally required of college students—is taught almost exclusively by such specialists or by graduate students who aspire to become such specialists.

This anomaly has never really been faced by the great majority of educators, administrators, or teachers. Yet it should be quite apparent that the interrelationship of specialists and uninterested non-specialists inevitably creates a serious division of interests; it opens between student and instructor a gap that is practically unbridgeable. It is idle to say that the gap ought to be bridged by the enthusiasm the instructor kindles in the student for these special interests. In fact—at least in the compulsory Freshman English course—such a "solution" not only gets us nowhere, it begs the question. For there is ample testimony from thoughtful and eloquent teachers that Freshman English is part of what is now called "General Education," and as such should not be the particular province of the literary specialist.

Nevertheless, we are compelled to return to the stubborn fact that, for the present at least, and for an indeterminate time to come, the teaching of Freshman English in most schools will fall to the lot of this specialist. It is surely unnecessary to review here in detail the unhappy consequences to student and instructor alike. The mutual frustration, boredom, even hostility and cynicism which are all too frequently the product of this unnatural union are evident to any careful observer.

What, then, is the solution to this dilemma? Very possibly the long-range solution will involve a divorcing of the Freshman English course from the rest of the English program and the training of a new group of teachers by new methods and under different auspices to handle this extraordinarily difficult but all-important assignment. But all this will take time. Meanwhile, facing the realities of the present situation, what can we do about it?

For the editors of *Think Before You Write* one solution has been to design a course that more practically meets the needs of *both* the present student and the present instructor. Such a course must seem sufficiently clear and immediately useful to the student to enlist his sympathetic attention, and must seem intellectually sturdy enough to the instructor to insure his wholehearted participation. It must concern itself with basic *problems* whose significance is as readily grasped by the student as by the instructor. It must deal with *ideas* which can be applied by both student and instructor to the exigencies of their everyday lives. And it must utilize a *language* simple enough to be comprehensible to the student and precise enough to avoid offending the trained sensibilities of the instructor. The "subject matter" of such a course—one that seems to us to fulfill the first three of these four requirements—is the examination of the processes of one's own thinking, especially as that thinking is related to language. To meet the fourth requirement, one must, of course, find the right vehicle to convey this subject matter.

The heart of such a course may be found in this book. Although the Table of Contents is enough to indicate to the experienced instructor our purpose, direction, and general method, a few words of explanation are perhaps in order here—more especially since some of the features of the book, notably the Problems, are, we believe, unique. Moreover, the basis for selecting the readings, and the purpose and use of certain editorial apparatus other than the Problems, represent a departure from common practices—a departure, we feel, that Freshman English instructors will find fresh and stimulating.

First a word about the book as a whole. Everything in this book—the readings, the "links" between the readings, the introductions to each main section of readings, and the problems which follow each selection and each main section—is built around and related to certain significant aspects of what one scholar has so well termed "language in thought and action." This, then, is a book of *related* problems. These problems are explicitly spelled out in the headings of the Table of Contents, but they may be paraphrased thus: How do we come by our beliefs? How can we test their validity? What are the pitfalls we must avoid before we can put any confidence in the assumptions on which we base our everyday decisions? What inferences are we entitled to draw from supported assumptions? How do we test an inference, and against what? What role does language play in all this? When is a word a meaningless noise? How can we approach agreement about controversial issues?

How can we protect ourselves from the verbal slings and arrows
that are hurled at us every day from the press, radio, screen, and
rostrum? These are the related problems which endow this book
with an organic structure—the sort of structure that teachers, seeking unity and coherence in a Freshman reader, are frequently compelled to evolve as best they can from more amorphous materials.

In choosing the readings for each section, the editors have been
governed by two primary considerations: (1) Does each selection
contribute to the clarification of the main problem raised by the
whole section? and (2) Does each selection stimulate the student
to apply to his own thinking and use of language (that is, to the
forms which the problem takes within his own experience) the
suggestions advanced by the author? None of the readings is included here as an end in itself; each is a means to an end. Thus
Hayakawa's "The Language of Reports" is not thrown in to give the
student "a dash of semantics," but because it will assist him to distinguish fact from opinion, a skill which he must possess to enable
him to examine his assumptions. Similarly, Koestler's "Babbitts of
the Left" is not offered as a corrective for the political ideology of
certain kinds of "liberals," nor is it designed to provoke for its own
sake one of those endless controversies about politics which succeed
only in wasting an entire class's time in directionless argument.
Instead it is included here because it presents in a remarkably
clear manner concrete illustrations of four major fallacies in deduction that cripple the thinking of people of all political hues—fallacies
that anyone wishing to test his inferences must be able to recognize
and guard against. To cite still another example, the selection by
Silone is not intended to serve here as a model of contemporary
prose fiction but rather to illustrate dramatically the sort of confusion which descends on the heads of people who are unable to
distinguish between a symbol and a reality—a kind of confusion
fatal to the intelligent use of such a symbolic instrument as language.
All this is not to say that the editors have remained indifferent to
considerations of stylistic excellence; they have simply not made
this their primary concern. But, since clarity is the greatest single
virtue sought in any Freshman English course, and since clarity
is the dominant stylistic virtue of all of these selections, the editors
have no apologies to offer on this score.

Just as the readings pose problems, so do the editorial introductions. Hence these transitions concern themselves, not with pat little "definitive" pronouncements about authors and ideas, but with questions designed to tempt, tease, and even torment the student into thinking for himself. Yet these questions are not intended to exasperate; they are intended to clarify. They are suggestive of direction, of relationships, of the underlying unity of the inductive method of approaching and solving problems. But since one avowed purpose of this book is to train the student to think for himself, they remain questions, not answers; suggestions, not prescriptions.

Still, if the student must be stimulated by provocative questions to seek answers for himself, he must also be given specific problems which involve those questions, problems which he is capable of solving. He must, in short, be given the chance to learn a thing by doing it. And so the Problems—the specific Problems which follow each selection, and the General Problems which appear at the end of each section—are in a real sense the core of the book. These represent the editors' principal effort to get the student to grapple with the questions implicit in the whole book, to relate these questions to his own experience, to see, finally, these questions as inevitably *his* questions.

These Problems vary widely in difficulty. They range from the question designed expressly to test the student's comprehension of what he has read (*"Where do Neuberger and Oliver look for clues to explain the conduct of politicians, in the 'nature' of politicians or in the 'conditions' under which they operate?"*) through the question designed to assist the student to see relationships between ideas (*"In what way was the reaction of the immediate supervisors, who did not like to see their men lying asleep, an indication of unscientific thinking? What is the connection between this example of unscientific thinking and the objection of many parents to the informal atmosphere of some modern elementary schoolrooms? the objection of a civic group to spending more money on medical or psychiatric treatment for penitentiary inmates?"*) to the question designed to encourage the student to apply to his own thinking and use of language the questions and the suggestions brought to his attention by the readings (*"What evidence of propaganda on political, economic, educational, or religious questions have you observed in comic strips?"*).

Furthermore, these problems vary greatly in their length. Here a warning is in order. Do not let the length and *seeming* complexity of some of the problems deter you from using them. It is their very specificity that makes them practical, and, paradoxically, easier. They are deliberate attempts to duplicate the way in which the underlying problems of thinking and language come to us in everyday life, not streamlined and neatly packaged, but multi-faced and full of homely detail. Every experienced instructor knows how much better are the results of his assignments if he has taken plenty of time "setting the stage" for them. So here. The time spent in spelling out the problem is ultimately time saved in solving it.

If there is variety in these Problems, there is also unity—a more basic unity, we make bold to assert, than has invested the pages of any Freshman reader we have examined. This is the unity that is the inevitable concomitant of the inductive method of thinking, the kind of unity, superficially so elusive, actually so basic, that has made the pragmatic method of science one of man's best problem-solving instruments. If the editors can be said to have a "cause," it is to encourage the application of this scientific method of thinking in those areas where it has, so far, been used sparingly.

Anyone who develops a taste for the kinds of Problems found here will have many of his own to add to ours. We will take it as a great kindness if instructors and students will submit to us their own favorites as well as any criticisms of those problems which, for one reason or another, do not quite "come off."

No book can be all things to all men, and *Think Before You Write* is no exception. Yet the editors feel that they have devised a more than usually flexible instrument for use in Freshman English programs. For instance, the materials assembled here are adaptable to either a one- or two-semester course. If explored intensively, the readings and problems are sufficient for a full-year program; if selected with care, they can be covered in a half-year program. Similarly, the book can rather easily be adapted to any one of the four main approaches to Freshman English mentioned earlier. Although nominally aimed at courses which emphasize reading and writing, for the very practical reason that most Freshman English courses at present are so designed, the greater bulk of the materials, especially the Problems, are adaptable to a number of uses: as starting points for class discussions, as bases for oral as well as written composition, as questions for group oral discussions by panels, as materials for the longer, investigative paper, as experiments in critical listening.

It is for these several reasons, then—its essential practicality, its organic unity, its flexibility—that the editors offer *Think Before You Write* as one way to meet the needs of the *present* student and the *present* instructor, as one means to close that gap between them which imperils the very existence of the Freshman English course as a significant experience in the life of the college Freshman or of his instructor.

The editors are not so fond of their product as to imagine that the course and method outlined in this book constitute *the* answer. They are confident, however, on the basis of their own personal experience and the experience of most of their students and several of their co-workers (the book has been tested in mimeographed form in the classroom for nearly two years) that this volume does constitute *one possible* answer. They rest their case on such specific manifestations of changed behavior as the markedly increased enthusiasm of both students and instructors who substituted for other methods and materials those offered here; the perceptible shift in the thinking of students away from rigidity, dogmatism, sentimentality, and superficiality toward greater flexibility, tolerance, fact-mindedness, and scientific caution; the spontaneous application by students of the ideas, methods, and skills promoted in the classroom to extracurricular activities; and, finally, a demonstrable increase in interest in language as a social instrument, leading to modest but very solid gains in its correct and effective use.

PART ONE

The Problem of Straight Thinking

1. EXAMINING YOUR ASSUMPTIONS

Testing Your Own Beliefs

"NOW look here, son, your mother and I have slaved for years to give you the chance we didn't have. Not that we begrudge it to you, boy. But don't come around telling me you're fed up with college. Why, man alive, if I'd had your chance, do you think I'd be working with my hands now? Now go back there next semester and settle down. Just show those profs what kind of lawyers we grow out here in the wheatfields. And don't ever again bring that hurt look into your mother's eyes by saying you're not suited for college."

"So you really think you can determine what your boy will be by putting him in a room full of objects and letting his choice indicate the career he'll follow?"

"Yes. Don't you see, if he chooses the toy bank, he'll become a banker; if he chooses the electric train, he'll become a railroad man; if he chooses the book, he'll become a scholar, and so forth."

"But what if he grabs them all?"

"That's easy. Then he'll become a politician!"

"I know Jerry's a swell fellow and all that, but you and I can't buck the committee. Besides, if we let down the bars for Jerry, all the rest of them would be trying to push in here. Don't get me wrong. I've got nothing against ——s so long as they keep their place."

"It's as simple as ABC. A tiger doesn't change his stripes, a leopard doesn't change his spots, and a man doesn't ever forget to look out for Number One. Nature made them what they are, and nothing you or I say is going to change them."

Expressions of popular beliefs? Yes. Of groundless beliefs? Maybe. At least six writers represented in the selections that follow—Alcaro, Neuberger, Oliver, McWilliams, Dunham, and Mirsky—think so; and before you're through reading what *they* have to say, *you* may be a little less sure of some of these beliefs.

But these selections are not put here primarily to shake your beliefs. Rather they are here to serve as suggestive examples of curious, inquiring minds at work. And just what is an inquiring mind? Well, it's more than just "being from Missouri" and having to be shown, although it's that, too. The man with an inquiring mind wants to know *how* he came by his beliefs. He wants to know their bases—their "grounds." More than that, he wants to see *all* sides of a question. He wants to *test* his beliefs.

The first two writers in this section set the stage for any inquiry into a specific belief—Mander by showing us how we come to hold many of our beliefs, Mill by showing us how important it is to test our beliefs.

Much wisdom is frequently contained in a paradox. After you have read Mander and Mill, you will understand what Thomas Henry Huxley meant when he said, "Irrationally held truths may be more harmful than reasoned errors."

But you don't have to believe this . . . yet.

A. E. Mander

Do you think for yourself? Are you sure you do? What do you believe "thinking for yourself" involves? What constitutes adequate "grounds for belief"? What "grounds" do you have for beliefs you hold with intense conviction or accept without question? Can a man say they are *his* if he has not examined the facts and reasoning on which they may—or may not—be based?

These are just some of the blunt, embarrassing questions Mander, an English psychologist, asks in the following excerpt from his book, *Logic for the Millions*.

GROUNDLESS BELIEFS *

In future we are going to follow the practice—until it becomes a habit ("second nature")—of classifying propositions according to their grounds. Of every statement we come across, we shall ask: "HOW DO WE KNOW THAT? WHAT REASON HAVE WE FOR BELIEVING THAT? ON WHAT 'GROUNDS' IS THAT STATEMENT BASED?" Probably we shall be astonished at the number of propositions met with in everyday life—propositions usually accepted blindly, without question, as a matter of course—which we shall find it necessary to class as groundless. They rest upon mere tradition, or on somebody's bare assertion unsupported by even a shadow of proof. . . .

It may be a belief which we originally accepted as a result of simple "suggestion," and we have continued to hold it ever since. It has now become one of our regular habits of thought. *Perhaps somebody—somewhere—sometime—told us a certain thing, and quite uncritically we accepted and believed it. Perhaps it was away back in our early childhood—before we had even developed the power of questioning anything that might be told to us.* Many of our strongest convictions were established then; and now, in adult life, we find it most difficult even to question their truth. They seem to us "obviously" true: we feel that even to question them would be "absurd."

But if the staunchest Roman Catholic and the staunchest Presbyterian had been exchanged when infants, and if they had been brought up with home and all other influences reversed, we can have very little doubt what the result would have been. It is consistent with all our knowledge of psychology to conclude that each would have grown up holding exactly the opposite beliefs to those he holds now . . . and each would then have felt as sure of the truth of his opinion as he now feels—of the truth of the opposite opinion. The same thing is true, of course, of many beliefs other than those of a religious nature. If we had grown up in a community where polygamy or head-hunting, or infanticide, or gladiatorial fighting, or duelling, was regarded as the normal and natural

---

* A. E. Mander, *Logic for the Millions,* The Philosophical Library, New York, 1947.

thing—then we should have grown up to regard it as "obviously" natural and perfectly moral and proper. If we had been bred by criminals amongst criminals in one of those quarters of a great city where criminals dwell—then we should have grown up with a set of moral standards quite different from those we have. Or if an English baby had been adopted and brought up in a German home, and had grown up with no knowledge that his parents were English, all the sentiments and beliefs of that person would be "German" and not "English." Many of our beliefs—many of our most deeply-rooted and fundamental convictions—are held simply as a result of the fact that we happen to have been "brought up" to them.

Of course we do not cease, when we cease to be children, to adopt new beliefs on mere suggestion. We continue doing it, more or less unconsciously all our lives: hence, to take only the most striking examples, the enormous influence of newspapers and the effectiveness of skilful advertising. *Much of what passes as such is not, strictly, thinking at all. It is the mere "parroting" of ideas picked up by chance and adopted as our own without question. Most people, most of the time, are mere parrots.* But as we leave childhood, we tend to accept only such new ideas as fit in with the ideas we already hold; and all conflicting ideas seem to us "obviously" absurd.

Propositions that are accepted simply because "everybody says so," must be classed under the same heading. The dogma may not be that of any particular individual: it may be a dogmatic statement which has been passed from one person to another, from generation to generation, perhaps for hundreds—perhaps for thousands —of years. It may be part of the traditional belief of the people or the race. In that case, it is part of our social inheritance from some period in the past. But we should fully face the fact (already stated) that beliefs which are merely inherited from the past must have originated at a time when men knew much less than they know today. So the fact that a belief is "old" is no argument in its favour.

We need especially to be on our guard when we come across propositions which seem to be "obviously" true—so obviously that it seems impossible to doubt them.

When we find ourselves entertaining an opinion about which there is
a feeling that *even to enquire into it* would be *absurd, unnecessary, undesirable,* or *wicked*—we may know that that opinion is a non-rational
one.   —TROTTER

When we are tempted to say that any general truth is so "obvious" that it would be absurd even to question it, we should remember that the whole history of the development of human
thought has been full of cases of such "obvious truths" breaking
down when examined in the light of increasing knowledge and
reason. For instance, for ages nothing could have seemed more
obvious, more utterly beyond question, than the proposition that
slavery was natural, reasonable, necessary, and right. Some kinds
of men were "obviously" "slaves by nature." To doubt it was impossible.

Again, for more than two thousand years, it was "impossible to
conceive" the planets as moving in paths other than circles. The
circle was "obviously" the perfect figure; and so it was "natural"
and "inevitable" to suppose that the planets moved in circles. The
age-long struggle of the greatest intellects in the world to shake
off that assumption is one of the marvels of history.

It was formerly "obvious" that the heart—and not the brain—was
the organ of consciousness. To most people today (even apart from
proof) it seems equally "obvious" that we think with our brains.
Many modern persons find it very difficult to credit the fact that
men can ever have supposed otherwise. Yet—they did. And, what
is more, the "truth" that we think with our hearts seemed to them
so "obvious" that it was absolutely impossible for them to doubt it.

That the earth must be flat, formerly seemed so obvious and self-
evident that the very suggestion of any other possibility would have
been—and was—regarded as a joke.

It was for two thousand years "taken for granted" as "obvious"
that a heavy weight must fall faster than a light one. An assumed
or dogmatic proposition which had been universally accepted as
"obvious"; and which, when challenged, was supported by reference
to a dogma of Aristotle. Until Galileo actually demonstrated the
contrary, nothing could have seemed more beyond possibility or
doubt.

Propositions which are accepted blindly, without question, on the grounds of mere assumption or dogma, need to be frankly recognized as such. Progress in human thought seems to consist mainly in getting rid of such ideas.

Other beliefs are held through self-interest. Modern psychology leaves us no room for doubt on this point. We adopt and cling to some beliefs because—or partly because—it "pays" us to do so. But, as a rule, the person concerned is about the last person in the world to be able to recognize this in himself. Indeed, he would probably be highly indignant if told of what anyone familiar with modern psychology can recognize so plainly. It would be quite wrong to attribute all opinions—even political opinions—to self-interest. But it would be equally wrong to deny that this is one potent factor.

"Self-interest" is to be understood first in the ordinary sense, as referring to a man's way of earning his livelihood and acquiring wealth. But we may extend the term to cover also his interest in social position; popularity with his fellows (at least his own "set"); the respect and goodwill of those whose respect and goodwill he values; agreeable associations with the people of a particular party, church, or social set, from which he would be excluded if his opinions were changed. It covers his interest in his own career; in whatever prestige he enjoys as one of the leaders—or at least as a valued supporter—of some movement or institution, some political party, some religious body, some other kind of society or group. There is many a man who is unconsciously compelled to cling to a belief because he is a "somebody" in some circle—and if he were to abandon that belief, he would find himself nobody at all.

Putting it broadly, we should always suspect any of our opinions when we recognize that our happiness depends, directly or indirectly, upon our continuing to hold them—when we might lose anything, material or otherwise, by changing our opinion.

Somewhat similar is the acceptance of an opinion through the desire—probably not recognized by the person concerned—to justify his own nature, his own position, or his own behaviour. The coward can so easily adopt a philosophy which seems to justify cowardice—though, of course, "cowardice" is not the name he gives it! The lazy and bungling person can adopt a set of opinions which prove to his satisfaction that "the grapes are sour"—the "grapes" being the rewards that more energetic and competent men can win. And many a preacher and propagandist is like the fox that lost his tail. (There is much wisdom in Aesop!)

Many groundless opinions are held through sentimental associations. The thought is associated with memories—pleasant or unpleasant as the case may be—of particular persons who held similar opinions. It is found that many a man who in childhood was hostile to his father, in after life is always prejudiced against whatever opinions his father used to express. And conversely in the case of one who has pleasant recollections of his father, his mother, a teacher perhaps, or some other person who played a big part in his early life.

In adult life, as we have often observed, a bitter quarrel may change a man's opinion entirely. Antagonism to a man usually produces some antagonism to his opinions; and the bitterness felt against the man usually spreads to the idea for which he stands. What keen satisfaction we find in belittling the opinions, or attacking the opinions, of somebody of whom we are jealous, or of somebody against whom we bear a grudge! But, on the other hand, it is equally true that friendly feelings to a man have an effect in disposing us to feel friendly to his views.

Other opinions again are determined by what we may best call Fashion. To take one example: how largely our opinions on the merits of certain authors, or poets, or composers, are dictated merely by fashion! But the effect of fashion is very much wider than that: we trace it almost everywhere, in every field of thought. *We tend very strongly to feel and to believe as others are feeling and believing. Not all others, perhaps; but others of our own set.*

But we do not, as a rule, continue all our lives changing our sentiments and opinions with every change of fashion. Sooner or later our minds become fixed. Many a man holds his opinions today—because they happened to be in fashion ten, twenty, thirty, forty, or fifty years ago.

Once an opinion is accepted, whatever be the cause of its acceptance, it has a strong tendency to persist. Every time we think along a particular thought-pattern, makes it easier for us to think the same way again. It is quite legitimate to speak of "habits" of thought. The "brain path" becomes so well worn; the pattern of brain-centres becomes so well connected up by continual use, that the nerve current finds a route of practically no resistance, and so it always takes almost exactly the same course.

We all know the person who has a string of stock anecdotes. We all know too the person who has certain stock arguments and opinions which he expresses, almost in the same words, whenever he receives the "cue." We all know men and women whose minds work like gramophones. Put them on to the "record" about the good old days; or about prohibition; or about the wicked capitalists; or about the lazy and improvident workers; or about their illnesses (the tale of their troubles and the number of operations they have undergone); or about some holiday they once spent; or about the country going to the dogs; or about the modern girl; or some long, tedious anecdote about what I said to him, and what he said to me, and I said . . . and he said . . . *and then I told him straight . . . !* All we have to do is to start him off—and nothing on earth can stop him—until the "record" has run out!

The same thing is true of opinions and beliefs of all kinds. After they have been held a certain length of time, they become, as it were, so stamped in by continual use that it is almost impossible now to change them. While we are young, we are continually taking in new ideas, altering our thought-patterns, "making up our minds" afresh. As we grow older, we become less and less able to accept any new idea which will not fit in with our existing thought-pattern. Thus we become, in James's term, Old Fogeys. Sometimes our thought-patterns set while we are still quite young. In a few rare cases they remain open or alterable even into old age. An Old Fogey may have become such at seventeen—or seventy. We are Old Fogeys from the moment when we become unable to accept any new fact, any new idea, which would necessitate changing our established habits of thought. "I am almost afraid to say so (says James), but I believe that in the majority of human beings Old Fogeyism begins at about the age of twenty-five."

Yet when full allowance has been made for all these non-rational factors in the determination of opinion, there remains—not in all minds, not in most minds, but in some—a desire to discover the facts; to think things out in a clear and rational way; to get at the truth at all costs, whatever it may turn out to be! For such minds this . . . is written.

PROBLEMS

1. Mander lists *six* sources for many of our groundless beliefs. To test your understanding of the nature of these sources and the kinds of beliefs which stem from them, provide as many examples of such beliefs as you can. To assist you in getting a start, the six sources, with two examples for each, are listed below.

   a. Result of early environment ("thought habits")
   > (1) The —— race (one's own) is mentally superior to all other races.
   >
   > (2) My town (or country) is a more desirable place to live in than ——.

   b. Parroting (Note: These conform pretty largely to pre-established "thought habits.")
   > (1) Childhood is the happiest time of your life.
   >
   > (2) Every self-respecting young man should go to college.

   c. Everybody says so
   > (1) Politicians can't be trusted.
   >
   > (2) After all, the simple pleasures are best.

   d. Self-interest (It pays to think that way, 1 and 2; justifying one's own belief or conduct, 3 and 4)
   > (1) Remove rent controls, and the housing shortage will solve itself.
   >
   > (2) Support high tariffs and protect our standard of living.
   >
   > (3) People could be as rich as I if they only had my initiative.
   >
   > (4) The —— (fill in with name of unpopular minority group) are naturally a carefree, idle people who like to live the way they do.

   e. Sentimental associations (pleasant and unpleasant)
   > (1) I wouldn't trade Brooklyn for any place in the world.
   >
   > (2) Don't ever marry a salesman; you'll be sorry if you do.

   f. Fashion (your own "set")
   > (1) Jazz is not art. (Symphonic music is dull.)
   >
   > (2) The book-of-the-month clubs provide excellent entertainment. (The book-of-the-month clubs are vulgar, commercial schemes to sell third-rate books.)

2. It is important to be able to recognize the "earmarks" of a groundless belief—in order to detect one *we* hold. What are some of these "earmarks"?

3. Survey the steps by which you arrived at any of the following beliefs which you may hold at present; then determine on what *grounds,* if any, you originally based your beliefs.

   a. A certain course, in which you have not been personally enrolled, is *difficult* or *easy.*

   b. A black cat crossing one's path, or any other particular occurrence or practice, is *lucky* or *unlucky.*

   c. Cheating, or some other particular kind of behavior, is morally wrong.

   d. College will help one get a job—or will "broaden" a person or "give him some culture."

   e. Stupidity, selfishness, valor, fear, or some other characteristic is a "natural," inborn, human trait.

4. As Mander suggests, many questions about physics, biology, morals, literature, etc., were once settled by simply referring to "a dogma of Aristotle." Do you know of any men whose mere word, no matter what it is about, is used today by large numbers of people as complete and final proof of the rightness of a notion? (What about, for example, statements by Gandhi, Franklin D. Roosevelt, Stalin, and Churchill?) Now, then, why is the fact that a man has proved himself wise and skillful with one type of problem *not* a sound reason for taking his word again, without examining his *grounds* for belief, on some other type of question? For example, why was it illogical for many people to give *special* attention to the anti-Semitic views of Henry Ford, a master of machine mass production? to the attitudes of Lindbergh, a great aviator and aviation engineer, on racial superiority? to the great physicist Einstein on the ways to bring about world peace? to the pronouncements of Franklin D. Roosevelt and Harry Truman on good and bad painting?

5. In what ways could self-interest, expressed in terms of economic benefits, reputation, or self-satisfaction, be a motive for an individual's holding any of the following beliefs without any *factual grounds,* or even in spite of the facts?

   a. My girl is beautiful (or intelligent).

   b. We Americans (Germans, Italians, British, etc.) are superior in intelligence and courage to the other peoples of the earth.

   c. Slavery is natural.

   d. Survival belongs to the most powerful; "only the fittest survive."

   e. A sucker is born every minute.

   f. Thrift is one of the highest moral virtues.

   g. The "classics" are the heart of any worth-while education; or, the only *real* education is training in technical skills.

6. Mander is highly critical of correct or incorrect beliefs held because the believer considers it to be in his interest to hold them. How may such a belief work against the holder's interest? For example, how may a man's groundless belief in his own ability to handle a problem in a certain way prevent his seeing the situation clearly and perhaps attacking it more effectively?

John Stuart Mill

The following selection is mainly concerned, not with the *justice* or *morality* of suppressing "the other side" of an issue, but with these fundamental questions: Can we really *understand* one side if we don't know the other side or sides? Can we *use* an idea which we do not fully understand?

John Stuart Mill (1806-1873), who had become a magazine editor by the time he had reached his early twenties, was a leading advocate of utilitarianism, a philosophy whose main tenet was that the basic value of thought and action lies in their usefulness as contributions to man's happiness. Mill wrote many books in support of free speech and press, women's rights, free economic enterprise, and, later in life, of government control in some economic fields. His *Autobiography* is the frank, moving record of an honest, highly intelligent man's attempt to investigate himself.

HOW DO WE KNOW WHAT WE BELIEVE? *

There is a class of persons (happily not quite so numerous as formerly) who think it enough if a person assents undoubtingly to what they think true, though he has no knowledge whatever of the grounds of the opinion, and could not make a tenable defence of it against the most superficial objections. Such persons, if they can once get their creed taught from authority, naturally think that no good, and some harm, comes of its being allowed to be questioned. Where their influence prevails, they make it nearly impossible for the received opinion to be rejected wisely and considerately, though it may still be rejected rashly and ignorantly; for to

* From John Stuart Mill, *On Liberty*.

shut out discussion entirely is seldom possible, and when it once gets in, beliefs not grounded on conviction are apt to give way before the slightest semblance of an argument. Waiving, however, this possibility—assuming that the true opinion abides in the mind, but abides as a prejudice, a belief independent of, and proof against, argument—this is not the way in which truth ought to be held by a rational being. This is not knowing the truth. Truth, thus held, is but one superstition the more, accidentally clinging to the words which enunciate a truth.

If the intellect and judgment of mankind ought to be cultivated . . . on what can these faculties be more appropriately exercised by any one, than on the things which concern him so much that it is considered necessary for him to hold opinions on them? If the cultivation of the understanding consists in one thing more than in another, it is surely in learning the grounds of one's own opinions. Whatever people believe, on subjects on which it is of the first importance to believe rightly, they ought to be able to defend against at least the common objections. But, some one may say, "Let them be *taught* the grounds of their opinions. It does not follow that opinions must be merely parroted because they are never heard controverted. Persons who learn geometry do not simply commit the theorems to memory, but understand and learn likewise the demonstrations; and it would be absurd to say that they remain ignorant of the grounds of geometrical truths, because they never hear any one deny, and attempt to disprove them." Undoubtedly: and such teaching suffices on a subject like mathematics, where there is nothing at all to be said on the wrong side of the question. The peculiarity of the evidence of mathematical truths is, that all the argument is on one side. There are no objections, and no answers to objections. But on every subject on which difference of opinion is possible, the truth depends on a balance to be struck between two sets of conflicting reasons. Even in natural philosophy, there is always some other explanation possible of the same facts; some geocentric theory instead of heliocentric, some phlogiston instead of oxygen; and it has to be shown why that other theory cannot be the true one: and until this is shown and until we know how it is shown, we do not understand the grounds of our opinion. But when we turn to subjects infinitely more complicated, to morals, . religion, politics, social relations, and the business of life, three-fourths of the arguments for every disputed opinion consist in dispelling the appearances which favor some opinion different from it. The greatest orator, save one, of antiquity, has left it on record that he always studied his adversary's case with as great, if not with still greater, intensity than even his own. What Cicero practised as the means of forensic success, requires to be imitated by all who study any subject in order to arrive at the truth. He who knows only his own side of the case, knows little of that. His reasons may be good, and no one may have been able to refute them. But if he is equally unable to refute the reasons on the opposite side; if he does not so much as know what they are, he has no ground for preferring either opinion. The rational position for him would be suspension of judgment, and unless he contents himself with that, he is either led by authority, or adopts, like the generality of the world, the side to which he feels most inclination. Nor is it enough that he should hear the arguments of adversaries from his own teachers, presented, as they state them, and accompanied by what they offer as refutations. This is not the way to do justice to the arguments, or bring them into real contact with his own mind. He must be able to hear them from persons who actually believe them; who defend them in earnest, and do their very utmost for them. He must know them in their most plausible and persuasive form; he must feel the whole force of the difficulty which the true view of the subject has to encounter and dispose of, else he will never really possess himself of the portion of truth which meets and removes that difficulty. Ninety-nine in a hundred of what are called educated men are in this condition, even of those who can argue fluently for their opinions. Their conclusion may be true, but it might be false for anything they know: they have never thrown themselves into the mental position of those who think differently from them, and considered what such persons may have to say; and consequently they do not, in any proper sense of the word, know the doctrine which they themselves profess. They do not know those parts of it which explain and justify the remainder; the considerations which show that a fact which seemingly conflicts with another is reconcilable with it, or that, of two apparently strong reasons, one and not the other ought to be preferred. All that part of the truth which turns the scale, and decides the judgment of a completely informed mind, they are strangers to;

nor is it ever really known, but to those who have attended equally and impartially to both sides, and endeavored to see the reasons of both in the strongest light. So essential is this discipline to a real understanding of moral and human subjects, that if opponents of all important truths do not exist, it is indispensable to imagine them and supply them with the strongest arguments which the most skilful devil's advocate can conjure up.

To abate the force of these considerations, an enemy of free discussion may be supposed to say, that there is no necessity for mankind in general to know and understand all that can be said against or for their opinions by philosophers and theologians. That it is not needful for common men to be able to expose all the misstatements or fallacies of an ingenious opponent. That it is enough if there is always somebody capable of answering them, so that nothing likely to mislead uninstructed persons remains unrefuted. That simple minds, having been taught the obvious grounds of the truths inculcated on them, may trust to authority for the rest, and being aware that they have neither knowledge nor talent to resolve every difficulty which can be raised, may repose in the assurance that all those which have been raised have been or can be answered, by those who are specially trained to the task.

Conceding to this view of the subject the utmost that can be claimed for it by those most easily satisfied with the amount of understanding of truth which ought to accompany the belief of it; even so, the argument for free discussion is no way weakened. For even this doctrine acknowledges that mankind ought to have a rational assurance that all objections have been satisfactorily answered; and how are they to be answered if that which requires to be answered is not spoken? or how can the answer be known to be satisfactory, if the objectors have no opportunity of showing that it is unsatisfactory? If not the public, at least the philosophers and theologians who are to resolve the difficulties, must make themselves familiar with those difficulties in their most puzzling form; and this cannot be accomplished unless they are freely stated, and placed in the most advantageous light which they admit of. . . .

If, however, the mischievous operation of the absence of free discussion, when the received opinions are true, were confined to leaving men ignorant of the grounds of those opinions, it might be thought that this, if an intellectual, is no moral evil, and does not affect the worth of the opinions, regarded in their influence on the character. The fact, however, is, that not only the grounds of the opinion are forgotten in the absence of discussion, but too often the meaning of the opinion itself. The words which convey it, cease to suggest ideas, or suggest only a small portion of those they were originally employed to communicate. Instead of a vivid conception and a living belief, there remain only a few phrases retained by rote; or, if any part, the shell and husk only of the meaning is retained, the finer essence being lost. The great chapter in human history which this fact occupies and fills, cannot be too earnestly studied and meditated on.

It is illustrated in the experience of almost all ethical doctrines and religious creeds. They are all full of meaning and vitality to those who originate them, and to the direct disciples of the originators. Their meaning continues to be felt in undiminished strength, and is perhaps brought out into even fuller consciousness, so long as the struggle lasts to give the doctrine or creed an ascendency over other creeds. At last it either prevails, and becomes the general opinion, or its progress stops; it keeps possession of the ground it has gained, but ceases to spread further. When either of these results has become apparent, controversy on the subject flags, and gradually dies away. The doctrine has taken its place, if not as a received opinion, as one of the admitted sects or divisions of opinion: those who hold it have generally inherited, not adopted it; and conversion from one of these doctrines to another, being now an exceptional fact, occupies little place in the thoughts of their professors. Instead of being, as at first, constantly on the alert either to defend themselves against the world, or to bring the world over to them, they have subsided into acquiescence, and neither listen, when they can help it, to arguments against their creed, nor trouble dissentients (if there be such) with arguments in its favor. From this time may usually be dated the decline in the living power of the doctrine. . . .

[This] holds true, generally speaking, of all traditional doctrines— those of prudence and knowledge of life, as well as of morals or religion. All languages and literatures are full of general observations on life, both as to what it is, and how to conduct oneself in it; observations which everybody knows, which everybody repeats, or hears with acquiescence, which are received as truisms, yet of which most people first truly learn the meaning, when experience, generally of a painful kind, has made it a reality to them. How often, when smarting under some unforeseen misfortune or disappointment, does a person call to mind some proverb or common saying familiar to him all his life, the meaning of which, if he had ever before felt it as he does now, would have saved him from the calamity. There are indeed reasons for this, other than the absence of discussion: there are many truths of which the full meaning *cannot* be realized, until personal experience has brought it home. But much more of the meaning even of these would have been understood, and what was understood would have been far more deeply impressed on the mind, if the man had been accustomed to hear it argued *pro* and *con* by people who did understand it. The fatal tendency of mankind to leave off thinking about a thing when it is no longer doubtful is the cause of half their errors. A contemporary author has well spoken of "the deep slumber of a decided opinion."

But what! (it may be asked) Is the absence of unanimity an indispensable condition of true knowledge? Is it necessary that some part of mankind should persist in error, to enable any to realize the truth? Does a belief cease to be real and vital as soon as it is generally received—and is a proposition never thoroughly understood and felt unless some doubt of it remains? As soon as mankind have unanimously accepted a truth, does the truth perish within them? The highest aim and best result of improved intelligence, it has hitherto been thought, is to unite mankind more and more in the acknowledgment of all important truths: and does the intelligence only last as long as it has not achieved its object? Do the fruits of conquest perish by the very completeness of the victory?

I affirm no such thing. As mankind improve, the number of doctrines which are no longer disputed or doubted will be constantly on the increase: and the well-being of mankind may almost be measured by the number and gravity of the truths which have reached the point of being uncontested. The cessation, on one question after another, of serious controversy, is one of the necessary incidents of the consolidation of opinion; a consolidation as salutary in the case of true opinions, as it is dangerous and noxious when the opinions are erroneous. But though this gradual narrowing of the bounds of diversity of opinion is necessary in both senses of the term, being at once inevitable and indispensable, we are not therefore obliged to conclude that all its consequences must be beneficial. The loss of so important an aid to the intelligent and living apprehension of a truth, as is afforded by the necessity of explaining it to, or defending it against, opponents, though not sufficient to outweigh, is no trifling drawback from, the benefit of its universal recognition. Where this advantage can no longer be had, I confess I should like to see the teachers of mankind endeavoring to provide a substitute for it; some contrivance for making the difficulties of the question as present to the learner's consciousness, as if they were pressed upon him by a dissentient champion, eager for his conversion.

But instead of seeking contrivances for this purpose, they have lost those they formerly had. The Socratic dialectics, so magnificently exemplified in the dialogues of Plato, were a contrivance of this description. They were essentially a negative discussion of the great questions of philosophy and life, directed with consummate skill to the purpose of convincing any one who had merely adopted the commonplaces of received opinion, that he did not understand the subject—that he as yet attached no definite meaning to the doctrines he professed; in order that, becoming aware of his ignorance, he might be put in the way to attain a stable belief, resting on a clear apprehension both of the meaning of doctrines and of their evidence. The school disputations of the Middle Ages had a somewhat similar object. They were intended to make sure that the pupil understood his own opinion, and (by necessary correlation) the opinion opposed to it, and could enforce the grounds of the one and confute those of the other. These last-mentioned contests had indeed the incurable defect, that the premises appealed to were taken from authority, not from reason; and, as a discipline to the mind, they were in every respect inferior to the powerful dialectics which formed the intellects of the "Socratici viri": but the modern mind owes far more to both than it is generally willing to admit, and the present modes of education contain nothing which in the smallest degree supplies the place either of the one or of the other. A person who derives all his instruction from teachers or books, even if he escape the besetting temptation of contenting himself with cram, is under no compulsion to hear both sides; accordingly it is far from a frequent accomplishment, even among thinkers, to know both sides; and the weakest part of what everybody says in defence of his opinion, is what he intends as a reply to antagonists. It is the fashion of the present time to disparage negative logic—that which points out weaknesses in theory or errors in practise, without establishing positive truths. Such negative criticism would indeed be poor enough as an ultimate result; but as a means to attaining any positive knowledge or conviction worthy the name, it cannot be valued too highly; and until people are again systematically trained to it, there will be few great thinkers, and a low general average of intellect, in any but the mathematical and physical departments of speculation.

On any other subject no one's opinions deserve the name of knowledge, except so far as he has either had forced upon him by others, or gone through of himself, the same mental process which would have been required of him in carrying on an active controversy with opponents. That, therefore, which when absent, it is so indispensable, but so difficult, to create, how worse than absurd is it to forego, when spontaneously offering itself! If there are any persons who contest a received opinion, or who will do so if law or opinion will let them, let us thank them for it, open our minds to listen to them, and rejoice that there is some one to do for us what we otherwise ought, if we have any regard for either the certainty or the vitality of our convictions, to do with much greater labor for ourselves.

PROBLEMS

1. Compare two of your beliefs—one that *you* have built up and considered thoroughly and one that you have been "taught," without attention being paid to a contrary view. Which of the beliefs do you really understand? Which do you find more useful? Does this examination of your own experience seem to uphold Mill's contention that "He who knows only his own side of the case, knows little of that"? (Do you notice that the beliefs for which you have factual confirmation are apt to be about homely problems, such as mending fences or finding an electrical "short," while other beliefs, for which you may not have factual confirmation, are apt to be about "world-shaking" problems that affect great numbers of people—problems such as war, the atom bomb, unemployment, inflation?)

2. When he wrote, about a hundred years ago, Mill believed that mathematical "truths" were an exception to the general rule that truths were not really understood if merely *taught*. But the work in recent years of such men as Albert Einstein, Alfred Whitehead, Bertrand Russell, and Arthur Eddington has caused even mathematics to lose some of the "certainty" which Mill took for granted. If uncertainty occurs in the "stable" science of mathematics, what does it suggest to you about such relatively less "stable" sciences as psychology, political science, and economics?

3. Mill suggests that unexamined, uncontested, generally accepted ideas tend to lose their "meaning." Test the soundness of his suggestion by noting any signs of vagueness in people's grasp or understanding of the following ideas—all of them accepted by large numbers of people as being beyond question:

    a. War does not "pay."

    b. Democracy involves freedom.

    c. *Education* is synonymous with *schools.*

    d. The human race has progressed rapidly during the past hundred years.

    e. Competition, the struggle for survival, is the basis of all human progress.

    f. The human race needs "ideals" if it is to go forward.

4. Does the history of any organization or movement about which you are fairly well informed show the pattern outlined by Mill: early vitality of beliefs, general acceptance of beliefs, and finally loss of real meaning in the beliefs? For example, do you know of a social fraternity that started out with a strong public service program but became just another social club, all the while retaining its original fine-sounding mottos? A "progressive education" school which, although it has long ago slipped into the old grooves, still talks the lingo of "progressive education"? A church ceremony which all members of the congregation still observe but do not understand? A set of minimum course-requirements, the original justification for which is understood by few faculty members or students?

5. What *forms* does the opposition to a thorough examination and re-examination of widely accepted ideas commonly take? In this connection, you might recall family discussions and work on committees. Try your hand at writing a brief dialogue involving the members of your family or a committee (or some other group of your own choosing). By means of this dialogue reveal your awareness of the *forms* in which such opposition customarily appears. (A few examples: the complaint that it is a waste of time "to go all over that

matter again"; the objection that further analysis is "splitting hairs" or "will just confuse the issue, get us mixed up.")

6. Have you observed any concrete evidence of a present-day tendency to consider "negative criticism" purely destructive? For example, have you noticed any attempts to throttle criticism of government or business on the grounds that such criticism is unconstructive fault-finding? Have you noticed attacks on contemporary "realistic" novels and movies because they are, allegedly, destructive, not sufficiently "positive" or "uplifting"? What further examples of this tendency can you provide?

Marion Walker Alcaro

In taking a course or doing an assignment or answering an examination question, have you ever found yourself wondering, "What's the point of this?" If you have, did you then conclude that college itself was worthless but that a college degree was still a good thing for one's pocketbook and social standing? Or did you rebel and refuse to do the seemingly nonsensical work, perhaps without analyzing the reasons for its being nonsensical? Or did you decide, although *you* could not at that time see the point, that there *must* be a point in it, some unseen, mysterious value that would make its appearance later in your life? Did you try to figure out more useful alternatives to the sort of thing you were doing?

Mrs. Alcaro suggests in this article what she considers wrong with college today and what should be done about it. She is, of course, expressing the view of a woman graduate who has settled down to be a housewife, mother, and part-time author; but the questions she raises, if not the conclusions she suggests, apply also, with slight changes, to the college man.

COLLEGES DON'T MAKE SENSE *

The day I graduated from college I believed—modestly, and yet with a nice warm glow of conviction—that I was an educated young woman. I had salted away an impressive supply of mis-

* Marion Walker Alcaro, "Colleges Don't Make Sense," *Woman's Day*, May 1946.

cellaneous information. My mind, after constant limbering up
with fancy mental gymnastics, was as supple as a ballerina. I was
all set to deal with Life. One year later, at close grips with two
very elemental problems of living—marriage and motherhood—I
was beginning to suspect that I was poorly equipped to handle
either one. Now, after ten years, I know that for a girl who was ear-
marked for domesticity from the time she diapered her first doll,
college was a criminal waste of time.

Let me hasten to explain—before the feminists and the sentimen-
talists and many of my own classmates rise in wrath—that I am not
an advocate of any back-to-the-cradle-and-kitchen movement. And
I have no quarrel with our colleges when it comes to the preparation they give the potential career girl. They turn out brilliantly
trained teachers, artists, and professional women. But the girl who
is destined to be primarily a woman is shortchanged. The girl who
during her college years is obviously marking time before marriage—and there's nothing wrong with that, by the way—is given the
same fare as the girl who is going "to make something of herself."
The former is dished out great hunks of obsolete literature, gobs of
history that she won't remember, scoops of science that she won't
remember either, dibs and dabs of philosophy and psychology, and
a smattering of languages thrown in for seasoning. She is given a
B.A. for swallowing the mixture, but nothing in this time-honored
goulash has any use or meaning in her post-graduate life.

A degree has come to have tremendous snob appeal. A college
graduate may belong to university clubs, and college women's
clubs, and revel in class reunions. But these privileges are dearly
bought at the price of four years of intellectual doodling. Since
about 80 per cent of the alumnae of women's colleges marry and
raise families, it seems to me that their alma maters have as great
a responsibility toward the girl whose destiny is marriage as they
have toward her career-minded classmates. It seems to me that she
should get something more out of college than a few friendships
and the satisfaction of leaping some stiff intellectual hurdles. And
yet her needs are either bungled, ignored, or looked down upon.

The root of the trouble is that education for women started out
with a chip on its shoulder. It had to fight the Battle of the Sexes;
but after proving conclusively that women are the mental equals of
men it has maintained the competition long after the original issue

has become ancient history. Women's colleges are slavishly patterned after men's colleges, on the belligerent theory that if the gander can take it so can the goose. Any deviation from the masculine formula, any purely feminine innovation, would be considered a loss of academic prestige. In their desire to show the men a thing or two, women's colleges have urged their students to rise above the chores that have been traditionally a woman's lot, ignoring the facts that those chores still have to be done and that women have to do them. Marriage and motherhood are not represented as professions demanding skill and training, but as humble sidetracks. As a result, the college girl who marries is not only poorly prepared for her role in life but vaguely apologetic about it. "I have nothing interesting to report," wrote one graduate in response to a questionnaire sent out for her tenth reunion. "I have a husband and three children."

Make no mistake—I know that to suggest the lowly domestic arts invade the ivy-covered walls of our snootier colleges for women—on the same footing with Beowulf—would be like shaking a bee tree. But all the same, for the girl who marries, there should be some relation between the hours spent in classroom and laboratory and library and the demands of post-graduate life.

Take my own case. Shortly after graduation I married a young doctor just beginning his internship. Let's take a look at the qualifications of the wife to whom this lucky guy turned over the responsibility for his physical well-being, his house, his bank account, his children, and to a large extent his career itself. I was as informed as all get out when it came to the significance of revolution and romanticism. I could chatter about the minor English poets of the sixteenth century. I had studied Anglo-Saxon grammar. I knew all about the love life of the earthworm. But I couldn't cook a decent meal. I couldn't manage a house. Pregnancy amazed me. Babies scared me. And my knowledge of finance was limited to what-shall-I-do-until-my-allowance-comes.

Oh, I learned all right. I learned the hard way. My college professors would say that because my mind had been conditioned by the study of the liberal arts I had learned to grasp a problem, analyze it, seek out the proper references, and then proceed to solve it. Don't you believe it! I learned because I jolly well had to, and I learned slowly and painfully by the method of trial and error—mostly error.

The preparation of undergraduates for marriage should be a vibrant challenge to the liberal arts college. If domestic arts were taught as brilliantly, as scientifically, as exhaustively, and on the same scale as the belles lettres, they could assume a respected place in the college curriculum. The need exists—a need which is not filled later by quick courses in cooking schools, or schools for brides, or courses for expectant mothers. With imagination and some bold pioneering, our colleges could meet it adequately.

Some standard college courses need only a change of focus or emphasis. For instance, look at the methods of teaching the sciences and of teaching what we call "hygiene." When I was in college I was exposed to one year of zoology. The class spent the first six weeks dissecting pickled frogs. The class did—I didn't. I spent my time on the fire escape trying to keep from losing my lunch. From there we progressed to the amoeba, the crayfish, and the earthworm. We studied them all in detail. We dissected, we drew diagrams, we squinted into microscopes, we peered into test tubes—for two long laboratory and three lecture periods every week. For the one member of the class who studied medicine this undoubtedly proved useful. The majority of us could have done with far less concentration on lowly creatures and far more information about pregnancy, childbirth, prenatal care, the menopause, and sex. These matters were taken care of in a one-semester, one-hour-a-week hygiene course consisting of some sketchy lectures by the college physician (unmarried) and an embarrassed physical education instructor (also unmarried).

When a cat has her first litter of kittens, nature thoughtfully provides her with the knowledge of how to bring them up. With humans it doesn't work that way. When my first son was born, I came out of the anaesthetic knowing no more about how to take care of him than I did before. After I got him home I spent most of my time with my nose in a book on babies. He yelled—I ran for the book! He didn't yell—I ran for the book! How much wear and tear on both of us would have been avoided if I could have studied child care as painstakingly as I studied French drama. I came across my drama notebook the other day—pages and pages of meticulous notes on musty plays by musty playwrights. If I had had as elaborate a notebook on child care to refer to during the crises of the past nine years, motherhood would have been a snap.

No matter what her domestic setup may be, necessarily the woman who marries spends time and thought on food. The college which holds its academic nose at the mention of anything which smacks of the culinary misses an opportunity to explore a fascinating subject which could be approached from many angles. Think what the combined forces of the departments of history, science, and economics could do with the study of food and nutrition—if they put their minds on it! Working with food would be high adventure for a college graduate if she were given some scholarly groundwork in its chemistry, its romance, and its role as world force and determinant of history. There are those—among them me—who would go even further and suggest that expert cookery could take its place among the fine arts with apologies to no one. But that is probably an earthy point of view.

Money matters are designated in the minds of most women as Great Mysteries. And yet many women at some time in their lives are forced to manage their own incomes. And many women marry doctors and clergymen and other babes in the woods of finance. How about a course in the fundamentals of investment, insurance, taxation, and managing a budget? Nothing elaborate—one semester would do. It seems to me that the department of mathematics could, without losing face, sandwich one in somewhere.

My roommate took history of art—ancient, Renaissance, modern, and contemporary. Unofficially I took it too; after drilling her for quizzes for two years, I felt like an authority. This came in handy when I went to Florence. I wasn't lost in the Pitti and the Uffizi. But I was lost in a furniture store when I chose the furnishings for my first house. What a conglomeration I picked out for my family to live with! It has taken years to replace that junk, and there are still a few horrors around the house to remind me of my youth and ignorance. If colleges for women would offer courses in architecture for home owners and in interior decoration—including the study of modern and traditional furniture, china, glassware, silver, and fabrics—they would earn the gratitude of the husbands of their alumnae.

The most progressive step in education for women that has been made in recent years is a course in personal grooming offered by a junior college in the Middle West. The colleges which have hailed it with lofty amusement or out-and-out sneers would do well to take another look at some of their own frowzy undergraduates. Or at some of their own finished products, for that matter. The mental giantess who looks like a scarecrow is intellectually lopsided. The woman who knows how to make the most of her appearance stands a far better chance of achieving well-balanced personal development. Training in the selection of clothes, and in personal grooming, and in the use of cosmetics, may seem frivolous to the devotees of Shakespeare, but it adds up to sound preparation for living.

Colleges rationalize the adherence to their moth-eaten curricula by insisting that a liberal arts education according to the stereotyped formula introduces a girl to intellectual vistas that will enrich the rest of her life. That sounds dandy. Unfortunately the argument doesn't hold water. The average bachelor of arts who marries is so totally unprepared to meet the demands of her new life that she is lucky if she finds time to read Dick Tracy. If she had some practical training along with the academic hardtack, she could step into her role as a professional woman instead of a bungling amateur—and then, yes, she would have a chance to develop the intellectual tastes acquired in college. Our colleges for women point with pride to the few celebrities which they produce—the scientists, the artists, the politicians, the prima donnas of business. When they can produce many women who know the business of womanhood and who have been taught to respect its dignity, then the cap-and-gown crowd will have real cause for self-congratulation.

PROBLEMS

1. How does Mrs. Alcaro show that opinions about "the ideal education" are not necessarily rational merely because they have received popular acceptance?
2. How does Mrs. Alcaro account for the grip which the liberal arts tradition has obtained on women's colleges?
3. What hard realities rise to challenge the usefulness of this liberal arts program?
4. The battle that manual skills and domestic arts are today fighting for recognition in the college curriculum very closely parallels the

struggle of science for similar recognition at the end of the nineteenth century. What do the two have in common that accounts, at least in part, for the reluctance of traditionalists to admit them to collegiate standing on equal footing with the arts and the humanities?

5. In a spirit similar to that of many supporters of the liberal arts program, some advocates of more vocational training assume that the mere existence of courses in technical skills assures students of receiving a "more practical" education (if "practical" means learning specific skills, like operating a tractor, welding, repairing a motor, or cooking). In what ways is *this* an unsupported assumption? What, specifically, would need to be known before one could conclude that such courses were "practical," or more "practical" than the so-called "long-haired" subjects?

6. How is today's swift obsolescence of processes and systems a danger to both the vocationalist's and the traditionalist's programs? Do the implications of atomic energy present any greater danger to technicians trained to use traditional sources of energy than to historians trained in traditional concepts of power politics and warfare?

7. In what ways may the Chaucer scholar become as narrow a vocationalist as the fisheries or soils instructor? Is either one educating "the whole man," or "half a man," or more than one tiny part of a man?

8. A recent survey of the alumni of Princeton University (see *Life,* June 16, 1947) revealed that the reading tastes of these college graduates were substantially the same as when they graduated years before. Fifteen years after graduation the class of '32 picked Fielding's *Tom Jones* and Kipling's "If" as the greatest works of prose and poetry, respectively, just as they had done in their senior year in college. Further, the average number of books read yearly by these graduates was ten. How does this survey challenge the assumption that a liberal arts education introduces one to "intellectual vistas that will enrich the rest of his life"? How does it support Mrs. Alcaro's contention as to the real function of a college?

Richard Neuberger *   *F. S. Oliver* *

The view that politics is a dirty, stupid game and that politicians are naturally inferior to men in other types of endeavor is a common one, surprisingly so in view of the fact that a democ-

---

* The two selections that follow, the one by Neuberger (p. 30) and the one by Oliver (p. 34), are considered jointly. The problems covering these selections begin on p. 39.

racy depends on politics and politicians for its very existence. It is an easy view to adopt, until one actually examines a politician and the conditions under which he operates; then it may become more difficult.

Neuberger, an Oregon newspaperman who has been in and out of state office, looks at politics from the vantage point of an *ex*-politician. If read hastily, his remarks may seem to support the common view; a more careful reading will show, however, that his criticism is centered not so much on the politician as on the politician's environment (that is, his public), which helps determine his conduct as a public servant. Interestingly enough, Neuberger did not follow his own advice, to get out of politics. He is currently back in office as a state senator, practicing "the art of the possible."

The selection by Oliver, a student of British politics, is from his book on Horace Walpole, an eighteenth-century prime minister of England. Walpole operated a notorious political "spoils system" and yet has come to be considered by many historians as the father of some of the most desirable features of the British parliamentary system.

If the problem of reconciling ideals with practical politics interests you (and it *has* to interest the citizens of any state that intends to remain a democracy), you may wish to turn to some other revealing, thought-provoking studies of politics, such as Harold Ickes' *The Autobiography of a Curmudgeon,* Jim Farley's *Jim Farley's Story,* George Norris' *Fighting Liberal,* David Lilienthal's *TVA—Democracy on the March,* Lincoln Steffens' *Autobiography,* Edward N. Doan's *The La Follettes and the Wisconsin Idea,* Henry L. Stimson and McGeorge Bundy's *On Active Service in Peace and War,* Raymond Gram Swing's *Forerunners of American Fascism,* Basil Rauch's *The History of the New Deal, 1933-1938,* Frances Perkins' *The Roosevelt I Knew,* Robert Sherwood's *Roosevelt and Hopkins,* Winston Churchill's *Memoirs,* Walter White's *A Man Called White,* Alexis de Tocqueville's *Democracy in America,* Richard Hofstader's *The American Political Tradition and the Men Who Made It,* Arthur M. Schlesinger, Jr.'s *The Vital Center.*

And here's a handful of novels thrown in for good measure for those who prefer the oblique approach of fiction: Mark Twain and C. D. Warner's *The Gilded Age,* John Dos Passos' *The Adventures of a Young Man* and *Number One,* Frank Norris' *The Octopus,* Robert Penn Warren's *All the King's Men,* Lionel Trilling's *The Middle of the Journey.*

I RUN FOR OFFICE *

I had not realized what quest of political office was doing to me until I received an invitation to speak in a neighboring city across the Columbia River. As I looked at the water through the trusses of the railroad bridge, I suddenly remembered that I had passed into another sovereignty. This was the state of Washington. Oregon's soil—and voters—were behind me.

For the first time in many weeks I would not be talking to people who could vote on my candidacy for the state Senate. Within the limits of taste and decency, I could say what I pleased. I might challenge the prejudices of my listeners and still be safe from retribution at the polls. No longer would fear and hesitation, those abject sentinels, mount guard over each word and syllable.

If I blurted out my true feelings on the sales tax or postwar military training in the colleges, I would not need to review the episode in terms of the school bloc or the Legion vote. An honest expression on state rent control would not inevitably be followed by cold sweat over housewives or landlords striking my name from their sample ballots. And if after the meeting I failed to listen attentively for half an hour to some crank's plan for correcting the evils of the money system, the sequel would not be a sleepless night worrying about his influence in Precinct 144.

Yet before indulging this new-found freedom of speech, I carefully examined the audience to make certain that no constituents had crossed the Columbia to eavesdrop on what I would say in alien surroundings.

Twice in my thirty-three years I have been nominated for public office in Oregon at the Democratic primaries. This experience has run a gamut of sorts, for I have both won and lost. In 1940 I was elected to the Oregon House of Representatives on President Roosevelt's coattails. In 1946 I was defeated for the state Senate in the Republican comeback.

The pursuit of votes in a great democracy should prove exhilarating. I have not found it so. I have learned much, and I

---

* Richard Neuberger in *Harper's Magazine,* February 1947. Copyright, 1947, by Harper & Brothers.

commend the undertaking to students of political science—in fact, to all who would better understand their country. But the temptation to pussyfoot, to evade and parry rather than to voice one's candid opinion, is so overwhelming that the experience will surely torment any except the flintiest conscience.

The candidate commences with one or two issues on which he declares himself as forthrightly as he dares. From such positions he does not withdraw—although I have met politicians who can retreat as skillfully as Marshal Ney. But the candidate knows that these issues form his reputation. They are the basis of his publicity in the newspapers. He utters them over and over again. He becomes recognized as a friend of labor or a champion of free enterprise. He is for or against public ownership of electric power; perhaps he decides to premise his campaign on keeping communism out of the American home or freeing the farmer from Wall Street.

Once away from the few questions on which he has decided to take a stand, the candidate twists and turns like Katooshka fleeing across the steppes ahead of the wolf pack. The electorate seems to him ready to rend him limb from limb should he falter in his personal behavior, family life, or economic concepts. If politicians are moral cowards—and I believe they are—it is partly because the public has made them so. Two campaigns for office have convinced me that the American people are essentially cynical about candidates. This cynicism breeds a curious sort of hostility. At many public gatherings I have felt that the audience waited tensely to deny me support if I should utter one phrase contrary to the predilections of the group I was addressing. Charity definitely does not begin at the political meeting.

I recall the leader of the longshoremen who admitted my one hundred per cent record on labor legislation, but declared his union could not possibly back me because I had expressed doubt, in answer to a question from the floor, whether we should share the atomic secret with the Soviet Union. His attitude may have been due to communist leanings, but the same could not be said of the clergyman who conceded our full agreement on social problems, yet advised worshippers to vote against me because of an article my wife had written for the *Oregonian* about a local art group which hired females to pose in the nude.

Had I been aware originally of the desire to embarrass candidates rather than to tolerate in them the shortcomings common to the human race, I confess that I probably would have ducked the atomic question and told my wife to refrain from reference to the unclad models.

Candidates are timid and evasive because such conduct is politically profitable. I might say we are cowards literally in self-defense. The politician siding with a particular organization on nine issues out of ten is scorned for the tenth. Blunt speech in campaigns has always cost me votes—whether the topic involved was ridiculous or sublime. When I inveighed against the billboards cluttering Oregon's roads, farmers renting barns and highway parkings to sign companies mobilized for my opponent. After I had denounced the persecution of returning Japanese-American war veterans, the American Legion commenced gunning for my political hide.

Minorities determine many elections, particularly in the primaries, and this is why equivocation pays. I have faith that a substantial majority of the voters approved my stand both on billboards and the attacks against the Nisei. But the majority was unorganized, while the Legion and the farmers with signs on their land were marshaled for action; and politicians know that one active enemy, constantly at the telephone or buttonholing acquaintances, can do damage to a candidacy which twenty indifferent supporters never offset.

As a writer on politics I liked to think romantically that forthrightness meant victory. I thought of George Norris, and forgot that he was the exception and not the rule. As a candidate, I am aware that forthrightness generally must be its own reward. The political retort perfect is that which sounds strident but offends nobody. "Say nothing, and say it well," I was advised by a United States senator who interested himself in my embryonic political career.

When I spoke in colored neighborhoods for civil rights legislation, I incurred the wrath of wealthy Negro night-club operators who did not want their people allowed to patronize public places frequented by whites. But when I cautiously straddled an old-age pension proposition on the Oregon ballot, I found that I picked up votes from both sides. Before even so sophisticated an organization as the League of Women Voters, outright endorsement of a new school tax did not return the same political dividends as approving the measure "in principle, with certain reservations." This was a way of riding two chariots—and also of convincing the disillusioned candidate that Barnum was right.

At the peak of the campaign, aspirants for all jobs from governor to constable traveled a circuit, addressing trade unions, women's clubs, pension groups, and Izaak Walton Leagues. Most of the candidates thought nothing of telling a property owners' association at eight o'clock that taxes had to come down, and before the evening was over promising a rally of old people the $24,000,000,000 Townsend Plan. When I remarked to a fellow candidate that this seemed a trifle inconsistent he growled, "Well, they're so darned anxious to trip us up that I don't really mind fooling 'em a little. I even kinda think they like it."

Maybe they do, for he had been on the public payroll nearly twenty years. . . .

I wonder, too, whether the writer can mix his craft with a personal political candidacy. He can support or oppose others, but should he himself run? Those who would govern us, we measure by a special yardstick. I was sharply criticized for being photographed soliciting a vote from a pretty girl in a brief bathing suit. A labor leader did not believe a genuine friend of the common people could drive a car as new as my 1942 Oldsmobile. These are not charges leveled against the butcher, the baker, or the candlestick maker.

A writer, if he is to be reasonably honest, must express sentiments repugnant to a good many people. This is not the way to win votes. During one of my legislative campaigns, a loyal friend went to the public library and checked out all the copies of a book I had written because he had heard its contents assailed at a meeting. "Would that mine enemy had written a book," becomes particularly pertinent when the enemy is running for office. Nor is the novelist any safer than the author of non-fiction. In California's 1934 gubernatorial campaign sentences shrewdly culled from the novels of Upton Sinclair were plastered on thousands of billboards from the Klamath Basin to Mexico.

As long as the business of rounding up votes dominated my thoughts, I discovered an unconscious inhibition on what I wrote. Truth, at least as I saw it, became not the sole test. I speculated on whether my words might antagonize this or that group. Several times, I regret to report, my eraser modified original conclusions so they would be more generally acceptable. This is not a situation in which a writer can do justice to his profession, his topic, or to himself.

And I was seeking only minor office. What might the inhibitions have been if I had glimpsed ahead the prospect of the governor's chair or a United States senatorship?

The case against making politics my career is strong. I accept the case implicitly. Already it has persuaded me against becoming the titular head of the Democratic party in our state.

Yet the argument is only 99 $\frac{44}{100}$ per cent pure. The other fraction disturbs me occasionally. When I see Oregon's teachers paid the lowest salaries on the Coast, when I see a private utility company selling the power from the dam at Bonneville which the people built and paid for, when I see a Japanese-American soldier with forty-one blood transfusions denied a hotel room on a rainy night, when I see a million-dollar race track rising while veterans cannot construct homes—then my blood pressure rises, too, and I wonder if any case is strong enough to impel abdication in favor of those who tolerate these things.

But the slightest return of political ambition brings that degrading fear which is the curse of politics. I even ask myself if I have said too much in these pages.

ARE POLITICIANS WICKED? *

Few men are placed in such fortunate circumstances as to be able to gain office, or to keep it for any length of time, without misleading or bamboozling the people. A classic instance of the difficulty of plain dealing is, that though men can often be induced, when their faculties are on the alert, to make an admirable resolution, they are not easily kept at the sticking point. Their decision is rarely fixed so firmly or so permanently in their minds that when the bills fall due, which by implication they have accepted, they will honour them without protest. It is often harder to induce them to do the things by which alone their resolution can be carried into effect than it was at the beginning to lead them to it. This arises not from perfidy, but from forgetfulness or confusion of mind, or because some new interest has driven out the old. Sometimes, as with

* F. S. Oliver, *The Endless Adventure*, Macmillan & Co. Ltd., London, 1931.

children, their attention must be occupied with an entertaining toy while the politician stealthily makes the matter secure; sometimes, like horses, they have to be blindfolded in order to get them out of a burning stable.

In dealing with foreign nations the politician who wishes to act uprightly is even harder put to it; for there the difficulty is not popular ignorance and simplicity, but the expert knowledge of able officials who, as part of their professional training, have had to make themselves conversant with the blunders, deceptions, and disappointments of the past, and who are filled with suspicions that are none the less justified because they happen to be centuries old.

If the conscience of an honest man lays down stern rules, so also does the art of politics. At a juncture where no accommodation is possible between the two, the politician may be faced by these alternatives: "Shall I break the rules of my art in order to save my private honour? or shall I break the rules of my conscience in order to fulfil my public trust?" . . .

Many of us, carried away at one time and another by hero-worship or partisanship, have attempted to discriminate between politicians and statesmen; that is, between the "insidious and crafty animal" and the disinterested public servant. . . .

Moralists, idealists, and humanitarians are equally severe. They hold converse with the politician from necessity, but rarely from choice. Their attitude is one of cold suspicion. They are shocked by his unveracity, by the deadness of his soul to all the higher emotions. Obviously he cares for nothing in the world except the grinding of his own axe. He is never more than a lip-servant of sacred causes, and then only when they happen to be in fashion.

The antipathy that soldiers, sailors, and country gentlemen show for the politician is rooted in their conviction that no one who talks so much, and obviously knows so little, about the conduct of war and the management of land can possibly understand any department whatsoever of public affairs.

The great army of company directors and others of a certain age, whom newspapers describe as "captains of industry," condemn him for his lack of practical ability, initiative, push-and-go; they suspect him of being a lazy fellow who likes to draw a salary for doing next to nothing.

Jingoes denounce him as a traitor if he is not forever plucking foreign nations by the beard. Pacifists, on the other hand, consider him to be the chief cause of war by reason, sometimes of his timid opportunism, at others of his truculence; the compromises he agrees to in order to curry favor with public opinion are fatal to peace; he is the puppet of military cliques, and shares all the passions and panics that degrade the mob.

The magnates of the popular press, secure behind their private telephone entanglements, sneer at his want of courage; and the man-of-the-world—most ingenuous of dotterels—takes up the same tale from his club armchair.

What humbug it is, for the most part! And what a welter should we be in, if the politicians, taking these lectures to heart, were to hand over the management of public affairs to their critics!

It must be placed to the politician's credit that he takes our contumelious treatment of him in such good part, with so little whining and loss of temper. He has a good case against us, if he cared to press it, inasmuch as we insist upon regarding him as part of a public show got up for our entertainment, and look on—hissing or applauding—while he is baited in the House of Commons, on the platform, and in the press.

This sport has been so long customary that we are callous to its cruelty. The contemporaries of a politician are apt to value him less for the useful services he does them than for the skill and sturdiness of his fighting. He rarely gets a just appraisement until historians come to deal with him long after he is dead. In order to keep his popularity he must stand torture as stoically as a Red Indian or a Chinaman; if he is seen to flinch, it is all up with him. And he has even worse things to bear than these personal assaults and batteries. For the average politician, though he thinks a great deal about his own career, is by nature a constructive animal. He has a craving—often an insatiable craving—to be making something. No sooner is he in office than he becomes engrossed in shaping policies, in legislation, and in administrative acts. It is through this passion that he is most vulnerable. For it takes a man of singular fortitude to watch with composure, on his outgoing from office, the foundations that he has dug with so much pain and labour left to silt up; or worse still, his all-but-finished building let go to rack and ruin for want of the little effort, the few slates and timbers, that would have made it weather-proof and habitable.

We shall do the politician an injustice if we take too seriously the heroics and pathetics with which he is so apt to decorate and conclude his speeches. These for the most part are only common form, tags which everybody uses, because the audience is supposed to relish them. It would be harsh to judge him a hypocrite on sentiments so undeliberate. The true temperance of his benevolence cannot be deduced from his rhetoric, which is for the most part meaningless and empty; but it may be gauged with some approach to accuracy from his acts, and by noting the things he does or tries to do, prevents or tries to prevent.

By nature he is probably no poorer and no richer than the rest of us in kindly warmth and desire to alleviate suffering; but the conditions of his calling place him at a manifest advantage. For the soil of politics is peculiarly congenial to the growth and burgeoning of an understanding sympathy with one's fellow-creatures. By force of circumstances the politician mixes, fights, and fraternises with all sorts and conditions of men. He cannot listen day after day to his opponents without shaking off much of his original narrow-mindedness. On his first arrival at Westminster he may be shocked and astounded to hear men asseverating doctrines that strike at the very roots of his philosophy. And he is also taken aback because it is evident that the House of Commons does not regard such speakers as either lunatics or criminals. But it is not long before he begins to realise that even the most outrageous of them are often sincere and sometimes right. If you would know whether a man is true or false, it is a great help to be placed where you can watch his eyes and listen to the tones of his voice. The politician has the good fortune to meet people face to face whose opinions he abhors, to be buffeted by them, to give as good as he gets and note how they take it. This method draws a great deal of the venom out of controversy.

The fact that we are so much bewildered and bedevilled at the present time, instead of moving us to sympathy for the politician, makes us all the angrier with him. If we saw our way clearly, we should probably be less censorious. We resent his being less flurried, less puzzled, than we are; and we therefore conclude that he must be a shallow creature, without sense enough to be aware of danger. For many of us have convinced ourselves that the old world is coming to an end; and while some appear to think that civilisation will be quenched utterly in the darkness of barbarism, others are hopeful that, from the fuliginous bonfire of antique systems, a new and more radiant order will arise.

These high-wrought fancies leave the average politician untouched. He would agree that the light is bad; but he cannot understand why this should set us wondering whether we are watching a sunset or waiting for the dawn. He sees no mysterious glimmerings in any part of the horizon. He is a commonplace fellow who goes by his watch, and his watch tells him it is broad day. The darkness is nothing more than an overhead autumnal fog, which will clear away when the wind rises. The obscurity interferes to some extent with his work; but he does not make it an excuse for idling or despondency. When people talk to him about an impending doom, he is uninterested and incredulous. It is perhaps one of his defects to place too much confidence in familiar custom. Left entirely to himself, he has been known to carry on his business as usual, until the falling skies caught him unawares and crushed him. He is little troubled with nightmares. His eyes are not fixed on the millennium nor yet precisely on the end of his own nose, but somewhere between the two. He deals with things as they occur, and prides himself on not thinking of them too far ahead. We abuse him: he expects this, and does not complain. Indeed, like a donkey that is accustomed to being beaten behind, he might stand stock-still from sheer astonishment were the abuse suddenly to cease.

If we eventually escape from our present perplexities, it will not be because theorists have discovered some fine new principle of salvation; or because newspapers have scolded and pointed angry fingers at this one or that; or because we, their readers, have become excited and have demanded that "something must be done." It will be because these decent, hard-working, cheerful, valiant, knockabout politicians, whose mysterious business it is to manage our affairs by breaking one another's heads, shall have carried on with their work as if nothing extraordinary was happening—just as Walpole did even in the worst of times—and shall have "jumbled something" out of their contentions that will be of advantage to their country. The notion that we can save ourselves without their help is an illusion; for politics is not one of those crafts that can be learned by the light of nature without an apprenticeship.

PROBLEMS

1. The widespread belief that politicians are morally and intellectually inferior to men in other vocations is revealed in many indirect ways. For example, the cartoonist's stereotype of a politician is a gross, paunchy, corrupt-looking, unimaginative-looking fellow. And have you noted how frequently the fact that one candidate is a businessman, military leader, or educator while the other candidate is a professional politician is taken as final proof of the superior qualifications of the former? What other evidence—expressions, actions, and so forth—of this view of politicians have you noted? (You might recall radio jokes, class-B movie "formula" politicians, everyday conversation about "dirty politics," so-called "respectable" people's shying away, as they say, from "politics.")

2. What unrealistic assumption about politics is entertained by people who grow disgusted at the failure of a "reform candidate" to carry out all his promised reforms when he is elected?

3. In what particular respects does Neuberger's testimony support the popular conception of the politician? In what ways does it call for modifications of that view?

4. What is the unexamined assumption about politics that permits people to overlook conduct on the part of a businessman or mechanic which, if pursued by a politician, would be loudly denounced? What is the connection between this kind of thinking and the notion of some people that schoolteachers should not smoke or take an occasional drink? How does this explain, in turn, the magnitude of our shock if a clergyman is detected in some social misdemeanor? Is this very far removed from the attitude of the citizens of a constitutional monarchy, such as England, toward their king and his immediate family? The king in a constitutional monarchy is admitted to be a symbol. Are politicians, schoolteachers, and clergymen also symbols? Does this suggest a possible source of our crooked thinking—confusing the symbol with the reality?

5. If we accept as a working definition of politics "the manipulation of power," what are we to think of the proposals of the Technocrats to "do away with all politics and politicians" and turn over the management of our society to a group of technological engineers? And how meaningful is the slogan of many a candidate in many an

American community, "Turn out the politicians and elect a business-man for mayor. Vote for efficiency in government"?

6. How realistic are those high school civics courses which focus exclusively on such details as the formal structure of federal, state, and local governments, the salaries of the various officials, the age, residence qualifications, and other prerequisites for holding certain offices, and so forth?

7. Where do Neuberger and Oliver look for clues to explain the conduct of politicians—in the *nature* of politicians or in the *conditions* under which they operate? In the final analysis are Neuberger and Oliver in essential agreement or disagreement in their respective attitudes toward politicians? Explain.

8. All of the preceding questions have one thing in common—they attempt to make clear the gap between illusion and reality in the thinking of many of us about political matters. How does this gap in our thinking help to account for the politicians' persistent use of "meaningless and empty rhetoric," "saying nothing, and saying it well"?

Carey McWilliams

In this selection from his book, *A Mask for Privilege,* McWilliams, one-time Commissioner of Immigration and Housing for California, a lawyer, a contributing editor of *The Nation,* and a recognized authority on United States minority groups, examines a widely accepted, seldom scrutinized generalization about a racial group. Using as a starting point a study made by *Fortune,* he compares the generalization with the facts and finds that, far from supporting the common belief, the facts lead to a quite different conclusion.

If you want to make similar comparisons of beliefs about other national or racial groups with the facts, you will find the facts in such books as Gunnar Myrdal's *An American Dilemma,* Alexander Leighton's *The Governing of Men,* Ruth Benedict's *Race: Science and Politics, To Secure These Rights* (The Report of the President's Committee on Civil Rights), St. Clair Drake and Horace Cayton's *Black Metropolis,* and Arnold Rose's *The Negro in America,* as well as in Carey McWilliams' *Brothers Under the Skin* and *Prejudice.*

IN THE MIDDLE
OF THE MIDDLE CLASS *

The best proof of the mythical character of the anti-Semitic ideology is to be found in an examination of the position which Jews occupy in our economy. For the notion that Jews dominate or control the American economy is one of the greatest myths of our time.

THE MARGINAL MAN

The quickest way to define the position that Jews occupy in the American economy is to mark off the fields in which Jewish participation is nonexistent or of negligible importance. This of course constitutes a reversal of the anti-Semite's technique, for he always starts by defining the areas in which Jews play a prominent part. A brief examination of the *Fortune* survey (*Jews in America*, 1936) will indicate, graphically enough, those sectors of the economy in which Jewish participation is of negligible importance.

Contrary to the ancient anti-Semitic myth, Jews are a minor influence in banking and finance. Of the 420 listed directors of the 19 members of the New York Clearing House in 1933, only 33 were Jews. "There are practically no Jewish employees of any kind," reads the *Fortune* survey, "in the largest commercial banks—and this in spite of the fact that many of their customers are Jews." While a few Jewish firms, such as Kuhn, Loeb and Company, J. and W. Seligman and Company, and Speyer and Company, have a well-established reputation in the investment banking field, Jewish influence in investment banking in the United States is wholly insignificant. Neither in commercial nor in investment banking are Jews an important factor. If the national rather than the New York scene were examined in detail, it could be demonstrated that Jewish influence in American banking is even less significant than the *Fortune* survey indicates. For the exclusion of Jews from the boards of local banks, outside New York, is a fact that can be readily verified by

* From *A Mask for Privilege: Anti-Semitism in America* by Carey McWilliams, by permission of Little, Brown & Co. Copyright, 1947, 1948, by Carey McWilliams.

the most cursory investigation. In related fields of finance, such as insurance, the Jewish influence is virtually nonexistent. "The absence of Jews in the insurance business," to quote from the survey, "is noteworthy." Generally speaking, Jews participate in the insurance business almost exclusively as salesmen catering to a preponderantly Jewish clientele. Nor do Jews figure, in any significant manner, in the various stock exchanges across the country.

If the Jewish participation in banking and finance is negligible, it is virtually nonexistent in heavy industry. There is not a single sector of the heavy industry front in which their influence amounts to dominance or control or in which it can even be regarded as significant. A minor exception might be noted in the scrap-iron and steel business, an outgrowth of the junk business, which has been a direct contribution of Jewish immigrants to the American economy. The scrap-iron business, it should be emphasized, is wholly peripheral to heavy industry in general. Similarly the waste-products industry including nonferrous scrap metal, paper, cotton rags, wool rag, and rubber is largely Jewish controlled. But, here again, control of waste products is a symbol of exclusion rather than a badge of influence.

The following significant industries are all "equally non-Jewish," according to the *Fortune* survey, namely, coal, auto, rubber, chemical, shipping, transportation, shipbuilding, petroleum, aviation, and railroading. The important private utility field, including light and power, telephone and telegraph, is most emphatically non-Jewish; and the same can be said of lumber, agriculture, mining, dairy farming, food processing, and the manufacture of heavy machinery. So far as heavy industry is concerned, one can best summarize the findings of the *Fortune* survey by saying that Jews are the ragpickers of American industry, the collectors of waste, the processors of scrap iron.

Jewish participation in the "light industries" field is largely restricted to the distribution end. In the manufacture of wool, the Jewish influence is slight (from 5 to 10 per cent of production); somewhat higher in silk, it is only 5 per cent in cotton. In the distribution of wool, silk, and cotton products, however, Jews do play a significant role. Their participation in the important meat-packing industry is limited, as one might expect, to the production of the kosher meat pack. In a few industries, such as the manufacture of furniture, they are an important factor. But in most of the light industries, their numerical significance is often greater than the volume of production which they actually control. In the manufacture of boots and shoes, for example, they are a 40 per cent minority in numbers but control only 29 per cent of the volume of production. In the entire light industries field, the principal exception to the generally non-Jewish pattern of control is to be found in the clothing industry, which, like the scrap business, might properly be regarded as a Jewish contribution to American industry.

While Jews play an important role in the buying of tobacco and control some of the large cigar manufacturing concerns, their participation in the mass production of cigarettes, which is emphatically big business, is negligible. Controlling about half the large distilling concerns, Jews fall far short of outright control of the liquor industry. In the general merchandizing field, the important fact to be noted is that, with the exception of apparel goods, Jews have been rigidly excluded from the various chain-store enterprises. Jewish participation is virtually nonexistent both in the drugstore chains and in the food distributing chains. Woolworth and Kress, for example, are 95 per cent non-Jewish. In the mail-order business, Montgomery-Ward and Sears, Roebuck are both non-Jewish, although it was Julius Rosenwald who built the latter company into the great institution it is today. While some of the department stores in New York and in the East are controlled by Jews, their influence in this field diminishes as one moves west.

Again contrary to popular belief, Jewish participation in publishing is not significant. In the magazine field, the *New Yorker*, the *American Mercury*, and *Esquire* are about the only magazines that are controlled by Jews. The measure of Jewish influence in this field might, therefore, be estimated by comparing the circulation of these publications with the circulation of such magazines as the *Saturday Evening Post*, *Collier's*, the *Woman's Home Companion*, *Good Housekeeping*, *Look*, and *Time*, *Life*, and *Fortune*. Jewish participation in the advertising field is about 1 to 3 per cent of the total. However, they are a fairly important factor in the book publishing business and in the job-and-trade printing industry in the larger cities; and, in two new industries, radio and motion pictures, their influence is significant. "The whole picture of industry, business, and amusements," concludes the *Fortune* survey, "may be summed up by repeating that while there are certain industries which Jews dominate and certain industries in which Jewish participation is considerable, there are also vast industrial fields, generally reckoned as the most typical of our civilization, in which they play a part so inconsiderable as not to count in the total picture."

Ironically enough, the negligible influence of Jews in American industry and finance is usually cited, as in the *Fortune* survey, as proof that they do not control the economy and therefore should not be regarded as a "menace" by non-Jews. So much is, indeed, eloquently self-evident. But what this same pattern also indicates is the far more significant fact that Jews have been excluded from participation in the basic industries of the country, the industries that exercise a decisive control over the entire economy. It is precisely this pattern of exclusion from industry and finance that one finds reflected in the pattern of social exclusion traced in the preceding chapter. Since Jews have been unable to penetrate entire segments of the American economy, it naturally follows that their concentration in certain fields is a result, not a cause, of discrimination. "What is remarkable about Jews in America," to quote from the *Fortune* survey, "is not their industrial power but their curious industrial distribution, their tendency to crowd together in particular squares of the checkerboard." But to explain this concentration, as the *Fortune* survey does, in terms of "psychological traits—their clannishness, their tribal inclination"—is certainly to ignore economic realities. One might with greater plausibility explain the crowding together on the checkerboard in terms of the tribal inclination of non-Jews. While certain cultural and sociological factors have been influential in bringing about the concentration of Jews in certain restricted fields of economic endeavor, and also help to explain their association together as Jews in these fields, the basic explanation must be found in the systematic exclusion of Jews from the dominant businesses and industries.

THE MARGINAL BUSINESS

Just what are the characteristics of these "particular squares on the checkerboard" in which Jews are concentrated? Generally speaking, the businesses in which Jews are concentrated are those in which a large risk-factor is involved; businesses peripheral to the economy; businesses originally regarded as unimportant; new industries and businesses; and businesses which have traditionally carried a certain element of social stigma, such, for example, as the amusement industry and the liquor industry. Not being able to penetrate the key control industries, Jews have been compelled to occupy the interstitial, the marginal, positions in the American economy. In short, it is the qualitative rather than the quantitative aspect of their participation in industry and finance that most graphically delineates their position.

The fact that Jewish businesses are essentially marginal in character has manifold collateral ramifications. It means, for example, that the Jewish lawyer occupies somewhat that same position in relation to the practice of the law that Jewish businessmen occupy in relation to American business. "The most important office law business in America," reads the *Fortune* survey, "such as the law business incidental to banking, insurance, trust-company operation, investment work, railroading, patents, admiralty, and large corporation matters in general is in the hands of non-Jewish firms many of which, even though they have numerous Jewish clients, have no Jewish partners." The success or failure of Jewish middle-class professional groups generally is related to the success or failure of those businesses in which Jews are a decisive or important influence. This circumstance gives the appearance of Jewish exclusiveness or clannishness to relationships which are primarily conditioned by non-Jewish exclusiveness and clannishness. Similarly, that Jews appear to wield more economic power than they do is the result of an illusion created by their concentration in businesses which make them conspicuous and which place them in a direct relation to the consuming public. Thus by and large the traditional European pattern of Jewish-Gentile economic relations has been repeated in America.

Today the marginal economic position of the Jew is more exposed in America than ever before. The structure of American capitalism has been profoundly altered since the first great waves of Jewish immigration in the eighties. Today heavy industry holds the reins of power in the United States, economically, politically, and socially. Our great industrial systems have long since achieved complete integration and the structure of power that they represent is an established and formidable reality. No longer directly dependent on finance capital, heavy industry nowadays finances its operations out of its vast reserves and accumulations. Generally speaking, Jewish businesses have been "nepotistic, speculative, and otherwise old-fashioned in comparison with the cartelized, impersonal industrial corporations." Of 1939 sales in the United States, 87 per cent by value of mineral products, 60 per cent of agricultural products, and 42 per cent of manufactured products were cartelized. Opportunities for the small-scale type of enterprise, in which Jews have long specialized, diminish in direct relation to the growth of cartels and the rise of monopolies.

The types of business in which Jews are concentrated, by their very nature, fail to invest ownership with social power and prestige. Too often these businesses lack the artisan beginnings, the long identification with certain family names, and the intimate relationship to a particular community that have invested so many American industries and the families that control them with an extraordinary social power. Clothing stores and motion picture theaters are not nearly so impressive as mines and mills, factories and railroads. Some of the industries in which Jews have prospered, such as radio and motion pictures, have been exceptionally lucrative in their infancy precisely because they were on the fringe of modern capitalism. By reason of their lucky identification with these industries, originally regarded as quite unimportant, some Jews have risen more rapidly economically than they have socially or culturally. These are, in Mr. Riesman's phrase, "the flamboyant social pariahs" to whose activities the anti-Semites devote so much attention. But the economic "upstart," the *nouveau riche* type, has always been a product of similar conditions. "The Newport millionaires," writes Miriam Beard, "who entertained with 'monkey dinners' and 'bullfrog dinners' were not Jewish; neither were the Bradley-Martins and James Hazen Hyde, whose fetes so shocked American public opinion. Gentiles, not Jews, exhibited the most grotesque eccentricities in the Gilded Age." As these new businesses have come to be recognized as a "good thing," they have been quickly stabilized by familiar economic processes and the upstarts have gradually been displaced by men "of sound judgment." Today, for example, Jewish influence in both radio and motion pictures is on the wane.

The steadily growing power which industrial groups have come to exercise in our society not only weakens such economic power as the Jews possess, but it also weakens the position of their allies, the liberal-minded elements of the non-Jewish middle class. Both in Germany and in the United States, the heavy industry groups have tended to be extremely reactionary in politics: protagonists of high tariffs, bitter opponents of organized labor, advocates of a blatantly nationalistic foreign policy. The nature of heavy industry tends to insulate its owners and managers from direct contact with, or dependence upon, public opinion. As Mr. Riesman points out, the heavy industry groups have everywhere shown a marked sympathy with the anti-Semitic rationalization of "productive" versus "predatory" capital. It is not by chance, therefore, that Henry Ford, once the most influential American anti-Semite, should have been smitten with this distinction or that he should have inveighed so strenuously against "international finance," "Wall Street," and "the bankers." As the leaders of heavy industry become increasingly preoccupied with the necessity of acquiring a direct control over government—a tendency already most pronounced in the United States—political power tends to merge with industrial power. This tendency has universally marked, if not the end, the beginning of the end, of that happy period of bourgeois liberalism in which the Jews have flourished and prospered.

PROBLEMS

1. The notion that "Jews are clannish" is widely held in this country. The assumption that the "clannishness" accounts for their concentration in certain types of work has seldom been examined. McWilliams examines this assumption. What does he conclude?

   What facts, established by the *Fortune* survey, lend credibility to McWilliams' contention that economic and social exclusiveness on the part of Gentiles causes Jewish clannishness?

   To what conclusion does he come concerning the kind (the *qualitative* factor) of business they do control? In what way does his *interpretation* of the Jewish concentration in "marginal business" differ from the anti-Semites' interpretation? In what specific ways does the nature of these "marginal businesses" easily lead people, especially those who desire certain answers, into mistaken conclusions about Jews in business?

2. How might superficial appearances easily lead to the drawing of mistaken conclusions from the following facts:

   a. Many Irish on the police force and in politics.

   b. Italian names in news reports on gangsterism.

   c. Frequency of Italian, French, German, and Russian names on musical programs.

   d. Predominance of girls in high school honor societies.

   e. Relatively small number of women in responsible positions in business and industry.

   f. British leadership in world exploration and colonization from the seventeenth through the nineteenth centuries.

3. This article raises the whole problem of cause and effect. Nothing can be trickier, especially when few facts are easily available. Consider, for example: Is "Jewish clannishness" responsible for Jewish concentration in certain squares of "the social and economic checkerboard," or is anti-Semitism responsible for what appears to be "Jewish clannishness"? Is the public's taste responsible for the mediocre quality of many of our radio programs, or is the steady diet of such weak radio fare responsible for the public taste? Did the sensation-mongering newspaper grow out of public demand, or did that kind of paper create a taste for sensation in newspaper readers? Can you see any way of breaking out of this seemingly endless, circular argument?

4. Many rational people recognize and admit that their unexamined assumptions about unpopular minority groups frequently break down when they meet an *individual* belonging to that group. Scientists, when they begin to find exceptions to what they once assumed to be a rule concerning some physical phenomena, grow suspicious of the "rule." Why do many persons persist in their stereotyped notions about an entire group of people even after they have met many exceptions? How may this relate to Mander's suggestion (p. 8) of self-interest as one source of "groundless beliefs"?

5. What does the frequent observation that very small children are comparatively devoid of class and race prejudice suggest as to the nature of prejudice and our means of acquiring it? Which of Mander's six sources of "groundless beliefs" plays a significant role here?

6. Careful students of society have noted that many people can become intellectually convinced of the irrationality of race prejudice but cannot free themselves emotionally from it. How does this support Mill's suggestion (pp. 17-18) that a belief may persist when there are no grounds for it?

Barrows Dunham *　　　　　　　　Alfred Mirsky *

The following two articles challenge the very common assumption "that you can't change human nature," an idea that has been used over and over again to justify war or a do-nothing attitude toward social problems or personal conduct of all sorts.

The first selection is from Dunham's *Man Against Myth*, in which he challenges such assumptions as "the rich are fit and the poor unfit," "there are superior and inferior races," and "you cannot be free and safe."

"Rats and Men" is a talk given by Alfred Mirsky, a member of the Rockefeller Institute for Medical Research, at the Conference on the Scientific Spirit and Democratic Faith held in New York City in May 1943. The talk was appropriate to the occasion, for the conference, concerned with the solution of human problems in scientific, democratic ways, would have had no point if man's behavior were unalterable.

YOU CAN'T CHANGE HUMAN NATURE †

Concerning the world and all that is in it man has had many strange opinions, but none more strange than those about himself. From time to time he has been thought the victim of chance or of fate, the sport of gods or of demons, the nursling of divinity or of nature, the "rubbish of an Adam" or evolution's last and fairest animal. He has spun mythical genealogies and embroidered those that were actual. He has mourned lost Edens, golden ages, states of nature; and with equal conviction he has awaited new heavens, new paradises, and new perfections. He has explored the cosmos, and he has mastered the atom. He has seemed to know everything except himself.

One reason is that knowledge is manifested in control. If a man builds a bridge capable of sustaining all sorts of traffic, you will

---

* The two selections that follow, the one by Dunham and the one by Mirsky (p. 58), are considered jointly. The problems covering these selections begin on p. 61.

† From *Man Against Myth* by Barrows Dunham, by permission of Little, Brown & Co. Copyright, 1947, by Barrows Dunham.

readily believe that he understands engineering. But evidence of this sort, which is the living testimony of practice, is singularly absent in social affairs. We have already had occasion to observe that, however much men may control the physical universe, they exert far less conscious, planned control over their relations with one another. In these, the most important of all matters, men seem more ignorant than perhaps they really are.

This seeming ignorance can be found, also, in the anarchic state of psychological theory. There is no single, reigning doctrine to which psychologists assent, as physicists do to the theory of relativity. On the contrary, there are various doctrines which compete for acceptance. Some of them, like the Freudian, hold that human behavior is decisively conditioned by inborn impulses; others, like the Behaviorist, hold that it is decisively conditioned by environmental influences. This welter of opinion suggests that the science is still immature and that its assemblage and analysis of data is very incomplete.

Immature as psychology may be, there is no reason to suppose that it will not grow, or that successful generalizations about the data will never be made. Further study will presumably reveal such generalizations, and an increasing stability in man's social relationships would undoubtedly speed the process. Meanwhile, one must look with some caution upon all psychological theories, including, I suppose, the one I shall present in this chapter.

The unsettled state of psychology, however, is favorable to the perpetuation of myths; and the myths, so long as they survive, retard the progress of the science itself. Men who have their social conclusions already in mind can borrow freely from what appears to be scientific data, there being no doctrine of sufficient authority to prevent such practices. Moreover, we are all of us men living among men, and our experiences of one another generate, almost unsolicited, certain convictions about human nature. That is to say, we are all of us amateur psychologists, and we bestow upon our views the sort of mystical accuracy which a believer in home remedies opposes to the advice of physicians.

In such a climate illusions multiply, and among them there is, I suppose, none more ubiquitous than the idea that "you can't change human nature." This ancient platitude might long ago have been relegated to a home for superannuated ideas, were it not so constantly useful. It has been voiced by a motley congregation of sinners and saints, rulers and slaves, philosophers, monks, theologians, psychiatrists, journalists, statesmen, and professors. Everyone has said it; many have believed it; few have understood it.

Its uses are multifarious. Is there poverty in the world? That's because men are naturally improvident. Are people unemployed? That's because men are naturally lazy. Are there wars? That's because men are naturally belligerent. Do men cheat, injure, and bankrupt one another in economic competition? That's because men naturally act on the profit motive. Have some men been slaves when others were slaveowners, or serfs when others were kings? That's because they were all born to be so, each in his kind.

Or again: Do we wish to prevent the development of criminals and to rehabilitate those already made? It's no use: you can't change human nature. Do we wish to enact justice and equality among races? It's no use: you can't change human nature. Do we wish to spread the enlightenment of science to all mankind? It's no use: you can't change human stupidity.

Or again, a much more cautious variant: Do we wish to extend the suffrage to millions now without it? Impossible: they must be educated first. Do we wish to abolish the several discriminations against Jews and Negroes? Impossible: people's "attitudes" must be changed first. Do we wish to make decisive improvements in the nature of society? Impossible: men's souls must first be changed, "materialism" giving way to "spirituality."

It may appear that the views in this last category assume the possibility of changing human nature. That appearance, however, is illusory, for the change which is assumed is completely divorced from the social milieu in which alone change can occur. It therefore becomes an abstract conception, floating agreeably in the minds of its possessors.

Take, for example, the disfranchisement of American Negroes. Our imaginary antagonist says that he is democratically fond of Negroes, but that he does not think they should vote until they have been educated. Very well, let us admire his democratic fondness. But the Negroes will not be adequately educated until they have adequate access to schools. They will not have adequate access to schools until there are adequate legislative appropriations. There will be no adequate legislative appropriations until legislators are

elected who will really represent the disfranchised. Few such legislators will be elected until the disfranchised are allowed to vote.
Thus our friend, in postponing the suffrage, postpones also the education which is supposed to qualify voters for the suffrage. The
change he says he desires is one which he has rendered impossible,
and cynics may surmise that he never really desired it.

It is easy enough to be an idealist so long as ideals are unrelated
to action. Such men, when pressed with arguments or when confronted with the necessity of decision, will retreat into the assertion
that there is no real change anyhow, that all we do is to tinker
with externals. For the advocacy of impossible change is in fact
the advocacy of no change at all. . . .

Human nature is said to be unalterable [because] men are
universally and incurably selfish. . . . From Thrasymachus through
Machiavelli down to their followers in the present day, a long line
of dismal commentators has proclaimed this doctrine in accents
of ill-concealed pleasure. Acceptance of it is supposed to be the
essence of worldly wisdom and even, theologically speaking, a means
of salvation. It seems odd that one should expect to enter heaven
upon the assumption that one is a creature of hell; but, unless I mis-
read the authorities, this is precisely what they assert.

At any rate, the term "selfishness" means what is sometimes called
man's inhumanity to man, the sacrifice of other people's interests to
one's own advantage. The extreme example of this is the form of
organized violence which is war. Accordingly, we hear on all sides
the assertion that war can never be abolished, because it has its
source in the unchangeable nature of man. Let us look at a few
expressions of this view:

> Man is a beast of prey. I shall say it again and again. . . . Conflict is
> the original fact of life, is life itself, and not the most pitiful pacifist is
> able entirely to uproot the pleasure it gives his inmost soul.[1]

> It was in his [Dr. Charles W. Mayo's] opinion absurd to imagine that
> it would ever be possible to abolish war. War is part of our human in-
> heritance and hence lies beyond our control.[2]

[1] Oswald Spengler: "The Return of the Caesars," *American Mercury*, Vol.
31, p. 137.
[2] John M. Fletcher: "Human Nature and World Peace," *Virginia Quarterly
Review*, Vol. 20, p. 351. Mr. Fletcher takes the opposite view.

Nothing done at San Francisco will alter the essential nature of man—in which are buried the complex causes of war.[3]

Mr. Baldwin proceeded to accept this "fact" with a stoicism worthy of a military analyst:

The guiding star still shines; it cannot be attained in a century or two. But it is nevertheless worth struggling forward, pushing on; it would be worth the effort even if we knew the star was a mirage. Death is an accepted part of life. Yet death is no cause for despair. The whole philosophy of man is keyed to the conception of the ultimate triumph of life over death. Why, then, despair because war recurs?

Why despair? Because in war one's friends get killed, one's children get killed, and one gets killed oneself. Because everything one has built may be destroyed. Because it is idiocy to fight one war for the sake of fighting another later on. If human nature really does inevitably produce war, let us accept the fact without surrounding it with this comfortless nonsense.

One may take some encouragement from the fact that Mr. Baldwin thinks it worth while to chase after mirages. In other words, he thinks that some illusions are valuable for the entire human race. Now a man who thinks that some illusions are valuable is a man who will be a little careless of the distinction between illusion and reality. Perhaps, then, he is deceived about the connection between human nature and war. I think we shall find that he certainly is, and that Herr Spengler (the converted Nazi) and Dr. Mayo are deceived also.

I have said that war is an extreme case of man's inhumanity to man. It is, therefore, a limit to a certain kind of behavior. If we can show that this kind of behavior is not an essential part of human nature, then the limiting case will not be an essential part of human nature either. For example, extreme brilliance would be the limiting case of a burning light. Then, if it can be shown that the light does not necessarily burn at all, we can infer that the light does not necessarily have extreme brilliance.

Let us ask ourselves, then, whether everything that men do involves loss and sacrifice for other people. There is no question

[3] Hanson W. Baldwin: "San Francisco Outlook," the *New York Times*, May 21, 1945, p. 10.

that *some* of the things men do are things which have this effect. But do *all* of them? The answer is plainly, no. So far as one's personal relations with one's fellows are concerned, the proportion of such acts is relatively small. On a social scale the proportion is rather larger; but even here the division of labor, which is a basic social fact, no matter how competitive the society may be, is a sort of unconsciously co-operative behavior on behalf of the general good. A society in which nobody ever did anything for the benefit of others would be one in which no division of labor could exist. It would, indeed, hardly be a society at all.

Well, then, we have established the fact that some of the things men do are things which benefit other people, although of course some of the things are not so. We can infer from this that behavior which benefits other people is at least as consistent with human nature as behavior which harms other people. This being true, it is plainly impossible to say that human nature is selfish in the sense that selfishness is present in all human actions.

Nevertheless, granting all this, it might still be true that selfishness exists in human nature side by side with social-mindedness, and that, as such, it is ineradicable. Expressed in concrete terms, such a view would mean that there are some things which men so profoundly need and desire that they will injure other people in order to get them. Apparently there are such things. But before you can predict that men will universally and inevitably commit these injuries for the sake of these gains, you must make one further and very important assumption: you must assume *that the gains are obtainable in no other way.* For if the gains are obtainable in some other way (by co-operation, for instance), what reason have you to suppose that men will not choose it? The only sufficient reason would be that human behavior is always selfish. But we have just established the falsity of that assertion. You have, therefore, no reason at all.

Suppose, now, it is said that all men have desires, that they seek to satisfy these desires, and that in this manner they constantly display an interest in themselves. Undoubtedly they do. No man has any desires except his own, and in satisfying them he may be said to display self-interest. But self-interest is not selfishness. Self-interest is the satisfaction of one's desires; selfishness is the satisfaction of one's desires at the expense of someone else. We may grant that self-interest is an essential part of human nature. I think, indeed, that it is. But we are still very far from being able to infer from this that selfishness is an essential part of human nature. We cannot possibly infer that it is so, unless we assume that all our desires are satisfied at cost to someone else. This concealed assumption, like the one previously discussed, is plainly false. We satisfy our desires in common with other people every day of our lives, and indeed the satisfaction of some of our desires *involves* the satisfaction of other people's. If this were not so, the institution of the meal, for example, would be wholly inconceivable.

Since we have now come to the question of desires, let us ask what it is that human beings may be said generally to want. If we set aside deceptive abstractions like "power," and if we attend to what may be called normal desires, as distinguished from manias and perversions (i.e. pathological states), we shall find that men chiefly want food, shelter, clothing, companionship, play, and sexual love. So far as one can tell from introspection into one's own behavior and from observation of other people's, both present and past, these desires are universal and basic. They are, furthermore, necessary conditions for the maintenance of the individual and of the race. It would make sense to say that human nature will always produce behavior in accordance with these desires.

But where is the "inevitable" selfishness? In themselves these desires certainly seem innocent, and at least two of them—companionship and sexual love—are social in their very essence. Upon so bland a substance how can the idea of human depravity be imposed? If such desires are in their own nature evil, then we shall be doing wrong every time we eat or play or put on a suit of clothes. Surely it is obvious that evil cannot exist in the desires themselves, but only in the way they are sometimes satisfied. The point of view which would consider these *desires* evil would be the point of view of a despot whose power is imperiled by the needs of common men. Indeed, it seems probable that precisely this is the social origin of the myth of human selfishness.

Let us recapitulate the argument. We have seen that not all, but only some, of men's acts involve injury to other people and thus merit the adjective "selfish." The selfishness of these acts, however, derives not from the desires which prompted them, but the conditions under which they are performed. But if human nature were inherently selfish, then it would have to be so under any and all conditions. It is so, however, only under some conditions. Human nature, therefore, is not inherently selfish. This argument is a *modus tollens* to the greater glory of the human race.

We can now return to the limiting case from which we started. If, as we see, there is nothing in human nature which necessitates men's injuring one another, then there is nothing in human nature which necessitates war. War can occur under certain conditions, but there is nothing in human nature which renders inevitable the existence of such conditions. As far as human nature is concerned, those conditions need not exist. I think, in fact, that human nature is such that men will one day render such conditions impossible. For, as things now stand, either men will render war impossible or war will render men impossible.

It is worth while to observe, also, that war is far more repugnant to human nature than consistent with it. If war were consistent with human nature in the same sense in which companionship, for example, is consistent with human nature, then war would be a state in which men felt free and at ease. Exactly the reverse, of course, is true. War is in fact so repugnant to normal human behavior that men have to be drafted into it, and all modern armies provide staffs of psychiatrists to care for the psychological ills which war engenders. Happiness is a good test of what conditions are in harmony with human nature, and by that test war must seem to be unnatural indeed.

One thing more remains to be said. The doctrine that human nature is incurably selfish is not just an assertion about a supposed fact; it is also a moral judgment of condemnation. Like other social myths, it contains a fusion (not to say, a confusion) of scientific and moral concepts. We are told not only that men are what they are, but that they are bad, too. Apparently, to see is to disapprove, to know is to condemn. We may wonder, perhaps, how creatures so dyed in villainy were ever able to conceive the moral standards by which they condemn themselves, how sinners so inveterate could ever have thought that they might be improved. But the moral judgment has certain social effects of its own, and these require examination.

If human nature is unalterably selfish, then to the extent that it is so, all men share an equal guilt. "In Adam's fall we sinnèd all." But if it is true as a fundamental fact that all men are equally guilty, then no man and no group of men can be singled out as especially iniquitous. Furthermore, there is a feeling that one sinner has no right to condemn another. From these conditions two social results follow:

(1) It becomes impossible to identify any one man or any one group of men as the source of social injustice and therefore as a menace to human welfare. Such a man or such a group of men can hide behind the alleged common and equal guilt of all, and thus escape condemnation. The exploiter and the profiteer and the colonial imperialist can say, "I'm only being human." In fact, that is exactly what they do say. The essence of Goering's defense at the Nuremberg trial was that he did exactly what anybody else would have done.

(2) It becomes impossible for any of us to claim the moral right to put an end to injustice. For if it is true that all men are equally sinners and that no sinner is entitled to condemn another, then none of us has the right to condemn profiteers and exploiters and imperialists. I well remember, during the Spanish Civil War, the assertions of the Reverend Mr. A. J. Muste that all nations had been guilty of aggression and that therefore no nation had the right to oppose German and Italian aggression in Spain. Such an argument is paralyzing. If we had taken it as our guide, we should simply have surrendered on high moral grounds to the Axis fascists.

Here, then, I think we have the true social reason for the doctrine of human selfishness. It exists because it has a special function to perform, not because it has any correspondence with fact. It exists because it conceals the men of power and their antisocial behavior. It exists because it robs us of the moral confidence necessary to attack them. It is, therefore, one of many ideological chains fastened upon mankind. Men may commit sins, but they can commit no sin so monstrous as believing themselves to be incurable.

RATS AND MEN *

Coming from that monastic retreat of ours over on the East Side, I want to tell you a few of the very simple things we do in the laboratories, because if you realize that most of these things we do are very simple, then I think you will understand that any barrier between our laboratories and the external world is quite an artificial one.

The kind of external problem that I want to suggest that this simple work has a bearing on, is the problem that this Conference is concerned with, the basis for democratic faith.

Perhaps many of you have noticed that those people who do not have the democratic faith usually have a very low opinion of human nature and it has always been that way. The classical example of that in our own country was the statement of Alexander Hamilton that "the people is a great beast" and practically all Tories and reactionaries in one way or another will agree with Hamilton's statement. On the other hand, people who do have the democratic faith usually have a much more optimistic point of view towards human nature.

Having said so much, I want to tell you just a little bit about rats, because in laboratories we usually do not study man, although man should be studied in laboratories much more than he is. But we often take rats or fruit-flies or frogs or some creature that we can handle with some ease and about which we can be much more objective than we can about man.

You all know something about rats, and in most biological laboratories there are large colonies of them. The rats are used for all kinds of purposes. It is very well known to anybody who has a rat colony that if he doesn't keep the cages clean, and if he doesn't feed his animals well and doesn't take good care of them, they will really be "rats." They become very wild, uncontrollable creatures. It is common for mothers to eat their litters, and if you wanted to handle such a rat, you would take a good thick leather gauntlet,

* From a paper read by Alfred Mirsky at the Conference on the Scientific Spirit and Democratic Faith. Published in *The Scientific Spirit and Democratic Faith*, Columbia University Press, New York, 1944.

so that the rat would not bite you. Now that is so well known that nobody in the laboratory, if he can help it, treats his rats other than with care. He keeps them very clean and he feeds them as well as he knows how. He takes care of them as well as he knows how to. The result is that a laboratory rat is quite a mild creature, quite different from the proverbial rat. If a rat has been treated properly there is no great need to use a leather gauntlet. You can take a rat right out in your hand and he is quite a gentle creature.

So much for these rather obvious ways of taking care of rats. This information doesn't come from any theoretical or speculative kinds of biology. I have found a very good description in a little manual put out by the Wistar Institute some time ago, describing the care of rats. This manual is actually meant for rat keepers; and it tells you how to go about taking care of rats so that you have a colony that can be used for experimental purposes.

Their point is that even after you have taken the kind of care that I have just described, you have got to go way beyond that. They say that individual attention shown by handling and petting is essential for the best growth of rats and for securing uniform reactions from them when used as research animals. The rats should have ample opportunity to know their caretakers, and so on; they describe all this gentling treatment to which a rat must be exposed if he really is going to be as useful as possible just as an experimental animal. They finally actually use the word "gentled." They refer to such rats as being well nourished and also as being "gentled."

In the laboratory, we try to get some simple criteria of what that means, and these people give you one very simple one. It is very impressive. When a physiologist has a rat colony, he uses these rats for experiments. One experiment that some physiologists used their rats for was to take out the parathyroid gland. They found that if they took out this gland from rats that had been well nourished but not gentled, eighty-five per cent of those rats died, due to the operation, but that seventy-five per cent of the gentled rats survived. In other words, those rats that had been treated in what you might call a civilized way actually were far more vigorous animals while at the same time far gentler.

Now, if you take a rat out of the park—there are some rats running around there—take him into your house and feed him well, and then talk to him the way these keepers do, you will find that this isn't nearly as simple as I may have implied. Such rats may remain nearly as wild as they are now. The reason is that there is another factor involved. The laboratory rat when ill cared for is not very different from a wild rat, but the wild rat can never be turned into this kind of gentled rat that I have described. Genetically, he is quite a different animal. His inherent germ-plasm or whatever you care to call it is different from that of the rats that I have spoken about, and it really is impossible to gentle his variety of rat.

The point is that until you have provided the proper treatment for these other rats with the more favorable genetic constitution, you never would know that they are any different from the wild rat, and in order to bring out the proper rat nature of these laboratory rats, you have to go to an awful lot of trouble. You have to take much more trouble with these rats than we ordinarily take with human beings, but the result is very clear. These laboratory rats do not inherit a gentle constitution. When we say that they inherit an eye color, the color of their fur, or anything of that kind, this is only a shorthand way of saying something. What we really mean when referring to all characters inherited is that these animals inherit also a certain potentiality—the ability to respond in a certain way. We can say that these gentled rats are not gentle by inheritance; they have the potentiality to be gentled, but they show this only when circumstances are favorable.

Well now, that is the kind of story that we used to hear when I was in the Ethical Culture School, but I can say that it is a very easily demonstrable kind of story, and the implications for man and for the democratic faith are, I think, simple and obvious.

Let us take as an example the influence of proper nutrition. In England for a long time anyone who took note could see a tremendous difference in physique between the upper and lower classes. That was true in this country also but much less so. In England, in Francis Galton's time, when eugenics was being founded, practically everybody thought the difference in physique represented a difference in inherent constitution. Perhaps the upper classes were descended from the Norman conquerors—something of that kind! But now, in recent years, it has been shown without any doubt that if you give boys in the poorer schools as much milk as richer boys get and a few other items in their diet, their physique will approximate pretty closely to that of the boys in the upper classes. So for this particular factor, the factor of nutrition, we haven't by any means done what we can do, but we do know now what the score is. But of these other factors, the gentling that I have referred to, we know very little, and on the whole, very little has yet been done. This still is a world in which most people are intimidated the way rats ordinarily are not in laboratories, and we scarcely know what the potentialities of man are. But I think we know enough to say that if man were treated the way these rats have been in the laboratory, then the kind of statement that Alexander Hamilton made would appear just preposterous. There are good grounds for the democratic faith; in other words, for the faith that there are some good potentialities in ordinary human beings.

What we do with these rats is not at all different from the kind of ideas members of this Conference have in mind about human beings. But just because we do go into monastic seclusion, we can make some of the problems involved a good deal simpler than can be done with problems in the outside world.

PROBLEMS

1. Do you find enough that is suspect in the statement "you can't change human nature" to warrant re-examining it? Recalling Mander's remarks about "groundless beliefs" (pp. 5-11), do you see evidence of his contention that myths flourish when we do not yet know much about a subject and when we feel it to be in our self-interest to believe a certain thing? Note (1) the comparative youthfulness of psychology as a science, and (2) the way in which the "human nature" argument can be used to justify a questionable course of action.

2. What basic distinction does Dunham make between selfishness and self-interest?

3. Dunham suggests that many of the things we do to satisfy our own desires do not hurt, in fact, may help other people. Test his proposition in the following way:
   a. list things you have done within the past twenty-four hours;
   b. determine in each case whether the action was taken to satisfy a personal desire;
   c. then check those actions which did not, as far as you can tell, hurt anyone. Are any actions left unchecked? What conclusion

about the alleged "selfishness of human nature" can you logically reach?

4. If the "selfishness" or "unselfishness" of men's actions depends, as Dunham concludes, not on "human nature" but on the *circumstances* of his actions, what changes of belief in the inevitability or "naturalness" of such things as war, stealing, cruelty, cheating, non-co-operation, or cutthroat competition would appear logical?

5. Dunham concludes that men would not sometimes believe themselves basically selfish if they really *were* entirely selfish. Explain his point.

6. What distinction may be made between *moral* judgments and judgments of *fact*—between "It's bad" and "It happened," between "He committed a crime" and "He drove at 80 miles an hour in a 40-mile-an-hour zone"?

7. Do Mirsky's observations of the laboratory rats tend indirectly to support or contradict Dunham's contention that "human nature" is not essentially "selfish"?

8. Is Mirsky justified in drawing a conclusion about *human beings* from his observations of rats? Give the reasons for your answer.

GENERAL PROBLEMS:
Testing Your Own Beliefs

1. Describe in detail, on the basis of your personal experience, the ways in which the members of a group (club, school, neighborhood, community, labor organization, business group, professional organization, craft, and so forth) reacted to an idea that was a departure from their generally accepted way of thinking or doing. (For example, what happened when a new system of grading or a new kind of examination was introduced into a school? How did your fraternity or club take the officers' decision to liberalize membership requirements? What did the employees think and do when a new procedure or a new type of machine was brought into the factory or shop? How did people in your community think and talk when a new type of residential dwelling was built there?)

2. First, list widely held beliefs about three or four of the following classes of people: "only" children, precocious children (child prodigies), schoolteachers, truck drivers, stenographers, union officials, foremen, landlords, renters, detectives, gangsters, news reporters, opera singers, Hollywood movie stars, women drivers, Irishmen,

Scotchmen, Swedes, Germans, Americans, Spaniards, Russians, Orientals, Poles, Jews, American Indians, Negroes, Englishmen.

Now, take one belief which *you* hold about one of these classes and examine as many personal experiences *with individuals* of that class as you can remember. (In doing so, take care not to overlook cases that may not support the belief.)

Does your personal knowledge of individuals of that class support your belief? That is, does the pattern of the individual cases *exactly fit* the pattern of your belief about that class of people? If it does not, what does this indicate about the "grounds" for your belief? If you have noticed any marked differences between the behavior of certain *individuals* in the class and your preconceived idea of how that *class* behaves, have you considered environmental differences as a possible explanation? How could an awareness of these environmental differences lead to a modification of your belief?

3. One overall point made in this section, "Testing Your Own Beliefs," is that most people hold a number of very popular, widely accepted ideas which they seldom question, assumptions which they take pretty much for granted and use (often quite unconsciously) as premises to prove such-and-such a thing true or such-and-such an action justifiable.

To test the soundness of this observation, do the following: *select seven topics,* one from each paragraph of subjects given below, and record any beliefs about those topics which large numbers of people accept without question. For example, the topic "democracy" might immediately remind you of the belief, accepted by a great many people as being beyond doubt, that a democracy exists wherever the people can vote for their representatives. Again, the topic "human progress" may bring to mind the widely accepted view that the human race has progressed during the past 2000 years; "superstition in our ancestors" may suggest the common notion that we are less superstitious than our ancestors; "frontier life," the picture of all frontiersmen as rugged and adventurous; "mental discipline," the deep-rooted belief that the study of certain subjects, mathematics, for instance, helps one to think more precisely about other subjects; "normal behavior," the assumption that there is such a thing as *normal* behavior; "genius," the belief that genius is a special quality limited to a few people; or "the frankness of present-day speaking and writing," the seldom questioned assumption that today people are much more frank and outspoken than they used to be.

Remember, in making this test, that you are looking not *for ideas you consider correct or incorrect but for ideas that are widely accepted as unchallengeable.*

History: history's repeating itself; human progress; superstition in our ancestors; the Dark Ages; the American Revolution; the Constitution; American neutrality; America's role in World Wars I and/or II; frontier life; "this mechanical age."

Economics and politics: "the law of supply and demand"; taxes; tariffs; profits; wages; living standards; efficiency and/or inefficiency in private business; efficiency and/or inefficiency in government; free enterprise; "big" and "little" business; monopolies; capitalism; socialism; communism; fascism; democracy; bureaucracy; public utilities; public ownership; labor unions; union leaders; strikes; Wall Street; political machines; "the man in the street"; public opinion; "states' rights"; nationalism; imperialism; "power politics"; UN; causes of war; military training.

Physical science: the "typical scientist"; the scientific attitude; nature of scientific "laws"; the scientist as a thinker outside his own field of investigation; applied science and theoretical science; the power of science; the new "wonder drugs"; atomic energy; the hydrogen bomb; evolution; "survival of the fittest"; heredity.

Education and psychology: the real purpose of education; present trends in education; college degrees; a "liberal education"; a "practical education"; "mental discipline"; the elective system in education; marks or grades; big and little colleges; "culture"; the "fundamentals" of education; "book learning"; "learning by doing"; schoolteachers; college professors as "practical men" or "theorists"; Freudianism; psychiatry; the inferiority complex; instinct; "normal" behavior; the IQ; genius.

Press and radio: propaganda; the effect of press and radio on public opinion; reliability of "what you read in the paper"; freedom of the press in America and elsewhere; the intelligence of the reading public.

Religion and ethics: atheism; the role of religion in present-day society; science and religion; selfishness as the basis of human behavior; "character"; the "lack of moral standards" today; the frankness of present-day speaking and writing; the twentieth century as a "materialistic age."

The arts: the nature of "modern art"; abstract art; "serious" or "classical" music; "popular" music; the "artistic type"; the nature of poetry; "modern" poetry or fiction; "poetry and the common man"; "great" literature; the "classics"; inspiration; the effect of the movies on our thinking; foreign films.

4. Again using the list in Problem 3, select *one popular belief* about *one* of the listed topics and indicate all reasons why it should not be

allowed to go unchallenged. (You are not trying to prove it *wrong;* instead, you are considering whether "the case is closed" or whether further investigation is necessary. In answering this and the next problem you might find it helpful to re-read Mill's essay, "How Do We Know What We Believe?")

5. Once more using the list given in Problem 3, this time present an idea *unpopular* today, an idea not widely accepted, and then indicate your reasons for giving it serious consideration, for not dismissing it with a snort or handwave as we frequently do when faced with the unfamiliar and unorthodox. You are being asked here not to show why this idea should be *accepted* but to point out the specific reasons for investigating it further. (If your own thinking is inclined to be orthodox and you cannot think of unpopular ideas, just stand a popular idea on its head, that is, look at it from the opposing point of view.)

Distinguishing Fact from Opinion

ANYONE who has ever developed an appetite for testing his own beliefs is quickly made aware of the need for distinguishing fact from opinion.

Why is it that so often in an argument we appeal to someone on our side for his "opinion," whereas we defiantly demand that our opponent produce "facts"? Why does a detective bureau sending an investigator out on a case charge him to "get the facts"? Why does a judge frequently interrupt the testimony of a witness with a firm reminder that it is "the facts" in which the court is interested, not the witness's opinions? Why does an engineer investigating a ruptured sewer line ask for specific "facts" about the composition of the pipe, its diameter, the nature of the soil in which it rests, and so forth? Why does a general interrogating his scouts press them so hard for "factual details"—the number of enemy tanks, the disposition of fuel supplies?

Let us look at the problem somewhat differently: To what sources do two sports enthusiasts turn when they are arguing about Ted Williams' batting average for 1950? To what source does a man in a strange city turn when he wishes to find the address and telephone number of a friend? To what source do the judges of a rowing regatta turn today when they are uncertain as to who placed second and third in a close finish?

Let us attack the problem from still another point of view: Are we apt to be more satisfied with fact or with opinion when we are discussing the merits of a movie? the price of a roll of film? the quality of a dinner? the price of a pound of steak? the color arrangement in a painting? the color of a pint of enamel with which we are going to paint our porch chair? the readability of a book? the time? the disposition of a girl? the disposition of a horse?

How do the answers to these questions help us to answer the following questions: Do we ever distinguish fact from opinion? If so, when? Why? About what kinds of problems can we usually find satisfactory *factual* answers? What kinds of questions do not seem to lend themselves so easily to factual answers? Under what circumstances might we confuse fact and opinion?

If, in your *opinion,* your answers to these questions are not completely satisfying and you wish to make them so, if you'd like to learn some *facts* about facts and opinions, if you wish to read an essay that will (in the editors' *opinion*) go a long way toward helping you remove some of the kinks from your thinking, then try the first essay in this section. After you have read Hayakawa's analysis of the distinction between fact and opinion, you will be in a position to appreciate the difficult task that faced Henry J. Taylor when he was assigned to "get the facts" about the celebrated Patton slapping incidents, to see the pitfalls that Milton Mayer saw in a news report, and to relish with Mark Twain the peculiar difficulties that face a police magistrate who is trying to determine "The Evidence in the Case."

S. I. Hayakawa

The distinction between *observed facts* and *opinions or conclusions about them*—or, in written and spoken language, between *reports* and *judgments*—is one that is very easy to overlook. Are you aware of the difference between your remarks, "He's a swell guy!" and "He loaned me five dollars"? Of the difference between "The cost of living is too high" and "My living expenses have doubled in the past four years, while my salary has gone up 50 per cent in the same period"?

Hayakawa is concerned here not just with *what* we say or *how* we say it. He is thinking about *both* content and language (the symbols we use to express content) and *the effect of one on the other*. Hayakawa is probably the clearest writer on the semantic approach to language, i.e., the study of all the problems involved in our use of word-symbols to represent our experiences and ideas. The simplest way to become familiar with the ideas and books of present-day semanticists is to look at a few copies of *ETC: A Review of General Semantics,* a small but stimulating quarterly magazine edited by Hayakawa. And don't make the mistake of thinking you have to have a professional interest in language to appreciate semantics. Students of physics, mathematics, psychology, anthropology, folklore, and political science are likely to find a study of semantics challenging and useful.

THE LANGUAGE OF REPORTS *

For the purposes of the interchange of information, the basic symbolic act is the *report* of what we have seen, heard, or felt: "There is a ditch on each side of the road." "You can get those at Smith's hardware store for $2.75." "There aren't any fish on that side of the lake, but there are on this side." Then there are reports of reports: "The longest waterfall in the world is Victoria Falls in Rhodesia." "The Battle of Hastings took place in 1066." "The papers say that there was a big smash-up on Highway 41 near Evansville." Reports adhere to the following rules: first, they are *capable of verification;* second, they *exclude,* as far as possible, *inferences* and *judgments.* (These terms will be defined later.)

VERIFIABILITY

Reports are verifiable. We may not always be able to verify them ourselves, since we cannot track down the evidence for every piece of history we know, nor can we all go to Evansville to see the remains of the smash-up before they are cleared away. But if we are roughly agreed on the names of things, on what constitutes a "foot," "yard," "bushel," and so on, and on how to measure time, there is relatively little danger of our misunderstanding each other. Even in a world such as we have today, in which everybody seems to be quarreling with everybody else, *we still to a surprising degree trust each other's reports.* We ask directions of total strangers when we are traveling. We follow directions on road signs without being suspicious of the people who put them up. We read books of information about science, mathematics, automotive engineering, travel, geography, the history of costume, and other such factual matters, and we usually assume that the author is doing his best to tell us as truly as he can what he knows. And we are safe in so

* From *Language in Thought and Action,* by S. I. Hayakawa, copyright, 1941, 1949, by Harcourt Brace and Company, Inc.

assuming most of the time. With the emphasis that is being given today to the discussion of biased newspapers, propagandists, and the general untrustworthiness of many of the communications we receive, we are likely to forget that we still have an enormous amount of reliable information available and that deliberate misinformation, except in warfare, still is more the exception than the rule. The desire for self-preservation that compelled men to evolve means for the exchange of information also compels them to regard the giving of false information as profoundly reprehensible.

At its highest development, the language of reports is the language of science. By "highest development" we mean greatest general usefulness. Presbyterian and Catholic, workingman and capitalist, German and Englishman, *agree* on the meanings of such symbols as $2 \times 2 = 4$, $100°C.$, HNO_3, 3:35 A.M., 1940 A.D., 5000 *r.p.m.*, *1000 kilowatts, pulex irritans,* and so on. But how, it may be asked, can there be agreement about even this much among people who are at each other's throats about practically everything else: political philosophies, ethical ideals, religious beliefs, and the survival of my business *versus* the survival of yours? The answer is that circumstances *compel men to agree,* whether they wish to or not. If, for example, there were a dozen different religious sects in the United States, each insisting on its own way of naming the time of the day and the days of the year, the mere necessity of having a dozen different calendars, a dozen different kinds of watches, and a dozen sets of schedules for business hours, trains, and radio programs, to say nothing of the effort that would be required for translating terms from one nomenclature to another, would make life as we know it impossible.

The language of reports, then, including the more accurate reports of science, is "map" language, and because it gives us reasonably accurate representations of the "territory," it enables us to get work done. Such language may often be what is commonly termed "dull" or "uninteresting" reading: one does not usually read logarithmic tables or telephone directories for entertainment. But we could not get along without it. There are numberless occasions in the talking and writing we do in everyday life that *require that we state things in such a way that everybody will agree with our formulation.*

INFERENCES

The reader will find that practice in writing reports is a quick means of increasing his linguistic awareness. It is an exercise which will constantly provide him with his own examples of the principles of language and interpretation under discussion. The reports should be about first-hand experience—scenes the reader has witnessed himself, meetings and social events he has taken part in, people he knows well. They should be of such a nature that they can be verified and agreed upon. For the purpose of this exercise, inferences will be excluded.

Not that inferences are not important—we rely in everyday life and in science as much on *inferences* as on reports—in some areas of thought, for example, geology, paleontology, and nuclear physics, reports are the foundations, but inferences (and inferences upon inferences) are the main body of the science. An inference, as we shall use the term, is *a statement about the unknown made on the basis of the known.* We may *infer* from the handsomeness of a woman's clothes her wealth or social position; we may *infer* from the character of the ruins the origin of the fire that destroyed the building; we may *infer* from a man's calloused hands the nature of his occupation; we may *infer* from a senator's vote on an armaments bill his attitude toward Russia; we may *infer* from the structure of the land the path of a prehistoric glacier; we may *infer* from a halo on an unexposed photographic plate that it has been in the vicinity of radioactive materials; we may *infer* from the noise an engine makes the condition of its connecting rods. Inferences may be carelessly or carefully made. They may be made on the basis of a great background of previous experience with the subject-matter, or no experience at all. For example, the inferences a good mechanic can make about the internal condition of a motor by listening to it are often startlingly accurate, while the inferences made by an amateur (if he tries to make any) may be entirely wrong. But the common characteristic of inferences is that they are statements about matters which are not directly known, made on the basis of what has been observed.

The avoidance of inferences in our suggested practice in report-writing requires that we make no guesses as to what is going on in other people's minds. When we say, "He was angry," we are not reporting; we are making an inference from such observable facts as the following: "He pounded his fist on the table; he swore; he threw the telephone directory at his stenographer." In this particular example, the inference appears to be fairly safe; nevertheless, it is important to remember, especially for the purposes of training oneself, that it is an inference. Such expressions as "He thought a lot of himself," "He was scared of girls," "He has an inferiority complex," made on the basis of casual social observation, and "What Russia really wants to do is to establish a world communist dictatorship," made on the basis of casual newspaper reading, are highly inferential. One should keep in mind their inferential character and, in our suggested exercises, should substitute for them such statements as "He rarely spoke to subordinates in the plant," "I saw him at a party, and he never danced except when one of the girls asked him to," "He wouldn't apply for the scholarship although I believe he could have won it easily," and "The Russian delegation to the United Nations has asked for A, B, and C. Last year they voted against M and N, and voted for X and Y. On the basis of facts such as these, the newspaper I read makes the inference that what Russia really wants is to establish a world communist dictatorship. I tend to agree."

JUDGMENTS

In our suggested writing exercise, judgments are also to be excluded. By judgments, we shall mean *all expressions of the writer's approval or disapproval of the occurrences, persons, or objects he is describing.* For example, a report cannot say, "It was a wonderful car," but must say something like this: "It has been driven 50,000 miles and has never required any repairs." Again statements like "Jack lied to us" must be suppressed in favor of the more verifiable statement, "Jack told us he didn't have the keys to his car with him. However, when he pulled a handkerchief out of his pocket a few minutes later, a bunch of car keys fell out." Also a report may not say, "The senator was stubborn, defiant, and unco-operative," or "The senator courageously stood by his principles"; it must say instead, "The senator's vote was the only one against the bill."

Many people regard statements like the following as statements of "fact": "Jack *lied* to us," "Jerry is a *thief*," "Tommy is *clever*." As ordinarily employed, however, the word *"lied"* involves first an inference (that Jack knew otherwise and deliberately misstated the facts) and secondly a judgment (that the speaker disapproves of what he has inferred that Jack did). In the other two instances, we may substitute such expressions as, "Jerry was convicted of theft and served two years at Waupun," and "Tommy plays the violin, leads his class in school, and is captain of the debating team." After all, to say of a man that he is a "thief" is to say in effect, "He has stolen *and will steal again"*—which is more of a prediction than a report. Even to say, "He has stolen," is to make an inference (and simultaneously to pass a judgment) on an act about which there may be difference of opinion among those who have examined the evidence upon which the conviction was obtained. But to say that he was "convicted of theft" is to make a statement capable of being agreed upon through verification in court and prison records.

Scientific verifiability rests upon the external observation of facts, not upon the heaping up of judgments. If one person says, "Peter is a deadbeat," and another says, "I think so too," the statement has not been verified. In court cases, considerable trouble is sometimes caused by witnesses who cannot distinguish their judgments from the facts upon which those judgments are based. Cross-examinations under these circumstances go something like this:

WITNESS: That dirty double-crosser Jacobs ratted on me.
DEFENSE ATTORNEY: Your honor, I object.
JUDGE: Objection sustained. (Witness's remark is stricken from the record.) Now, try to tell the court exactly what happened.
WITNESS: He double-crossed me, the dirty, lying rat!
DEFENSE ATTORNEY: Your honor, I object!
JUDGE: Objection sustained. (Witness's remark is again stricken from the record.) Will the witness try to stick to the facts.
WITNESS: But I'm telling you the facts, your honor. He did double-cross me.

This can continue indefinitely unless the cross-examiner exercises some ingenuity in order to get at the facts behind the judgment. To the witness it is a "fact" that he was "double-crossed." Often hours of patient questioning are required before the factual bases of the judgment are revealed.

colored terms

Many words, of course, simultaneously convey a report and a judgment on the fact reported, as will be discussed more fully in a later chapter. For the purposes of a report as here defined, these should be avoided. Instead of "sneaked in," one might say "entered quietly"; instead of "politicians," "congressmen," or "aldermen," or "candidates for office"; instead of "bureaucrat," "public official"; instead of "tramp," "homeless unemployed"; instead of "dictatorial set-up," "centralized authority"; instead of "crackpots," "holders of uncommon views." A newspaper reporter, for example, is not permitted to write, "A crowd of suckers came to listen to Senator Smith last evening in that rickety firetrap and ex-dive that disfigures the south edge of town." Instead he says, "Between seventy-five and a hundred people heard an address last evening by Senator Smith at the Evergreen Gardens near the South Side city limits."

colored Terms

SNARL-WORDS AND PURR-WORDS

Throughout this book, it is important to remember that we are considering language not as an isolated phenomenon, but language in action—language in the full context of the nonlinguistic events which are its setting. The making of noises with the vocal organs is a muscular activity, and like other muscular activities, often involuntary. Our responses to powerful stimuli, such as to something that makes us very angry, are a complex of muscular and physiological events: the contracting of fighting muscles, the increase of blood pressure, change in body chemistry, clutching one's hair, and so on, *and* the making of noises, such as growls and snarls. We are a little too dignified, perhaps, to growl like dogs, but we do the next best thing and substitute series of words, such as "You dirty double-crosser!" "The filthy scum!" Similarly, if we are pleasurably agitated, we may, instead of purring or wagging the tail, say things like "She's the sweetest girl in all the world!"

Speeches such as these are, as direct expressions of approval or disapproval, judgments in their simplest form. They may be said to be human equivalents of snarling and purring. "She's the sweetest girl in all the world" is not a statement about the girl; it is a purr. This seems to be a fairly obvious fact; nevertheless, it is surprising how often, when such a statement is made, both the speaker and the hearer feel that something has been said about the girl. This error is especially common in the interpretation of utterances of orators and editorialists in some of their more excited denunciations of "Reds," "greedy monopolists," "Wall Street," "radicals," "foreign ideologies," and in their more fulsome dithyrambs about "our way of life." Constantly, because of the impressive sound of the words, the elaborate structure of the sentences, and the appearance of intellectual progression, we get the feeling that something is being said about something. On closer examination, however, we discover that these utterances merely say, "What I hate ('Reds,' 'Wall Street,' or whatever) I hate very, very much," and "What I like ('our way of life') I like very, very much." We may call such utterances "snarl-words" and "purr-words." They are not reports describing conditions in the extensional world in any way.

To call these judgments "snarl-words" and "purr-words" does not mean that we should simply shrug them off. It means that we should be careful to *allocate the meaning correctly*—placing such a statement as "She's the sweetest girl in the world" as a revelation of the speaker's state of mind, and not as a revelation of facts about the girl. If the "snarl-words" about "Reds," or "greedy monopolists" are accompanied by verifiable reports (which would also mean that we have previously agreed as to who, specifically, is meant by the term "Reds" or "greedy monopolists"), we might find reason to be just as disturbed as the speaker. If the "purr-words" about the sweetest girl in the world are accompanied by verifiable reports about her appearance, manners, skill in cooking, and so on, we might find reason to admire her too. But "snarl-words" and "purr-words" as such, unaccompanied by reports, offer nothing further to discuss, except possibly the question, "Why do you feel as you do?"

It is usually fruitless to debate such questions as "Was President Roosevelt a great statesman or merely a skillful politician?" "Is the music of Wagner the greatest music of all time or is it merely hysterical screeching?" "Which is the finer sport, tennis or baseball?" "Could Joe Louis in his prime have licked Bob Fitzsimmons in his prime?" To take sides on such issues of conflicting judgments is to reduce oneself to the same level of stubborn imbecility as one's opponents. But to ask questions of the form, "Why do you like (or dislike) Roosevelt (or Wagner, or tennis, or Joe Louis)?" is to learn something about one's friends and neighbors. After listening to their opinions and their reasons for them, we may leave the discussion slightly wiser, slightly better informed, and perhaps slightly less one-sided than we were before the discussion began.

HOW JUDGMENTS STOP THOUGHT

A judgment ("He is a fine boy," "It was a beautiful service," "Baseball is a healthful sport," "She is an awful bore") is a conclusion, summing up a large number of previously observed facts. The reader is probably familiar with the fact that students almost always have difficulty in writing themes of the required length because their ideas give out after a paragraph or two. The reason for this is that those early paragraphs contain so many judgments that there is little left to be said. When the conclusions are carefully excluded, however, and observed facts are given instead, there is never any trouble about the length of papers; in fact, they tend to become too long, since inexperienced writers, when told to give facts, often give far more than are necessary, because they lack discrimination between the important and the trivial.

Still another consequence of judgments early in the course of a written exercise—and this applies also to hasty judgments in everyday thought—is the temporary blindness they induce. When, for example, an essay starts with the words, "He was a real Wall Street executive," or "She was a typical cute little co-ed," if we continue writing at all, we must make all our later statements consistent with those judgments. The result is that all the individual characteristics of this particular "executive" or this particular "co-ed" are lost sight of entirely; and the rest of the essay is likely to deal not with observed facts, but with the writer's private notion (based on previously read stories, movies, pictures, and so forth) of what "Wall Street executives" or "typical co-eds" look like. The premature judgment, that is, often prevents us from seeing what is directly in front of us. Even if the writer feels sure at the beginning of a written exercise that the man he is describing is a "loafer" or that the scene he is describing is a "beautiful residential suburb," he will conscientiously keep such notions out of his head, lest his vision be obstructed.

SLANTING

In the course of writing reports of personal experiences, it will be found that in spite of all endeavors to keep judgments out, some will creep in. An account of a man, for example, may go like this: "He had apparently not shaved for several days, and his face and hands were covered with grime. His shoes were torn, and his coat, which was several sizes too small for him, was spotted with dried clay." Now, in spite of the fact that no judgment has been stated, a very obvious one is implied. Let us contrast this with another description of the same man. "Although his face was bearded and neglected, his eyes were clear, and he looked straight ahead as he walked rapidly down the road. He looked very tall; perhaps the fact that his coat was too small for him emphasized that impression. He was carrying a book under his left arm, and a small terrier ran at his heels." In this example, the impression about the same man is considerably changed, simply by the inclusion of new details and the subordination of unfavorable ones. Even if explicit judgments are kept out of one's writing, implied judgments will get in.

How, then, can we ever give an impartial report? The answer is, of course, that we cannot attain complete impartiality while we use the language of everyday life. Even with the very impersonal language of science, the task is sometimes difficult. Nevertheless, we can, by being aware of the favorable or unfavorable feelings that certain words and facts can arouse, attain enough impartiality for practical purposes. Such awareness enables us to balance the implied favorable and unfavorable judgments against each other. To learn to do this, it is a good idea to write two essays at a time on the same subject, both strict reports, to be read side by side: the first to contain facts and details likely to prejudice the reader in favor of the subject, the second to contain those likely to prejudice the reader against it. For example:

FOR	AGAINST
He had white teeth.	His teeth were uneven.
His eyes were blue, his hair blond and abundant.	He rarely looked people straight in the eye.
He had on a clean blue shirt.	His shirt was frayed at the cuffs.
He often helped his wife with the dishes.	He rarely got through drying dishes without breaking a few.
His pastor spoke very highly of him.	His grocer said he was always slow about paying his bills.

SLANTING BOTH WAYS AT ONCE

This process of selecting details favorable or unfavorable to the subject being described may be termed slanting. Slanting gives no explicit judgments, but it differs from reporting in that it deliberately makes certain judgments inescapable. The writer striving for impartiality will, therefore, take care to slant both for and against his subject, trying as conscientiously as he can to keep the balance even. The next stage of the exercise, then, should be to rewrite the parallel essays into a single coherent essay in which details on both sides are included.

His teeth were white, but uneven; his eyes were blue, his hair blond and abundant. He did not often look people straight in the eye. His shirt was slightly frayed at the cuffs, but it was clean. He frequently helped his wife with the dishes, but he broke many of them. Opinion about him in the community was divided. His grocer said he was slow about paying his bills, but his pastor spoke very highly of him.

This example is, of course, oversimplified and admittedly not very graceful. But practice in writing such essays will first of all help to prevent one from slipping unconsciously from observable facts to judgments; that is, from "He was a member of the Ku Klux Klan" to "the dirty scoundrel!" Next, it will reveal how little we really want to be impartial anyway, especially about our best friends, our parents, our alma mater, our own children, our country, the company we work for, the product we sell, our competitor's product, or anything else in which our interests are deeply involved. Finally, we will discover that, even if we have no wish to be impartial, we write more clearly, more forcefully, and more convincingly by this process of sticking as close as possible to observable facts. There will be, as someone once remarked, more horsepower and less exhaust.

A few weeks of practice in writing reports, slanted reports, and reports slanted both ways will improve powers of observation, as well as ability to recognize soundness of observation in the writings of others. A sharpened sense for the distinction between facts and judgments, facts and inferences, will reduce susceptibility to the flurries of frenzied public opinion which certain people find it to their interest to arouse. Alarming judgments and inferences can be made to appear inevitable by means of skillfully slanted reports. A reader who is aware of the technique of slanting, however, is relatively difficult to stampede by such methods. He knows too well that there may be other relevant facts which have been left out. . . .

. . . The importance of trying to "slant both ways" lies not in the hope of achieving a godlike impartiality in one's thinking and writing—which is manifestly an impossible goal. It lies in discovering what poor reporters most of us really are—in other words, how little we see of the world since we of necessity see it from our own point of view. To discover one's own biases is the beginning of wisdom.

PROBLEMS

1. A proper grasp of Hayakawa's discussion hinges upon your understanding of the meaning of four terms as *he* employs them. Define *report, judgment, inference, slanting.*
2. According to Hayakawa, what is the ideal method of verification? What makes it possible to rely on some kinds of secondhand reports? Which kinds? What is the "language" of these reliable kinds?
3. What is the difference between saying: "That picture shows both the front view and the side view of a woman's figure at the same time," "That picture shows a distorted figure of a woman," "I don't like that picture," and "That picture is no good"? Between saying: "The bridge is unsafe," "The piling of the bridge has been eaten by termites," and "The bridge timbers are in a weakened condition"?
4. A faculty committee of seven announces that it has unanimously agreed to expel a certain student for cheating. Does the *fact* that seven men drawn from different departments agree in this conclusion establish the *fact* that the student did cheat? A publisher's advertisement claimed "500 Colleges Can't Be Wrong!" in announcing the adoption of a new textbook by a number of schools. What is the relation of this statement to the cheating incident?
5. Substitute for the following *inferences* some facts which might make the inferences plausible:
   a. My employer is dictatorial.
   b. The Yale crew wanted to win that race in the worst way.
   c. The majority of Republican Congressmen are not primarily interested in the welfare of the average consumer.

    d. The Democratic Party is keeping itself in power by doing special favors for various pressure groups.

6. Here are seven statements. Are any of them statements about facts?
       a. Last year was a good business year.
       b. The people in Jonesville are a healthy lot.
       c. Our dormitories are overcrowded.
       d. The information comes from authoritative sources in Prague.
       e. C—— obtained a liberal education, while D—— became an expert in business administration.
       f. The UN building is very modern in design.
       g. The new college president brought about higher scholastic standards.

7. Rewrite the following fictitious headlines so as to exclude judgments and inferences. You are provided with the necessary facts in each case.
       a. GOVERNOR SELLS VETERANS DOWN THE RIVER
       (The governor vetoed a bill to give veterans a cash bonus.)
       b. HATE GROUP HOLDS MASS RALLY
       (The Ku Klux Klan held its annual meeting in a large auditorium in Atlanta, Georgia.)
       c. LABOR WINS COSTLY "VICTORY"
       (The United Auto Workers and the Chrysler Motor Company signed a contract under the terms of which workers over 65 will receive $100-a-month pensions, and all workers will receive improved medical and hospital insurance. Prior to signing the contract the UAW had been on strike for 100 days.)
       d. COMMUNISTS HIGH IN STATE DEPARTMENT
       (An ex-Communist says that two State Department employees who have access to Department files were in the Communist Party in 1936.)

8. Which words in the following series may be said to be "'purr-words"? "snarl-words"? neither?
       a. stubborn, firm, mulish
       b. lingered, loitered, hung around
       c. runty, short, not tall
       d. outlandish, eccentric, queer
       e. humble, servile, fawning
       f. mousy, shy, quiet
       g. dignified, reserved, stiff

9. Distinguish in each of the following statements those parts which are factual from those which are expressions of opinion:

a. My brother sold his car because he felt the upkeep was too high.
b. The union went on strike to enable the union leaders to build up their personal power.
c. Picasso is a painter, but that does not excuse his eccentricities.
d. The American Medical Association has levied an assessment on all its members to further its own selfish ends.
e. The United Nations has failed to prevent war; so it's no better than the old League of Nations.
f. The National Association of Manufacturers contributed heavily to the Dewey campaign in order to smash organized labor.
g. The University of California has discharged a large number of its employees in order to silence the criticism of the red-baiting press.
h. The Democratic majority in Congress has attempted to pass the Fair Employment Practice Act in order to win the Negro vote.

Henry J. Taylor

During World War II you probably read about General Patton's slashing (judgment!) armored drives against the Germans in Sicily and later in France, but you very likely remember still more clearly how strongly public opinion ran for and against Patton over his slapping of hospitalized soldiers for what he considered cowardice. It became very difficult to *get the facts* of the case and to keep them in mind, for the incidents had touched off, in an explosive wartime period, the feelings of soldiers and civilians about loyalty, treason, military discipline, tradition, fair play, and the relatively new science of psychology. In fact, it was not until 1947, when tempers had somewhat cooled, that the news report by Henry J. Taylor, correspondent and radio commentator, was published, along with other previously censored dispatches, in the collection, *Deadline Delayed*.

GENERAL PATTON AND THE SICILIAN SLAPPING INCIDENTS *

Headquarters Seventh Army
A.P.O. #758, U. S. Army
29th August, 1943

My dear General Eisenhower:

Replying to your letter of August 17, 1943, I want to commence by thanking you for this additional illustration of your fairness and generous consideration in making the communication personal.

I am at a loss to find words with which to express my chagrin and grief at having given you, a man to whom I owe everything and for whom I would gladly lay down my life, cause for displeasure with me.

I assure you that I had no intention of being either harsh or cruel in my treatment of the two soldiers in question. My sole purpose was to try and restore in them a just appreciation of their obligation as men and soldiers.

In World War I, I had a dear friend and former schoolmate who lost his nerve in an exactly analogous manner, and who, after years of mental anguish, committed suicide.

Both my friend and the medical men with whom I discussed his case assured me that had he been roundly checked at the time of his first misbehavior, he would have been restored to a normal state.

Naturally, this memory actuated me when I inaptly tried to apply the remedies suggested. After each incident I stated to officers with me that I felt I had probably saved an immortal soul. . . .

Very respectfully,
(*signed*) G. S. Patton, Jr.
Lieut. General, U. S. Army

General D. D. Eisenhower
Headquarters AFHQ
APO #512—U. S. Army

* Taken from a news report by Henry J. Taylor in *Deadline Delayed* by Members of the Overseas Press Club of America, published and copyright 1947 by E. P. Dutton and Co., Inc., New York.

When General Patton gave me a copy of this letter he lay back on the bed in his field-trailer and said, "What does that sound like to you?"

"It sounds to me like only half of the story," I said.

So, first, let's see what actually happened.

Private Charles H. Kuhl (in civilian life a carpet layer from South Bend, Indiana), ASN 35536908, L Company, 26th Infantry, 1st Division, was admitted to the 3rd Battalion, 26th Infantry aid station in Sicily on August 2, 1943, at 2:10 P.M.

He had been in the Army eight months and with the 1st Division about thirty days.

A diagnosis of "Exhaustion" was made at the station by Lieutenant H. L. Sanger, Medical Corps, and Kuhl was evacuated to C Company, 1st Medical Battalion, well to the rear of the fighting.

There a note was made on his medical tag stating that he had been admitted to this place three times during the Sicilian campaign.

He was evacuated to the clearing company by Captain J. D. Broom, M.C., put in "quarters" and given sodium amytal, one capsule night and morning, on the prescription of Captain N. S. Nedell, M.C.

On August 3rd the following remark appears on Kuhl's Emergency Medical Tag: "Psychoneuroses anxiety state—moderately severe. Soldier has been twice before in hospital within ten days. He can't take it at front evidently. He is repeatedly returned." (signed) Capt. T. P. Covington, Medical Corps.

By this route and in this way Private Kuhl arrived in the receiving tent of the 15th Evacuation Hospital, where the blow was struck that was heard round the world.

"I came into the tent," explains General Patton, "with the commanding officer of the outfit and other medical officers.

"I spoke to the various patients, especially commending the wounded men. I just get sick inside myself when I see a fellow torn apart, and some of the wounded were in terrible, ghastly shape. Then I came to this man and asked him what was the matter.

The soldier replied, "I guess I can't take it."

"Looking at the others in the tent, so many of them badly beaten up, I simply flew off the handle."

Patton squared off in front of the soldier.

He called the man every kind of a loathsome coward and then slapped him across the face with his gloves.

The soldier fell back. Patton grabbed him by the scruff of the neck and kicked him out of the tent.

Kuhl was immediately picked up by corpsmen and taken to a ward.[1]

Returning to his headquarters Patton issued the following memorandum to Corps, Division and Separate Brigade Commanders two days later:

> Headquarters Seventh Army
> APO #758 U. S. Army
> 5 August, 1943

It has come to my attention that a very small number of soldiers are going to the hospital on the pretext that they are nervously incapable of combat.

Such men are cowards, and bring discredit on the Army and disgrace to their comrades whom they heartlessly leave to endure the danger of a battle while they themselves use the hospital as a means of escaping.

You will take measures to see that such cases are not sent to the hospital, but are dealt with in their units.

Those who are not willing to fight will be tried by Court-Martial for cowardice in the face of the enemy.

> (*Signed*) G. S. Patton, Jr.
> Lieut. General, U. S. Army,
> Commanding

Five days later General Patton, not a medical man, again took matters into his own hands.

He slapped another soldier.

Private Paul G. Bennett, ASN 70000001, C Battery, Field Artillery, was admitted to the 93rd Evacuation Hospital on August 10th at 2:20 P.M.

Bennett, still only twenty-one, had served four years in the Regular Army. He had an excellent record. His unit had been attached to the II Corps since March and he had never had any difficulties

---

[1] There Kuhl was found to have a temperature of 102.2 degrees F., gave a history of chronic diarrhea for the past month, and was shown by a blood test to have malaria.

until four days earlier when his best friend in the outfit, fighting near by, was wounded in action.

Bennett could not sleep that night and felt nervous. The shells going over "bothered" him. "I keep thinking they're going to land right on me," he said. The next day he became increasingly nervous about the firing and about his buddy's recovery.

A battery aid man sent him to the rear echelon, where a medical officer gave him some medicine which made him sleep. But he was still nervous, badly disturbed.

On August 10th the medical officer ordered him to the 93rd Evacuation Hospital, although Bennett begged not to be evacuated because he did not want to leave his unit.

General Patton arrived at the hospital that day.

Bennett was sitting in the receiving tent, huddled up and shivering.

Patton spoke to all the injured men. He was solicitous, kind and inspiring. But when he and Major Charles B. Etter, the receiving officer in charge, reached Bennett and Patton asked the soldier what his trouble was, the soldier replied, "It's my nerves," and began to sob.

Patton turned on him like a tiger, screaming at him:

"What did you say?"

"It's my nerves," sobbed Bennett. "I can't take the shelling any more."

In this moment Patton lost control of himself completely. Without any investigation of the man's case whatever, he rushed close to Bennett and shouted: "Your nerves, hell. You are just a . . . coward, you yellow b——."

Then he slapped the soldier hard across the face.

"Shut up that . . . crying," he yelled. "I won't have these brave men here who have been shot seeing a yellow b—— sitting here crying."

Patton struck at the man again. He knocked his helmet liner off his head into the next tent. Then he turned to Major Etter and yelled, "Don't admit this yellow b——, there's nothing the matter with him. I won't have the hospitals cluttered up with these SOB's who haven't got the guts to fight."

Patton himself began to sob. He wheeled around to Colonel Donald E. Currier, the 93rd's commanding Medical Officer. "I can't help it," he said. "It makes me break down to see brave boys and to think of a yellow b—— being babied."

But this was not all. In his blind fury, Patton turned on Bennett again. The soldier now was managing to sit at attention, although shaking all over.

"You're going back to the front lines," Patton shouted. "You may get shot and killed, but you're going to fight. If you don't, I'll stand you up against a wall and have a firing squad kill you on purpose.

"In fact," he said, reaching for his revolver, "I ought to shoot you myself, you —— whimpering coward."

As he left the tent Patton was still yelling back at the receiving officer to "send that yellow SOB back to the front line."

Nurses and patients, attracted by the shouting and cursing, came from the adjoining tent and witnessed this disturbance.

Patton made no initial report of these affairs to his superior, General Eisenhower, who was then in his Headquarters at Tunis on the North African mainland.

"I felt ashamed of myself," General Patton told me, "and I hoped the whole thing would die out."

But an official report by Lieut. Colonel Perrin H. Long, Medical Corps consulting physician, was already on the way to Allied Headquarters through Medical Corps channels.

"The deleterious effects of such incidents upon the well-being of patients, upon the professional morale of hospital staffs and upon the relationship of patient to physician are incalculable," reported Lieut. Colonel Long. "It is imperative that immediate steps be taken to prevent a recurrence of such incidents."

General Eisenhower received this report on August 17th. His communication to General Patton was sent off that night.

In his message, which Patton showed me, the Commanding General told Patton of the allegations, told him that he could not describe in official language his revulsion, informed Patton that he must make, on his own initiative, proper amends to the soldiers involved and take steps to make amends before his whole army.

"This all happened practically on the eve of a new attack in which I had been written in for a large part of the plans, already issued," Patton explained, "and General Eisenhower stated therefore that he would temporarily reserve decision regarding my relief of command until he could determine the effect of my own corrective measures.

"Then Eisenhower did four things: He sent Maj. General John Porter Lucas to Sicily to make an investigation of the charges, sent the Theatre's Inspector General to investigate command relationships in my entire army, sent another general officer to interview the two soldiers and made a trip to Sicily himself to determine how much resentment against me existed in the army.

"Eisenhower's problem was whether what I had done was sufficiently damaging to compel my relief on the eve of attack, thus losing what he described as my unquestioned military value, or whether less drastic measures would be appropriate.

"I went to see both Kuhl and Bennett," Patton continued, "explained my motives and apologized for my actions.

"In each case I stated that I should like to shake hands with them; that I was sincerely sorry. In each case they accepted my offer.

"I called together all the doctors, nurses and enlisted men who were present when the slappings occurred. I apologized and expressed my humiliation over my impulsive actions.

"Finally, I addressed all divisions of the 7th Army in a series of assemblies, the last of which was an address before the 3rd Division on August 30th.

"I praised them as soldiers, expressed regret for any occasions when I harshly treated individuals and offered my apologies as their Commanding General for doing anything unfair or un-American.

"Beyond that, except to leave the Army and get out of the war, I do not know what I could have done."

PROBLEMS

1. After you have read the entire selection, re-read Patton's letter to Eisenhower at the beginning of the selection. Recalling Hayakawa's definitions of *report, judgment, inference, slanting, snarl-* and *purr-words*, determine which of these terms best describe the following:
   a. "your fairness and generous consideration" (paragraph 1)
   b. "a man to whom I owe everything" (paragraph 2)
   c. "I assure you that I had no intention of being either harsh or

cruel in my treatment of the two soldiers in question." (paragraph 3)

   d. the letter taken as a whole

2. Apply the same procedure to paragraph 2 of Patton's memorandum to Corps, Division, and Brigade Commanders, dated 5 August, 1943.

3. Now compare these two written communications with the last nine paragraphs of the selection, all quotes from Patton to Taylor. How do you account, in part, for the extraordinary difference in tone, manner, and thought between Patton's spoken words and Patton's written ones?

4. Next, examine, in a similar manner, the brief excerpt from the official report of Lieutenant Colonel Perrin H. Long of the Medical Corps. Is this a *report*, by Hayakawa's definition?

5. Finally, consider those portions of the total selection written by Taylor himself. Specifically, where does he depart from the canons of reporting and permit inferences, judgments, or emotional language to enter? Do you feel that this selection—*taken in its entirety*—is slanted? Defend your answer.

Milton Mayer

Colonel McCormick's Chicago *Tribune* has, after the New York *Daily News*, the greatest newspaper circulation in America. Yet there are some readers who have long doubted the *Tribune's* claim to being "the world's greatest newspaper." The *Tribune*, however, is a powerful voice in the Midwest. For many years it has been strongly anti-British, anti-Russian, anti-New Deal, isolationist, anti-union labor, pro-high tariff.

Milton Mayer has been variously a newspaperman, a magazine writer and editor (he is a contributing editor to *The Progressive*), and a college teacher (he was formerly assistant professor in the University College at the University of Chicago and most recently has been visiting professor of Applied Religion at William Penn College). He has been a consistent champion of the educational program of Chancellor Hutchins of the University of Chicago.

HOW TO READ THE CHICAGO *TRIBUNE* *

The following article, except for the footnotes and the numbers referring to them, is a reprint in full of a news report in the Chicago Tribune of Sunday, November 14, 1948 (circulation 1,675,000). It should be read from beginning to end and then read in conjunction with the footnotes. The footnotes are mine. This news report was printed at the top of the first column of page 1 of the Tribune of that date, with a two-column "runover" beginning at the top of the first column of page 2. It should be emphasized that there was no indication that this article was to be read as other than a news report; on the contrary, the columns it occupied in the Chicago Tribune are ordinarily used in that paper for news reports, the typography was identical with that of other news reports on the same page, the headline was a news headline, and the by-line of the writer was that of Frank Hughes, a Chicago Tribune news reporter. The reporter should have had plenty of time to prepare the article, since all the materials used had been available for months or years. The headline read: NAME ANGELS OF MOVES TO CURB PRESS. *The subhead read:* Foundation Aids Hutchins Group.[1]—*The Author.*

Multimillion dollar, tax exempt foundations [2] which have given cash grants to Communists or to the publication of communist propaganda [3] also are financing attempts to tamper with freedom of the press [4] in the United States.

[1] No foundation in any way contributed to the support, financial or other, of the Commission on Freedom of the Press. The report of the Commission (*A Free and Responsible Press*, Chicago: University of Chicago Press, 1947) states that "the inquiry was financed by grants of $200,000 from Time, Inc., and $15,000 from Encyclopaedia Britannica, Inc." These business institutions, like the Tribune Company, are incorporated for profit and operated for profit. They are not foundations. (The financial supporters of the Commission were named by Chairman Robert M. Hutchins in a press release accompanying publication of the report on March 27, 1947.)

[2] See above.

[3] No attempt is made to support this statement in the body of the article.

[4] If "freedom of the press" is defined as unlimited, it is already "tampered with" by the laws of libel, misbranding, obscenity, sedition, and treason. A cursory examination of the report would reveal repeated denunciations of government ownership, control, or regulation of the press as steps which "might cure the ills of freedom of the press, but only at the risk of killing

* Milton Mayer, in *Harper's Magazine*, April 1949. Copyright, 1949, by Harper & Brothers.

Three persons who occupy behind the scenes positions [5] in this picture are Henry R. Luce, publisher of Time, Life, and Fortune magazines; Robert M. Hutchins, chancellor of the University of Chicago, and William Benton, advertising executive [6] who formerly was assistant secretary of state. Luce has a foundation of his own, the Henry R. Luce Foundation, Inc.[7] He also is on the board of the Foreign Service Education Foundation.[8]

Luce, acting in the personal capacity of a foundation,[9] granted [10] $200,000 from Time, Inc., to Chancellor Hutchins to form a Commission on Freedom of the Press, which has taken a very active part in the campaign to dictate the content [11] of "mass communica-

the freedom in the process" (p. 2). The Commission would even protect the right of newspapers, if they cared to exercise it, to be liars, venalists, and scoundrels: "Many a lying, venal, and scoundrelly public expression must continue to find shelter under a 'freedom of the press' built for widely different purposes, for to impair the legal right even when the moral right is gone may easily be a cure worse than the disease." The Commission recommends one new law, "an alternative to the present remedy for libel" whereby "the injured party might obtain a retraction or a restatement of the facts by the offender or an opportunity to reply" (p. 86). *Cf.* American Society of Newspaper Editors, *Canons of Journalism:* "A newspaper should not publish unofficial charges affecting reputation or moral character, without opportunity given to the accused to be heard. . . . It is the privilege, as it is the duty, of a newspaper to make prompt and complete correction of its own serious mistakes. . . ."

[5] Luce and Hutchins occupied front-of-the-scenes positions in the Commission on Freedom of the Press, Luce as the man who suggested the inquiry to Hutchins, Hutchins as chairman of the Commission. Benton's only connection with the Commission was also public; it was as Chairman of the Board of Directors of Encyclopaedia Britannica, Inc.

[6] Benton is no longer an advertising executive or in any way associated with the advertising business (*v.* ftn. 12).

[7] The Henry Luce Foundation was incorporated in the State of New York, December 23, 1936, for religious, charitable, and educational purposes. Luce is neither a director nor an officer. Proof that this Foundation is engaged in activities outside its stated purposes could cost it its tax-exempt status under the Membership Corporations Law of New York.

[8] Luce is not on the board of the Foreign Service Education Foundation or in any way connected with it.

[9] It is impossible to act in the personal capacity of a foundation.

[10] Luce did not grant anybody anything in connection with the Commission. Time, Inc., states: "The grant of $200,000 to the Commission made by Time, Inc., was with the specific consent and authorization of the Board of Directors of this Company." Luce is one of seven members of the Board of Directors of Time, Inc.

[11] See footnote 4.

tions," a term the commission uses for dissemination of news.[12]

Chancellor Hutchins is honorary chairman of Norman Waite [*sic*] Harris Foundation.[13] He also was a trustee of the Julius Rosenwald fund [14] at the time it was giving fellowships to Langston Hughes, Negro poet,[15] described in congressional committee reports as "a card holding member of the Communist party." [16] Hughes has said he is not a Communist.[17]

[12] The Commission uses the term "mass communications" for dissemination of news; it also uses several other common terms; and undiscoverable numbers of persons and institutions use the term "mass communication" for dissemination of news. The etymology of the term is undiscovered. In the opinion of William Benton, former advertising executive (founder, president, chairman of the board, Benton & Bowles, 1929-36), the term originated many years ago among newspaper and magazine advertisers and agencies.

[13] The Norman Wait Harris Memorial Foundation was, according to its chairman, Professor Quincy Wright, "a gift contributed to the University of Chicago by the heirs of Norman Wait and Emma Gail Harris in 1923." The letter of gift states that its purpose is "to combat the disintegrating tendency of the spirit of distrust which pervades the old world and is not without its effect on our own country." The chief executive officer of the University of Chicago is, *ex officio*, honorary chairman of the Foundation.

[14] The Julius Rosenwald Fund was established in 1917 by Julius Rosenwald (1862-1932), Chairman of the Board of Directors of Sears, Roebuck & Co., "for the well-being of mankind." Rosenwald provided that the entire fund, which in 1928 was worth $40,000,000, be expended within twenty-five years after his death. The Fund terminated its existence June 30, 1948, having devoted its resources primarily to "education and betterment of race relations" in accordance with Rosenwald's own two principal philanthropic interests.

[15] Hutchins was a trustee of the Rosenwald Fund from November 11, 1934, to November 13, 1940. Langston Hughes was awarded Rosenwald Fellowships September 17, 1931, and April 11, 1941.

[16] Langston Hughes writes: "I have stated quite clearly in the press and elsewhere over a period of years that I am not now and have never been a member of the Communist Party. . . . I was attacked in the [Communist] Party press just before the war as a 'war-monger' since I did not agree that we should not prepare to fight Hitler. . . . I have not had any relations with congressional committees, have never been called before any of them, and have never seen copies of any of the charges from which the Hearst press quotes me frequently. As you will see from carbons [attached], I have written the various papers and radio commentators who repeat these charges, but (except for the *Reader's Digest*) have not had the courtesy of an answer from any of them." Edwin R. Embree (President, the Rosenwald Fund, 1928-48) writes: "I am personally convinced that Mr. Hughes is not a member of the Communist party and that he is a completely loyal American." Among Hughes' medals, prizes, and awards for literature are grants from the Guggenheim Foundation (1935) and the National Institute of Arts and Letters (1946).

[17] If Hughes is not a Communist, his only recourse is to bring a libel action against a newspaper which prints, or reprints, the unsubstantiated charge that

The Rosenwald fund is the only one of the foundations which have been mentioned that has been engaged in giving aid or money to such people or purposes.[18]

Hutchins' Commission on Freedom of the Press, despite its impressive title, had no public or governmental authority.[19] Financed mainly by Henry Luce,[20] it consisted of 12 university professors and former professors,[21] appointed solely by Hutchins.

It brought out a report saying that newspapers "must be accountable to society" (government) [22] and that "it becomes an imperative

he is. On June 3, 1916, the Chicago *Tribune* printed the charge that Henry Ford was an anarchist. Ford brought a libel action. The *Tribune* was found guilty, but the suit is said to have cost Ford $500,000 in lawyers' and other fees (*v.* Tebbel, *An American Dynasty,* pp. 93-100, Garden City, 1947). A man who does not bring a libel action against a newspaper which prints an unsubstantiated charge that he is a Communist may be a Communist; or he may be a Negro poet without the necessary funds.

[18] This statement is partly wrong and partly meaningless. If "such people" means Negroes, the statement is wrong; the Commission on Freedom of the Press, the Henry Luce Foundation, the Foreign Service Education Foundation, and the Norman Wait Harris Memorial Foundation have all given "aid or money" to Negroes. If "such people" means card-holding members of the Communist party, the statement is wrong; the Norman Wait Harris Memorial Foundation gave "aid or money" to Alexander A. Troyanovsky, Ambassador of the USSR to the U.S.A. and a card-holding member of the Communist party, to cover his expenses at an institute on "The Soviet Union and World Problems" in 1935. "Such purposes" is meaningless, the purposes of neither the Julius Rosenwald Fund nor of Hughes having been stated *supra.*

[19] Neither has the Chicago *Tribune,* despite its impressive title, "The World's Greatest Newspaper."

[20] See footnote 10.

[21] Hutchins told the National Conference of Editorial Writers, November 19, 1948: ". . . I think you are teachers. I did not say you were good teachers. . . . A good teacher has to try to be fair. He can not use the straw man or the red herring. . . . The big red herring, or bloater, was, of course, the fact that many members of the Commission were professors. . . . A teacher who was trying to be fair would have told his pupils that Chafee was the leading authority on freedom of expression in the United States, that Clark was the leading economist, that Hocking was the dean of philosophers, that Lasswell was one of the leading students of communication, that Merriam was the dean of political scientists, that Niebuhr was the leading theologian, that Redfield was one of the leading students of culture, that Schlesinger was the leading American historian, and that Dickinson, in addition to being General Counsel for the Pennsylvania Railroad, was one of the leading political scientists and constitutional lawyers of our time."

[22] All thirteen members of the Commission on Freedom of the Press state that they have never used the two terms "society" and "government" as synonyms in any of their writings; that the terms are unmistakably distinguished as concepts throughout their report; and that the terms are, in the political

question whether the performance of the press can any longer be left to the unregulated initiative of the few who manage it." [23]

According to the New Leader, weekly socialist newspaper, Chancellor Hutchins recently associated himself with another well known figure in "mass communications," Prof. Clyde R. Miller of Columbia university.[24]

The New Leader said Hutchins sponsored the Commission for Academic Freedom [25] of the National Council of the Arts, Sciences, and Professions, chairman of which is Prof. Harlow Shapley of Harvard university, and that Prof. Miller is secretary of the commission. The New Leader added that the national council is a Communist front.

Prof. Miller was head of the Institute of Propaganda Analysis at Columbia,[26] established in 1937 with a grant of $10,000 from the Good Will fund, a foundation endowed by the late Edward A. Filene, Boston merchant.[27] Prof. Miller's institute devoted itself to

credos of all thirteen of them, inequitable and inconvertible. The American tradition, in contrast to the Hobbesian-Hegelian-Chicago *Tribune* practice, has always distinguished "government" from "society" sharply and persistently. (Paine, *Common Sense:* "Society is the creature of their [men's] wants, government of their wickedness." Also, the Declaration of Independence: ". . . to secure these rights, *governments* are instituted among *men.* . . ." Also, the Constitution of the United States, Amendment 1: "Congress shall make no law . . . abridging the freedom . . . of the press; or the right of the *People* peaceably to assemble and to petition the *Government.* . . .")

[23] ". . . The local and regional chains, together with the Hearst, Scripps-Howard, and McCormick-Patterson ownership groups, control more than half (53.8 per cent) of the total newspaper circulation of the nation. Fourteen newspaper owners control 25 per cent of the daily circulation, with less than fifty owners controlling nearly half the total Sunday circulation." (Report of the Commission on Freedom of the Press, p. 43.) The Commission is opposed to government regulation of the initiative of the few who manage the press (*v.* ftn. 4).

[24] Professor Clyde R. Miller is not connected with Columbia University.

[25] Hutchins did not sponsor the Commission for Academic Freedom of the National Council of the Arts, Sciences, and Professions.

[26] The Institute of Propaganda Analysis was not at, or in any other way connected with, Columbia University.

[27] The Edward A. Filene Good Will Fund, Inc. was established October 8, 1936, as the Good Will Fund by President Edward A. Filene (1860-1937), President, William Filene Sons Co.; planner and co-organizer, U. S. Chamber of Commerce; Chairman, War Shipping Commission. The Good Will Fund, one of the many institutions established by Filene "for the benefit of mankind," stated, in its certificate of incorporation: "It shall not be within the purposes or powers of the corporation to engage in propaganda or otherwise attempt to influence legislation."

analyzing American and British "propaganda" against Hitler, at the time Germany and Soviet Russia were allies in World War II.[28]

When Germany turned on Russia, the "institute" disappeared.[29] It was well subsidized while it lasted,[30] receiving another $13,000 from the Good Will fund and $4,000 from the Whitney Foundation [31] in one year alone.

[28] Germany and Soviet Russia were not allies in World War II; they signed a non-aggression treaty August 24, 1939, which Germany violated June 22, 1941. During the period August 24, 1939-June 22, 1941, the Institute did not devote itself to analyzing American and British "propaganda" against Hitler. Many of its analyses were devoted to Nazi and Soviet propaganda against the United States and England. See, *e.g.*, "The War Comes" (*Propaganda Analysis*, Oct. 1, 1939): "Typical of those who had accepted Comintern propaganda at face value were the 400 leading American intellectuals who signed a manifesto opposing the lumping of Moscow and Berlin on the ground, among other things, that the U.S.S.R. was an ally of the democracies against fascism." One of the most heavily documented and most widely reprinted analyses of Communist propaganda ever made was "Communist Propaganda, U.S.A., 1939 Model" (*Propaganda Analysis*, March 1, 1939), a companion piece to "Propaganda Techniques of German Fascism" (*Propaganda Analysis*, May 1, 1938).

[29] Germany turned on Russia June 22, 1941. The last issue of *Propaganda Analysis*, the official publication of the Institute, appeared January 9, 1942, after Japan turned on the United States. Professor Alfred McClung Lee of Wayne University, Executive Director of the Institute at that time, writes: ". . . The only basis on which we could have continued the Institute was as an objective analyzer of propagandas from various sides. In wartime, the only program possible was to make the Institute into a propaganda agency. Hence the Institute died."

[30] According to Miller, who established the Institute and served as its executive secretary or secretary of its advisory board during its entire existence, "The blunt fact is that there simply wasn't money enough for the Institute to go forward. It could have gotten money, I am reasonably certain, had it been willing to weight its analyses [in the fall of 1941] to support our entrance into the war. I could not accept money on any such basis. Probably it could have gotten money had it been willing to weight its analyses against going to war. I couldn't accept money on that basis, either, though personally I was against going to war up until Pearl Harbor." (Among the millions of Americans who were against going to war up until Pearl Harbor were, besides Miller, Chancellor Hutchins of the University of Chicago and Col. R. R. McCormick of the Chicago *Tribune*.)

[31] The William C. Whitney Foundation, established in 1936 "for the benefit of mankind" by Mrs. Dorothy Whitney Elmhirst, is incorporated under the Membership Corporations Law of the State of New York and since that time has been, and still is, subject to loss of tax-exempt status upon proof that it disburses its funds for other than "charitable and eleemosynary purposes." Among its beneficiaries, besides the Institute for Propaganda Analysis, which received grants totaling $4,500 ($4,000 of it in one year ·alone), are the Y.M.C.A., the American Friends Service Committee, the Council for the Clinical Training of Theological Students, the North Country Community Hospital, and the National Gallery of the American Indian.

Luce, Benton, and Hutchins are intimately associated.[32] Benton is chairman of the board and part owner of Encyclopedia Britannica, which was given to the University of Chicago.[33] Hutchins is a director of the encyclopedia and chairman of its editorial board, and Luce is a member of the board of trustees.[34]

Benton is a former vice president of the University of Chicago and is now on its board of trustees. Encyclopedia Britannica gave $15,000 to the Hutchins-Luce Commission on Freedom of the Press.[35]

[32] The history of the law of conspiracy suggests that the association of men for one or more purposes does not *eo ipso* associate them for other purposes or for all their purposes. The U. S. Supreme Court (*Bridges* v. *Wixon,* 326 U. S. 135, 143, 1945) has stated: "Alliances for limited objectives are well known. Certainly those who joined forces with Russia to defeat the Nazis may not be said to have made an alliance to spread the cause of Communism." On the other hand, Colonel McCormick (Yale '03) might argue a general conspiracy among the Messrs. Luce (Yale '20), Benton (Yale '21), and Hutchins (Yale '21) on the ground that they pledged (*Bright College Years*) that "time and change shall not avail/To break the friendships formed at Yale." Whether or not this would cover the offense alleged, namely, move or moves to curb the press, would require juridical interpretation. But Benton, himself a member of a secret organization known as ZΨ, might allege *prima facie* evidence of a more general conspiracy by McCormick, Luce, and Hutchins, who, as associates in a secret society known as AΔΦ, have taken a mutual pledge that "no power can break the tie that binds [us]" and "naught shall sever us forever." (*The* AΔΦ *Song Book,* New York, 1923). Another association is that of Colonel McCormick and Marshall Field, publisher of the Chicago *Sun-Times.* These two men are jointly engaged in many enterprises, among them the Racquet and Tennis Club (N. Y.), the Chicago Club, the University of Chicago Citizens Board, the American Newspaper Publishers Association. Of some of these enterprises, *viz.,* the Racquet and Tennis Club and the Chicago Club, virtually nothing is known to the public. Luce is likewise associated with McCormick in the Racquet and Tennis Club, and Luce, Hutchins, and Benton are *all* associated with McCormick in the Chicago Club.

[33] By Sears, Roebuck & Co., chairman of the Board of Directors of which is General Robert E. Wood, another associate of Colonel McCormick in the Chicago Club amalgam.

[34] The Encyclopaedia Britannica, Inc., like the Tribune Co., Inc., a commercial corporation, is in charge not of a Board of Trustees, but of a Board of Directors. Luce is associated, on this Board of Directors, with Paul G. Hoffman, who is associated with Colonel McCormick in the Chicago Club picture and who is also President of the Studebaker Corp. and Director of the European Relief Administration; and with John Stuart, Chairman of the Board of Directors of the Quaker Oats Co. and, like Hoffman, an associate of Colonel McCormick in the venture known as the Republican party (*Who's Who in America,* Chicago, 1948).

[35] *Time,* edited by Henry R. Luce, said of the Commission's report: ". . . disappointing"; *Fortune,* also edited by Mr. Luce, that "the obscurities of this report are literally inexcusable."

Luce is said to have been instrumental in getting Benton appointed to the position of assistant secretary of state for public affairs in 1945.[36] Alger Hiss, who has been named as a Communist agent in the state department charged with influencing foreign policy was head of the state department's office of special political affairs.[37]

Hiss told *The Tribune* that Benton was the man who suggested the name of Zechariah Chafee Jr., Harvard law professor, as American delegate to the United Nations subcommission on freedom of information and of the press.[38]

This U. N. subcommission drafted a code to establish what newspapers in this country and thruout [sic] the world may and may not publish.[39] It could supercede [sic] the first amendment to the Con-

[36] Luce states that he "had no connection, direct or indirect, with Mr. Benton's appointment to the State Department." Benton states that "Mr. Luce never had the remotest idea that I was even being considered."

[37] Benton is here associated with Hiss, "who has been named as a Communist agent," by virtue of their both having been in the State Department. There is no evidence here that they were in any other way associated, or that they knew each other or had ever corresponded or communicated with each other.

[38] Chafee states: "I do not know whether this is true or not. . . . I know that I was formally proposed by Mrs. Roosevelt, the United States member of the Commission and its Chairman, and that I was approved by the United States government. . . . It is significant that here all the blame is thrown on Benton, whereas in its issue of September 4, 1948, the *Tribune* throws all the blame on Alger Hiss." The *Tribune* of September 4, 1948, stated in a news report: "Hiss put over the appointment of Professor Zechariah Chafee of the Harvard law school as this country's representative on the U.N.'s sub-commission of freedom of information and the press." Hiss states: "I said [to the Chicago *Tribune* reporter who interrogated him] that I believed Mr. Benton had been the initiator within the Department of State of Mr. Chafee's nomination. I added, however, that the Department's records would undoubtedly contain the whole story and that I was not familiar with the details of how Mr. Chafee's name had first come up." Benton states: "Chafee was recommended to me as the country's, if not the world's, leading authority on press freedom. At this point I had never met him. I recommended him solely on his reputation."

[39] The Articles formulated, at the request of the UN Human Rights Commission, by the Sub-Commission of which Chafee was a member, *limit the restriction of freedom of expression* to treason, incitement to violence, obscenity, libel, fraud, etc. A signatory nation *may, if it chooses,* limit freedom of expression to this extent *and only to this extent.* It *may, if it chooses,* permit unlimited freedom of expression, including treason, etc., but it *must not* confine expression *beyond* these limitations, within which, of course, they are now confined in the United States by existing laws. The Articles nowhere and in no manner establish "what newspapers in this country and throughout the

stitution if adopted as a treaty by the senate.[40] Hiss,[41] who left the state department to become president of the Carnegie Endowment for International Peace, another foundation, has denied he is a Communist.[42]

Chafee was the vice chairman of the Hutchins-Luce Commission on Freedom of the Press, and a book of which he was co-author was subsidized by the Commonwealth fund,[43] still another foundation.

world may and may not publish" beyond providing that a signatory nation *may, if it chooses,* permit newspapers to publish anything and everything. (*United States Conference on Freedom of Information, Geneva, Switzerland, March 23—April 21, 1948, Report of the United States Delegates with Related Documents, Annex B; Draft Declaration and Draft Covenant on Human Rights,* pp. 24-25 [Department of State, Washington, 1948].)

[40] The Draft Covenant on Human Rights, containing the Articles formulated by the Sub-Commission of which Chafee was a member, could not supersede the First Amendment to the Constitution if adopted as a treaty by the Senate. The Articles do not compel a signatory nation to limit freedom of expression in any way whatever.

[41] Hiss was in no way associated with the UN Sub-Commission on Freedom of Information and of the Press, not even to the extent that he was associated with Benton, *viz.,* by virtue of their both having been in the State Department. There is no evidence here that Hiss and Chafee were in any way associated, or that they knew each other, or had ever corresponded or communicated with each other. It is true, however, that "Hiss left the State Department to become President of the Carnegie Endowment for International Peace, another foundation," and "has denied he is a Communist." Paul G. Hoffman, a director of Encyclopaedia Britannica, Inc., is an associate, in the machinations of the Chicago Club, of Col. McCormick (*v.* ftn. 34). This associate of Col. McCormick is publisher of a biographical sketch of Lenin by Leon Trotsky (*v. Encyclopaedia Britannica,* V. 13, pp. 911-914, Chicago, 1947), both of them card-holding members of the Communist party. Joseph Stalin, another card-holding Communist, denies that Trotsky, the author of a biographical sketch published by Col. McCormick's associate, was a Communist.

[42] Hiss filed a libel action, forty-eight days before the *Tribune* article appeared, against the man who called him a Communist. Hiss is, at the time this footnote is written, under federal indictment for perjury in connection with the alleged transmission of secret papers in possession of the U. S. government to the government of the USSR, a presumably non-hostile power at the time of the alleged theft and subsequently a war ally of the United States. On Dec. 4, 1941, the Chicago *Tribune,* through a news report headed F.D.R.'S WAR PLANS!, made accessible to the governments of Germany, Italy, and Japan, presumably hostile powers at the time of the transmission and subsequently war enemies of the United States, what Secretary of War Stimson called "the most highly secret paper in the possession of the government." (*New York Times,* Mar. 23, 1946).

[43] The Commonwealth Fund was established October 17, 1918, by Mrs. Stephen V. Harkness "to do something for the welfare of mankind." Its

Chafee has been one of the most vigorous definers [44] of the "soviet view" on freedom of the press.[45] In Russia, he has said, the soviets "feel that our (American) press is not free because owners and publishers can interfere with presentation of views unacceptable to them." [46]

John Sloan Dickey, now president of Dartmouth college, was one of the propaganda workers [47] in the state department office of public information under Benton.[48] Dickey, who never held a teaching

grants are almost entirely to rural hospitals, medical schools, and scientific institutions. The publication subsidized by the Commonwealth Fund of which Chafee was co-author was *The Law of Evidence; Some Proposals for Its Reform* (1927). The president of the Commonwealth Fund, Judge Thomas Day Thacher, appointed Judge of the U. S. District Court by President Calvin Coolidge and Solicitor General of the U. S. by President Herbert Hoover; and the Vice President of the Fund, Malcolm Pratt Aldrich, Director of the New York Central Railroad, were both associates of Colonel McCormick in the abortive scheme of the Republican party to take over the government of the United States last November 2d. (*Who's Who in America,* Chicago, 1948).

[44] "Definer" is "one who defines," and "to define" is "to determine the essential qualities of" (Webster). "Definer" is not a commonly used word, nor is "vigorous definer" a commonly used expression. "Defender" and "vigorous defender," on the other hand, are. Chafee denies the vigor here ascribed to him, stating: "I have nowhere undertaken to give an extensive description of the Soviet view."

[45] "It is a mystery to me," says Chafee, "why it is wrong for us to try to understand the Soviet position on an important matter. Certainly we ought to know what we are going to answer before we set about answering it. I have no hesitation in admitting that I have tried to do that, although I have not spread my views in print. Of course, the *Tribune* knows that I have publicly opposed the Soviet views of the freedom of the press. One of my speeches at the Sub-Commission to that effect is reported on the front page of the *New York Times* for January 23, 1948."

[46] It is not easy to determine whether a newspaper owner and publisher interferes with presentation of views unacceptable to him, though the Chicago *Tribune,* which published many articles, editorials, and adverse speeches of its owner and publisher on the subject of the Commission on Freedom of the Press, did not publish, in full or in summary, the Commission's report.

[47] According to former Assistant Secretary of State Archibald MacLeish, Dickey's last superior officer in the Department, Dickey "was not a 'propaganda worker.' " (Dickey declined to comment on this *Tribune* statement.) Dickey (LL. B., Harvard, '32) was legal adviser to Secretary of State Cordell Hull, with the title of Special Assistant to the Secretary of State, 1940; Special Assistant to the Co-ordinator of Inter-American Affairs, 1940-44; and Director, Office of Public Affairs, Department of State, 1944-45.

[48] Dickey resigned from the State Department August 24, 1945, to accept

job before becoming president of Dartmouth,[49] now is on the board of trustees of the Rockefeller Foundation and the Woodrow Wilson Foundation.[50]

Dickey has established a propaganda course [51] at Dartmouth, called Great Issues, which he financed by obtaining a $75,000 grant from the Carnegie corporation. This course teaches students to judge the truth of newspapers by comparing them to a couple of America-last internationalist dailies in New York.[52]

the presidency of Dartmouth College. Benton entered the service of the State Department as Assistant Secretary of State November 17, 1945.

[49] Dickey taught at the School of Advanced International Studies, with the title of Lecturer in American Foreign Policies, 1944-45 (*Who's Who in America*, 1946-47). The School of Advanced International Studies is maintained by forty-nine American industrial and business corporations through the Foreign Service Educational Foundation. It is true, however, that many distinguished men have become presidents of institutions without previously having held a job in that kind of institution. *Cf.* General U. S. Grant (President of the United States, 1869-77), also Colonel R. R. McCormick (President of the Tribune Co., 1911-   ).

[50] Dickey is not a member of the Board of Trustees of the Woodrow Wilson Foundation. There is no Board of Trustees of the Woodrow Wilson Foundation. There is a Board of Directors, but Dickey is not a member of it. Dickey resigned from the Woodrow Wilson Foundation in May 1948.

[51] The purpose of the Great Issues Course is, according to Dartmouth College, "to pull together the diffused interests of the seniors and put them through a common intellectual experience on the threshold of adult life, aimed at developing a sense of common public purpose, a heightened individual public-mindedness, and a sharper ability to relate learning to the contemporary world." The purpose, thus stated, would not appear to fit any of the six definitions of "propaganda" given by that vigorous definer, Webster; neither would the participation, as lecturers in the course, of such divergent thinkers as Alexander Meiklejohn; Rep. Christian A. Herter (R., Mass.); Lewis Mumford; President James B. Conant of Harvard University; Guy C. Suits, Director of Research, General Electric Co.; Edward U. Condon, Director, National Bureau of Standards; President Chester I. Barnard, New Jersey Bell Telephone Co.; Secretary of State Dean Acheson; and Rep. Richard M. Nixon (R., Calif.). Newspapers are sometimes said to be vehicles of propaganda, and, since newspapers are used in the course (*v.* ftn. 52), it may be that the course is a "propaganda course" in that sense.

[52] New York newspapers used in the Great Issues Course are the *New York Times*, the New York *Herald Tribune*, and the Communist *Daily Worker*. Which two of the three are referred to here is not indicated.

The Dartmouth College *Bulletin* (Oct. 16, 1948) reported an exhibit, in connection with the Great Issues Course, of the *Times*, the *Daily Worker*, and the Chicago *Tribune*, "designed to show various forms of distortion in newspapers, particularly the Chicago *Tribune* and the *Daily Worker*."

The inspiration for Dickey's Great Issues course was Archibald MacLeish,[53] who once taught at Harvard and who preceded Benton as assistant secretary of state. MacLeish, who formerly was head of the Library of Congress, also was a member of the Hutchins-Luce Commission on Freedom of the Press.

Since the beginning of the New Deal administrations, the Rockefeller Foundation has given the Library of Congress more than $300,000.[54] In 1942 alone, this foundation gave the library, headed by MacLeish, approximately $90,000.

In the same year, the Rockefeller Foundation completed a three year grant of $81,800 to the library "toward a study of communication trends in war time, under the direction of Dr. Harold D. Lasswell."

Lasswell, a former University of Chicago professor under Hutchins,[55] now is at Yale. He, also, was a member of the Hutchins-Luce Commission on Freedom of the Press. In addition, Lasswell served as consultant for the department of justice, the federal communications commission, the office of war information, and for Benton in the state department.[56]

Using "content analysis," a pseudo-science [57] which he invented,[58] Lasswell attempted to prove that criticism of the New Deal administration, of England, or of Russia by American newspapers con-

[53] This is denied both by Dartmouth and by MacLeish.

[54] This is an understatement by $229,270. Between March 4, 1933 (the beginning of the national administration sometimes referred to as "the New Deal") and November 14, 1948 (the date this article was published), the Library of Congress received grants from the Rockefeller Foundation of $529,270.

[55] And under Hutchins' three predecessors.

[56] And for Benton in another connection (*v.* ftn. 94).

[57] Content analysis is not a pseudo-science, according to the Supreme Court. Lasswell, as an expert witness for the prosecution in *U. S. vs. William Dudley Pelley* (U. S. District Court, Southern District of Indiana, Indianapolis Division, Summer Term 1942), presented testimony based on content analysis of defendant's writings. On appeal by defendant, convicted of sedition, the admissibility of content analysis was expressly attacked. Conviction affirmed by U. S. Circuit Court of Appeals, 7th Circuit, 1942 (132 F. [2d] 170). The admissibility of content analysis was expressly attacked on request for rehearing and writ of certiorari denied (318 U. S. 764, 63 Sup. Ct. 665, 666, 1943; 318 U. S. 801, 63 Sup. Ct. 829, 1943).

[58] This is denied by Lasswell.

stituted Nazi propaganda,[59] which, presumably, ought to be silenced.[60]

Assisting Lasswell in this study were three men on the federal communications commission pay roll.[61] One of them, Frederick L. Schuman,[62] taught on the Midway when Lasswell was there.[63] Schuman has been affiliated with organizations labeled as Communist fronts by congressional committees for many years,[64] and most recently served on the platform committee of Henry Wallace's Progressive party.[65]

The other two who helped Lasswell,[66] Goodwin B. Watson and William E. Dodd Jr., were fired by an act of congress because of subversive activities.[67]

[59] Lasswell attempted to prove, in, for example, *U. S.* vs. *William Dudley Pelley,* that there was a parallelism of utterance between Pelley's own writings in the *Galilean* and the fourteen major themes of German-source propaganda output summarized by the Federal Communications Commission's short-wave radio monitoring service while the United States and Germany were at war. The United States, attempting to prove that this parallel constituted seditious utterances by Pelley, called Lasswell to testify as an expert witness. One of the German-source themes, of which Lasswell testified he found 112 parallels and no contradictions, in the *Galilean,* was: "The U. S. and the world are menaced by the Jews." This theme does not constitute, *prima facie,* what the Chicago *Tribune* here calls "criticism of the New Deal administration, of England, or of Russia."

[60] The presumption is the Chicago *Tribune's.* Lasswell is a political scientist, presenting the results of content analysis as scientific investigation. Like newspaper reporting, science neither declares nor presumes that anything ought or ought not to be done.

[61] The three men named did not assist Lasswell, nor were they associated with Lasswell.

[62] Woodrow Wilson Professor of Government at Williams College since 1938.

[63] This is a true statement. Between 2,000 and 3,000 persons taught "on the Midway" (the University of Chicago) during the twenty years (1918-38) Lasswell was there. Schuman and Lasswell have never been associated on any project of any kind or in any work of any kind, including content analysis.

[64] This statement is misleading, by the standards of "thoroughness" and "completeness" established by the American Society of Newspaper Editors, because it does not state that the Congress of the United States, in full possession of the knowledge of Schuman's affiliations referred to here, found him fit for employment by the United States government.

[65] This is a true statement.

[66] See footnote 61.

[67] Congress tried to fire Watson and Dodd, who were not associated with Lasswell, but the United States Supreme Court found (328 U. S. 303) this act of Congress unconstitutional and therefore null and void.

The contributions of the wealthy foundations to this type of propaganda technique [68] were not confined to MacLeish and Lasswell.[69] In 1941, the Rockefeller Foundation gave $15,960 for a "study of totalitarian communication in war time" to the New School of Social Research in New York City. The next year, the foundation made an additional grant of $19,740 to this institution "so that it may go on with its study of totalitarian communication in war time."

Prof. Lasswell is a perennial lecturer at the New School for Social Research.[70] This is the institution which in 1940 procured a $20,160 Rockefeller grant to finance Hanns Eisler, now deported as a Communist,[71] in "experimental demonstrations of music in film production." [72]

[68] If by "propaganda technique," content analysis is meant, as would appear to be the case by virtue of the reference to Lasswell in the same sentence, then this statement is incorrect (*v.* ftns. 57, 59, 60). Content analysis is, however, a technique for discovering propaganda.

[69] As Librarian of Congress, MacLeish was not engaged in "propaganda technique" activity and was not associated with Lasswell, who directed a study of communication trends in wartime on a Rockefeller Foundation grant to the Library, through whose Accounts and Disbursing Offices the grant was disbursed.

[70] Lasswell, who has not lectured at the New School for Social Research since 1943, never held the Perennial Lectureship in that institution. He was, however, eligible for the coveted Sporadic Lectureship.

[71] Hanns Eisler was not deported, and he was not deported as a Communist. Eisler, winner of the Composer's Award of the City of Vienna in 1924, is, according to President Emeritus Alvin Johnson of the New School for Social Research, "the first pioneer in the world of music composed particularly for the cinema. . . . Since the Constitution of the New School excludes the employment of teachers who are members of Communist or Fascist organizations, we inquired into Hanns Eisler's political status. He admitted frankly that he had been a member of the Communist party in Germany in 1926. Not being political-minded, he let his membership lapse and never restored it. . . . [He] was brought before a congressional committee, and admitted that he had once held a Communist card, something he had never denied. Held for deportation, he was granted the right to depart voluntarily, the government having no adequate case against him." The results of Hanns Eisler's study of music in film production were published under the title *Composing for the Film,* New York; Oxford, 1942.

[72] This statement identifies the Rockefeller Foundation and the New School for Social Research with the acts of Hanns Eisler performed (1) outside his relationship with these institutions and (2) prior to the establishment of the relationship. The question of "command responsibility" is involved here, that is, the responsibility of the benefactor, principal, superior, or employer for any and all acts of his beneficiary, agent, subordinate, or employee. This question is raised at several other points in this article, *e.g.,* Luce's responsibility

The war time director of the foreign broadcast intelligence service [73] of the federal communications commission was Robert D. Leigh, who was also director of the Hutchins-Luce Commission on Freedom of the Press.

Leigh also is director of the public library inquiry section of the Social Science Research council,[74] which is a chief spending agency for 10 big foundations.[75]

During the first decade of its life, the Social Science Research council received more than $4,000,000 [76] from the Carnegie cor-

for Hutchins, Hutchins' for the National Council of the Arts, Sciences, and Professions, Benton's for Dickey, Dickey's for the conduct of the Great Issues Course, the Rockefeller Foundation's for the Library of Congress, the Library's for MacLeish, MacLeish's for Lasswell, and Lasswell's for Schuman, Watson, and Dodd. Under this doctrine of "command responsibility," Colonel McCormick may be held responsible for any and all acts of his one-time employees or subordinates, Mayor Edward J. ("Sanitary Ed") Kelly of Chicago, Alfred ("Jake") Lingle, and Donald Day (*v*. ftn. 73). Kelly, subordinate and protégé of McCormick when the latter was president of the Chicago Sanitary District (1905-10), failed to report personal income of $450,000 in 1926-28 and had to settle with the U. S. government not only for $70,000 in taxes but also for $35,000 in penalties. Lingle, *Tribune* police reporter, was discovered, after his murder June 9, 1930, to have been a gangster.

[73] One of the functions of the Foreign Broadcast Intelligence Service was the recording of enemy broadcasts during World War II. One of the enemy broadcasts it recorded (January 8, 1945) began: "Hello, Americans! This is Donald Day, correspondent for the Chicago *Tribune* for twenty years in northern Europe, reporting to you from Berlin." Day had been with the *Tribune* until 1942.

[74] There is no public library inquiry section of the Social Science Research Council, but there is in progress a Public Library Inquiry undertaken by the S.S.R.C. in behalf of the American Library Association, which obtained a grant of $200,000 from the Carnegie Corporation. Leigh is director of the inquiry.

[75] The Social Science Research Council is not a chief spending agency of any big foundation. For example, as of the date the *Tribune* article appeared, the S.S.R.C. had received appropriations totaling $6,361,500 from the Rockefeller Foundation, which had made total appropriations, as of the prior date of December 31, 1947, of $413,907,068; and the S.S.R.C. had received appropriations totaling $1,023,500 from the Carnegie Corporation, which had made total appropriations, as of the prior date of September 30, 1947, of $203,296,078. The Rockefeller Foundation and the Carnegie Corporation are the two biggest of the thirteen (not ten, and not nine as listed in the paragraph following) big foundations for which the S.S.R.C. is a spending agency, but not a chief spending agency.

[76] This is a drop out of the bucket of some of the foundations listed. For example, during the first decade of its life (1923-32), the S.S.R.C. received $1,587,960 from the Rockefeller Foundation (whose total grants during

poration, the Carnegie Foundation for the Advancement of Teaching, the Commonwealth fund, the Falk Foundation,[77] the General Education board (Rockefeller), the Spelman fund (Rockefeller), the Rockefeller Foundation, the Rosenwald fund, and the Russell Sage Foundation.[78]

J. Frederic Dewhurst [79] of the Twentieth Century fund (Filene) [80]—still another foundation—is a member of Leigh's public library inquiry committee.

Undoubtedly the biggest wheel in the foundation "mass communications" structure [81] is Beardsley Ruml, chairman of the board of R. H. Macy & Co., New York, former chairman of the New York Federal Reserve board, and a member of the Hutchins-Luce Commission on Freedom of the Press.

Ruml once was a University of Chicago professor. He now is on the board of Encyclopedia Britannica Films, headed by Benton and

that decade were $133,355,712) and $75,000 from the Carnegie Corporation (whose total grants during that decade were $48,071,494).

[77] The Maurice and Laura Falk Foundation was established in 1929 by Maurice Falk, Pittsburgh industrialist, "for the improvement and betterment of mankind." Chairman of its Board of Managers is Leon Falk, Jr., Chairman of the Board of Directors of Falk & Co., and the Vice Chairmen are Frank B. Bell, Chairman of the Board of Directors of the Edgewater Steel Co., and E. T. Weir, Chairman of the Board of Directors of the National Steel Corp.

[78] The Russell Sage Foundation was established in 1907 by Mrs. Russell Sage "to improve the social and living conditions in the United States." Seven of the ten members of its Board of Trustees are bankers, corporation lawyers, and/or corporation directors.

[79] Corporation director and economist; chief of the Statistical Division of the Federal Reserve Bank of Philadelphia, 1923-28; Chief of the Division of Economic Research, U. S. Department of Commerce, under President Herbert Hoover, 1930-32; economist of the American Iron and Steel Institute, 1933; economic and technical adviser to numerous public agencies (*e.g.,* U. S. Bureau of the Census) and private organizations (*e.g.,* National Industrial Conference Board).

[80] The Twentieth Century Fund was established as the Co-operative League in 1919 by Edward A. Filene for the purpose of "promoting the improvement of economic, industrial, civic, and educational conditions." Chairman of the Executive Committee of its Board of Trustees is Henry S. Dennison, President, Dennison Manufacturing Co. Other board members: Paul G. Hoffman; Morris E. Leeds, Chairman of the Board of Directors, Leeds and Northrup Co.; H. Chr. Sonne, President, Amsinck, Sonne & Co.; Charles P. Taft, Ex-President (1947-48), the Federal Council of Churches of Christ in America.

[81] There is no foundation "mass communications" structure (*v.* ftn. 1).

Hutchins.[82] He was secretary of the Carnegie corporation.[83] He directed Spelman (Rockefeller) fund's giving of millions [84] to the so-called "social sciences." [85]

He was a trustee of the Rosenwald fund, is a member of the Social Science Research council,[86] a director of Muzak corporation, another of Benton's organizations,[87] and a director of the National Bureau of Economic Research, endowed by the Rockefeller Foundation.[88]

John Grierson, the Canadian adviser to the Hutchins-Luce Commission on Freedom of the Press,[89] once was the recipient of a

[82] This is a misstatement. Benton heads Encyclopaedia Britannica Films, Inc., as Chairman of its Board of Directors. H. E. Houghton heads it as Chairman of the Executive Committee of its Board of Directors. C. Scott Fletcher heads it as President. Hutchins is one of sixteen members of its Board of Directors.

[83] Ruml was never secretary of the Carnegie Corporation. He was assistant to its president (1921-22).

[84] Ruml did not direct the Spelman Fund's giving of millions to the social sciences, and the Spelman Fund did not give millions to the social sciences. And if "so-called social sciences" refers to the Social Science Research Council, the Spelman Fund's gifts were $67,500.

[85] The so-called "social sciences," like the so-called "Chicago *Tribune,*" are so called because that is their name.

Eleven years ago—January 3, 1938—R. M. Lee, Managing Editor of the *Tribune,* made a written apology for the *Tribune's* insertion of the word "so-called" into Associated Press dispatches referring to the National Labor Relations Board, and ascribed the insertion to a copy-reader who "did so for no reason that he could explain except that it seemed a clarifying phrase. Obviously, instructions have gone out to avoid a repetition of any such error" (*v.* Gunther, *Inside U.S.A.,* p. 365, New York, 1947).

[86] Ruml is not a member of the Social Science Research Council, nor is he in any way associated with it.

[87] Like R. H. Macy & Co. and the Chicago *Tribune,* a commercial, not a philanthropic, educational, or scientific institution.

[88] The National Bureau of Economic Research is not endowed, and it is not endowed by the Rockefeller Foundation. Its expenses are met by periodic contributions from philanthropic, business, and labor organizations, and from individuals. (The Rockefeller Foundation contributed less than half of the bureau's expenses for 1947, the last year for which an audit of the bureau is available.) Twelve universities share in its direction through officially appointed directors. Directors-at-large include Shepard Morgan, Vice President, Chase National Bank of New York; George B. Roberts, Vice President, National City Bank of New York; and Harry Scherman, President, Book-of-the-Month Club.

[89] The French adviser of the Commission was Jacques Maritain, subsequently Ambassador of France to the Holy See. The Chinese adviser was Hu Shih, Former Ambassador of China to the United States, now listed as a "war

Rockefeller Foundation fellowship at the University of Chicago which Leigh, director of the commission, said Ruml was instrumental in obtaining.[90]

Grierson was refused an immigration visa to re-enter the United States shortly after he was questioned by a Canadian commission investigating the soviet spy ring in the dominion.[91]

Grierson later was given a job with the United Nations educational, scientific, and cultural organization, which was headed by Archibald MacLeish [92] before Julian Huxley, former London zoo-keeper,[93] took it over. William Benton was chairman of the Ameri-

criminal" by the Chinese Communist headquarters (Chicago *Tribune*, Feb. 11, 1949).

[90] Leigh states that he told the *Tribune* reporter who questioned him that Ruml, in his capacity of Dean of the Division of Social Sciences of the University of Chicago (1931-33), might have been instrumental in Grierson's appointment to a Rockefeller fellowship there, and suggested that the reporter ask Ruml. Grierson was appointed to his Rockefeller fellowship on the nomination of the Scottish and Northern English Universities in 1924, when Ruml was not connected with either the Rockefeller Foundation or the University of Chicago.

[91] This statement does not meet the standards of "thoroughness" and "completeness" established by the American Society of Newspaper Editors. Grierson, Film Commissioner of the National Film Board of Canada and General Manager of the Wartime Information Board of Canada, testified before a Canadian Royal Commission investigating espionage in World War II. His testimony had to do exclusively with the appearance of his name, in the papers of suspects, as superior of a civil service secretary who was suspect. Prime Minister Louis St. Laurent, the then Minister of Justice and Attorney General of Canada, stated, November 14, 1946, in a letter to the editor of the Montreal *Star:* "I am at a loss to understand the report which you state is now current in certain newspaper circles in the United States to the effect that Mr. Grierson was a leader of the spy ring now before our courts. . . . I sincerely deplore the loose and ill-founded conclusions pointing to Mr. Grierson as 'head of the spy ring' or as consciously connected with it in any way." The U. S. State Department subsequently refused Grierson a quota visa without saying why, without giving Grierson a public hearing, and without, according to the Canadian government, making any inquiry of that government concerning Grierson.

[92] MacLeish was never head of the United Nations Educational, Scientific, and Cultural Organization.

[93] If Julian Huxley, Secretary of the London Zoological Society (1935-42), is a former London zoo-keeper, then Colonel R. R. McCormick, President of the Chicago Sanitary District (1905-10), is a former Chicago sewage disposer. (Colonel McCormick, in an address before the Executives' Club of Chicago, March 3, 1944, stated: "It was the Communists who taught the New Deal the tactics of smear and vilification, and the vilest of the vilifiers are Communists" [Tebbel, *op. cit.*, p. 247]). Huxley, the first head of UNESCO (Director-

can delegation to UNESCO.[94]

Beardsley Ruml and George Shuster, president of Hunter college and also a member of the Hutchins-Luce Commission on Freedom of the Press,[95] were among American national commission members for UNESCO.

Another commissioner of the Hutchins-Luce group was Reinhold Niebuhr, professor at Union Theological seminary, who has preached socialism and denounced capitalism for many years.[96]

Niebuhr was the beneficiary of a Rockefeller Foundation financed exchange of professors in 1943 which sent him to England and brought to the United States William Beveridge,[97] author of England's socialist [98] "cradle to the grave" security plan.

General, 1946-48), was Professor of Zoology, King's College, London, 1925-27; Honorary Lecturer, King's College, London, 1927-35; Fullerian Professor of Physiology in the Royal Institution, London, 1926-29; also General Supervisor of Biological Films, Gaumont-British Instructional, Ltd., 1933-36, and of Zoological Film Productions, 1937. As Secretary of the Zoological Society, he was director of the London Zoo. He is the Editor for Biology, Fourteenth Edition, *Encyclopaedia Britannica,* and the author of *Essays of a Biologist, The Individual in the Animal Kingdom, Evolution, The Modern Synthesis,* and other works. Winner of many medals, prizes, and awards for eminence in theoretical and experimental biology, he is President of the Institute of Animal Behavior, Chairman of the Association for the Study of Systematics, and Vice-President of the Eugenics Society of Great Britain.

[94] Benton is Vice Chairman of the Board of Trustees and one of the organizers of another organization, unmentioned in this article, the Committee for Economic Development. (Lasswell is a member of its Research Advisory Board.) The Trustees of the C.E.D., associated with Benton, who is associated with Luce, Hutchins, Negro poets, professors, propaganda analysts, content analysts, and persons fired unsuccessfully by Congress, are the presidents and chairmen of the boards of directors of eighty-five of the biggest commercial corporations in America.

[95] Shuster is a liar, a traitor to Yalta and Teheran, an enemy of the Soviet Union, a real enemy of the German people, and a Catholic reactionary who ought to be hanged, according to the Communist *Daily Worker* (March 3, 1945).

[96] Niebuhr, awarded the degree of Doctor of Divinity, *honoris causae,* by thirteen universities, including Harvard, Yale, Princeton, and Oxford, attacks "the Marxist illusion" in many of his works, *e.g. The Children of Light and the Children of Darkness* (pp. 109-110), New York, 1944.

[97] Sir William Beveridge, editorial writer, London *Morning Post,* 1906-08; Director of Labor Exchanges of the British Board of Trade, 1908-16, under the Presidency of Winston Churchill; Assistant General Secretary to the Ministry of Munitions, 1915-16; Second Secretary, 1916-18, Permanent Secretary, 1919, to the Ministry of Food; Director, London School of Economics, 1919-37. Sir William is a member of no political party.

[98] The "Beveridge Plan" was attacked by Adolf Hitler and by Joseph

Also associated with the foundations and their great wealth is another member of the Hutchins-Luce Commission on Freedom of the Press, Prof. Charles E. Merriam of the University of Chicago. He was a trustee of the Rockefeller Spelman fund, past president of the Social Science Research council, and one of the originators of the National Resources Planning board.

Prof. John M. Clark of Columbia university, seat of Carnegie endowment activities,[99] was a Hutchins-Luce press "commissioner," and also was associated with Merriam on the planning board.[100]

Still another Hutchins-Luce press commissioner was Prof. William E. Hocking of Harvard. Hocking is an associate of the Institute of Pacific Relations,[101] on the board of which were Henry Luce and Henry A. Wallace.[102]

Goebbels as "bolshevism" and by the Communist *Daily Worker* of London for "leaving quite untouched the private ownership of the big capitalist monopolies, which are the causes of economic crisis, unemployment, and poverty."

[99] The only connection between the Carnegie Endowment for International Peace and Columbia University is that of landlord and tenant. The endowment rents a house owned by the University.

[100] Clark states: "I was never a member of the Board, and do not even know whether Merriam was or was not on the board at the time I (1) made a study of timed public works for them, about 1934; or (2) criticized some of their staff studies around 1938-1940."

[101] William Ernest Hocking, Alford Professor Emeritus of Philosophy at Harvard University, does not confine his relations to the Pacific, where he is an associate of the East Asiatic Society and the American Oriental Association, in addition to being a trustee of Lignan University, Canton, China. He also has Atlantic relations, as an associate of the British Institute of Philosophy, the New Hampshire Historical Society, and the American Society of Puritan Descendants.

[102] This is a true statement. Luce and Wallace *were* associated with Hocking, just as Colonel McCormick *was* associated with Kelly, Lingle, and Day (*v.* ftn. 72). Other members of the Board of Trustees of the Institute for Pacific Relations are: President Raymond B. Allen of the University of Washington; Dwight L. Clarke, President of Occidental (*not* Oriental) Life Insurance Co. of California; Arthur H. Dean, Partner, Sullivan and Cromwell, New York; Charles K. Gamble, Director, Standard-Vacuum Oil Co., New York; W. R. Herod, President, International General Electric Co.; President Robert Gordon Sproul, University of California; Former Under Secretary of State Sumner Welles; Chancellor Ray Lyman Wilbur, Stanford University, Former Secretary of the Interior (under President Herbert Hoover); J. D. Zellerbach, President, Crown Zellerbach Corp. In a letter November 18, 1949, to a critic of the Institute, Clayton Lane, Executive Secretary of the Institute, states: "If you now have actual evidence or a persistent belief that this Institute or any of its present officers or staff is connected with the Communist party, or is engaged in any activity prejudicial to the American national interest, will you please inform me in the fullest possible terms. I am deter-

The institute is financed by the Rockefeller Foundation to the tune of $130,000 to $230,000 a year, and receives in the neighborhood of $30,000 a year from the Carnegie corporation.[103] Carnegie gave it $127,000 from 1923 to 1932.[104]

The 1948 California legislative committee on un-American activities listed the Institute of Pacific Relations as among "typical mass organizations that are victims of Communist domination." [105]

There were only three other man [sic] on the Hutchins-Luce Commission on Freedom of the Press, Prof. Robert Redfield [106] of the University of Chicago, Prof. Arthur Schlesinger [107] of Harvard, and Prof. John Dickinson [108] of the University of Pennsylvania. All

mined, as are my Trustees and colleagues, that there shall be no reasonable basis for such charges as you have made. . . . Disclosure [of Communist activities] and protest [against them] is not enough. We Americans must somehow find the positive answers to Communism. If we do not find them and apply them effectively in Asia, the Russians may eventually have most of it securely on their side at great hazard to us. Food and guns have not provided the answer in China; perhaps much more of both would not have provided it."

[103] According to the Institute of Pacific Relations, Rockefeller Foundation grants to the Institute for the current year are $51,150; Carnegie Corporation grants, $20,000.

[104] This is incorrect, according to the Institute of Pacific Relations.

[105] " 'Collective responsibility' or institutional guilt, whereby every person listed on the membership rolls of an organization is an equal partner in crime, is a new principle of international justice, sponsored by the American members of the court. . . . All Americans ought to be profoundly disturbed because Mr. Justice Jackson's theory is contrary to every tradition of our law and to every principle of justice. The smear court at Nuremberg is precisely the kind of court which is outlawed in our Bill of Rights, and its law, insofar as it can be said to have any, comes far closer to the Nazi model than to ours" (Chicago *Tribune* editorial, November 28, 1945). Hocking, with whom Luce and Wallace were formerly associated in the Institute of Pacific Relations, is one of 2,000 associates of the Institute.

[106] Like Lingle and Day, Redfield is a former associate of Colonel McCormick on the *Tribune*, where Redfield was employed for one week in 1920. He was President of the American Anthropological Association (1944), and, in addition to having received grants and appointments from the Carnegie Institution and the Rockefeller Foundation, is the holder of a degree (*honoris causae*) from Fisk University.

[107] Schlesinger, Francis Lee Higginson Professor of History at Harvard University, has been President of the American Historical Association (1942) and winner of many prizes, medals, and awards for history, and is Massachusetts State Chairman of the Americans for Democratic Action, which bars Communists from membership.

[108] Dickinson was appointed General Solicitor of the Pennsylvania Railroad in 1937, and has been General Counsel of the Pennsylvania Railroad since

three are associated in the multimillion dollar Social Science Research council,[109] supported by 10 enormously wealthy foundations.[110]

These 12 professors,[111] headed by Chancellor Hutchins, repeated the accusation in their report that newspaper owners and workers possess "the unconscious arrogance of conscious wealth." [112]

PROBLEMS

1. Following Mayer's suggestion that you first read the original "news report" in the Chicago *Tribune*, what specific ideas about the Commission on Freedom of the Press did you receive?

    a. Without reading Mayer's footnotes, what evidence did you gather that you were getting a straight news *report* of *facts*? that you were getting a *slanted* report, a series of judgments?

    b. What *questions* occurred to you as you read the *Tribune* article? Did you have immediately at hand any information that could

1946. He was also Professor of Law at the University of Pennsylvania, but was not at the time this article was published.

[109] Dickinson's last activity in the Social Science Research Council was 1941; Redfield's in 1945; and Schlesinger's in 1945. All three belong to the Corporation of the Council, an honorary body composed of past directors of the S.S.R.C. Its members do not associate as such.

[110] The thirteen (not ten, and not nine as listed in the article *supra*) foundations which contribute to the support of the Social Science Research Council are not enormously wealthy, *e.g.*, the Maurice and Laura Falk Foundation (ftn. 77), which had assets on December 31, 1946, as of its last available biennial report, of $6,967,025.87. Many Americans who have not established foundations are wealthier, individually, than most of the thirteen foundations which contribute to the support of the S.S.R.C. One of them is Colonel R. R. McCormick, Editor and Publisher of the Chicago *Tribune* and President of the Tribune Co., which owns the two biggest newspaper publishing properties in the United States, the Chicago *Tribune* and the New York *Daily News*.

[111] MacLeish has not been a professor since 1922, Hutchins since 1929, Ruml since 1933, Shuster since 1935, Hocking since 1943, Merriam since 1944, and Dickinson since June 1948.

[112] This is a misrepresentation of a misquotation from William Allen White (1868-1944), editor of the Emporia (Kansas) *Gazette* (1895-1944). (The Commission on Freedom of the Press, *op. cit.*, p. 60.).

"The Chicago *Tribune* lives and grows because it is first of all a *news*paper. It spares no expense, no effort, to gather the news of every significant development and trend at home and abroad. And it prints it, completely and without compromise, in the public interest." (*The First Hundred Years*, Chicago 1947: The Tribune Co.).

help you answer these questions? What easily available materials could help *you* check the objectivity of the *Tribune* article? (Consider, for instance, the usefulness of *Who's Who in America*.)

2. After reading Mayer's footnotes, did you find any changes in:

a. Your picture of the Commission's report, *A Free and Responsible Press?*

b. Your picture of the purpose of Luce, Hutchins, and the others in setting up the Commission?

c. Your picture of the Commission's *personnel?*

3. Can you detect in Mayer's footnotes any evidence of his own use of judgments, inferences, slanting? What does such an extensive and intensive criticism of the *Tribune* article suggest about Mayer's own attitude toward Hutchins, Luce, the Commission?

4. What light does the fact that *Fortune,* published by the Luce interests, printed a report of the Commission's findings which was, on the whole, unfavorable (see *Fortune,* April, 1947) throw on the reliability of the *Tribune* story?

Mark Twain

If you wish to put to a real test the difficulty of reporting "exactly what happened," you might, like Clemens, visit a police court.

During the eighteen-sixties, Samuel L. Clemens ("Mark Twain") worked as a miner and newspaperman in Nevada and California. During his wanderings he constantly noted the incongruity between facts and men's pictures of the facts. Indeed, a good deal of the world's humor would seem to have grown out of an acute awareness of this difference.

THE EVIDENCE IN THE CASE *

I reported this trial simply for my own amusement, one idle day last week—but I have seen the facts in the case so distorted and misrepresented in the daily papers that I feel it my duty to come forward and do what I can to set the plaintiff and defendant right before the public. This can best be done by submitting the plain, unembellished statements of the witnesses as given under oath be-

* Mark Twain, *The Evidence in the Case,* Harper & Brothers, publisher.

fore his honor Judge Sheperd, in the San Francisco Police Court. There is that nice sense of justice and that ability to discriminate between right and wrong among the masses, which will enable them, after carefully reading the testimony, to decide without hesitation in the remarkable case of Smith vs. Jones.

To such as are not used to visiting the Police Court, I will observe that there is nothing inviting about the place, there being no rich carpets, no mirrors, no pictures, no elegant sofa or armchairs to lounge in, no free lunch—and, in fact, nothing to make a man who has been there once desire to go again.

There is a pulpit at the head of the hall, occupied by a handsome gray-haired judge, with a faculty of appearing pleasant and impartial to the disinterested spectator, and prejudiced and frosty to the last degree to the prisoner at the bar. To the left of the pulpit is a long table for reporters; in front of the pulpit the clerks are stationed, and in the center of the hall a nest of lawyers. On the left again are pine benches behind a railing, occupied by seedy white men, Negroes, Chinamen, Kanakas—in a word, by the seedy and dejected of all nations—and in a corner is a box where more can be had when they are wanted. On the right are more pine benches, for the use of prisoners, and their friends and witnesses.

An officer in a gray uniform, and with a star upon his breast, guards the door.

A holy calm pervades the scene.

The case of Smith vs. Jones being called, each of these parties, stepping out from among the other seedy ones, gave the court a particular circumstantial account of how the whole thing occurred, and then sat down.

The two narratives differed from each other.

In reality, I was half persuaded that these men were talking about two separate and distinct affairs altogether, inasmuch as no single circumstances mentioned by one was even remotely hinted at by the other.

Mr. Alfred Sowerby was then called to the witness stand, and testified, "I was in the saloon at the time, your Honor, and I see this man Smith come up all of a sudden to Jones, who warn't saying a word, and split him in the snoot."

LAWYER. "Did what, sir?"

WITNESS. "Busted him in the snoot."

LAWYER. "What do you mean by such language as that? When you say that the plaintiff suddenly approached the defendant, who was silent at the time, and 'busted him in the snoot,' do you mean that the plaintiff struck the defendant?"

WITNESS. "I'm swearing to that very circumstance. Yes, your Honor, that was just the way of it. Now, for instance, as if you was Jones and I was Smith. Well, I comes up all of a sudden and says to your Honor, says I, 'Damn your old tripe—' "

THE COURT. "Order in the court! Witness, confine yourself to a plain statement of the facts in this case."

LAWYER. "Take the witness. I have no further use for him."

The lawyer on the other side said he would endeavor to worry along without the assistance of Mr. Sowerby, and Mr. McWilliamson was next called, and deposed as follows:

"I was a-standing as close to Mr. Smith as I am to this pulpit, a-chaffing with one of the lager beer girls—Sophronia by name, being from somewheres in Germany, so she says, but as to that I—"

LAWYER. "Never mind the nativity of the beer girl, but state as concisely as possible what you know of the assault and battery."

WITNESS. "Well, German or no German—which I'll take my oath I don't believe she is, being red-headed, with long, bony fingers—"

LAWYER. "Stick to the assault and battery. Go on with your story."

WITNESS. "Well, sir, she—that is Jones—he sidled up and drawed his revolver and tried to shoot the top of Smith's head off, and Smith run, and Sophronia she walloped herself down in the sawdust and screamed twice, just as loud as she could yell. I never see a poor creature in such distress—and then she sung out: 'Oh, hell's fire! What are they up to now?' Saying which, she jerked another yell and fainted away as dead as a wax figger. Thinks I to myself, I'll be damned if this ain't getting rather dusty, and I'll—"

THE COURT. "We have no desire to know what you thought. We only wish to know what you saw. Are you sure Mr. Jones tried to shoot the top of Mr. Smith's head off?"

WITNESS. "Yes, your Honor."

THE COURT. "How many times did he shoot?"

WITNESS. "Well, sir, I can't say exactly as to the number—but I should think—well, say, seven or eight times—as many as that, anyway."

THE COURT. "Be careful now, and remember you are under oath. What kind of pistol was it?"

WITNESS. "It was a derringer, your Honor."

THE COURT. "A derringer! You must not trifle here, sir. A derringer only shoots once. How could Jones have fired seven or eight times?"

The witness is evidently as stunned by that last proposition as if a brick had struck him. "Well, your Honor—he—that is, she—Jones, I mean—Soph—"

THE COURT. "Are you sure he fired more than one shot? Are you sure he fired at all?"

WITNESS. "I—I, well, perhaps he didn't—and—and, your Honor may be right. But, you see, that girl, with her dratted yowling—altogether, it might be that he did only shoot once."

LAWYER. "And about his attempting to shoot the top of Smith's head off—didn't he aim at his body or legs? Come now."

WITNESS. "Yes, sir—I think he did—I—I'm pretty certain of it. Yes, sir, he must a-fired at his legs."

Nothing was elicited on the cross examination, except that the weapon used by Mr. Jones was a bowie knife instead of a derringer, and that he made a number of desperate attempts to scalp the plaintiff. It also came out that Sophronia, of doubtful nativity, did not faint, and was not present during the affray, she having been discharged from her situation the previous evening.

Washington Billings, sworn, said: "I see the row, and it warn't in no saloon. It was in the street. Both of 'em was drunk, and one was a-coming up the street, and tother was a-going down. Both of 'em was close to the houses when they first see each other, and both of 'em made their calculations to miss each other, but the second time they tacked across the pavement—drifting-like, diagonal—they come together, down by the curb—*al*-mighty soggy, they did—which staggered 'em a moment, and then over they went into the gutter. Smith was up first, and he made a dive for a cobble and fell on Jones. Jones dug out and made a dive for a cobble, and slipped his hold and jammed his head into Smith's stomach. They each done that over again, twice more, just the same way. After that, neither of 'em could get up any more, and so they just laid there in the slush and clawed mud and cussed each other."

On the cross examination, the witness could not say whether the parties continued to fight afterward in the saloon or not—he only knew they began it in the gutter, and to the best of his knowledge and belief they were too drunk to get into a saloon, and too drunk to stay in it after they got there. As to weapons, he saw none used except the cobble stones, and to the best of his knowledge and belief, they missed fire every time while he was present.

Jeremiah Driscoll came forward, was sworn, and testified, "I saw the fight, your Honor, and it wasn't in a saloon nor in the street. It was up in the Square, and they fought with a pine bench and a cane—"

LAWYER. "There, there, there—that will do—that—will—do! Take the witness."

The testimony on the cross examination went to show that during the fight one of the parties drew a sling-shot and cocked it and at the same time the other discharged a hand-grenade at his antagonist. He could not say, however, which drew the sling-shot or which threw the grenade. Upon questioning him further, and confronting him with the parties to the case before the court, it transpired that the faces of Jones and Smith were unknown to him, and that he had been talking about an entirely different fight all the time.

Other witnesses were examined, some of whom swore that Smith was the aggressor, and others that Jones began the row. Some said they fought with their fists, others that they fought with knives, others tomahawks, others revolvers, others clubs, others axes, others beer mugs and chairs, and others swore that there had been no fight at all. However, fight or no fight, the testimony was straightforward and uniform on one point, at any rate, and that was that the fuss was about two dollars and forty cents, which one party owed the other, but it was impossible to find out which was the debtor and which the creditor.

After the witnesses had been heard, his honor, Judge Sheperd, observed that the evidence in this case resembled the evidence before him in some thirty-five cases every day, on an average. He then said he would continue the case, to afford the parties an opportunity of procuring more testimony. . . .

Now, with every confidence in the instinctive candor and fair dealing of my race, I leave the accused and the accuser in the case of Smith vs. Jones before the bar of the world. Let their fate be pronounced. The decision will be a holy and just one.

PROBLEMS

1. Like many another humorist, Twain was amused by the difference between facts and people's ideas about the facts. (Moreover, Twain spent considerable time on the Western frontier, where the "tall tale" flourished and hurly-burly social conditions made for uncertainty of information.) Can you find (or recall) other instances of the use by humorists of such inconsistency as the basis for jokes? Consider cartoons (especially those in *The New Yorker*), movies, and radio, as well as accounts of real or fictional incidents.

2. When you have had to "get at the facts" of some incident or situation, e.g., an accident, a quarrel, the outcome of a close election, or the value of an object, what were your main obstacles? Write a clear, full account of such a situation, indicating the difficulties you encountered and how you met them.

3. Considering the difficulty of sifting fact from opinion in courtroom testimony, under what circumstances would you as a litigant prefer that the decision be arrived at by a judge alone? by a jury? Can you suggest why litigants in civil (non-criminal) actions are more frequently willing to let the decision be determined by a judge alone than are litigants in criminal actions? Why do litigants in civil suits involving contractual disputes more frequently waive their right to jury trial than do litigants in civil suits involving bodily injury (torts)? *Warning:* Don't jump to any easy conclusions here; keep your eye focused on the nature of the matter in dispute, not on the assumed nature of the disputants.

GENERAL PROBLEMS:
Distinguishing Fact from Opinion

1. Skill in distinguishing fact from opinion may be acquired by practice in analyzing one's own writing or the writing of others. Since most of us read more than we write, it might be logical to practice analyzing the writing of others first. Perhaps, too, we can more easily attain that objectivity necessary to acquire this skill if we "break down" the other fellow's writing before turning to our own. Which of the statements printed below may be classified as *reports* (verifiable fact)? which as *judgments* or *inferences* (opinion)? Distinctions of the kind

we are attempting to make here are not always clear-cut, so you may wish to point out those *parts* of some of these statements which are *reports,* and those *parts* which are *judgments* or *inferences.* One further warning: It is the *nature* of these statements, not their truth or falsity, with which we are concerned. A statement of presumed fact may be an error and still be a *report;* e.g., "There are 45 apples in that basket" (whereas by count there may be only 43).

  a. "The General Education Board was founded by Mr. John D. Rockefeller in 1902 and was incorporated by Act of Congress, January 12, 1903. It was established one year after the Rockefeller Institute for Medical Research and was the first foundation for philanthropic purposes established by Mr. Rockefeller. . . . The purpose of the Board, as specified in its charter, is 'the promotion of education within the United States of America, without distinction of race, sex, or creed.' "

—General Education Board, Annual Report, 1947-1948

  b. "The keenest political observer alive in the 20th Century, in a typically Churchillian phrase, once privately called the men in the Kremlin 'those ruthless and bloody-minded professors.' "

—*Time,* July 17, 1950

  c. "The harpoon was darted; the stricken whale flew forward; with igniting velocity the line ran through the groove;—ran foul. Ahab stooped to clear it; he did clear it; but the flying turn caught him round the neck, and voicelessly as Turkish mutes bowstring their victim, he was shot out of the boat ere the crew knew he was gone. Next instant, the heavy eye-splice in the rope's final end flew out of the stark-empty tub, knocked down an oarsman, and smiting the sea, disappeared in its depths."

—Herman Melville, *Moby Dick*

  d. "A better education will help me in some form of work. I have seen it help others and if I acquire the knowledge I should it will help me in the same manner."   —Student theme

  e. "The tenor who sings the First Shepherd [in the Italian HMV recording of Monteverdi's "Orfeo"] would be better suited to 'Cavalleria Rusticana,' and the Eurydice has a strong tremolo; but the other singers are good. The performance is agreeably recorded; surfaces are noisy. Elaine Shop provides a libretto with an Italian text and an English translation by Ellen A. Lebow."

—B. H. Haggin, "Records," *The Nation,* May 6, 1950

2. There are a number of ways in which one can sharpen his ability to distinguish fact from opinion in his own writing. Some of these

ways were suggested in the Problems that followed Hayakawa's essay earlier in this section. Here are two further suggestions:

a. Attempt to write a straight *report,* excluding all *judgments* and *inferences,* about some experience which by its very nature might ordinarily arouse strong feelings in you. For example, you might write about being discharged from a job, about an unfortunate investment (of time or money) you made, about a "raw deal" you received, about a "bitter disappointment," about the loss of a friendship. *Helpful hint:* You had better leave this report untitled. Can you see why?

b. No matter how successful you were in writing a genuine *report* on one of these suggested subjects, you, or your readers, may feel that your report was *slanted* because you selected only certain details. To test the validity of this possible criticism, and further to sharpen your skill, write a second *report* about the same experience, this time from the point of view of some other person directly involved in the experience, e.g., the man who discharged you, the person who sold you the article you thought a poor buy, the person who gave you the "raw deal," one who observed but did not share your "bitter disappointment," the former friend.

3. A recent publication of the American Council on Education, *Helping Teachers Understand Children,* illustrates in a rather dramatic way, to anyone who is striving to be clear-headed about his relations with other people, the importance of training in the writing of reports. The following are verbatim extracts from "conduct reports" about children written by teachers *before* the teachers had learned the principles of *report* writing:

a. Henry is a good leader and adjusts well to the group. He is very dependable and self-reliant. (grade 2)

b. Charles annoys others. He is boisterous and wants to be the center of attention no matter what is going on. He is so dirty that no one likes to be near him. His family has been helped by organizations so long I doubt that they have any concern about their condition any more. They could do much better if they were not so trifling. (grade 6)

Compare these with the next two *reports* written *after* the teachers had been given some practice in writing "specific descriptions of the behavior of children in characteristic situations" instead of "making snap judgments and immediate interpretations on inadequate evidence," "characterizing a child in terms of only a single personality trait," and "reacting according to the significance of the episode for the writer [teacher] rather than for the child being studied."

c. While reading the "Run-Away Engine," Pressley (grade 1) often interrupted to say that just the same things that happened to the engine had happened to his grandfather when he drove *his* engine. . . . Some mules passed our window. Pressley said his grandfather had two mules, one is white and one is red. Pulled up one trouser leg before scrubbing tables—said that helped him work. . . . I saw him from a little distance going home, his trouser leg still up and one arm tucked into his shirt with the sleeve hanging empty as though he were playing "broken arm."

d. Sam (aged 12) showed a decided preference for Dora today. Asked to help her committee put up curtains. Said that "girls hardly know how to put up curtain fixtures straight. . . ." Painted a picture with Dora. Told me he would probably learn to paint a little better if he could paint with an artist like Dora. . . . [During poetry period] when James asked for "Hiding," he said, "Oh, boy, stop asking for those baby poems."

Using these "before and after" examples as a rough working model, and drawing on the experience acquired by writing the previous reports, write a factual *report* of the actual behavior in a specific situation of someone on whom you have passed hasty judgment. For example, have you complained that a fellow student is an "ear-banger" or a "longhair"? Have you praised some classmate as a "smooth operator"? Have you curtly foreclosed further discussion of a sorority sister with, "She's a perfect drip"? Have you dismissed an unmarried woman instructor as "just another old maid schoolteacher"? Specifically, what did each of these persons do, what did he say, how did he act in the particular situation that prompted your judgment? Recall *all* of the relevant circumstances. Would a strictly factual account of their conduct in these situations justify your judgment in the eyes of a third party looking only at the *facts?* Does their conduct justify your judgment in your own eyes now that you are *reporting?* Try it and see.

Guarding Against
Oversimplification

DO you recall the old riddle that runs, "Why is a spider like a baseball outfielder"? (They both catch flies.)

Well, here are some questions along the same line. Why is the famous passage from Keats—" 'Beauty is truth, truth beauty,'—that is all / Ye know on earth, and all ye need to know"—like the advice of the Calypso singer, Sir Lancelot, "Never make a pretty woman your wife"? like the solution to the international stalemate proposed by some people, "Drop a couple of atom bombs"? like the New York dress designer's contention that "Paris fashions are destroying the morals of the American woman"? like the advice of the economists who urge business executives and government officials to "leave the national economy to the law of supply and demand"? like the little girl's explanation of her baby brother's appearance in the family—"Mummy got him at the hospital"?

The answers to these questions, like the answer to the old riddle, is discovered when one sees what these apparently dissimilar statements have in common—here the desire to provide an oversimple explanation to a very complex problem.

The forms which this deep-rooted desire for simple answers can take are many and varied. The present section begins with Overstreet's analysis of the peculiar nature of oversimplification (he calls it "monism"). This selection is followed by three essays that illustrate the most common forms of oversimplification. Platt reveals how our tendency to oversimplify when we are talking about the natural world blinds us to what is really there. (How would those of you who have lived in Southern California for any length of time describe the "seasons" there? How many are there? In what order do they come? Is there more than one spring?) Allport and Postman, and Doolaard point out what happens when we look at people or events through eyes that are "set" to see only those things that fit our preconceived assumptions about those people or events. Sometimes that "set" serves as a fine-meshed screen which lets very little through; but we seize happily on that little and create from it a life-sized picture of the person or event, a picture so oversimplified that "any resemblance between these characters and persons living or dead is purely coincidental."

Perhaps you are beginning to think, "Is nothing in life simple?" We could say, "See, you're revealing at this very moment the desire for simplism." But we won't. Instead, we'll end this note with a word of encouragement. Paradoxically, if and when we stop over-simplifying, solutions to many problems become simpler, because they become possible. Wouldn't you agree that a possible solution, even one that requires some hard and persistent thinking, is "simpler" than a seemingly simple solution that turns out to be no solution at all and, therefore, only leads to further confusion?

That much is simple, isn't it?

H. A. *Overstreet*

Monorail, monotone, monotony, monoplane, monogram, mono-graph, monopoly—what idea do all these terms suggest?

You have very likely said, "— — has a one-track mind." But is not the thinking of all of us perhaps characterized, in varying degrees, of course, by a tendency to operate on a "single track"? Overstreet examines this possibility.

Until his retirement in 1939, Overstreet was head of the Philosophy Department at the College of the City of New York. He is the author of numerous popular books on social and individual behavior, of which *The Mature Mind* is the most recent.

ONE PROBLEM? ONE SOLUTION? *

In order to accomplish anything, the choice of a method is a prime essential. There are good methods of hoeing potatoes,

* Reprinted from *A Declaration of Interdependence* by H. A. Overstreet, by permission of W. W. Norton & Company, Inc. Copyright 1937 by W. W. Norton & Company, Inc.

handling mules, building automobiles, running a college—and poor ones. A good method involves a knowledge of the end desired but also of the best way to go about achieving it. A writer of short stories would probably make a mess of building an automobile, while a builder of automobiles, untrained in the niceties of language, would probably make a mess of writing short stories.

How to go about doing things is therefore, in its way, as important as knowing what one wishes to do. This needs to be especially emphasized in regard to things done or attempted in the social field. We are all pretty generally agreed upon what we want of our democracy. Painful differences arise when we try to get this agreed end realized. One of the illuminating—and disheartening—spectacles is the ease with which social progressives fall out among themselves. Many a good movement goes on the rocks because those who sincerely want the good cannot agree upon the way in which what they want is to be accomplished.

We witness, today, a fairly paralyzing disagreement between those who insist upon what might be called a monistic method of attacking the social problem and those who insist upon a pluralistic method. The monists are those who trace all the major evils of the world to one conditioning cause. This cause may be the economic system, or irreligion, or the poor education of the young, or the Jew, or any other single factor that is assumed to cast gloom over existence. Discovering one cause accountable, they call for one kind of action, a frontal attack. The pluralists, on the other hand, are those who, finding themselves unable to trace all evils to a single cause, call for action along many lines. Wherever there is an evil, they would handle it in terms of its special circumstances and conditions. The monists disavow such a method as unscientific, declaring that it merely treats symptoms instead of attempting to eliminate the cause. The pluralists counter by declaring that the monists, in their wish to find the one and only cause, inevitably reduce the multiplicity of life to too great a simplicity and so miss most of what is significant.

So the conflict goes on. It is impossible for us to disregard it if we are serious about our efforts to establish in America a more acceptable democracy. Is there one underlying evil that needs attacking, or are there many evils that may be separately and successively attacked?

THE URGE TO UNITY

The monistic attitude falls in with man's persistent effort to find unity in diversity. Sheer diversity has always been disconcerting. The typical propensity in man has been to find similarities, sequences, lines of relationship so that mere chaotic manyness might be reduced to order. Thus the "mere many" has been grouped into classes, and the multitude of "mere happenings" has been traced to causes. Man's outstanding effort throughout the ages has been to find the Class of all classes, the Cause of all causes. When Aristotle found his Moveless Mover, or the religionist his Creator, each of these was exhibiting the apparently ineradicable propensity of man to reduce all diversity to ultimate unity.

There seems to be no way of escaping this drive toward unity. As St. Augustine expressed it: "Our hearts are restless till they rest in Thee." But it is significant to notice that when we have found an ultimate unity we have never been able to do anything specific with it. Thus, powerful as the Aristotelian Moveless Mover was, it was quite incapable of giving information as to how a peristyle should be built or how the Athenian constitution might be improved. Irresistible as the Creator has been to the religionist, the knowledge of Him has given no indication as to how the movements of the planets are to be measured or how pneumonia is to be cured.

An ultimate unity, in short, has served merely the end (no doubt an important one) of intellectual and emotional satisfaction. It has not served the end of specific achievement.

It is for this reason that the fruitful history of man has consisted in the doing of many things, each of which has had its special and limited relations, but no one of which has been clearly and specifically related to the ultimate unity. Thus, without any need for invoking a Moveless Mover, or Creator, or Absolute, the anatomist has dissected the human body and learned of its parts and processes; the painter has mixed his pigments and applied them to canvas; the mechanic has built his cogwheels, the architect his dome; the fisherman has cast his line and drawn out his catch; the tinsmith has soldered his can; the baker has baked his bread. Life, in short, has consisted of the art of doing a multitude of things. The overspanning unity may have been there. It has pleased us to think so. But for all practical purposes we have had to learn to place no dependence upon it for specific information and technique, but to go ahead with the mastering of the particular situations we have had in hand. While intellectually and emotionally, therefore, we have been monists, practically and specifically we have been pluralists.

WEAKNESSES OF SOCIAL MONISM

This may seem to have nothing to do with the kind of monism which insists upon finding the single cause of our social ills and attacking it directly. But there is a close connection between the two kinds of thinking.

In the first place, social monism suffers from the weakness of all monism: it not only assumes a single cause, but, far more precariously, it assumes that we have the power to discover what it is. In regard to the cosmos, such an assumption would now seem to be untenable. The diversity of the world is too vast and man's mental powers too slight to enable him to enclose the universe within a word or phrase, or even within a sentence or a paragraph. Thus for the cosmic monist to say that the world is matter means merely that he has set down a question mark, for what ultimate matter is neither he nor any of the rest of us knows. To say that the world is mind is likewise to set down a question mark. But even when we reduce the area of our search to the world of the human and the social we are not much better off. Human happenings are so indefinitely diverse, the springs of human motivation and the mechanisms of human achievement are still so far beyond our finding, that to crowd all social life into a single category—economic or religious or what not —is to assume a mental comprehensiveness we actually do not possess.

When we do so we invariably commit the fallacy of simplism. We cast out the unmanageable and the unexplainable. We wave them aside as irrelevant, when, for all we know, they may be profoundly relevant. In our haste to possess the solvent idea, we are impatient of protracted research. We oversimplify. We have the will to declare the truth; and not even reality shall stop us.

Out of simplism grow the panaceas. A panacea is an offered cure for an ill that is only partly diagnosed. Thus it is suggested that we cure crime by more severe punishment, or that we cure the depression by going on the silver standard, or by taxing the rich, or by liquidating capitalism. As often as not a panacea merely aggravates the disease—which is the sad experience of the world today. While it is indeed a good thing to look for the cause of our troubles, when the wrong cause is found, heaven help the trouble.

Out of simplism, too, grow the scapegoat techniques. Hunting around for a single cause, we find it in a person or a group. It is that everlasting goat, the Jew; or it is the Catholics, or Mr. Hearst, or Mr. Morgan. The scapegoat technique is one of the typical recourses of the immature mind. The child cannot know the intricately related factors that have brought about an evil situation. It selects one obvious factor and vents its wrath upon it. But, again, the scapegoat technique is merely the outcome of the wish to reduce all the multiplicity of a problem to a swift and easy unity.

Social monism seems to exhibit a further weakness. It tends to disregard (because it has no interest in) all phases of life save those in which the single cause is prominently in evidence. Thus, for the economic monist, the work of a psychiatrist dealing with the depressive states of a patient would, in strict logic, be postponed until the economic system was rectified. To every suggestion that the depressive states might well be treated long before economic equilibrium is established, the monist would logically reply that since the depressive states have their origin in a world badly maladjusted, there can be no cure until the basic maladjustment is corrected.

This, clearly, is a counsel of postponement that we can ill afford to follow. While it may be true that various ills from which we suffer have their rootage deep down in a badly organized society, it does not follow that nothing can be done about them until full social adjustment is achieved.

Thus, for example, it is quite possible to take in hand many problems of teaching without referring to the economic system. There is a difference between an ignorant teacher and one who has knowledge. Under any system of life whatever, the former is a liability. At the present time, therefore, we can go vigorously at the task of training teachers in such ways that they will be informed within the areas of their teaching. Again, there is a difference between autocratic teachers and those who recognize that their task is to respect the potential powers of their charges. One suspects that even under the most admirable economic arrangements this difference in psychological outlook might be present. It need not be necessary, therefore, to postpone dealing with this psychological inadequacy until the whole system of life has been revised.

A PLURALISTIC APPROACH

There would seem to be wisdom, then, in a pluralistic approach to the problems of our life. Are there political evils? They may have arisen out of sheer ignorance, out of our inability thus far to devise a political mechanism that can work smoothly and effectively. Many of our political evils today are doubtless of this kind. To try to govern a modern city with a clumsy board of aldermen meets with its own defeat. We can try a commission form of government. We have tried it and it has worked. To be sure, the commission form has not solved all our city problems, but it has solved some of them. So far, then, so good. We can now tackle further problems. To try to catch criminals by a city police department that has no way of cooperating effectively with county, state, and federal officials is to court defeat. We can try to regionalize our police administration. We have tried it and it has worked. To be sure, it has not eliminated the criminal, but it has helped us to catch him. So far, then, so good. We can go on to further problems of crime.

Are there educational evils? We have them by the dozens and the scores. For education depends in a peculiar manner upon personality, and personality has queer quirks. We can investigate the quirks, can train better teachers, can learn more about students, can learn more about the society in which students live. We shall not thereby change the world into one wholly admirable, but we shall have done some of the things that can be undertaken notwithstanding that we still live in an unsatisfactory world. Moreover we shall have done what will be necessary even in an admirable world.

And so in regard to other areas of our life—economic, religious, social, artistic, recreational, domestic. Each has a host of specific problems that can be specifically handled. To postpone them all for the furtherance of one central objective is to suffer the danger of being foolish in many things while we wait for a chance to be wise in the one way we may never live long enough to achieve.

THIS GIVES US A CHANCE

There is one outstanding value in the pluralistic approach that needs particular mention. Such an approach gives every one of us something that he can effectively do, and do now. Thus the worker for civil service reform is not to be despised and rejected because such reform does not settle all our problems. Because it settles some of them, it is a task that needs to be undertaken. The worker in adult education need not be told that his effort to keep adult minds alive—his own included—will not of itself usher in the new society. He doubtless knows this, but he might reply that any new society without adult minds that have kept alive will not be worth the having.

There is a particular kind of despair that all too frequently possesses the finer type of mind: it is the despair that comes from realizing the magnitude of what needs to be done and the insignificance of what he himself can do. We have all had this despair as we have watched the immense tragedy of a World War and the different but probably equal tragedy of the depression. "What can we do?" we have asked. The monist answers: "Do this one thing. Seek out the evil that oppresses us and attack that evil." Many of us have been fascinated by the reply. It has seemed to penetrate to the very center of our distresses and show us the one way out. But when we have sought to attack the one evil—not this or that phase of it, but *the* evil—we have not known where the attack was to be begun nor how it was to be conducted. In the end, knowing no specific thing to do, we have merely achieved the intellectual and emotional satisfaction of hating the evil and hoping for the society from which the evil would be banished.

In spite of the intellectual and emotional satisfaction, there is a kind of frustration in this. Invariably man learns by doing. When he is balked of the doing of particular things because the one central thing cannot be done, he fails of learning. His intellectual and emotional satisfaction becomes a substitute for effective action. He contemplates—perhaps excoriates—but does not achieve.

This applies with particular force to the situation in America. There would seem to be no *one* evil to attack, no *one* solution to propose. If, as we said at the beginning of this book, we are passing through an unintended revolution that has taken us by surprise, bringing with it problems and perplexities we have never yet had to face, we shall be ill-advised if we look for one enemy, as we properly should have done if the revolution had been an intended one. The fact is that the order of our life is changing. Problems rise up to meet us on every hand, problems that root in our unprepared minds, in the outdated mechanisms of our society, and in our ignorance of how new social techniques are to be found for managing a new abundance.

A large number of our problems are of the engineering sort. We have to learn how to build a more effective political mechanism—from the smallest community to the nation and the world. We have to learn how to educate the minds of young and old into a knowledge and wisdom appropriate to this far more difficult age. We have to learn how to build better cities and countrysides, and, above all, how to distribute equitably as well as produce abundantly.

What is significant about these problems is that many of them can be undertaken singly; and the individual who is in the fortunate position of being able to attack even one of them can have the satisfaction of doing something more effective than merely contemplating the coming order or trying to persuade people that the present order should go.

The social pluralist is too apt to be abashed by the contempt of the monist. The latter seems to be thorough-going, to cut straight to the heart of things. The pluralist seems, by contrast, to be occupied merely with ragged edges. And indeed, from an emotional standpoint, the monist has it all his own way. As human beings, we want the unified outlook and the unified attack. But to want it and to have it are two quite different things. All through human history man has sought an all-resolving unity, and all through his history this type of unity has turned out to be valueless for specific achievement. The pluralist may well remember that life has consisted always in the doing of many things unrelated in man's consciousness to any overspanning unity, and if, in the bewildering complexity of the present situation, he finds that there are a number of things he can do to advance order and sanity in his world, he can rightly be happy in the doing of them.

In any event, the establishment of a more acceptable democracy would seem to wait upon the willingness of many Americans to do many things in more acceptable ways.

PROBLEMS

1. *a.* When a man concludes that the existence of armaments is *the* cause of war, what *one* cure will he probably conclude to be *the* cure? What other possible contributing causes will he be likely to ignore? What causes will he be likely to ignore if he concludes that capitalism or communism is *the* cause?

   b. When a man arrives at the belief that literacy is *the* source of all democracy, what type of education will he probably advocate? What kinds of education will he tend to overlook or neglect?

   c. When one determines that *the great leader* is *the* cause of social progress, what ways of bringing about social improvement may easily be discounted?

   d. When students conclude, consciously or unconsciously, that books are *the* source, not just *one* source, of knowledge, what sources of information may they tend to overlook?

2. What would be some typical *monistic* reactions to the following problems:

   a. Consistent failure to pass school examinations?

   b. Several successive disastrous football seasons?

   c. A series of acts of vandalism in a town during the fraternity initiation period at the local college?

   d. A succession of bad colds?

   e. A severe water shortage continuing after the building of a number of expensive "check dams"?

3. In a carefully detailed paper show how a monistic approach might lead to both *inefficiency* and *injustice* in the following situations:

   a. There has been an outbreak of petty thefts in a small, rural community which recently received an influx of soldiers coming for their annual national guard training.

   b. There has been a relatively steep increase in the costs of city government after the adoption of a city-manager plan.

   c. A staff doctor at a mental institution has been murdered by a convicted criminal who was sent to the institution for psychiatric treatment.

4. Some modern-day semanticists who are also clinical psychologists have suggested a close relationship between *monistic* thinking and such common maladjustments as "inferiority feelings," excessive anxiety, and a feeling of frustration. Can you see the connection? What is it? (Students interested in this thesis will find it persuasively outlined in Wendell Johnson's *People in Quandaries*.)

5. In what ways does the commonness of such advertisements as "Are you unpopular? Use Whiff-Sniff" illustrate the prevalence of monism in our thinking?

6. In writing a theme or term paper (e.g., on the rising cost of living, the increase in cheating during examinations, traffic accidents, juvenile delinquency, or success in selling) have you encountered the "urge to unity"? What conditions under which most themes are written lead one to think "monistically"? What is there peculiar to the examination system that may lead teachers and students alike to fall into this way of thinking?

Rutherford Platt

Most of us like to consider ourselves "realistic" in our perception of the physical world around us, but a little poking into our observation of color (as in the following selection), sound, taste, smell, and so forth, usually indicates that we *miss* more than we *observe*. If that is true of observations of our physical environment, how much more applicable must it be to our apprehension of less tangible facts, such as the motives and reactions underlying human conduct? Platt, a businessman and author, shows us one way of seeing a little beyond our noses.

THE SEEING EYE *

Color is always to be seen in the countryside whenever there is light. That includes the dullest day of winter, and overcast and stormy days of every season. The brightest primary colors are always present as well as the most delicate hues. You might suppose that bright red is not a year round color. Let us see. In the June meadow burns the flame red of the devil's paintbrush and the scarlet of wild strawberries. The next month, on the edge of the woods, a wood lily will fling out its red vibrations. In August, at the foot of the hill, along the brook flare glossy rubies of honeysuckle and bittersweet nightshade berries. Later in August the cardinal flower throws out a sharp band from the long end of the spectrum. In September, the Jack-in-the-pulpit fruits and Rus-

---

* Reprinted by permission of Dodd, Mead & Company from *This Green World* by Rutherford Platt. Copyright, 1942, by Dodd, Mead & Company, Inc.

sula mushrooms are among the countless objects that flash the long red waves of light. In October, the leaves of the red maples, sassafras and sumac will surrender their chlorophyll and throw off scarlet vibrations instead of green. In early winter the climbing bittersweet and the fruit of the cranberry tree will flare from the hedge rows. All through the winter there is no brighter scarlet than the tips of Cladonia lichens called "British soldiers," or the twigs of the red osier dogwood, or the winter buds of willows, red maples and blueberries.

You can see through the seasons a similar succession of yellow, purple, blue, green or any other color or hue you may look for. Color is no seasonal phenomenon; there is always more of it than most of us ever see.

Exploring for bright color the year round brings undreamed-of surprises. When you accustom your mind's eye to detect hues, the beauty of the world we live in becomes a revelation. I used to consider that green leaves are all about the same green tone. That is so far from the fact that it is often possible to tell the species of a tree from its distinctive shade of green. Birches are yellow green; poplars, gray green. Sugar maple leaves are a bright rich green above and silvery green beneath. When the wind blows the whole tree gleams with silver. The elm leaves are a polished dark bluish green; the cherry is similar but even glossier. The locust presents a beautiful duotone effect, with lighter and darker green leaves on the same twig. The ash is a dark blue green. The American beech has foliage of clear bright green. Poison ivy starts as bronze red and turns to polished green as sparkling, if it is growing in full sunlight, as though covered with cellophane.

Each conifer, too, has its distinctive shade of green. The white pine is well named not only for its white wood but also for the accents of white light which play through its needles. This effect is due in part to a light blue tint, almost white, in the lines of the breathing pores on the under side of each needle and in part to highlights from the polished surface of the needles. Other species of pine are on the dark side. The three common species of pine native in the eastern United States are named after the tones of their green needles: red, white and black. The famous cultivated variety of spruce, known as blue spruce, has beautiful blue green needles. The hemlock is a dark yellow green and very lustrous.

Among herbaceous plants one of the loveliest shades of green is found in the leaves of clover. The surface is dull, with a bluish tone mottled with light blue angular check marks. In contrast, the mullein is as gray as a woolly blanket, but when you hold it up to the sun the transmitted light is clear yellow green. Of all the bright greens in the world there is none brighter than the pleated leaves of lady's-slipper and Clintonia. They have a high polish in contrast with the blue green of honeysuckle leaves which have a beautiful rich suède finish. Bloodroot leaves, when they first appear in early spring, are unique not only for their fantastic design but also because they are a lovely blue green. And the exquisite flowers shoot up on dynamic straight stems through the heart-shaped base.

A vast array of unseen color will suddenly flare when you look for the hues in bark. I used to think that all bark, with the exception of white birch, was a nondescript grayish or brownish tone. That was before I really *looked* at bark and discovered not only a variety of hues of one color but also many different colors. That of the yellow birch is glistening yellow. Sweet birch bark and the younger bark of cherry are maroon. The younger bark in the upper branches of Scotch pine is such a bright orange that the species can be identified by this feature. The white in white oak bark gives the bole its distinctive gray tint by which it can be identified from all other species of oaks. The barks of the American beech and of the red maple are smooth battleship gray. The deeply sculptured bark of the black locust has bright yellow streaks in its fissures. The Osage orange bark is orange, although the name is a coincidence, as the tree is named after its fruit and not its bark. There is a distinct difference in the whites of the two white birch trees: the gray birch is a cold silvery white; the paper birch is a warmer buff white, due to the orange inner bark just below the surface.

So mobile is color outdoors that it changes with every intensity of light. Perhaps this is one reason why certain seasons of the year are considered to be rather drab or colorless. November is the darkest month of the year. Then the sky is frequently overcast and the noon sun is closer to the horizon. The snow which builds up intensities of light in winter has not yet arrived. In these days of reduced illumination, reds turn purple. This is seen in the colors of lichens, twigs of dogwoods or buds of red maple and willow. Yellow turns olive green. Bright green becomes bluish. Look at the foliage of conifers, club-mosses and evergreen ferns in November. Blue turns deeper blue, witness the bloom on the canes of brambles and the metallic blue of the fluted shafts of the scouring rushes. The orange in the carpet of fallen leaves, in catkins, seeds, grasses, and the November hues of hay-scented ferns turns brownish. Brown is a degraded orange. It is produced when the pigments that give off the light waves of orange act as a sort of brake to reduce their intensity—or the same effect is produced when the original source light is of low intensity.

Conversely, outdoor hues are entirely changed by increased illumination. Red appears as purplish pink; yellow becomes warmer; green grows bluer; blue, purpler; and orange, reddish. Violet remains violet but of a paler tint.

This is one reason why it is difficult to discuss precisely the colors of things. Objects which have not changed their color natures take on different hues when the atmospheric illumination varies. All such changes are optical illusions; they are of the psychological nature of color which is so fluid as it plays on the sensitive nerve ends in our eyes.

This fact makes color in the outdoors one of the least known and least understood of nature's phenomena. The terminology for color is incomplete and inaccurate. We speak in generalities, dividing this vast array of hues, tints and tones under a few key labels like red, yellow, green, blue, orange. Violet, purple and magenta are ambiguous words. Even the botanists with all their striving for precision of expression have never finally agreed on a way of describing colors accurately. In the *Manual of Botany* by the great Asa Gray most of the hues from pink to violet are simply called "purple." But if a quality as elusive as color cannot be accurately described, at least it can be felt and the comparison of tones, tints and hues made and enjoyed on the spot while you look at the objects. In this way one can learn to think in terms of color and feel an artist's thrill over its infinite gradations.

PROBLEMS

1. Platt has found that there are no "colorless" days or seasons. Why, then, are so many of us, and why was Platt formerly, unaware of this ever-present color? Analogies are risky, but does Platt's discovery, based on close observation, suggest one reason why a psychiatrist's careful analysis of a "dull" or "average" person often makes fascinating reading?

2. Platt says that when he "really *looked*" at bark he found a great variety of colors and also hues of one color. How does this kind of "looking" differ from the kind of looking most of us do? Why is it that we seldom look hard at physical objects? Is it that we are satisfied to identify things as belonging to vague, general categories like "bark"? How does this relate to the way we look at certain human beings as "just salesmen"; the way teachers look at children as "just pupils"? Do you begin to see how deeply rooted the tendency to oversimplify really is?

3. What exactly is the difference in ways of "looking" between:
   a. the doctor, and the layman who generalizes all his muscle aches into "rheumatism"?
   b. the social thinker who talks about the "masses," and the social worker who works with individuals who make up those masses?
   c. the person who asks no questions when told someone is "a writer," and the man who asks, "What kind of writing does he do?"
   d. the art gallery visitor who calls all abstract art "modern," and the one who sees elements of abstraction in some ancient Egyptian tomb-paintings, Etruscan figurines, African masks, and a contemporary sculptor's work in wire?
   e. the student who writes about "The Advantages of Family Life," and the student who writes a paper on "Two Kinds of Family" or "The Mother-dominated Family"?

4. Platt, in his book, *This Green World,* is primarily concerned with the increased enjoyment which can be derived from breaking down one's oversimplified observation of nature. Moreover, he frequently points out that the distinction between two colors or hues enables one to identify different trees and flowers. How does the specific, concrete thinking which Platt has in mind help in the solving of human problems more than does the broad, generalized thinking which Platt rejects? For example, a student's choice of a teacher because he is a certain kind of man, and not because he has an M.A. or a Ph.D.; a

wise consumer's choice of one of two refrigerators or two automobiles on the basis of the function it is to serve, not the amount of chrome it has. Consider, if you please, reasons for the choice of a wife or husband.

5. Platt notes that the terminology of color is far too general, too broad, to give an accurate picture of the world of color. What does this suggest as one great, never-ending task in our development and use of language as a means of understanding and solving human problems? What effect does Platt's suggestion have on the common assumption (which we will consider later with more thoroughness) that the word-symbol is "the thing itself," that if we know the word for a thing we know that thing, that if there is no word for a thing that thing does not exist?

6. What criticism of one common way of teaching "science," especially botany and biology, is implicit in Platt's viewpoint?

Gordon W. Allport and Leo Postman

What really *happens to facts* when a reporter, teacher, debater, novelist, or gossip "distorts" them?

During the past decade Allport and Postman have done important work in the relatively new field of the analysis of public opinion and the effects of mass communications upon it. They and other social psychologists have tried to observe with scientific accuracy the ways in which public opinion grows, and the relationship between facts and people's conceptions of them. The opinion poll-takers, such as Gallup and Roper, have centered their attention on measuring changes in public opinion. Investigators like Allport, Postman, Lasswell, and Cantril have been more interested in finding *how* public opinion is formed—the origins of social attitudes (especially those held by large groups of peoples), the forces responsible for the mass notions about the Irish, Negroes, Jews, Germans, and the reasons for changes in public opinion.

THE BASIC PATTERN OF DISTORTION *

We choose a trifling rumor incident and select it almost at random from the wartime crop of stories current in a rural Maine community in the summer of 1945, shortly before Japan's surrender.

A Chinese teacher on a solitary vacation drove his car into the community and asked his way to a hilltop from which he could obtain the pleasant view pictured in a tourist guide issued by the Chamber of Commerce in a neighboring town. Someone showed him the way, but within an hour the community was buzzing with the story that *a Japanese spy had ascended the hill to take pictures of the region.*

The simple, unadorned facts that constitute the "kernel of truth" in this rumor were never reported but were from the outset distorted in three directions. . . . They were *leveled, sharpened,* and *assimilated.* Let us consider each type of change in order.

(1) *Leveling.* Omitted from the rumor are many details which are essential for a true understanding of the incident: the courteous and timid, but withal honest, approach of the visitor to the native of whom he inquired his way; the fact that the visitor's precise nationality was unknown although he was certainly Oriental. Likewise not mentioned was the fact that the visitor had allowed himself to be readily identified by people along the way; and the truth that no one had seen a camera in his possession.

These omissions are scarcely attributable to the unreliability of people's memory. Rather they are systematic omissions. They dropped out because if told, they would tend to negate the preferred interpretation: "a Japanese spy is among us." We do not know to what extent the omissions are due to a misperception of the situation by the native who first talked with the stranger, and to what extent the details kept dropping out as the story spread from person to person. It is probable that the eyewitness himself did not perceive all the relevant evidence because the sight of an Oriental had immediately activated his long-standing biases and preconceptions. Perceiving and remembering are parts of a single process. . . .

* From *The Psychology of Rumor* by Gordon W. Allport and Leo Postman. Copyright, 1947, by Henry Holt and Company, Inc.

(2) *Sharpening*. When some details are dropped, those that are preserved necessarily gain in emphasis and importance. Sharpening, as we have seen, is the reciprocal of leveling. Having accepted their special interpretation of the Chinese scholar's visit, the rumor agents accentuated certain features while minimizing others. The sharpening of selected details accounts for the overdrawn dramatic quality of the final story. What in the original situation was Oriental became specified as Japanese; what was merely a "man" became a special kind of man, a "spy." The harmless holiday pursuit of viewing the scenery became the much sharper, sinister purpose of espionage. The truth that the visitor *had* a picture in his hand became sharpened into the act of "taking pictures." The objective fact that no pictures of any possible value to the enemy could be taken from that particular rural location was overlooked. There were no industrial or military installations visible from that hill. Furthermore, the war was known to be in its last stages and spy activity, especially in remote regions, was, objectively considered, most improbable. Yet, such were the wartime emotions and suspicions that the sharpening occurred, putting point on the incident, making it crisp, understandable, and portentous. Here was something worth telling, worthy of rumination and respect.

(3) *Assimilation*. Leveling and sharpening, of course, do not occur haphazardly but take place in essential conformity with the past experience and present attitudes of the rumor spreaders. In the Maine countryside resident natives have had little contact with Orientals. Like most Occidentals they are unable to distinguish a Chinese person from a Japanese. They had only one available rubric for Orientals, firmly implanted in their minds by wartime news and stories: the "Japanese spy." No other category was available for the classification of this unusual visitation. A Chinese-teacher-on-a-holiday was a concept that could not arise in the minds of most farmers, for they did not know that some American universities employ Chinese scholars on their staffs and that these scholars, like other teachers, are entitled to summer holidays. The novel situation was perforce *assimilated* in terms of the most available frames of reference.

"To take pictures of the region" is another clear instance of assimilation. The visitor carried no camera, yet as a result of the government's campaign for "security of information," as a result of prohibitions against cameras in strategic war areas and lurid movies dealing with espionage, the rumor agents were provided with a plausible motive for the strange visitor. The association of ideas is crude: a yellow man—a Jap—a spy—photographic espionage. One idea led to the other with almost mechanical inevitability until the final conclusion emerged.

Such mechanical association of ideas accounts, in part, for the story that spread, but an unmistakable dynamic factor was also present. In this remote Maine community the war was profoundly felt. Nearly every house had its son in the service. Hatred for the Japanese was intense, desire to defend America deep, and suspicion of foreigners a long-standing cultural characteristic of the region. To these inveterate attitudes the perception of the event was assimilated, and from these attitudes came the impetus to concoct the rumor. Wartime created the conditions that brought these dynamic factors into play. The event had potential *importance* to the people. It also had considerable *ambiguity*, for they lacked correct information regarding the visitor's nationality and purpose.

The three-pronged process of leveling, sharpening, and assimilation reflects the rumor agents' "effort after meaning." The facts of the situation, but dimly understood, did not provide the meaning that the strange visitation required. Hence a single directive idea took hold—the *spy motif*—and in accordance with it, discordant details were leveled out, incidents sharpened to fit the chosen theme, and the espisode as a whole assimilated to the pre-existing structure of feeling and thought characteristic of the members of the group among whom the rumor spread.

PROBLEMS

1. In the Japanese spy rumor, Allport and Postman see evidence of distortion, which they reduce to "leveling," "sharpening," and "assimilation." In what ways do these three tendencies manifest the "urge to unity" discussed by Overstreet?
2. Can you detect the presence of these three tendencies in a rumor which you have heard? Consider, for instance, the recurrent rumors of the imminent discharge of a coach following a poor football season; the rumors about the suspension of a student journalist following the

appearance in the school paper of an indiscreet or emotionally charged article about some controversial issue; the rumors of a "housecleaning" by the college administration following a fraternity party in the course of which certain college regulations were not observed.

3. Can you see how leveling, sharpening, and assimilation may have been at work in the following:

a. A man, looking back on his high school days, concludes that they were great fun. (He had played hookey frequently and was graded low on "interest," but he had starred in football games and had "gone steady" with a pretty girl.)

b. A young, inexperienced, nervous girl from a middle-class urban family is employed to teach in a rural high school by a principal well known for his emphasis on "absolute honesty" in all classroom tests and work. She sees two boys, who have been doing badly in her course, whispering during an examination, and she promptly sends them to the principal for cheating. Subsequent investigation reveals that the boys were discussing the advisability of cutting afternoon classes to go hunting, it being the first week of deer season.

c. A mother visiting her daughter's home notices that the home is very simply furnished, without the niceties of sterling silver and cut glass and without certain household conveniences (deep freezer, sewing machine, electric ironer) to which she is accustomed. She is unaware of the presence in the home of a large library of books and records. Missing the things that are in her own home, and knowing that her daughter's husband makes a good salary, she concludes that her son-in-law is stingy.

A. Den Doolaard

A. Den Doolaard, a Dutch journalist and novelist who has traveled in this country, here outlines common European conceptions of Americans and their way of life. If his picture seems overdrawn, you might look closely at some of the generalizations commonly made by Americans about "foreigners"—that the Italians are "musical" or "dirty," that the Scottish are "stingy," that the Scandinavian peoples are "independent and progressive," that the French "have no moral scruples," that the Arabs are "thieves," that all Irish are "witty" and "pugnacious," that all English say, "I say—," and do not show their

real feelings, that Europeans are, in general, over-intellectual-
ized, highly cultured, unscientific, impractical. Why is there a
difference between such conceptions and the facts you discover
through personal experience or reading? Do we do what Doolaard's fellow countrymen did in oversimplifying America?

A STUDY IN MISUNDERSTANDING *

I am a Dutchman. Can you swear that this does not evoke
instantaneously the following surrealistic picture in your mind:
my head an Edam cheese, my left arm a tulip, my right one the
wing of a windmill, whereas the rest of my anatomy consists of
baggy trousers and wooden clogs? Are you quite sure that during
the recent Dutch-Indonesian conflict the tulip was not temporarily
replaced by a six-shooter, and were you not firmly convinced that I,
being a Dutchman, could only be a diehard imperialist?

Don't laugh before I have painted the corresponding picture
which will prove to you that Europeans see Americans in exactly
the same crazy way as Americans see Europeans. After my first
visit to America last year I galloped 'round to various neighbors in
my Dutch village, and, before telling them what I had seen and
witnessed, I asked them how they saw the average American. The
result was another surrealistic concoction, as follows: The head of
the average American was a radio, producing a syrupy love song.
His left arm a steering column fixed up with a Dynaflow device, his
right arm a baseball bat. His heart a red circle with the words
Lucky Strike inside, his belly a safe deposit box, his left leg a
drilling tower and his right leg a skyscraper. One of my informants
had just read in his newspaper something about Negro-baiting in
the South, and he substituted for the crooning radio a white
hood with two holes.

These pictures are a beautiful example, not of empirical but of
mythical thinking. The myth, at its best, is made up of one part prejudice and two parts illusion. With people who have a nasty mind
and moreover regularly read the Hearst press, the concoction is the
other way 'round.

* From A. Den Doolaard, "A Study in Misunderstanding," from *The Saturday
Review of Literature*, September 24, 1949.

There is one other striking thing about these myths: their dimensions. The average American is convinced that Europe is a small place, and in a wholly illogical way he is apt to think that Europeans must be small too. A Texan I met last year needed three double whiskeys to help him swallow the measurable truth that I as a European stood an inch over six feet in my socks. Vice versa, Europeans think of America as something enormous.

In the mind's eye of the average European (west of the Iron Curtain) the average American therefore looms much larger than life-size—at least as large as that stupendous lady, the Statue of Liberty. She is admittedly a woman, although nobody would dare to think of her as such any more, hiding as she does in her enormous bosom an elevator shaft and various other technical devices. Opposite the Manhattan skyscrapers she easily holds her own, but at the entrance of any European harbor she would look perfectly ludicrous.

Why? Not because the Hudson estuary is any larger than several European estuaries. It is not. The answer is simply that the days of the European giants are over, and that Europeans are aware of it.

. . . Show an American dollar to any European, and his eyes will become as large and round as the wheel of fortune it represents for him. He will hardly look at thin-lipped George Washington or at the hodge-podge of semi-cabalistic-free-masonic-heraldic symbols the greenback is adorned with, because his eyes are blinded by a glittering vision. He will see enormous cars, skyscrapers that reach to the moon, monstrous combines rushing through wheat-fields bigger than his own small country, and girls with endless legs digging their proudly pointed bosoms into his ribs aching for the kind of love that the Johnson Office has shelved between the coils of its hypocritical icebox. His wife will see her American rival moving swiftly on four-inch heels through her mechanized kitchen, deftly setting mysterious dials for a self-cooking dinner. Then an elevator will deposit her on the bearskin rug before her satin bed upon which a fresh pair of Nylon stockings is waiting for her.

Why, the civilized, book-reading American will ask, do Europeans entertain such crazy thoughts? Don't they know that the minimum wage in this country was, until very recently, fixed at forty cents an hour, and that the income of the average American is little more than $1,400 a year? Have they never heard about the

Dust Bowl and the Great Depression? Surely Steinbeck and Erskine Caldwell have been translated, and, if what we have heard is true, European publishers are fighting each other tooth and nail to grab the copyrights of "The Naked and the Dead" and "The Seven Storey Mountain"!

The answer is that the projection of a nation on the mind of other nations is usually determined not by qualitative factors. For every copy of Emerson, Melville, Hemingway, or the Beards sold in Europe the news agents sell a thousand copies of the "slicks" and of *Time* and *Life*. On top of that comes the projection of dozens of Hollywood films a year. The result is a series of illusions, all erroneous but equally compelling.

In this way the majority of Europeans are led to believe that the majority of Americans are a bunch of alcoholic semi-lunatics, rushing in chromium cars from a drive-in movie to a divorce court. Millions of bobbysoxers and frustrated spinsters are firmly convinced that all American men are great lovers and that all American girls are virgins until their wedding night. And even the second, female, part of the Kinsey report will not be able to disillusion them. They won't read it, and even if they do Don Ameche will sing their doubts away.

Mass illusions are universal. Still, I dare to pretend that, if ever there was a continent that as a whole fell a victim to continuous mass illusion, it was not America but Europe.

Europe's first mass illusion was that America did not exist. The dreamland of medieval European man stretched far away into the fabulous East. In the Asiatic illusion the Holy Grave and the golden roofs of Cathay both played their equal part. When Columbus discovered America he first took it for the Far East and ultimately came to the conclusion that it was a hostile barrier reef cutting him off from his lifelong dream. Columbus's desperate search for the Biblical paradise on the shores of the Caribbean Sea was the last tragic attempt on the part of a European to transfer the Asiatic mass illusion to America. His successors were wiser: they left the spiritual component of the illusion behind and straightaway went looking for gold.

During the nineteenth century the European mass illusion had completely migrated westward. Already centuries ago it had been amputated of its spiritual part, and in the heydays of materialism it was, of course, impossible to bring back this spiritual element into the picture. Henceforth the European dream found its fulfillment in the gaping admiration of American millionaires.

But man cannot live by bread alone. By reason of the time lag that conditions the duration of all mass illusions the European mind once more stretched its antennae towards the East, in its search for the spiritual elements without which no mass illusion is complete. Many Europeans suddenly found it in Soviet Russia, and it can safely be said that during the Twenties of this century a considerable portion of the European intellectuals were fellow travelers. Since then the majority of these illusionists have discovered to their dismay that the living conditions in their Eastern dreamland were pitifully inadequate. Many of those former drawing-room Communists are now dabbling in Eastern Wisdom. They revere Gandhi, although they would never think of skipping a meal themselves. And when they are through with their daily portion of Lao-tse they feast their eyes on the culinary color ads in the slicks.

At the same time millions of European workers still staunchly believe in the wonderland of the Five Pointed Red Star. But even these zealots of a proletarian paradise, which, as they think, will put an end to the injustices of the capitalistic system, quite often secretly dream of a small American car. There is an ironic fact which the Ford dynasty does not realize: when they abolished the Model T they took away a cheap and effective capitalistic sop to the disgruntled European worker.

In this way the dream of the European is torn in two. This dualistic character of the present-day European mass illusion has, however, two terrible consequences. First of all, the European has become a schizophrenic without realizing it, and the partition of Europe along the river Elbe is only a threatening political symbol of this mental rift. Secondly, it condemns America in the European mind to 100 per-cent avid and ruthless materialism. When Asia is the altar, America cannot be anything but the money bag. And America is doing little or nothing to fight this partly erroneous conception. Europe today looks exactly like Laocoön, desperately fighting the serpents, modern version: the endless coils of slimy film and hissing soundtrack spat out by the Hollywood studios. And these are more dangerous than the mythical adders; they do not kill the body, but they poison the mind.

America has an antidote but it does not figure on the list of commodities explorable under the Marshall aid, perhaps because America tacitly assumes that Europe only wants its dollars and whatever can be bought for them in the American market. The antidote I mean is the knowledge that there still exists another America, hidden away under the avalanche of billboards and Betty Grables, atom bombs and soap operas, superfortresses and deepfreezers, nylon stockings and skyscrapers, pluguglies and sob sisters, lobbyists and tycoons, spewed out by the assembly lines of the greatest industrial nation in the world. This other America is the America of Jefferson and Lincoln, and of the bus conductor who said last year on the second of November: "My vote can sway the election." The America of Rosenwald, the millionaire who traveled upper berth because this meant two dollars more in his endowment fund for Negro universities. The America which in every generation still produces thousands of quiet men living like true descendants of Johnny Appleseed, who planted the orchards and preached the word. The America which produces a writer like John Hersey, who wrote a small but great book because this was the only thing he could do to atone for the Bomb. And another writer like William Faulkner, who has the lonely courage to write as it damned well pleases him, with the result that his only best seller is the twenty-five-cent edition of "Wild Palms," and that only on account of the naked lady on the cellophane cover. The America of the humble schoolmaster in a small town on Long Island Sound who singlehanded fought a bunch of millionaires and real-estate vultures in order to preserve the right of the townspeople to bathe at the only small stretch of free beach which had not yet been converted into dollars. The America which produces such men by the thousands. If they lose their fights as they often do, they encourage others by their example to win theirs. The America which made the unforgettable movie "Mr. Smith Goes to Washington." The America of the community chests and the smoke jumpers. The America which flashed a three-letter code message, TVA, around the world. It gave new hope to millions of starving people, living in deserts and swamps.

The America which the illusionists believe is the only one does an enormous advertising job for the angry men and the mighty pressure groups who have sworn that there will never be another

TVA. But they cannot blow up the dams. They cannot silence the old farmer who said to me, when I asked him what TVA had done for him: "Mister, twenty years ago I was a frightened hillbilly; today I am a free man, and a proud man, too." They cannot abolish the only constitution in the world which expressly reserves the right of revolution against tyrants.

This other America is very little known even in America itself. But Columbus is not dead. Every year small groups of European and Asiatic discoverers sail towards these shores determined upon finding it. Few Americans realize that today it is almost as difficult for the average European to reach America as it was for Columbus 450 years ago. His National Bank will be as parsimonious with the indispensable dollars as Queen Isabella was with her doubloons. And once on American shores the difficulties are by no means over. Then it seems as if the whole continent from New York to San Francisco conspires against him to divert him from his high purpose. It tries to kill him under its motorcades, to deafen him with its blaring radios, to dazzle him with neon lights and video. The loveliest women in the world stalk him as their helpless prey, and if his limited resources condemn him to eat in the cheaper establishments, the worst cooks in the world try to poison him with ice water, sundaes, Southern chicken produced as a side line by a cement factory, and homemade apple pie straight from a plant with a capacity of twenty tons an hour. A handful survive: those who have the sense to stick to hamburgers, spaghetti, and the wonderful seafood. They will need, moreover, a large helping of moral austerity in order to make their safe getaway from the most glamorous leg show in the world, the pavements of midtown Manhattan during the evening hour when the young and comely secretaries leave their offices.

After New York, the wonder city, the next stumbling block is Washington, D. C. One of my erudite European friends, who has never visited a movie theatre in his life, told me that he had prepared himself for his American tour by reading Thoreau's "Walden," Lincoln's address, and Beard's "The Republic." Fearing the worst, I tried to thrust upon him half a dozen volumes by Damon Runyon, John O'Hara, and James Cain, but he retorted that he mistrusted cheap fiction. He paid an impromptu visit to the gallery of the U. S. Senate, by the worst of chances on the day when a gentleman named Pat McCarran held the floor. The overstrung bow of his idealism snapped right in the middle, and for the rest of his stay he buried himself in the Library of Congress, a sadder but not a wiser man.

Such idealistic pilgrims should remember the bold word of a British philosopher: "In every country in the world every decent man is always ashamed of the government he must live under." Moreover, the business of government is being conducted on many different levels, and the highest level is not always the loftiest. On the very day that Senator McCarran murdered the America that my oversensitive friend had dreamt about, I assisted at the annual meeting of a large farmer's cooperative in Paducah, Kentucky. Apart from having had a whale of a time I came away from that meeting with the firm conviction that the real American democracy was not ready to perish from the earth. And that conviction sustained me even during the sad day when, further south, I ran into an ugly race riot. I closed my eyes against the glare of the flaming cross and thought hard of the other America I had seen a few weeks before: a calm and highly cultured Negro judge in a Bronx court, deftly dealing with white defendants, without a trace of self-consciousness or pride. Without raising his voice once he displayed in case after case the lofty wisdom which history has successfully monopolized for the highly overrated Solomon, whose fame after all is based upon one case only. When I had seen him at work I felt that even in Washington this suburban Negro judge would not have looked a displaced person.

Of course, I do not mean to imply that he would be able to make his way to the Supreme Court as easily as Tom Clark. I only toyed with the idea because it suddenly occurred to me that here was the crucial test which could convince millions of deluded and skeptical Europeans that the other America really exists. Time and again the specter of the sadfaced Southern Negro is the dark intruder in the glittering dust raised on the European roads by the American 3,000-dollar cars. Along every country road they flash their smooth and soothing message of an almost perfect technical civilization, in which everyone can trade in his car every year for a higher powered model, indispensable for the ever swifter pursuit of elusive happiness.

This is the America so succulently advertised in the slicks. One of the mysterious consequences of the Marshall Plan is that they have invaded the European newsstands in fat and gleaming stacks, crowding out the thin and shoddy home periodicals. Therefore the returning pilgrim, who patiently tells his tale about the other America is more often than not received with incredulity or even anger. Most people, when you try to take away their illusions and prejudices will yap at you like a dog which grows mad when you touch his beloved gnawing bone.

Why does the official America offer so little help to the unpaid propagandists who try to convince Europeans that there exists another and nowadays almost invisible America, hidden somewhere between Radio City and the River Rouge Plant, between Washington and the studios, an America which has resolutely torn the shameful masks from the bigoted faces of the Alabama night riders? Is it because the strong and rich America of Alexander Hamilton is stealthily usurping the humbler America of Thomas Jefferson? Is America really proud of Westbrook Pegler and secretly ashamed of Walter White? Does it really prefer the Hickenloopers to the Lilienthals? Or is it the other way round?

That is what more and more Europeans and even Asiatics ask themselves. America should know that in the eroded river valleys of India and Pakistan sleek-haired agricultural engineers tell the poor and fever-ridden peasants a fairy tale about a faraway country, where a valley as miserable as their own was converted into a paradise. Quite likely, when the lecture is over, the peasants will forget what TVA exactly stands for, and they won't be able to remember Senator Norris's name for long. But they will remember how he and his helpers victoriously fought the pressure groups and the politicians, and realized their dream of plenty for all who are willing to work, in a democracy which starts at the grass roots.

In this way a new illusion is born: that America has something more to offer than dollars and technical knowhow alone. It is not yet a mass illusion, but in Europe there is an uneasy feeling that the Marshall Plan is somehow incomplete without the moral message that might turn the Atlantic community into something stronger than a frightened defensive alliance against the Big Bad Brother in the Kremlin. The message is there: Jefferson wrote it. Every American schoolchild knows its words, but does America remember its meaning?

America today is the world's giant. Therefore its time for great-ness has arrived. Even without the advertising pages of the *Sateve-post* and the editorial columns of *Life* America would be capable of creating a new mass illusion: that freedom can be a reality, and happiness an attainable goal, not only for the chosen few who succeed in living graciously at somebody's expense, but for the nameless multitude as well.

A few, but not the best Americans, try hard to convince the world that all attempts at a modern interpretation of Jefferson's message have already been secretly classified as Un-American Activities. But even if this were true the peasant in the Indus Valley and the anxious European who is never farther away from the Soviet frontier than Pittsburgh from New York, would not believe it. Ever more people outside the Soviet orbit believe, albeit secretly, that America can be something more than the world's leader in the production of cars and nylon stockings. But some of them are also secretly afraid that if America refuses to assume the moral leadership of the free world as well, it will go down into history as the country whose last and supreme gift to mankind was the atom bomb.

PROBLEMS

1. What is the connection between what Doolaard calls "illusion" and what Allport and Postman speak of as "leveling, sharpening, and assimilation"?
2. According to Doolaard, what qualities are common to the Europeans' mythological conception of the East and their conception of the West?
3. Do you find in *Americans* any evidence of "mass illusions" about Europeans and European life? about Asia? What tendencies in human thinking do the European and American conceptions of the rest of the world reveal? Anthropologists tell us that some primitive tribes have two words that stand for "men": one word to describe them-selves; another word to describe all other men. In the light of Doo-laard's article, does this now seem merely "quaint" to you?
4. Psychologists and sociologists employ still another term, stereotypes, to describe "mass illusions." What vocational, professional, national, racial, and religious groups here in America are frequently subjected by the rest of us to the stereotyping process? Consider, for instance,

policemen, dentists, Irishmen, Negroes, and Mormons, just as a starter. How many more can you add to this list?

5. What technique, suggested by Platt to be used when observing natural phenomena, would be equally useful here in breaking down these stereotypes?

6. Doolaard tells of a European friend whose fears about America were reinforced by one visit to the U. S. Senate. The demagoguery he witnessed that day was quite real, but what mistake did he make in retreating dejectedly to the Library of Congress? Was it the same mistake he had made earlier when he refused to read "cheap fiction"? In what respects was this man's reaction like that of many World War II American soldiers who, upon being immediately greeted by bad smells and all sorts of human parasites seeking cigarettes and G.I. rations, decided that all Europe or Africa was "a mess"?

7. If you were going on a two months' trip to Europe, Africa, or Asia, what precautions would you take to prevent yourself from acquiring an illusory picture of that foreign culture, or from reinforcing an illusion which you already had? In this connection, what do you think of the logic of that tiresome heckler who, when he has exhausted all his arguments in a discussion of some foreign problem, falls back on that old argument, "Well, were you ever there?"

GENERAL PROBLEMS:
Guarding Against Oversimplification

1. Before plunging into problems 2, 3, and 4 in this section, all of which call for some thoughtful writing, warm up on these two examples of oversimplification:

   a.   GREAT AMERICAN POET GIVES RECIPE FOR ILLS
   Cambridge, Mass., Mar. 24 (UP)—Poet Robert Frost, nearing his 75th birthday, gave his solution today to the world's problems.
   "Twenty acres of land for every man would be the answer to all the world's problems," he said. "It would show them all their burdens as well as their privileges."

   b. A recent cartoon in *The Saturday Evening Post* showed a forlorn little man, all but lost in a shapeless, outsized suit, inquiring bewilderedly of the clerk at the information booth of what appeared to be Grand Central Station, "Why am I here? What does all this mean in the infinite scheme of things?" How did the cartoonist, Burr Shafer, pin down in this brief word-and-picture story the tendency of many people to seek an oversimplified "answer" to what has proved to be perhaps the most troublesome question men have asked themselves? (Friendly tip: Don't overlook the concealed assumption that is lurking behind our hero's question.)

2. If one investigates thoughtfully the thinking of philosophers and farmers, senators and salesmen, teachers and taxi drivers, scientists and soldiers, Rotarians and revolutionists, he will find that everywhere there is a tug-of-war in men's minds between the "monistic" and the "pluralistic" way of looking at problems. Here are a half-dozen samples of "philosophizing" from as many different sources. Which of these statements reflect "monistic" thinking? which "pluralistic" thinking?

   a. "The world's condition cannot but cause disquiet and anxiety. Hostility piles up between nation and nation, labor and capital, class and class. . . . Is there a remedy that will cure the individual and the nation and give hope of a speedy and satisfactory recovery? . . . The crisis is fundamentally a moral one. The nations must re-arm morally. Moral recovery is the forerunner of economic recovery. . . . We need a power strong enough to change human nature and build bridges between man and man, faction and faction."

   b. "The freedoms that matter in ordinary life are definite and concrete; and they change with the changing ways of different ages and different civilizations. . . . But a random list of typical contemporary freedoms is useful as a reminder that free*dom* has to be perpetually reinterpreted into free*doms*."

   c. "Yea, for men who match our mountains—
   There's a need throughout the land,
   For men of giant stature,
   Who'll in war and peace command.
   May that need ne'er be unanswered;
   Let their strong arms e'er insure
   The success of every venture,
   That this nation may endure."

   d. "What I want to know is when my boy is going to get an education? He's a musician, but he doesn't know a noun."

   e. "If [a naturalist] turns his attention to bees he will find that complex interrelationship of individuals to make a hive that has often been described. There are the workers, the drones and the queen, each with patterns of behavior that aid the continued existence of the colony with a striking disregard for the well-being of any one individual. The drones are starved, mutilated and thrown out when their functions have been performed. Workers that arrive home with frayed wings or begin to fail in their productive capacity receive the same treatment. . . . The naturalist . . . will make these discoveries in a spirit of finding out how it all works and without pronouncing judgment on the bees, without calling the drones 'useless' or the destruction of damaged workers 'wicked.' "

f. "The point, of course, is to understand the behavior of any one nation in relation to other nations. 'Understanding,' as used here, does not mean intuition and is not limited to sympathy. . . . Such understanding should enable us to distinguish more accurately between the behavior that is possible for a country and behavior that we as a nation might want that country to adopt, but which is impossible given its situation and particular cultural patterns. Within the range of behavior that is possible for a country we should be able to distinguish the easy and probable from the difficult and improbable. In particular, we should be able to gauge better the effect of our own policies and actions and whether they produce the results desired or call forth responses that make worse the situation we wish to see mended."

Now can you write an analytical paper in which you show the common denominators in those selections you identified as "monistic"? What, specifically, has the inquirer in each instance overlooked? What unexamined assumption(s) does he begin with?

3. Write a descriptive *report* of some natural or man-made object which you regard as *beautiful* or *ugly*. This is not the conventional assignment it seems to be. This is, rather, a test of your ability to avoid the kind of oversimplification Platt was talking about when he pointed out how little we really *see*. You are necessarily beginning with a preconceived judgment: you sincerely think this object beautiful or ugly. But, and here's the test, you are to report only what you *actually see*, what is *actually there*. You are to avoid "reading into" the object any value judgments that are "in your mind." This, in sum, is to be a factual, objective *report*, testing your powers of close observation, not a vague, highly impressionistic "appreciation."

To help you get started, the editors have reprinted here excerpts from two papers by a student who made this test. Selection *a*, his first attempt, illustrates a failure to observe and report what was *actually there*. Even this brief excerpt is full of judgments and inferences. Moreover, it is rather difficult to understand. Measured by the criteria most English instructors use to evaluate student papers, it "lacks unity," is "not coherent." Selection *b*, the same student's second attempt, although not faultless, illustrates fairly well the method of direct observation and reporting. Is it just a coincidence that it is also more unified and coherent?

a. "There are a great number of things in the Pilot Wheel Restaurant that could quite naturally keep the mind's interest and attention. The waiter can come up with bits of information about friends not seen for weeks; the organist has a choice repertoire of jokes as well as tunes; and speculation on the odd fish painted on the walls can lead one into the most interesting reveries. If for the moment the mind escapes all this, the light blue glass of the window immediately draws intent interest and focuses attention on the view beyond."

b. "As you enter the rectangular anteroom of the Silver Lounge, the first thing you are apt to see is glass brick, curved concavely, flanking each side of the wide, blue mirror door that opens to the club proper. Light blue, triple-twist frieze, wall-to-wall floor cover carpets this anteroom. The walls are upholstered with pale blue leather on the lower four feet and cream-colored leather on the upper walls and ceiling. Tacks with brass heads that secure the material to the wall and ceiling are placed in a criss-cross pattern. The location of a telephone is indicated by blue leather letters placed on the cream-colored wall to the side and above the glass-and-leather door that leads to the booth. Light fixtures on the ceiling are made of chromed metal and frosted glass. Glazed cream-colored, cylindrical, pottery ash trays are placed on circular rubber mats on each side of a metal door, opening onto an elevator shaft."

One final comment. The classmates of the student who wrote these papers were in disagreement as to whether Selection *b* described a "beautiful" or "ugly" object. Students who raise an eyebrow at this are missing the whole point. No one is attempting to legislate what another man's taste should be. One merely wishes to know as exactly as possible the basis for that taste: the specific physical parts and characteristics which a person has in mind when he labels an object "beautiful" or "ugly." Then, if there is disagreement as to the object's esthetic appeal, one at least knows the basis for the disagreement. And, when we are attempting to communicate intelligently with one another, such knowledge takes us a long way. Contrast this kind of communicated information with such commonly heard expressions as, "I don't like modern art," or "I saw a terrific sunset." How much real information is conveyed by such expressions?

4. Oversimplified thinking probably appears most frequently in the form of an *unsupported generalization*. Unsupported generalizations are

statements of complex ideas or groups of ideas telescoped into a few words.

An example is provided by the statement frequently heard during World War II: "Those Nazis are brutal!" This sweeping generalization, unsupported by anything but indignation, might have been qualified by a more thoughtful person in this way: "Men assigned by the German government to positions of authority in Nazi concentration camps where they are given frequent opportunities, even encouragement, to give vent to their desire to inflict pain on others (a desire which many psychologists tell us is latent to a greater or lesser degree in most men) will often become brutalized by this environment, even though they were not, perhaps, consciously brutal when they first undertook the assignment."

"That takes a lot of words," you say, "and a lot of thinking."

Perhaps. But by defining what we mean by "brutal," by limiting our statement to a set of particular persons, places, events, and environments, and by distinguishing between these particulars and the indefinite number of other particulars connoted by the original generalization, we have succeeded in communicating a fairly definite idea. Furthermore, although our idea even in its new form is still in the realm of opinion, it is an opinion capable of being supported by evidence and so translatable into fact.

With this analysis as a rough working guide, see what you can do to change some of the following unsupported generalizations to more meaningful, supportable statements by the process of *limiting, distinguishing,* and *defining.*

a. You can't trust a beautiful woman.

b. Genius is one per cent inspiration and ninety-nine per cent perspiration.

c. Strong men are produced by crises.

d. A picture is worth a thousand words.

e. A nation's greatest resource is the minds of its youth.

f. Americans are gross materialists.

g. Advertising is the lifeblood of modern business.

h. The twentieth century is an age of anxiety.

i. Heroes are born, not made.

j. People are not what they seem.

Detecting Rationalization

YOU have probably been asked these questions, or others very much like them:

"*How come Harry got his lieutenant's commission and you didn't?*"

"*I thought you were going to slaughter that physics final? What happened?*"

"*What ever made you give Johnson $300 for that car?*"

"*When are you coming through with that five bucks I loaned you?*"

"*Look here, Baxter, I told you to stay with that job until you were finished. Now what's the explanation?*"

"*I don't want to criticize, but how is it that the Holloway girl does so much better in school than you do?*"

"*Look, Marty, when we made you president we thought you'd put in lots of time building up the membership. How about it?*"

"*Whew, Jean, why did you bring that boy to the dance Saturday night?*"

"*Tapering off pretty slowly, aren't you? Didn't I hear you say you were off cigarettes until the end of basketball season?*"

"*Say, when's that little one-horse school of yours going to win a football game?*"

"*I think that was a mean trick, blackballing that Franklin girl. Why'd you do it?*"

"*I thought you were the campus 'Liberal'? Well, where were you last Saturday when the rest of us were taking those low-rent housing petitions all over town?*"

In answering these questions, and others like them, did you give the "real" reasons for your behavior? Or did you give "good" reasons? Do you know the difference? If so, do you know *why* you gave "real" reasons some of the time and "good" reasons other times?

Symonds, in his essay, "Rationalization," will help you understand your behavior under these and similar circumstances. Then three satirists, Gilbert, Voltaire, and Carroll, will show you that if you have been rationalizing (if you think you haven't you're probably rationalizing now), you are not alone.

And if you like jazz, you might ask your favorite disc jockey to dig up a copy of Billie Holiday's recording, with Teddy Wilson and his orchestra, of "Foolin' Myself." Listen and ponder.

Percival M. Symonds

"Rationalizing," a term borrowed by the general public from the psychologists, has become a popular catchword. Thus it has lost much of its original clarity of meaning; but, if carefully explained and concretely illustrated, as in Symonds' book, *Dynamic Psychology*, it can throw light on the many ways we try to avoid admitting the *real* reason for an act or belief when that reason is in some way unsatisfactory to us.

Note: By now you have grown used to finding "Problems" after each selection. But here we think you will have more fun if, before tackling any problems, you see how three world-famous satirists handle rationalizing. After that, the problems.

RATIONALIZATION *

Rationalization may be defined as faulty thinking which serves to disguise or hide the unconscious motives of behavior and feeling. Rationalization, therefore, takes its place as another one of the defense mechanisms—a defense against having to recognize unconscious motivation in everyday life. It is a device frequently resorted to by many a person in attempting to reassure himself of his

* Percival M. Symonds, *Dynamic Psychology*, Appleton-Century-Crofts, Inc., 1949.

own prestige. It is a way of fooling oneself, of making oneself seem more able, more successful, more moral, and more honorable than one really is. Rationalization is the blanket which we throw over our own infirmities and weaknesses so that it will not be necessary for us to have to face them directly. A boy excuses himself for failing an examination by saying he did not study for it, whereas the examination was actually too difficult for him to be successful in.

FUNDAMENTAL CONSIDERATIONS

Rationalization as Fallacious Thinking. Rationalization is fundamentally fallacious thinking. In terms of the syllogism, rationalization is a selection of facts that can be used as minor premises in order to justify certain conclusions already reached. One notes three things in this analysis of the process of rationalization: first, that the conclusion is given. Usually this is an act performed, since rationalizations are very frequently explanations justifying behavior which has already taken place. Second, in a rationalization the major premise is also given, and with this no particular fault is found, except that it may not always be a sound generalization. The essential feature of rationalization is the search for a particular circumstance to be used for the minor premise which, taken with the major premise, will lead decisively to the conclusion. Rationalization, therefore, represents a selection of possible circumstances or reasons which will justify the course of action already pursued.

For example, Max comes late to school and on being sent to the office of the principal finds it necessary to have a reason for his lateness. Lateness is the action which must be justified. Among the real reasons are the boy's dislike of school, the pressure that he is under at home to make a good record, and the convenient way of showing his hostility toward his parents provided by the demerits he receives. Max, however, is only vaguely aware of the former reason and is entirely unaware of the latter. When faced with the necessity of finding an excuse to satisfy the principal, he begins to search for a reputable one. First it is necessary to persuade himself that it was not possible for him to get to school any earlier: "Yes, as I was coming down the walk I noticed a trolley car just leaving, and it was five minutes before the next one came. I am sure that there must have been a delay in the street-car service." This seems reasonably convincing to him, and so he plans to use it as his excuse. The syllogism in this instance would run something like this: Major premise—if there is a delay in the street-car service, I shall be late to school. Minor premise—there was a delay. Conclusion—therefore, I was late to school.

The distinction between a rationalization and correct thinking is the distinction commonly made between the good and the real reason. The real reason is the state of affairs essentially and necessarily connected with the conclusion which is to be justified. A good reason is a circumstance selected out of many that could have been chosen which contains a superficial or concomitant explanation.

In this analysis, the implication is that certain facts are overlooked, and necessarily so, since they are repressed and therefore are facts of which the individual is unaware. In rationalization there is a disproportion of emphasis. Uncomfortable facts are disregarded in favor of ones which will not serve as deep-seated threats to the essential integrity of the person concerned.

Motivation. Rationalization is an effort to guard one's pride by escaping the necessity of recognizing the real basis for behavior for which one feels ashamed and guilty. . . .

A subsidiary motive for rationalization is the attempt to minimize the successes and virtues of another person toward whom we feel hostile or with whom we are in competition. As in the primary form of rationalization, one tends to find arguments and reasons for depreciating and degrading the behavior and motives of another person.

Characterized by Inflexibility. Rationalization as a method of thought is characterized in general by inflexibility, fixity, and stubbornness. Since in rationalizing the person is not entirely free to cast around for possible explanations from which to select one that seems, by all the canons of logic, most fundamental, he must protect his reasoning artificially, and this is frequently accomplished by the force of the assertion and the stubbornness with which the reason is held. One reason why rationalization is inflexible is that it usually is accompanied by or follows the arousal of emotion, and emotion notoriously leads to an exaggeration of response and inflexibility.

Logic-Tight Compartments of the Mind. The person who rationalizes also tends to show dissociation in his mental processes. The term, "logic-tight compartments" of the mind, has been used as a picturesque description of the mental processes of selecting reasons in rationalization. The person who rationalizes, for instance, is usually inconsistent. He may stand for liberalism in philosophy but he is quite reactionary in his political or economic views. He may stand for social security and be an active worker in various charitable enterprises, but when it comes to passage of laws which would limit the income of a corporation in which he has invested or which would increase his taxes, he takes a very reactionary stand. It is almost as though barriers were erected in his mind preventing him from seeing the essential relation between his point of view with regard to social security, on the one hand, and the necessity for the redistribution of wealth on the other. The same person will claim that cigarettes steady his nerves and stimulate him. People whose minds are divided into logic-tight compartments tend to accept things on authority rather than investigate all of the implications of their beliefs.

Signs of Rationalization. In the following illustrations of rationalization, one may feel as though all reasoning tended to be a form of rationalization and may even begin to distrust any of his own reasoning. Of course this is not true; all reasoning is not necessarily a rationalization. Rationalization can be recognized by a number of clearly defined signs. One signal is the person's attempt to hunt for reasons. If the principal in asking Max, for instance, finds that Max stumbles and halts in his effort to produce a good reason for being late, he may suspect that Max will never give the real reason even if he knew it, but is searching for an approved one that will be a rationalization. Secondly, the extent to which a person avoids rationalization in his thinking can be determined by the consistency of his thought. If in discussion one uncovers certain inconsistencies that the other person fails to recognize, or, recognizing them, attempts to justify further, one may suspect that rationalization is at work.

For instance, Mr. M., who is at a bridge party where it is proposed that they play for small stakes, refuses on the grounds that it is against his principles. On other occasions, however, it has been noticed that Mr. M does not have the same scruples in regard to living up to some of his other standards with rigid consistency. If Mr. M. is willing to compromise in one situation, one may suspect that there is some unexpressed reason behind the refusal to do so when playing bridge. Perhaps at the bottom of his expressed conviction is some deep-seated feeling with regard to playing for money which outweighs any possible gain in wealth or prestige.

Another sure method of detecting rationalization is by noting the amount of emotion shown during a discussion. A person who rationalizes is almost sure to lose his temper if the adequacy of the reasons which he gives is questioned. The man who is not rationalizing meets challenges on their merits and pits one argument against another with a flexibility and a willingness to change his position, giving reputable explanations for doing so.

Rationalization as a Disguise. Rationalization may be thought of primarily as a disguise of the self for the self. First and foremost, we wish to protect ourselves against recognizing our own motives which a part of our personality would consider ignoble, mean, and discrediting. In order to maintain a certain integration of the personality and to find ways of making all kinds of behavior and circumstances acceptable, one resorts to rationalization. However, the integration is not complete; hence, the logic-tight compartments. It is after one has persuaded himself of his rightness and integrity that he then attempts to justify himself to the world and persuade others also that his reputation is still unsullied. One naturally thinks of rationalization as an attempt to prove to others that one's motives are noble, but it should not be forgotten that preceding this attempt is the necessity of persuading oneself.

Rationalization Used to Justify Fundamental Values. Rationalization may be used to *justify fundamental values,* which are acquired through the process of identification in early childhood. Every person grows up a citizen of a country, a member of a church, and a member of a political party with certain basic personal values and philosophy. Later he finds it necessary to justify his membership in his political party, his adherence to a certain church, his loyalty to a club or state, and searches for reasons and arguments which will justify his choice. It is because of this that one must suspect much of the campaign oratory, for the arguments used in political speeches are more for the purpose of justifying choices made long ago rather than the attempt to help people form their opinions anew.

Use of Rationalization to Justify Behavior of Another Person. One can use rationalization not only to justify one's own behavior, but also that of another person with whom one has identified one-self or for whom one feels responsible. A mother, for example, may explain away the behavior of her naughty child by saying that he is tired. However, in this example, it may well be that she is pro-tecting herself, as well as the child, by trying to hide her inade-quacies as a mother. But as a parent identifies himself with his children, he will run to their defense and offer excuses for their delinquencies. Generalizing, we find a tendency to rationalize for the failure or shortcomings of our school, political party, golf club, or even state or nation. Whatever we feel a part of, that we must uphold and justify. . . .

TYPES AND EXAMPLES OF RATIONALIZATION

To attempt to classify all the varieties of rationalization and to give illustrations of them would be an impossible task, since ration-alization enters into every phase of human affairs. The best that can be done is to point out a number of these varieties in the hope that with them in mind the reader will become sensitive to the presence of rationalization in any form. . . .

Personality Limitation. Practically any personality limitation, either real or imagined, is subject to justification by the individual who feels the need to be protective. Any error or mistake will frequently call forth an attempt to justify the self. "The poor workman quarrels with his tools," and he readily finds occasion to excuse imperfections in his handiwork. The cabinet maker will find excuses in the grain of the wood; the tennis player in the uneven surface of the court; the billiard player in the fact that the table is not exactly level. Most persons in our culture find it necessary to rationalize their status and excuse their failures, whereas the real reasons may lie in their own deficiencies. The person who is in debt to another can usually find many excuses for postponing payment. One also finds it necessary to rationalize his social status. Persons in minority groups are especially given to rationalizing about their conditions and failures in life. This is pos-sibly one of their greatest handicaps in that it keeps them from evaluating their circumstances in true perspective. The Negro business man rationalizes that he cannot succeed because Negroes prefer buying from white dealers when, as a matter of fact, he may not have used business tactics that insure success.

Incapacity. It would make an interesting study to ascertain what kind of incapacity makes people feel sensitive and inferior. Most persons do not feel it necessary to give excuses for not being good athletes, good musicians, good artists, or good scientists. On the other hand, most persons find it very necessary to justify their mental abilities. Probably there is no area in which people are more sensitive or in which it is more difficult to admit incapacity. This may be due to the pressure put on children to succeed in school. The school boy or girl must find a reputable excuse for failure if failure comes his way. In a study undertaken sometime ago the question was asked of pupils who had left school at the end of the eighth grade, "Why did you find it necessary to leave school?" All sorts of reasons were given, but excuses on the ground of poor health and necessity of going to work were among the most frequent. Undoubtedly, there was some truth in these reasons, but the explanation of lack of ability to do the work in the succeeding grades or lack of interest in school was given much less frequently than should be expected.

A person who has an incapacity for being aggressive will feel particularly virtuous for the kind consideration which he has for the feelings of others. The person who is unable to defend himself against the attacks of others will satisfy himself on the basis of his capacity to understand other people. The man who is unable to go after what he wants will feel a glow of self-justification at his unselfish aims. There are many persons who because of infantile experiences find it difficult to have adequate sex experiences in later life. Most of these persons find it necessary to adopt certain rationalizations. Many unmarried women, for instance, have love-affairs but are blocked from consummating them in marriage because of fixations on earlier persons, perhaps on the father. They will rationalize each of these experiences, however, finding that the man in whom they were interested did not really measure up to their ideals of what a husband should be. One man, for instance, spends too much time following the racing news. Another is slack and untidy in his person, and still another, in the final analysis, lacks the push and drive to be the success which his sweetheart feels he must be. In each of these cases the affair is broken off and some such superficial excuse is given, whereas the real reason lies in the unresolved fixations coming from early life experiences.

Eccentricity. Most persons with eccentricities, for instance, obsessions, which are their bulwark against disturbing duties and anxieties, find it necessary to rationalize them, usually on the grounds of their social value. Indeed, most neurotic persons will find rational excuses for pampering their neurotic tendencies. The man who must have his whole household quiet from two to three every afternoon so he may have a nap justifies his behavior on the grounds of his health. The mother who has an obsessive need to nag at her son day in and day out about his work in school justifies the action on the ground that in no other way will Arthur be able to get through school.

Anxiety and Fear. Many people carry around a burden of anxieties and fears which they find it necessary to rationalize either verbally or in behavior in order to protect themselves. Many women, for instance, are afraid of approaching old age, and they do everything in their power to retard its advance. The cosmetology industry has been developed largely to help women ward off the encroachments of age. Most persons adopt a variety of rationalizations against disease and pain. They will try to persuade themselves that the pain does not exist, or that its treatment can be postponed. Other commonly held anxieties against which most persons find it necessary to bolster themselves are the fears of being neglected, of being poor, and of being ugly. Fear of social disapproval and losing caste with others is a basic cause for rationalization both in word and in behavior.

Character Weaknesses. Then there are any number of character weaknesses which must be justified by rationalization. One person may attempt to justify his selfishness on the grounds that he must look after his own interests first, because only when he himself is healthy and satisfied can he be of service to others. Then there is the need for justifying the taking of personal advantage of others and being domineering. For instance, a man takes an active interest in politics, justifies this interest on the grounds of national and state welfare, and makes generous contributions to the campaign funds of the Republican party. He maintains that the economic well-being of the nation is possible only when the Republican party is in control. Actually, however, this may be a 'façade to cover up his interest in possible greater profits in connection with his own business.

Jealousy is frequently covered up by rationalization. Members of a society will institute rigid tests for membership and will carry on elaborate initiation rituals, all designed by the unconscious as a way of proving their own superiority and humiliating the newcomers who threaten their position.

A group of high-school seniors were discussing the personnel of an important committee. Theirs was the job of nominating the members. Betty, a prominent girl in the group, objected, unjustly, to Lorraine; Lorraine would be a competitor of hers later on for citizenship honors, and she did not want her to be given this additional honor.

Mrs. Y. protested against the appointment of Mrs. X. on a committee in the women's club. Mrs. Y. maintained that Mrs. X. lived too far out in the country and attempted to mollify her protests by saying that Mrs. X. was already carrying so many responsibilities that she would not have time to take on this additional one. Actually, however, underneath this reasonable protest was jealousy of Mrs. X. as a rival.

A man may attempt to justify his penuriousness by saying that he must save up for his old age or that he is looking forward to a vacation trip or to buying a new home. The reason this is called a rationalization is that the man cannot help being "tight"—it is a character trait ingrained by early infantile experiences.

The tendency to hate, which many persons seem to hold irrationally, is often justified by finding superficial reasons for disliking or hating the other person. The man who frequently finds it necessary to escape from responsibilities must also accompany his refusals with reasons almost certain to be rationalizations.

Idealization. The process called *idealization,* in which a person in love tends to overvalue his loved object, rests in part on rationalization.

James rhapsodizes over his sweetheart and in his fantasy attributes to her the most extravagant excellences. He gives expression to these spiritual merits by poems addressed to her. He fails to recognize the sensual basis of his attraction and worship, but rationalizes the sensual by reference to spiritual charms.

Sex. Finally, in our society where sex expression is taboo except in the institution of marriage, it becomes necessary to rationalize all premarital experiences.

Kathryn, an emotional girl of seventeen, had sex relations with one of the boys in her high-school class. She justified her actions by saying that she was getting the experience which every woman should have before she marries. "No man wants to marry a woman who is a novice in such matters."

It is also common for adolescent girls who regret early sexual experiences to blame their parents for not informing them of the dangers involved or exercising firmer control, although this very control was bitterly contested at the time. . . .

VALUES OF RATIONALIZATION

Positive. Rationalization cannot be thought of as a commendable mechanism. Its values are mainly negative. The only positive values that one can see are those which make it possible for a person to avoid facing disagreeable and distressing motives. This device may for the time being alleviate the anxiety, but it is an unstable form of adjustment and is always in danger of being toppled over by force of circumstances. In general, one may say that good adjustment involves facing all kinds of reality, which is the very thing that rationalization attempts to prevent. . . .

Negative. Rationalization has more dangers than advantages. It tends to blind the man to the rational solution of his problems in the real world. It encourages postponing of the solution of real problems and helps a person to excuse himself from facing his problems. In rationalization there is also the danger of actually harming others. For instance, the mother who rationalizes concerning her child is putting off a realistic meeting of the child's problems. The mother of a dull-normal child may refuse to recognize the reality of his dullness. Her anxiety over school progress increases as the child continues to show increasing retardation. This anxiety leading to increased pressure creates neurotic disturbances in the child.

W. S. Gilbert

Here is just one of many scenes from Gilbert and Sullivan's witty light operas which pokes fun at the heavy, full-time rationalizing in the English life of seventy years ago. Ko-ko, a

Titipu tailor condemned to death for flirting but meanwhile fulfilling the duties of Lord High Executioner, reveals himself more efficient as a rationalizer than as an executioner. Pooh-Bah, Lord High Everything Else, is not slow at finding convenient "reasons" either.

SOME ADMINISTRATIVE HEADACHES *

KO. (*looking after* YUM-YUM). There she goes! To think how entirely my future happiness is wrapped up in that little parcel! Really, it hardly seems worth while! Oh, matrimony!—(*Enter* POOH-BAH *and* PISH-TUSH.) Now then, what is it? Can't you see I'm soliloquizing? You have interrupted an apostrophe, sir!

PISH. I am the bearer of a letter from his Majesty the Mikado.

KO. (*taking it from him reverentially*). A letter from the Mikado! What in the world can he have to say to me? (*Reads letter.*) Ah, here it is at last! I thought it would come sooner or later! The Mikado is struck by the fact that no executions have taken place in Titipu for a year and decrees that unless somebody is beheaded within one month the post of Lord High Executioner shall be abolished, and the city reduced to the rank of a village!

PISH. But that will involve us all in irretrievable ruin!

KO. Yes. There is no help for it, I shall have to execute somebody at once. The only question is, who shall it be?

POOH. Well, it seems unkind to say so, but as you're already under sentence of death for flirting, everything seems to point to *you.*

KO. To me? What are you talking about? I can't execute myself.

POOH. Why not?

KO. Why not? Because, in the first place, self-decapitation is an extremely difficult, not to say dangerous, thing to attempt; and, in the second, it's suicide, and suicide is a capital offence.

POOH. That is so, no doubt.

PISH. We might reserve that point.

POOH. True, it could be argued six months hence, before the full Court.

KO. Besides, I don't see how a man *can* cut off his own head.

POOH. A man might try.

* From W. S. Gilbert and Arthur Sullivan, *The Mikado.*

PISH. Even if you only succeeded in cutting it half off, that would be something.

POOH. It would be taken as an earnest of your desire to comply with the Imperial will.

KO. No. Pardon me, but there I am adamant. As official Headsman, my reputation is at stake, and I can't consent to embark on a professional operation unless I see my way to a successful result.

POOH. This professional conscientiousness is highly creditable to *you,* but it places us in a very awkward position.

KO. My good sir, the awkwardness of your position is grace itself compared with that of a man engaged in the act of cutting off his own head.

PISH. I am afraid that, unless you can obtain a substitute—

KO. A substitute? Oh, certainly—nothing easier. (*To* POOH-BAH) I appoint you Lord High Substitute.

POOH. I should be delighted. Such an appointment would realize my fondest dreams. But no, at any sacrifice, I must set bounds to my insatiable ambition!

Voltaire

> In his bold satires Voltaire, today the best remembered of the eighteenth-century French philosophers, sought to point out the unreasonableness of the institutions and social customs of his age. In doing this he exposed the rationalizations by which men tried to "screen off" such irrationality. Some historians credit Voltaire with a role in shaping the public opinion that led to the French Revolution. *Candide,* perhaps his best-known satire today, was his criticism of the idea, common in the eighteenth century, that men are essentially rational.

A LITTLE MATTER OF DISTANCE *

Talking thus, they arrived at Portsmouth. There were multitudes of people on the shore, looking attentively at a rather fat man who was kneeling down with his eyes bandaged on the deck

* From Voltaire, *Candide or: The Optimist.*

of one of the ships in the fleet; four soldiers placed opposite this man each shot three bullets into his brain in the calmest manner imaginable; and the whole assembly returned home with great satisfaction.

"What is all this?" said Candide. "And what Demon exercises his power everywhere?"

He asked who was the fat man who had just been killed so ceremoniously.

"An admiral," was the reply.

"And why kill the admiral?"

"Because," he was told, "he did not kill enough people. He fought a battle with a French admiral and it was held that the English admiral was not close enough to him."

"But," said Candide, "the French admiral was just as far from the English admiral!"

"That is indisputable," was the answer, "but in this country it is a good thing to kill an admiral from time to time to encourage the others."

Lewis Carroll

Lewis Carroll was the pen name of Charles Lutwidge Dodgson, a lecturer in mathematics at Oxford in the late nineteenth century. Carroll, best known for his *Alice's Adventures in Wonderland,* liked to turn things upside down. But he did so consciously. Many of us, like Carroll's King of Hearts, may do so unconsciously, especially when we are rationalizing. Consciously or unconsciously, few people can stand things on their heads better than a judge bent on having the case go his way. Carroll, not surprisingly, saw this and here has a little fun with "the Law." For a candid camera shot of the judge as rationalizer, and for a number of other fresh insights into that verbal jungle we call "the Law," see *Law and the Modern Mind* by Jerome Frank, himself one of America's most distinguished judges.

THE LEGAL MIND AT WORK *

At this moment the King, who had been for some time busily writing in his note-book, called out "Silence!" and read out from his book, "Rule Forty-two. *All persons more than a mile high to leave the court.*"

Everybody looked at Alice.

"*I'm* not a mile high," said Alice.

"You are," said the King.

"Nearly two miles high," added the Queen.

"Well, I shan't go, at any rate," said Alice; "besides, that's not a regular rule: you invented it just now."

"It's the oldest rule in the book," said the King.

"Then it ought to be Number One," said Alice.

The King turned pale, and shut his note-book hastily. "Consider your verdict," he said to the jury, in a low trembling voice.

GENERAL PROBLEMS:
Detecting Rationalization

A test of our understanding of the rationalizing process is provided by the following specific problems which tap experiences common to most of us. In addition to answering the specific questions posed by each of these problems, you should be able to detect the motive lying at the root of each of the offered "reasons."

1. For some months a father had intended to fix a loose railing on the front porch. One day, when his two children are climbing on the railing, it breaks. Result: one of his children breaks an arm.

List the following "reasons" for the accident *in the order of importance into which they will probably slip* in the father's thinking (unless he is a very honest thinker):

a. Growing-up is a risky affair, anyway; you're peculiar if you reach maturity without your share of broken bones.

b. The kids had no business skirmishing on the front porch; someone was bound to get hurt.

c. He had not got around soon enough to fixing the railing.

* From Lewis Carroll, *Alice's Adventures in Wonderland*.

2. A housewife cheats on meat rationing during a war. Place the possible reasons for cheating in the order of importance they are likely to assume in the woman's thinking and in her explanations to others:
   a. She wanted to keep her family of heavy meat-eaters satisfied and to feel pride in putting out meals which she knew they would approve.
   b. Other people were cheating; why shouldn't she?
   c. The government was not justified in infringing on the rights of an individual by such restrictions as rationing.
   d. She had heard, and believed, that the Army was wasting meat.

3. The authorities at a university are suggesting the de-professionalizing of football at their institution (no scouting for players, no partial economic aid to good football prospects, less elaborate game-schedules). They argue that the game has become too commercialized and that it has assumed too great importance in the life of the university.

   In what order would the alumni probably put down their reasons for retaining "big time" football?
   a. A strong team, no matter how it is gathered together, is good publicity for the school.
   b. Football competition breeds good sportsmanship (sense of fair play, and so forth).
   c. They (the alumni) like football.
   d. Big gate receipts from football help to pay for sports that cannot pay their own way.

4. Businessmen along a busy highway learn that a proposed divided-highway will miss them by a half-mile. They know that a good deal of their present business depends on the highway traffic.

   In their protests against changing the route—and in their own thinking as the debate continues—which one of the following reasons for *not* changing the route is likely to be forgotten or, at least, de-emphasized?
   a. Making a new route would be more expensive than widening the present highway.
   b. The saving of a few miles is not worth the expense and trouble of making a brand-new highway.
   c. The protesting businessmen will lose business.

5. A school board refuses to rehire a woman teacher because three out of five members disapprove of the teacher's smoking. (They have observed her smoking at social functions off the school grounds.)

   List the following facts in the order of importance they are likely to hold later in the thinking and explanations of the board members:
   a. The teacher was popular with students.

b. The principal considered her one of his best teachers.

c. Her smoking had "caused talk" in "certain circles," which included a few mothers of students in her classes.

d. Numerous prominent women in the community smoke at social functions without meeting snubs or other forms of open criticism.

e. The teacher did not go to a church regularly; most—not all—of the teachers attend regularly.

f. Three members—a majority—of the board disapproved of smoking by schoolteachers.

g. The teacher had a temporary credential.

6. During a war thousands of members of a minority race group work in the war industries of a large city. No disturbances occur during the war, when there is a shortage of hands. After the war some industries leave; others cut production. A year after the war there is a series of clashes between members of the minority and the majority racial groups.

No matter what the facts of the case really are, which of the following statements are likely to be emphasized and which suppressed by those who have attacked the minority group?

a. Members of the minority race group are helping to break down law and order in the community.

b. Members of the racial minority are by nature inferior mentally and morally.

c. Now that the emergency is over, the minority ought to go back to where they came from.

d. They are getting "too cocky" ("need to be taken down a peg").

e. They are in the tightening labor market and are making it hard for the majority racial group to get jobs.

7. A bond issue for new schools is proposed. The town's present school buildings are greatly overcrowded. There has been little school construction for thirty years, while the population has tripled. An organization of taxpayers campaigns against the bond issue.

What order of importance are the following reasons, regardless of their merit, likely to take in the group's campaign and, eventually, in the thinking of its members?

a. Education is not so important to us as a low tax rate.

b. School construction is not so important as improved teaching methods, more rigorous discipline, and so forth. We should do first things first.

c. We do not want to pay out in taxes more than we are now paying.

d. The costs of government services are already too high.

e. A rise in the tax rate would constitute another government threat to private initiative in America today.

8. Congress is considering a bill to reduce the tariff on a certain product.
   Which one of the following reasons for keeping the tariff is likely
   to be omitted or somewhat buried in the attack on the reduction by
   both employers and employees in the affected industry? Which reason
   will probably move into the foreground?
   a. The manufacturers and employees fear that the imported goods
   will compete successfully with their own products unless economic
   hurdles are put up.
   b. The American standard of living should be kept at its present level.
   c. The foreign competition, made possible by lower wages, is unfair.
   d. The foreign product is of inferior quality.
9. A nation acquired a colony by conquest 150 years ago. A strong
   movement for independence is growing in the colony.
   No matter what the actual merits of each reason, indicate what
   order of significance the people of the ruling nation will probably
   give to the various reasons for keeping their colonial possession.
   a. To the winner belong the spoils.
   b. A century and a half ago the people of the home country sacrificed
   blood and treasure to gain the territory.
   c. The home country needs the colony's products to keep its own
   factories going; the prosperity of the home country partly depends on its control of the colony.
   d. If this country does not keep the colony, some other power will
   take over.
   e. The colonizing power has brought the enlightenment and technological progress of modern Western civilization to a dark, barbarian
   area; it has given the natives modern sanitation, law and order, and
   the benefits of trade.

II. TESTING YOUR INFERENCES

Reasoning Inductively

SUPPOSE you were asked such questions as: Which light bulb, the Alpha or the Beta, will take longer to burn out in the socket of your desk lamp? Which of two grass seeds, Tru-Green or Ever-Green, will grow faster in the soil in front of your house? Which of two soda crackers, Crunchies or Munchies, will stay fresh longer in your cupboard when they have been removed from their containers?

Now suppose you were asked such questions as: Who are the better fighters, the U. S. Army or the U. S. Marines? Which is the more effective way of teaching history, Professor X's lecture method or Professor Y's discussion method? Which people are the more moral, the French or the British?

If you had not been put on your guard, if these questions came at you at different times in several different conversational situations, you would probably respond to any of the first set of questions by saying something like this: "I don't know, but if you can show me why it's worth knowing the answer, I can find out." Would that be your response to any of the second set of questions? Would you not—remember, you're not on your guard—have ready an "answer" to these questions?

This little experiment in questions-and-answers raises some more questions. What is the striking difference between these two *sets* of questions? Which questions more readily lend themselves to

(1) setting up a specific, sharply defined problem, (2) close, first-hand observation, (3) the control by the investigator of most of the factors that will probably affect the outcome, (4) repeated tests to check the results, (5) the fewest possible emotional pressures dictating a desired outcome, (6) the opportunity to present proof on a non-verbal level?

The answers to these questions are pretty obvious. Not nearly so obvious are the answers to some further questions. Why do we persist in believing we have "answers" to questions like those in the second set? What is the relation between this persistent belief in unverifiable answers to vague questions and the twentieth-century paradox of unparalleled technological progress co-existing with wars, depressions, famines, and dictatorships? Can the methods which have proved so successful in answering some kinds of questions be adapted to those kinds of questions with which they have never been tried, and which so far remain unanswered?

The selections in this section on "Reasoning Inductively" address themselves to these questions. In the first selection, Chase attempts to describe and define one principal method men have used to obtain workable answers to some of their questions, the method known variously as "the scientific method" or "the inductive method." The second selection provides an example of the scientific method at work in experimental biology, a field in which it is customarily employed. Selections three and four report the attempts of two very thoughtful men, Mayo and Lilienthal, to apply the scientific method to problems of earth-shaking dimensions, from which, until very recent times, the methods of science have been excluded. In the fifth selection, a distinguished scientist, Eddington, discusses a problem which has proved equally fascinating to scientists and sensationalists, with the latter thus far always getting the better press. (What light does this popularity of the pseudo-scientific "wonder tale" throw on that favorite oversimplification of ours that "we live in a scientific age"?) Finally, selections six and seven reveal the other side of the coin. Cantril examines what happens when people who cannot think inductively are faced with a real or imagined emergency; and Evans demonstrates wittily that the scientist who forgets his methods is at least as badly off as the plumber who forgets his tools.

Stuart Chase

Chase, a practicing economist and an unusually effective popularizer of the social sciences, tries to get to the heart of the scientific method and to present as simply as he can its main characteristics and its peculiar advantages in problem-solving.

You will find other useful analyses of the scientific method in George Lundberg's *Can Science Save Us?*, John Dewey's *Human Nature and Conduct*, Alexander H. Leighton's *Human Relations in a Changing World* and *The Governing of Men*, Ruth Benedict's *Race: Science and Politics*, P. W. Bridgman's *The Logic of Modern Physics*, Sidney Hook's *Education for Modern Man*, *The Conference on the Scientific Spirit and Democratic Faith* (by various authors), and *Living Philosophies* (Albert Einstein, *et al.*).

Readers frightened away by "science" might try David Bradley's *No Place to Hide* or Albert Camus' *The Plague* (a novel). Readers of these last two books may well become much more frightened of "no-science."

inductive method.

THE SCIENTIFIC METHOD IN ACTION *

A scientist and his friend were driving through Wyoming and saw a flock of sheep up on a mesa.

"They've just been sheared," said the friend.

"They seem to be, on this side," replied the scientist.

You do not take anything for granted when you enter the monastery of science. You take the vow of utter ignorance until the evidence comes in. This is quite contrary to normal behavior, which abhors explanatory vacuums; and so it is not surprising that congressmen sometimes think scientists queer, and that the Army called the men on the Manhattan project "long-hairs." There is a curious paradox here—the men who know the most assert they know nothing at all except under rigorously limited conditions.

"We come to have a great caution," says Dr. Oppenheimer, "in all assertions of totality, or finality or absoluteness. . . . We learn to

* Stuart Chase, *The Proper Study of Mankind*, Harper & Brothers, 1948. Copyright, 1948, by Stuart Chase.

throw away those instruments of action, and those modes of description, which are not appropriate to the reality we are trying to discover, and in this most painful discipline, find ourselves modest before the world." . . .

I have read a great many definitions of the scientific method, but most of them seem incomplete. The most satisfactory are perhaps Morris R. Cohen's in his *Logic and Scientific Method*, and J. R. Oppenheimer's in the *Technology Review*, February, 1948. So in my amateur way I have sought to combine them by writing out the characteristics of every definition or description encountered. After the duplications are crossed out, ten characteristics seem to remain, a kind of matrix of the scientific method. This is the closest I can get, in words, to an explanation of what science means.

1. Most important of all is the fact that human emotions are thrown out of scientific work. Alone among man's disciplines science can resolve problems independently of our desires and wills. We may desire to find an answer to a question, as Newton did, but when the real work begins the emotional bias must go out. Scientific method is systematic doubt. It does not doubt everything, only what cannot be proved. For determining proof there is a rigorous procedure, first laid down by Pythagoras.

2. A scientist usually begins with a problem to be solved. The problem must be stated in terms which admit an answer in the space-time world. Only people with nothing better to do study facts just to study facts; they usually end up on quiz programs. Somebody must be uneasy, under tension, because he does not know the answer to something he feels to be important. Maybe it is an urgent problem, like beating the Germans to a chain reaction; maybe it is more leisurely, like the probable population of the United States in 1970.

3. The evidence already available is usually explored and classified, perhaps some calculations are made, and the student arrives at a theory, a *hypothesis*, which may answer the problem which has plagued him. At this point the philosopher and the scientist often part company. The philosopher is inclined to believe that his hypothesis is the answer because it sounds so reasonable. The scientist expects the worst. The whole point of science, says Oppenheimer, is to invite the detection of error and welcome it.

4. Following the hypothesis, experiments and observations must be made to prove or disprove it. Often dis-proof is helpful because it narrows the field. Surrounding the scientist should be a *community* in close and accurate communication, dealing in similar concepts, and capable of rapidly checking his work for errors in experiment or logical consistency. These corrections are registered chiefly through scientific papers in the journals.

5. If the experiments indicate a high probability for the hypothesis, then the world has an addition to knowledge. It goes into the storehouse for permanent reference. Prediction becomes possible in similar situations. We have something to rely on, something beyond debate. All competent observers can agree that $E = MC^2$, or that the reproductive index governs population growth. At the state of unproved hypothesis, scientists can argue like an old-time Socialist local, but when the experimental proof comes in they must cease their clamor. Sometimes a group of verified hypotheses can be combined into a great general law—like thermodynamics or gravitation. Scientists are always pleased when they can make their conclusions more general.

An illustration of the ending of debate is found in the development of the atom. After the discovery of the nucleus and surrounding electrons early in the twentieth century, it was found that the positive and negative electric charges inside the atom did not balance out. For twenty years physicists argued about how an electron can be inside the nucleus and why the charges do not annihilate each other. Then Chadwick discovered the *neutron* in 1933. At once the electrical accounts balanced satisfactorily, and the argument was silenced.

6. The scientific method demands that when facts are compared, they must be of the same order. Do not add cabbages to electrons and expect to get a total which means anything.

7. Science is dynamic and self-correcting. A vigilant community is always watching. It has ceased to search for absolutes, and now tends to concentrate on processes. Further experiments may increase or decrease the probability of a given "law," and if they do the law must be restated. Then more experiments are required to nail down the restatement for the storehouse—and so endlessly onward. At each advance, probability is increased, and a closer fit

with nature made. No scientist expects an absolute fit; he leaves that to the metaphysicians.

When Kurt Lewin, the psychologist, died in 1947, the *Lancet* paid him a tribute for, among other fine accomplishments, the distinction he drew between Aristotle and Galileo. Aristotle was concerned with the *properties* of stones; Galileo, on the contrary, concerned himself with the *relations* of stones to the environment.

8. There are no self-evident propositions in science.

9. The logic of consistency is extensively used but the final appeal is to experiment or observation on the nonverbal level. An argument may answer a philosopher; it will never answer an experiment. An experiment can be answered only by a more careful experiment.

10. To doctor an experiment, to slant a conclusion, to report anything but the whole truth as one knows it alone in the night, brings ignominy and oblivion. There can be no secret processes, no patent medicines, no private understandings, no payoffs on the side. The calculations must be laid on the table, face up, for all the world to see. In this sense science is the most "moral" of all man's disciplines. The gravest defect in the Manhattan project, and the reason for the publication of the Smyth report immediately after Hiroshima, lay here. Scientists had to break their moral code and many of them bitterly resented it. Science will be corrupted if ever its direction falls permanently into the hands of nationalists and ideologists. It is as international as the north wind.

Bridgman and Oppenheimer with their great honors are up there on the mountain. How can we men of the foothills and the plain comprehend them? We cannot comprehend them completely unless we take the vows and join their close-knit community. But there are at least three reasons why we can come closer than has been the case, and abandon altogether the idea that a scientist is a victim of midnight seizures.

To begin with, all of us from Einstein down are members of the human race, with similar physiological equipment. There is reason to suppose that we have about the same number of potential connections in our brains. If scientists play on these connections to a somewhat different tune, others conceivably could learn to do so. Furthermore, top scientists when they leave their chosen mountain and make judgments about other matters, such as life and morals and the hereafter, can sound just as foolish as anybody else.

Secondly, in every one of us there is that ceaseless "quest for certainty" which John Dewey talks about. We are all at least embryo or tadpole scientists in wanting explanations for things which puzzle and perplex us. The folkways, of course, provide many explanatory theories to order: "It rained because the moon was full." Individuals, however, gather up stray items of experience and formulate their own theories: "The car is knocking because that last filling-station must have sold us some low-grade, watered gasoline." The scientist states his hypotheses much more carefully, and then verifies them with controlled experiments or more observation. The rest of us usually abandon them in the raw hypothesis stage.

Finally, many people are constantly carrying on little controlled experiments without being aware that they are, for the moment, scientists. You plant half the peas an inch deep and the rest two inches deep, and see which makes the better crop. You try this fertilizer against that. You switch on an electric light and no light comes. "Burned out," you generalize. But often before throwing the bulb away, you screw it into another socket where a working bulb has proved the current to be on. This simple action is a controlled experiment, and a fairly rigorous one.

The germs of the scientific method are in all classes and conditions of men, especially those who work with their hands. There need not be the world of the scientist sealed off from the world of the layman if we really want to get together and establish better lines of communication. A little research by social scientists could disclose the proper methods. Every day that passes makes it more necessary that the two worlds meet. . . .

PROBLEMS

1. One of the editors, while in the Army, knew a captain who insisted that anybody who said, "I'm not sure" or "I don't know" would "never make a good soldier." Can you see the dangers in this view?

    You have very likely been annoyed, even angered, by people who said, "Well, uh—I'm not sure" or "Maybe yes—but maybe no." Have you known persons who lumped together all such uncertain answers as signs of "moral cowardice" or "lack of moral character"? How may this kind of classification be a result of that fear of "explanatory vacuums" described by Chase?

2. Chase has tried to "boil down" the thinking of others about the scientific method to ten major points. Can you in turn boil down Chase's points to eliminate duplication or overlapping?

3. Chase lists "systematic doubt" as one characteristic of the "scientific method." What distinguishes this kind of doubt from the "Oh, yeah?" or "You can't be sure of anything" kind of skepticism or cynicism?

4. Chase distinguishes between examining facts to solve a problem and just collecting information. With this difference in mind, consider which of your high school and college courses have, in this respect, reflected the scientific method. Write a paper in which you compare a "survey" course or a "general culture" course with the "problems" type of course.

5. What difference do you observe between a *hypothesis* and an *answer*? Later in this course we shall study the tendency to lean too heavily on language, that is, to feel, because we have *words* for something, we have an *answer*. Can you see how Chase's criticism of "the philosopher," under characteristic number 3, may apply to the rest of us in our everyday thinking?

6. Chase holds that dis-proof, the *no* answers, can be helpful. Is this attitude common outside the physical sciences? Have you noticed how frequently, in public discussion of controversial social problems, the speaker who points out obstacles in the way of a plan is criticized for being "unconstructive"? In each instance that you can recall was the term justified? In your own writing of class reports and term papers have you noticed any tendency in yourself to feel you had failed if you came up with negative answers? Did you notice yourself trying to avoid such answers?

7. A student in an economics course says that the only way "to get things done" (i.e., to prevent price inflation, prevent unfair practices in business, to get people out of overcrowded fields into less crowded ones) is "to *force* people to do such-and-such, the way they do in the Army." He argues in this manner: "You can't fight a war successfully if you allow every Tom, Dick, and Harry to make his own decisions." In what way may this be a comparison of facts of different kinds ("electrons and cabbages")?

A student in a psychology class argues that a certain minority group (e.g., Negroes, Filipinos, Italians) are "less intelligent" than the native-born, white Americans of North European descent, because their school records are generally lower. May this also be a comparison of facts of different kinds? If so, how?

8. How does the question, "Are human beings naturally *bad?*" differ from the question, "What causes juvenile delinquency in big American cities today?" What is the main difference between the questions, "What's wrong with Europe's economy?" and "What specific effects does a high tariff wall or wornout industrial equipment or a lack of dollars have on the economy of Western European countries?" How do these differences illustrate the unscientific-minded man's "search for absolutes" and the scientific-minded person's concern with processes and means?

9. Chase, in presenting point number 9, says that in the scientific method "the final appeal is to experiment or observation on the nonverbal level." Can this requirement be met in our handling of problems outside the physical sciences? (In this connection be sure to read Mayo's "The First Inquiry.") For example, can we test, at least partially, a man's smartness by what he can *do?* Can we make the "final appeal" to experiment or observation in making up our minds how history can be most effectively taught in high school or what the causes of a strike in a local factory may be? What is the difference between talking about "America's high standard of living" and examining the actual division of income revealed in any census? Between worrying over "the postwar crime wave" and comparing prewar with postwar crime totals?

10. Have you observed unscientific thinking by scientists outside their own special fields? Have you, for instance, detected any difference in the basis for the attitude of the professor of soil chemistry toward, say, alkaline soils, and his attitude toward the farm policies of certain government bureaus? Have you noted any difference between your own thinking in the physics, biology, or chemistry laboratory and your thinking outside the laboratory about motives for your friends' actions, causes of automobile accidents, advantages in taking a job?

Bernard Jaffe

Sunday-supplement writers and the authors of pseudo-scientific fiction have helped to create in the minds of many of us a dramatic, highly unrealistic picture of the scientist at work. Still, the actual, day-to-day hard work of scientists is, in a more fundamental way, even more dramatic, if we do not lose sight of the mental hazards scientists must always be on the watch for, of the never-ending fight scientists have had to wage against other appealing methods of arriving at answers, and of the distance between the scientists' controlled experimentation and our vague, generalized thinking about most personal and social problems.

The following selection from Jaffe's *Men of Science in America* reports the steps taken by Herbert Evans of the University of California in determining the existence and the effects of a substance apparently related to the ability in mammals to reproduce. Evans is one of the world's leading experimental biologists; he is especially noted for his research on the structure of the germ cell.

DISCOVERING A VITAMIN *

Evans began his study of the vitamins while working, at the Biological Institute of the University of California, on the sex cycle of the rat. He was investigating this problem in connection with his hormone studies. The diet of his animals interested him as just another factor which might affect this cycle. Vitamins A and B had already been discovered by Elmer V. McCollum at the University of Wisconsin during the three years which preceded the entrance of the United States into the First World War. McCollum had made available a number of diets rich in these vitamins, and Evans fed his rats on these standard diets. (Fat-soluble vitamin D was still unknown at this time.) To the surprise of Evans and his assistant, Miss Katherine S. Bishop, animals fed on this diet would exhibit normal sex cycles, mate, and conceive, but could not go through a normal pregnancy. Death of the developing embryo invariably occurred. No live progeny was born. Neither vitamin A nor vitamin B could prevent this strange intra-uterine death.

Then began a search for foods which might contain some element essential to normal development of the embryo. Fresh leaves of lettuce seemed to contain it, for when added to the diet sterility was prevented. The wheat germ was also potent. Even in infinitesimal amounts, Evans found, the rich golden oil extracted from it

* Bernard Jaffe, *Men of Science in America*. Reprinted by permission of Simon and Schuster, publishers. Copyright, 1944, by Bernard Jaffe.

meant all the difference between barrenness and fecundity. Evans waited until he was positive that absence of this hitherto unrecognized dietary factor led to sterility in male rats and to destruction of the developing embryo in females. Then in December, 1922 (the year of the discovery of vitamin D by McCollum), he announced the discovery of vitamin X. This name was later changed to vitamin E by Barnett Sure, who the following year independently confirmed the results of the Berkeley investigator.

Evans, with a splendid technique cleverly guarded by controls, uncovered some interesting facts in connection with this new vitamin. He reared hundreds of mother rats on a strict ration lacking all traces of vitamin E, and then induced fertility by administering minute doses of highly concentrated vitamin E extracts. He found that he could cure female rats of the threat of dead embryos by giving them vitamin E extracts as late as the fifth day of pregnancy. Evans killed normal young female rats and fed their pancreas, spleen, or muscle tissues to sterile mother rats, who later bore normal litters. "Therefore," he concluded, "normal young female rats begin life with initial fertility, their tissues containing vitamin E conveyed to them in intra-uterine life by their mothers." However, the supply of vitamin E must be continued in their diet, otherwise a deficiency results which causes sterility. Some of his rats were given an overabundance of his magic yellow wheat-germ oil, but this excess vitamin E had no effect on the size or the frequency of their litters.

The application of this discovery to human life occurred to Evans and many others. They thought of the thousands of women who, though otherwise normal, lose children again and again before birth. Though Evans made no claims for the vitamin E potency in humans, Dr. P. Vogt-Möller, of the County Hospital at Odense, Denmark, tried vitamin E therapy on a group of cows known to be chronic aborters, and obtained favorable results. Then on July 25, 1931, he reported to the English medical journal, *Lancet,* the results of his next step. Case No. 1 was that of a twenty-four-year-old woman who, after four miscarriages, was given Evans' wheat oil orally. Her next pregnancy followed a normal course and a healthy baby was born. Case No. 2 was that of a twenty-nine-year-old woman who, after the birth of her first child, miscarried four times in succession. This woman was given about two tablespoons of wheat oil each week, and responded as successfully as the first case. Others, too, believe that vitamin E is necessary for the human mother, but the medical world still awaits more conclusive testimony. Evans himself cautioned medical men against "the indiscriminate use of vitamin E in attempting to cure human sterility which is most frequently due to other causes." Henry C. Sherman of Columbia University had found evidence that a lack of vitamin A also impairs the reproductive functions. Vitamin E is, therefore, not *the* fertility vitamin but one of several chemicals which are necessary for normal reproduction.

In August, 1935, thirteen years after the announcement of the discovery of vitamin E, Evans reported that he had finally succeeded in obtaining this vitamin in pure crystalline form. During the next year his laboratory reported the isolation from wheat-germ oil of another chemical which had the antisterility properties of vitamin E. It is colorless or slightly yellowish, odorless oil. Its formula was found to be $C_{29}H_{50}O_2$ and its melting point about 158° Centigrade. At the suggestion of Professor G. M. Calhoun of the University of California, this alcohol compound was named *alpha-tocopherol*—from *tokos*, meaning childbirth; *phero*, meaning to bear, and *ol* an alcohol. When given to vitamin E-deficient rats in single doses of three milligrams, it enabled the rats to bear normal litters. That same year Evans reported that cottonseed oil, and, later, lettuce leaves and palm oil, furnished the same alcohol.

The structure of alpha-tocopherol was found by D. L. Fernholz in the Rahway, New Jersey, laboratories of Merck and Company. In 1938 its synthesis was accomplished in three widely separated laboratories. Lee I. Smith of the University of Minnesota completed the achievement in Evans' laboratory, Paul Karrer prepared it in Switzerland, and Todd did the same in England. Then followed in quick succession the isolation of beta-tocopherol, gamma-tocopherol, and alpha-tocoquinone, all of which possess vitamin E potency. This seemed to indicate that more than one substance appears to function as vitamin E, of which alpha-tocopherol is the most active constituent.

The question of relationship between vitamin E and reproduction is still not completely cleared up. According to Evans a number of outstanding enigmas in this field include such problems as: What is the specificity of chemical structure in vitamin E responses? Are different chemical portions of the tocopherol molecule necessary for reproduction and neuromuscular activity? What is the actual mode of action of the vitamin in the physiology of the embryo? What is the cause of death of E-free sucklings, and how does spontaneous recovery ensue? What analogous human clinical conditions exist? To find answers to some of these questions Evans and his laboratory continue to wrestle with their colonies of rats on the campus of the University of California.

PROBLEMS

1. The importance of the discovery of vitamin E doubtless went far beyond the connection of the vitamin to the rat's sex cycle which Evans was investigating and which is a more limited field than that of the sex cycles of animals in general. What aspect of the scientific method as outlined by Chase does this illustrate?
2. What "controls" did Evans set up in determining exactly what factor affected fecundity in rats?
3. In Jaffe's account what specific evidence do you find of the hypothesis-testing that Chase considers essential to the scientific method? What contrast do you find between the caution of Evans and the other workers on vitamin E and the attitude of many newspaper and magazine writers toward scientific discoveries? What do these journalists do which men who more closely follow the scientific method in their thinking refuse to do?
4. The contributing of facts about vitamin E by many men all over the world suggests what error in the popular conception (reflected in movies, stories, and general conversation about "greatest scientists") of the lone scientific genius making his revolutionary discovery? What is the relation of this to much present thinking about the atomic bomb?

Elton Mayo

"The First Inquiry" is a firsthand report of one attempt to apply the scientific method to thinking outside the physical sciences—in this case, a social problem. In 1923 the Mayo investigators were called in to find the reason for low output and fast labor-turnover in a textile plant near Philadelphia. (Note that they had been preceded by several groups of "efficiency experts," who might, if one did not examine their methods, be lumped inaccurately under the term "scientists" or "scientific experts.")

Mayo's investigations were continued with several companies whose managements "wished to find out why human co-operation could not be as exactly and accurately determined" as could other factors of applied science or organized industrial operation. These inquiries have produced significant results for industry and the development of methods of scientific social investigation. The Hawthorne project, conducted under the auspices of the Western Electric Company, is doubtless the most revealing, and certainly the best known, of these experiments. Students who wish for further details of this precedent-making experiment in genuine social science will find full accounts in F. J. Roethlisberger and William J. Dickson's *Management and the Worker*, and in T. North Whitehead's *The Industrial Worker*, as well as in Mayo's book. An account of this and other comparable experiments, with some tentative generalizations derived therefrom, is to be found in George C. Homans' *The Human Group*. Do you see something significant in the fact that these experiments, conducted in the 20's and early 30's, were not published until the very late 30's and the 40's?

THE FIRST INQUIRY *

Economic theory in its human aspect is woefully insufficient; indeed it is absurd. Humanity is not adequately described as a horde of individuals, each actuated by self-interest, each fighting his neighbor for the scarce material of survival. Realization that such theories completely falsify the normal human scene drives us back to study of particular human situations. *Knowledge-of-acquaintance* of the actual event, intimate understanding of the complexity of human relationships, must precede the formulation of alternatives to current economic abstractions. This is the clinical method, the necessary preliminary to laboratory investigation. Only when clinically tested by successful treatment can a diagnosis be safely developed toward logical elaboration and laboratory experiment.

The first inquiry we undertook ran headlong into illustration of the insufficiency of the assumption that individual self-interest actually operates as adequate incentive. Rather more than twenty years ago we were asked to discover, if possible, the causes of a high labor turnover in the mule-spinning department of a textile mill near Philadelphia. The general labor situation elsewhere in the plant seemed highly satisfactory; the employers were unusually enlightened and humane; the work was exceedingly well organized in respect of operations and the company was generally regarded as an extremely successful venture. But the president and his director of personnel were much troubled by the situation in the mule-spinning department. Whereas the general labor turnover in other departments was estimated to be approximately 5% or 6% per annum, in the spinning department the turnover was estimated at approximately 250%. That is to say, about 100 men had to be taken on every year in order to keep about 40 working. And the difficulty tended to be most acute when the factory was busily employed and most in need of men.

Several firms of efficiency engineers had been consulted; these firms had instituted altogether four financial incentive schemes. And these schemes had been a total failure; labor turnover had not dropped one point, nor had production improved: it was almost as a last resort that the firm consulted a university. Although other plants in the vicinity had apparently drifted into acceptance of low morale amongst mule spinners as inevitable, the president of this company refused to believe that the situation was beyond remedy.

On a first inspection the conditions of work in the department did not seem to differ in any general respect from conditions elsewhere in the mill. For some time Saturday work had been discontinued throughout the plant, so that the work week was of 50 hours—five days of 10 hours, two shifts of 5 hours each separated by a 45-minute lunch interval. The mule-spinner attendant was known as a piecer; his work involved walking up and down a long alley, perhaps 30 yards or more, on either side of which a machine head was operating spinning frames. These frames moved back and forth stretching yarn taken from the carding machines, twisting it, and rolling it up on cops. The number of frames operated by a machine head varied from 10 to 14. All had to be closely watched; threads constantly broke and had to be pieced together. The number of piecers in an alley, usually two or three, varied according to the kind of yarn being spun. To an observer the work looked monotonous—walking up and down an alley twisting together broken threads. The only variation in work occurred when a machine head was stopped in order to doff or to replace some spools.

Dr. S. D. Ludlum, professor of neuropsychiatry in the graduate school of medicine in the University of Pennsylvania, was of immense aid to us at this stage as later in the study. He arranged that a registered nurse, one of our group, should be able to relate her small clinic for minor troubles in the plant direct to the Polyclinic Hospital in Philadelphia. Serious cases she referred to the hospital clinicians; minor injuries, a cut or splinter, she could deal with herself. This arrangement seemed to do away with any need for further explanation. Workers gratefully accepted the services of the nurse and, in some instances, the further clinical aid of the hospital. These services were real and understandable. From the first the mule spinners formed a large part of the nurse's regular callers—and either when at work or in the clinic talked to her and to us quite freely. It was of course clearly understood that nothing said to any of us was ever repeated to anyone in the plant.

As the men began to talk to us, the picture of the situation developed quite differently from that obtained at first inspection. We discovered that almost every piecer suffered from foot trouble of one or another kind for which he apparently knew no effective remedy. Many also claimed neuritis in various localities of arms, shoulders, or legs. But above and beyond all this, the striking fact was the uniformly pessimistic nature of the preoccupations of these workers while at work. To this there seemed no exception: their own opinion of their work was low, even lower than the estimate of mule spinning held by other workers in the plant. We discovered also that the job was essentially solitary: there might be three workers in an alley, but the amount of communication between them in a day was almost nil. One might be piecing threads together here; another, 20 yards away. And the doffing process when it took place involved rapid work with a minimum of communication. Some of the men were young—in the twenties, others were in the fifties—all alike claimed that they were too fatigued to enjoy social evenings after work. Occasionally a worker would flare out into apparently unreasonable anger and incontinently leave his job.

The whole group was characterized by a species of strongly held loyalty to the company president. He had been a colonel in the regular United States Army and had seen active service both before and during the First World War. Many of the workers had been in the trenches in France under his immediate command and had the highest opinion of him; they had come with him from his regiment to the textile mill. Perhaps for this reason their pessimistic moods showed no anger against "the Colonel" or "the company." For the most part the individual seemed to be almost melancholic about himself; this mood alternated with spurts of rage against some immediate supervisor.

After some discussion the management permitted us to experiment with rest periods—two of 10 minutes' length in the morning and two again in the afternoon. We arranged these rests so that the work period should be divided thus: 2 hours' work, 10 minutes' rest; 1½ hours' work, 10 minutes' rest; and a final work period of 1 hour and 10 minutes. The actual uninterrupted work period thus diminished in morning and afternoon. In these rest periods the workers were permitted to lie down; we instructed them in the best methods of securing the maximum of muscular relaxation. We encouraged them to sleep for 10 minutes and most of them were able to do so.

We began with one team of piecers, about one-third of the total number, and the results were encouraging from the outset. The men themselves were pleased and interested; they speedily adopted the method of rest we advised. The effect was immediate—symptoms of melancholy preoccupation almost wholly disappeared, the labor turnover came to an end, production was maintained, and the morale generally improved. Such immediate effects could not be attributed to the mere elimination of physical fatigue. This was confirmed by the fact that an almost equivalent improvement showed itself in the work of the other two-thirds of the piecers. These men had discussed the experiment at lunch time with their fellows and were confident that "the Colonel" would extend the system to them if it were found satisfactory. And in the October of that year, 1923, this expectation was fulfilled; the management, pleased with the improved condition of the men and the work, decided to extend the rest period system to include the entire personnel of the spinning department. This made it possible for us to do what we could not do before—to measure the effect of the rest periods upon the productivity of the department.

Until October, 1923, the spinning department had never earned a bonus under one of the incentive systems introduced; in October and for the months recorded thereafter, with one interesting exception, the spinners consistently earned a bonus in addition to their wages. I have elsewhere described the bonus plan and shall not repeat this detail here. Enough to say that, if the production of the department in any month exceeded 75% of a carefully calculated possibility, every spinner was paid an excess percentage of his flat-rate wage equivalent to the average excess percentage of production over 75%. Thus a monthly man-hour efficiency of 80% meant a 5% bonus on his monthly wage to every employee in the department. As said above, no fraction of bonus had even been earned by the department. We were unable to get figures showing the average productivity of the department before October, 1923, when the experiment proper began; but it was generally admitted by executives and supervisors that production had never been above an approximate 70%.

The period from October, 1923, to mid-February, 1924, inclusive, showed a surprising change. The mental and physical condition of the men continued to improve, and, whereas the financial incentive of the bonus had not operated to stimulate production while they felt fatigued, they were now pleased by the fact that under conditions of work that seemed much easier they were earning bonuses as never before. The system was not, however, altogether satisfactory at this time. The immediate supervisors had never liked the sight of workers lying asleep on sacks while the mules were running; it occurred to one of them that the men should be made to "earn" their rest periods. That is to say, a task was set and, if finished within a given time, the men had their rest. For the most part, the workers had three or four rests every day and the innovation worked well enough. For example, the monthly average of productivity ran as follows:

	Efficiency	Bonus
October, 1923	79½%	4½%
November, 1923	78¾	3¾
December, 1923	82	7
January, 1924	78¾	3¾
February, 1924	80¼	5¼

This, for workers who had never before earned a bonus, meant much.

This general condition continued until Friday, February 15, when in response to a heavy demand for goods the supervisor who had introduced the idea of earned rest periods ordered the whole system abandoned. Within five days production fell to a point lower than it had been for months. And on February 22, we found that the old pessimistic preoccupations had returned in full force, thus coinciding almost exactly with the drop in production. The executive officer in charge ordered the resumption of the rest period system on Monday, February 25; this was done, but the idea of earned rest periods was also reinstated even more strongly than before. At this point, the workers gave every symptom of profound discouragement; they professed a belief that the system would be discontinued before long. In spite of this, the daily record for March showed definite improvement, but the general average for the month was back at the old point, 70%.

At this point the president of the company, "the Colonel," took charge. His military service had taught him two important things— one, to care for his men, and, two, not to be afraid of making decisions. He called a conference in his office to discuss the remarkable diminution from 80% to 70% in the department's productive efficiency. We were able to point out that in March there had been a recrudescence of absenteeism, an ill that had notably diminished in the October to February period. This meant that the men were taking their rest periods in the form of "missed" days, a proceeding that did not greatly remedy their condition and that produced chaos in the plant. We put it therefore that the question was not whether a certain proportion of their working time was to be given up to rest. We pointed out that they took the rest, whether it was given them or not. We were asking that a less proportion should be thus allotted, but that it should be done systematically. Furthermore, we were able to claim that the whole rest period system had never had a fair trial. In other words, it had not been possible for a worker to know as he entered the factory in the morning that he was assured of his four rests in the day.

In order to test our claim, the president ordered that during the month of April the spinning mules should be shut down for 10 minutes at a time four times a day and that all hands from the floor supervisor down should rest as they had been instructed to do. There was some difficulty in securing the requisite amount of floor space for approximately 40 men to lie down by their machines and in securing sufficient sacking to provide for their comfort. With the exception of the president himself, there were few who believed that this drastic alteration of method could result in increased production. The men themselves believed that 40 minutes lost by 40 men per day during a whole month could not be recovered. They pointed out that the machines could not be "speeded up" and that there was no other way of recovering the lost time. In spite of this general belief, the returns for April showed an improvement on March. The March production-efficiency figure had been 70%, the April figure was 77½%. This, while it represented a 7½% gain in the company's rating, was actually a 10% gain. The men had had their rests, the pessimism had again disappeared; simultaneously, their morale had much improved, absenteeism had diminished, and every worker had earned a 2½% bonus on his wages. In the month of May and thereafter, the president ordered a return to the system of alternating rest periods, with this important difference that each group of three men in an alley was to determine for itself the method of alternation, the understanding being that every worker was to have four such rest periods daily and regularly. In the month of May, the average efficiency of man-hour production was 80¼%. In June it reached the then record high figure of 85%. During the following three months the department maintained its improved capacity: July, 82%; August, 83½%; September, 86½%.

It is interesting to observe the difference that an absolute certainty of a minimum number of rest periods made. The months from April to September differed from the preceding months in this respect and they revealed a steady progress. Mondays and Fridays were no longer the worst days in the week. The irregularity reported in May was due to the fact that the spinning mules were constantly "running away from the cards," that is, outdistancing the carding machines which supplied them with spooled yarn. By June, the company had put in two new carding machines, and June was as steadily above 85% as March was below 75%.

The investigation began with a question as to the causes of a very high labor turnover. In the 12 months of experiment there was no labor turnover at all. This does not mean that no worker left the factory—during a period of trade slackness, some were laid off, one at least moved his place of residence and found work elsewhere, another was found to be phthisical and sent to the country. But the former problem of a highly emotional labor turnover ceased to exist. The factory began to hold its mule spinners and no longer had difficulty in maintaining a full complement in times of rushed work. The attitude of management to the innovation was revealed in the fact that the company purchased army cots for the workers to rest upon. When these cots proved unequal to the wear and tear, management installed a bed and mattress at the end of each alley as provision for the workers' adequate rest. And the workers developed the habit of sleeping for the last three rest periods of the day, the late morning rest and both afternoon rests. Experience seemed to show that the benefit was directly proportionate to the completeness of the relaxation—hence the beds. Several years later, the president of the company said publicly that from this time the labor turnover sank to an approximate 5% or 6% per annum and stayed there until the mules were taken out and ring spinning substituted.

At the time when we completed our part in this work, we were sure that we had not wholly discovered the causes of the high labor turnover. We could not even attribute the change to the mere introduction of rest periods; inevitably many other changes had been simultaneously introduced. For example, we had listened carefully and with full attention to anything a worker wished to say, whatever the character of his comment. In addition to this, we—supported by the president—had demonstrated an interest in what was said by the introduction of experimental changes, by instruction in the best methods of relaxation. The Colonel also had demonstrated unmistakably a sincere interest in his workers' welfare; he had lived up to his Army reputation. The supervisor who instituted the earning of rest periods was swept aside by the president and the company—thereby "placing" the company's attitude in the minds of its workers.

But, in addition to this—and we did not see this clearly at the time—the president had effected another important change. He had helped to transform a horde of "solitaries" into a social group. In May, 1924, he placed the control of rest periods squarely in the hands of the workers in an alley with no one to say them nay.

This led to consultation, not only between individuals, but between alleys throughout the group—and to a feeling of responsibility directly to the president. And the general social changes effected were astonishing—even in relationships outside the factory. One worker told us with great surprise that he had begun taking his wife to "movies" in the evenings, a thing he had not done for years. Another, equally to his surprise, gave up a habit of spending alcoholic week ends on bootleg liquor. In general the change was complex, and the difficulty of assigning the part played in it by various aspects of the experiment impossible to resolve. We should have liked to experiment further, but this desire—probably wisely in the circumstances—was disallowed. Thus the inquiry left us with many questions unanswered, but it pointed a direction for further studies, the results of which later proved helpful in reinterpreting the data of this first investigation.

But we had moved onwards. The efficiency experts had not consulted the workers; they regarded workers' statements as exaggerated or due to misconception of the facts and therefore to be ignored. Yet to ignore an important symptom—whatever its character—on supposedly moral grounds is preposterous. The "expert" assumptions of rabble hypothesis and individual self-interest as a basis for diagnosis led nowhere. On the other hand, careful and pedestrian consideration of the workers' situation taken as part of a clinical diagnosis led us to results so surprising that we could at the time only partly explain them.

PROBLEMS

1. Do you remember Hayakawa's suggestion that judgments block further observation, e.g., the difficulty of going further in a theme after the writer has called a girl "a typical cute little co-ed"? Well, then, how do such abstractions as "economic man" (Mayo's "individual self-interest" hypothesis) and "the common man" (Mayo's "rabble" hypothesis) prevent direct observation of conditions under which men work? How does this relate to the thinking of the efficiency engineers who preceded Mayo's investigators? To the thinking of a student who writes that he will profit by college because college "improves one's earning power"? To the decision of a man to give his wife perfume for Christmas because "women like to smell pretty"?

2. How do you account for the fact that a special benefit, rest periods, conferred on only one-third of the spinners brought about an almost equivalent boost in the morale of the other two-thirds? What cautious inference might be drawn from this seemingly curious fact? How does this observation of the behavior of the two-thirds reveal the ability of Mayo's experimenters to steer clear of preconceived assumptions?

3. In what way was the reaction of the immediate supervisors, who did not like to see their men lying asleep, an indication of an unscientific type of thinking? What is the connection between this example of unscientific thinking and the objection of many parents to the informal atmosphere of some modern elementary schoolrooms? the objections of a civic group to spending more money on medical and psychiatric treatment for penitentiary inmates? the objection of "old hands" in the military services to the introduction of women's auxiliaries like the WAVES and the WACS?

4. How do the statements, ". . . we did not see this clearly at the time," "In general the change was complex . . . ," "We should have liked to experiment further . . . ," and ". . . it pointed a direction for further studies . . . ," in the last three paragraphs of the article reveal the scientific mind at work?

5. From the inference that "social groups" operate more effectively than an equivalent number of "solitaries," what application can you make to such organizations as a football team? a college faculty? a labor union? a trade association? a group of doctors jointly operating a clinic? international student and teacher exchanges? Pan-American conferences? the United Nations?

David Lilienthal

It is clear, in the following selection—a talk given in 1946 before a meeting of chemists—that David Lilienthal counts on his audience understanding what he is talking about—the attempt of a group of informed men to reach scientifically an answer to one of man's most baffling, complex problems, control of the atomic bomb for constructive rather than destructive use.

Lilienthal continually compares the "political" method of problem-solving with the scientific method. Lilienthal had ample opportunity to make such comparisons as Director of the Tennessee Valley Authority, and later as Chairman of the Atomic Energy Commission. In the latter capacity he had many skirmishes with critics in Congress, and he has become a leading defender of scientists against suspicious or antagonistic Congressmen, newspaper editors, or private citizens.

HOW CAN ATOMIC ENERGY
BE CONTROLLED? *

Can atomic energy be so developed and so controlled that it will be used only for the advancement of human welfare and not be used for war and destruction? As we meet here tonight this is probably the world's number one question. Since June 14 a group of men meeting in New York City has been patiently seeking for an answer to this tough problem. This is the Atomic Energy Commission of the United Nations, made up of representatives of twelve countries, with Bernard Baruch, the American delegate.

No answer to this question will be genuinely workable unless it is agreeable to every one of the Great Powers and all, or substantially all, the nations of the world. This is quite an order. In fact, quite an order. It may be something like insisting that a fellow who never in his life had broadjumped more than ten feet must jump twenty feet. But if he feels he just *has* to jump twenty feet, if a deep chasm lies before him, and something pretty hungry is chasing him, then twenty feet is still one hell of a jump—but because he has no easy alternative, it's not impossible. Well, the world has no easy alternatives about atomic energy—none that I can see. If an answer can't be found, one that this country and Russia and the other nations find acceptable and workable, then we're bound to have a feverish arms race. This will not be just an atomic arms race, though atomic weapons will probably lead the list, but one clear across the board. If that happens, scientists and technical men will simply have to do what all the rest of us must then do—that is, change our whole way of living. And there won't be much peace of mind while we're making the change. Instead of devoting your skills as chemists to improving the lot of men, as you

* David E. Lilienthal, "How Can Atomic Energy Be Controlled?" Reprinted from *Chemical & Engineering News*, Vol. 24, No. 18, September 25, 1946, pp. 2483-85. Copyright 1946 by the American Chemical Society and reprinted by permission of the copyright owner.

would prefer to do, you, like all the rest of us—if we get into this kind of arms race—will be working like mad to find ways of scattering our cities so as to defend ourselves, and spending our energies devising ways of destroying our potential enemies. Not a pretty prospect for science or industry, or civil liberties, or nerves, or anything else.

It was scientists and technical men—prominent among them chemists—who gave the world the large-scale release of atomic energy. This is the supreme achievement to date of the scientific spirit and the scientific method. It is my own opinion that the only hope to control atomic energy and prevent its use for destruction lies in applying the scientific spirit and the scientific method to this problem. In a world thus far largely run by the ideas of politics and legalism, I freely admit that this would be something quite novel. But considering how unattractive are the alternatives, I don't believe that the twenty-foot broad jump is out of the question, and I doubt if you do either.

The averting of war and the maintenance of peace are traditionally described as political problems, or as it is sometimes put, "These are matters calling for political decisions, reached and carried out by political methods." Typical political methods in domestic affairs as well as international relations are quite familiar to all of us. Their practitioners sometimes include business, labor, and farm leaders, as well as politicians and statesmen—even, once in a while, a scientist. And when a scientist goes in for political dogmatism, he can make a politician look scientific by comparison!

The political method, generally speaking, is based on the process of *first* deciding what answer you and your side want, and *then* scurrying around for evidence and arguments and public opinion and force to support the answer you started with in the first place. Political methods—I am oversimplifying a bit, but not much—are based on three procedures so far as the people are concerned:

1. Tell the people what you know *they want to hear*—regardless of the facts. This gives great scope for orators, sloganmakers, and dogmatists.

2. Tell the people what you want them to hear—regardless of the facts. This is the technique of the well-poisoner.

3. Tell 'em nothing, and make 'em like it. This is an ancient art, but its modern practitioners have brought it to a new high level.

POLITICAL VS. SCIENTIFIC METHODS

Political methods are generally quite in contrast to the scientific spirit and method. In his "Novum Organum," Francis Bacon said many many years ago: "We cannot command Nature except by obeying her." The scientist, essentially a humble man, obeys Nature by honestly observing and then truthfully recording *not* what he *wants* to find, but what in truth he *does* find. The essence of the scientific method and spirit to me—a layman—is that it does not start with the answer, but with the facts, and draws its insight and its overtones from the facts.

It's not often that there is an opportunity to analyze what is called a political problem in a scientific spirit. But something of the sort did happen last winter. The product was an idea embodied in a document published by our State Department called "A Report on the International Control of Atomic Energy." The proposals of that report for the creation of a world-wide Atomic Development Authority have since been accepted by our President, Secretary Byrnes, and Mr. Baruch and his associates as basic to the American proposals presented by Mr. Baruch in a historic address to the UN Atomic Commission and to the world.

This report represented the work and the unanimous agreement of a Board of Consultants of five men. We were men of widely differing backgrounds and experience. But all five of us had this in common—we had all had responsibility for technical enterprises, and therefore had grown accustomed to the methods of tackling problems that are characteristic not of politics but of technology. Chester Barnard, one of our associates, president of the New Jersey Bell Telephone Co., thinks scientifically about organization. Robert Oppenheimer, a physicist, was wartime director of the atom bomb plant at Los Alamos. Charles Thomas, a chemist and one of this society's distinguished members, is director of Monsanto's research activities, and in charge of research at the atomic energy plant at Oak Ridge. Harry Winne is vice-president of General Electric in charge of engineering policy. Your speaker is chairman of TVA. So that all of us had rather extensive and responsible experience in undertakings based on scientific and technical knowledge. This was indeed a strange team to be asked to try to find an answer to what is classified as a "political" problem.

We five locked ourselves up for two months, had the whole array of facts before us, and came up with a plan all of us believed was workable. That plan has been widely discussed and is fairly well known. We urged that the people of the world agree to entrust to a world agency, the Atomic Development Authority, the control and management of all activities concerning atomic energy that are dangerous—that is, dangerous to the security of the world—activities that are steps on the road toward the making of atomic bombs. These dangerous steps begin with the raw material: uranium and thorium. Under our proposed plan, factories to produce fissionable materials would all be owned and operated, not by rival nations, but by this world corporation functioning under world law and responsible to all people.

But it is *how* our Board of Consultants went about trying to find a plan that is in some ways as important as the answer we came up with. For we didn't follow the typical political method of starting with the answer all neatly laid out, and then look around for facts and arguments to support our pet notion. We didn't start, for example, by asserting that the answer was world government and then pick out facts that would fit that answer. Nor did we say, "National sovereignty must in no wise be infringed," and then try to squeeze out a plan that would fit that dogma. No, we started somewhat as a chemist might, tackling a technical problem—with the facts as he found them.

You recall that a year ago when the world saw for the first time the fantastic destructiveness of the atomic bomb, many Americans said, "Now, this won't do; this must be the last time that an atomic bomb is used. The people of the world must agree to outlaw the bomb." What was meant was that the nations would all sign a treaty that solemnly promised that none of them would ever in secret or otherwise make these bombs and use them in a war. All the nations would devote themselves exclusively to the many wonderful peaceful uses of atomic energy—for electric power, for a war on cancer and other diseases, and research in a hundred fields.

My four associates and I placed the facts alongside this idea of eliminating the bomb by international agreement, and as a consequence we were forced to discard the idea. For those facts made it clear that there was no security whatever for people anywhere, no prospect of a moment's freedom from fear of an atomic armament race if this is all we had to offer—this outlawing by international covenant.

What facts? Well, fact No. 1 is this: the same materials and operations required to put atomic energy to peaceful purposes are adaptable, virtually without change, to the making of the stuff that goes into atomic bombs. This is true through almost the whole course of producing atomic energy.

In the light of the facts it was just political hoorah to talk about nations concentrating on peaceful purposes as if that called for entirely different processes and materials from those used for destruction. Once you have produced some of this dangerous material, there are ways of doctoring or denaturing it, to make it rather safe, and not effective for bombs in that form; but you must *begin* with substances that, however useful for producing electric power or for research, can just as readily be used to destroy the cities of mankind. There's a fact—and a fact is a stubborn thing and no amount of political dogma can do anything to change a fact. And there is another thing about a scientific fact: It pays no attention to national boundaries. There are no such things as American neutrons, say, and some different kind of Russian neutrons, and British neutrons. A neutron doesn't know about boundary lines.

These being the facts, what does an international covenant never to use atomic bombs amount to? The nations would all go through the process of signing their names to a treaty, agreeing never to make atomic bombs, agreeing at most that they will forbid their citizens to use fissionable materials except for peaceful purposes. But under the treaty each nation will be permitted to go on mining uranium and thorium and putting them through a plant that will produce materials that however valuable for peace are also readily suitable for a bomb.

Well, how much security, how much peace of mind, would anyone get out of that? Mighty little. For as is well known, the atomic bomb is a surprise weapon and a relatively cheap one. We are reliably advised that several hundred of these bombs used on a nation's cities would finish off any industrial nation of the world. The bomb was originally developed in secret, and, assuming closed borders, could probably be developed by a nation in secret again. We concluded, unanimously, that if nations were rivals in the development of atomic energy materials that could be diverted rather simply from open, peaceful uses to secret, warlike purposes, an agreement by each nation to outlaw the bomb might even be worse than nothing at all. For it would create suspicion and fear as to what the other fellow is doing behind closed factory doors and in hidden and secret laboratories and bomb plants; and fear and suspicion breed wars.

Then we said to ourselves: Suppose the world agreed to join together to crack down on anyone who violated the international agreement, who despite the agreement went ahead and made and used atomic bombs. We rejected that plan, too, for we could find precious little security in a plan to punish a nation *after* it had dropped hundreds of bombs and killed millions of human beings. As for such punishment as a deterrent, the fact is that there is a premium in atomic warfare in pulling the trigger first, so that your enemy won't be able to retaliate effectively. And there is therefore a great premium on making preparations secretly while your law-abiding and trusting neighbors are depending on international agreements that say on paper that the bomb will not be used. And with that kind of creepy atmosphere to live in, in time everyone would suspect everyone else, no one would have any sense of security, and everybody would be making atomic bombs in secret. The world would not be a very happy place.

INSPECTION AS A SAFEGUARD

But then this was suggested: Why couldn't we have an international inspection agency, to snoop into every factory and plant to see whether nations are fulfilling their agreement not to put fissionable material into bombs? Again we looked at the facts, explored them painstakingly, and the facts forced us to conclude that a plan of inspection as a sole safeguard was quite unworkable. One of those facts was simply this: If an international inspector is to provide security against secret invasions, that inspector must know at least as much about atomic energy as the people he's supposed to watch. And there's the rub. An inspector—a high grade policeman— simply wouldn't know enough to detect a skillful evasion. This is a new field; new developments, as you well know, are coming along, stepping on each other's heels. Because of new knowledge the plants that are built next year will almost certainly not be like the ones we have in the Tennessee Valley at Oak Ridge or at Hanford in Washington state; and if a nation wanted to mislead the world, it could design them quite differently, so they might look rather innocent to an inspector. In a race between a nation that has scientists trying to design new kinds of plants so the international inspector wouldn't recognize them, and an army of inspectors looking for the only kind of plants they know about, which are yesterday's plants— in that kind of race, the inspectors probably wouldn't have much chance. The only people who would be genuinely qualified to protect the world against secret shenanigans would be those who know how to design and operate atomic energy plants—the chemists, the physicists, and the engineers. And that is one weighty reason we urged that world security be protected by a development and operating agency manned by just such technical people, acting not for rival nations, racing each other, but for all nations and all peoples.

Well, this is the way we took one set of facts after another and explored this problem, and the things we rejected as not workable furnished a clue as to what we thought would be workable. It was these objectives, and this same method of analyzing the facts, that led the President, and Mr. Baruch and his associates, to present the American proposal for such an Atomic Development Authority. There is a point in remembering that it was Woodrow Wilson who dubbed Mr. Baruch with the nickname "Dr. Facts."

The proposed Atomic Development Authority would not be a mere international detective force, but, as its proposed name implies, a development agency engaged in operations and extensive research. To provide security the ADA must *know*. Henry DeWolf Smyth has said that the men on the Atomic Development Authority might well become the elite of the scientific world. "Able men," he continued, "devoted to the traditional ideas of science, and men eager to contribute to the increase and dissemination of knowledge regardless of national boundaries, will be glad to join this group." And this high caliber of talent would be essential to world security, so that the agency entrusted with control would know as much as anyone in the world about new possibilities.

There is an even more important though perhaps less obvious reason why the agency should be more than a policing force. "To be genuinely effective for security," my associates and I stated in our report, "the plan must be one that is not wholly negative, suppressive, and police-like. . . . [It] must be one that will tend to develop the beneficial possibilities of atomic energy and encourage the growth of fundamental knowledge, stirring the constructive and imaginative impulses of men rather than merely concentrating on the defensive and negative. It should, in short, be a plan that looks to the promise of man's future well-being as well as to his security."

Some people have objected to our proposal because it doesn't guarantee an end to war. That's not valid criticism, for what we set out to do was to find a way to prevent the surprise use of atomic weapons. Everyone would be profoundly happy if someone would come up with a workable scheme that would eliminate all war with one stroke; but I don't anticipate that that's the way it will happen. That's the goal; it must be, of course; but to get to that goal we've got a long way to go and much to learn. Perhaps the best way to get there is to start with the most urgent problem, and that would seem to be atomic weapons. If we can't take this first step, what chance is there for the full-blown world government some people believe is essential, or an end to all war? My own guess is, not much. But if in this one field of atomic energy the people of the world can develop a system of world law and a world operating and control agency, by following the facts and disregarding political dogma, then perhaps all of us can tackle the next worst problem in the same way, and get that behind us, and on to the next, and in this way begin to work together, begin to figure out our problems on the basis of facts, in something of the spirit that scientists go about their problems, and really look forward to a generation of great progress and security, of real development, not only physically, but morally and spiritually.

PROBLEMS

1. What primary difference, according to Lilienthal, exists between what he considers the "scientific" and the "political" methods of answering problems?
2. What specific facts destroyed each of the hypotheses considered by the Board of Consultants—"eliminating the bomb by international agreement" and "an international inspection agency"?

3. How does Lilienthal's outline of the Consultants' elimination of proposals that did not fit the facts illustrate Chase's suggestion of the value of *negative* findings to the scientific thinker?

4. What aspect of the scientific attitude, as outlined by Chase, is illustrated by Lilienthal's answer to those who object to the Consultants' plan as not guaranteeing "an end to war"? How does this relate to Overstreet's distinction between "monism" and "pluralism"?

What do you think would be the answer of such a man as Lilienthal to the objection to the United Nations that "it is designed, at present, more to get quarrels under control than to keep them from starting"? to the objection to development of backward areas that "it probably will not guarantee the physical well-being of everybody in those parts of the world"? to the statement that "although the UN medical agencies have been distributing medical services in many places, there are still terrible epidemics in many countries"? to the comment about a slum-area boys' club that "it does not do away with all the conditions that breed crime"?

Arthur S. Eddington

Eddington gently pours the cold water of facts on the very common belief that life of a highly developed sort must exist on other planets.

A famous British scientist, Eddington (1882-1944) conducted researches into the motions of stars and contributed to the theory of relativity; he also interpreted for the general public recent developments in science, especially in the field of relativity, in such books as *The Nature of the Physical World* and *The Expanding Universe.*

LIFE ON OTHER WORLDS *

I will here put together the present astronomical evidence as to the habitability of other worlds. The popular idea that an answer to this question is one of the main aims of the study of celestial objects is rather disconcerting to the astronomer. Anything that he has to contribute is of the nature of fragmentary hints

---

* Arthur S. Eddington, *The Nature of the Physical World,* Cambridge University Press, New York, 1928.

picked up in the course of investigations with more practicable and commonplace purposes. Nevertheless, the mind is irresistibly drawn to play with the thought that somewhere in the universe there may be other beings "a little lower than the angels" whom Man may regard as his equals—or perhaps his superiors.

It is idle to guess the forms that life might take in conditions differing from those of our planet. If I have rightly understood the view of palaeontologists, mammalian life is the third terrestrial dynasty—Nature's third attempt to evolve an order of life sufficiently flexible to changing conditions and fitted to dominate the earth. Minor details in the balance of circumstances must greatly affect the possibility of life and the type of organism destined to prevail. Some critical branch-point in the course of evolution must be negotiated before life can rise to the level of consciousness. All this is remote from the astronomer's line of study. To avoid endless conjecture I shall assume that the required conditions of habitability are not unlike those on the earth, and that if such conditions obtain life will automatically make its appearance.

We survey first the planets of the solar system; of these only Venus and Mars seem at all eligible. Venus, so far as we know, would be well adapted for life similar to ours. It is about the same size as the earth, nearer the sun but probably not warmer, and it possesses an atmosphere of satisfactory density. Spectroscopic observation has unexpectedly failed to give any indication of oxygen in the upper atmosphere and thus suggests a doubt as to whether free oxygen exists on the planet; but at present we hesitate to draw so definite an inference. If transplanted to Venus we might perhaps continue to live without much derangement of habit—except that I personally would have to find a new profession, since Venus is not a good place for astronomers. It is completely covered with cloud or mist. For this reason no definite surface markings can be made out, and it is still uncertain how fast it rotates on its axis and in which direction the axis lies. One curious theory may be mentioned though it should perhaps not be taken too seriously. It is thought by some that the great cavity occupied by the Pacific Ocean is a scar left by the moon when it was first disrupted from the earth. Evidently this cavity fulfils an important function in draining away superfluous water, and if it were filled up practically all the continental area would be submerged. Thus indirectly the existence of dry land is bound up with the existence of the moon. But Venus has no moon, and since it seems to be similar to the earth in other respects, it may perhaps be inferred that it is a world which is all ocean—where fishes are supreme. . . .

Mars is the only planet whose solid surface can be seen and studied; and it tempts us to consider the possibility of life in more detail. Its smaller size leads to considerably different conditions; but the two essentials, air and water, are both present though scanty. The Martian atmosphere is thinner than our own, but it is perhaps adequate. It has been proved to contain oxygen. There is no ocean; the surface markings represent, not sea and land, but red desert and darker ground which is perhaps moist and fertile.

A conspicuous feature is the white cap covering the pole which is clearly a deposit of snow; it must be quite shallow since it melts away completely in the summer. Photographs show from time to time indubitable clouds which blot out temporarily large areas of surface detail; clear weather, however, is more usual. The air, if cloudless, is slightly hazy. W. H. Wright has shown this very convincingly by comparing photographs taken with light of different wave-lengths. Light of short wave-length is much scattered by haze and accordingly the ordinary photographs are disappointingly blurry. Much sharper surface-detail is shown when visual yellow light is employed (a yellow screen being commonly used to adapt visual telescopes for photography); being of longer wave-length the visual rays penetrate the haze more easily. Still clearer detail is obtained by photographing with the long infra-red waves.

Great attention has been paid to the determination of the temperature of the surface of Mars; it is possible to find this by direct measurement of the heat radiated to us from different parts of the surface. The results, though in many respects informative, are scarcely accurate and accordant enough to give a definite idea of the climatology. Naturally the temperature varies a great deal between day and night and in different latitudes; but on the average the conditions are decidedly chilly. Even at the equator the temperature falls below freezing point at sunset. If we accepted the present determinations as definitive we should have some doubt as to whether life could endure the conditions.

In one of Huxley's essays there occurs the passage: "Until human life is longer and the duties of the present press less heavily I do not think that wise men will occupy themselves with Jovian or Martian natural history." Today it would seem that Martian natural history is not altogether beyond the limits of serious science. At least the surface of Mars shows a seasonal change such as we might well imagine the forest-clad earth would show to an outside looker. This seasonal change of appearance is very conspicuous to the attentive observer. As the spring in one hemisphere advances (I mean, of course, the Martian spring), the darker areas, which are at first few and faint, extend and deepen in contrast. The same regions darken year after year at nearly the same date in the Martian calendar. It may be that there is an inorganic explanation; the spring rains moisten the surface and change its colour. But it is perhaps unlikely that there is enough rain to bring about this change as a direct effect. It is easier to believe that we are witnessing the annual awakening of vegetation so familiar on our own planet.

The existence of oxygen in the Martian atmosphere supplies another argument in support of the existence of vegetable life. Oxygen combines freely with many elements, and the rocks in the earth's crust are thirsty for oxygen. They would in course of time bring about its complete disappearance from the air, were it not that the vegetation extracts it from the soil and sets it free again. If oxygen in the terrestrial atmosphere is maintained in this way, it would seem reasonable to assume that vegetable life is required to play the same part on Mars. Taking this in conjunction with the evidence of the seasonal changes of appearance, a rather strong case for the existence of vegetation seems to have been made out.

If vegetable life must be admitted, can we exclude animal life? I have come to the end of the astronomical data and can take no responsibility for anything further that you may infer. It is true that the late Prof. Lowell argued that certain more or less straight markings on the planet represent an artificial irrigation system and are the signs of an advanced civilization; but this theory has not, I think, won much support. In justice to the author of this speculation it should be said that his own work and that of his observatory have made a magnificent contribution to our knowledge of Mars; but few would follow him all the way on the more picturesque side of his conclusions. Finally we may stress one point. Mars has every appearance of being a planet long past its prime; and it is in any case improbable that two planets differing so much as Mars and the Earth would be in the zenith of biological development contemporaneously.

If the planets of the solar system should fail us, there remain some thousands of millions of stars which we have been accustomed to regard as suns ruling attendant systems of planets. It has seemed a presumption, bordering almost on impiety, to deny to them life of the same order of creation as ourselves. It would indeed be rash to assume that nowhere else in the universe has Nature repeated the strange experiment which she has performed on the earth. But there are considerations which must hold us back from populating the universe too liberally.

On examining the stars with a telescope we are surprised to find how many of those which appear single points to the eye are actually two stars close together. When the telescope fails to separate them the spectroscope often reveals two stars in orbital revolution round each other. At least one star in three is double—a pair of self-luminous globes both comparable in dimensions with the sun. The single supreme sun is accordingly not the only product of evolution; not much less frequently the development has taken another turn and resulted in two suns closely associated. We may probably rule out the possibility of planets in double stars. Not only is there a difficulty in ascribing to them permanent orbits under the more complicated field of gravitation, but a cause for the formation of planets seems to be lacking. The star has satisfied its impulse to fission in another manner; it has divided into two nearly equal portions instead of throwing off a succession of tiny fragments.

The most obvious cause of division is excessive rotation. As the gaseous globe contracts it spins fast and faster until a time may come when it can no longer hold together, and some kind of relief must be found. According to the nebular hypothesis of Laplace the sun gained relief by throwing off successively rings of matter which have formed the planets. But were it not for this one instance of a planetary system which is known to us, we should have concluded from the thousands of double stars in the sky that the common consequence of excessive rotation is to divide the star into two bodies of equal rank.

It might still be held that the ejection of a planetary system and the fission into a double star are alternative solutions of the problem arising from excessive rotation, the star taking one course or the other according to circumstances. We know of myriads of double stars and of only one planetary system; but in any case it is beyond our power to detect other planetary systems if they exist. We can only appeal to the results of theoretical study of rotating masses of gas; the work presents many complications and the results may not be final; but the researches of Sir J. H. Jeans lead to the conclusion that rotational break-up produces a double star and never a system of planets. The solar system is not the typical product of development of a star; it is not even a common variety of development; it is a freak.

By elimination of alternatives it appears that a configuration resembling the solar system would only be formed if at a certain stage of condensation an unusual accident had occurred. According to Jeans the accident was the close approach of another star casually pursuing its way through space. This star must have passed within a distance not far outside the orbit of Neptune; it must not have passed too rapidly, but have slowly overtaken or been overtaken by the sun. By tidal distortion it raised big protuberances on the sun, and caused it to spurt out filaments of matter which have condensed to form the planets. That was more than a thousand million years ago. The intruding star has since gone on its way and mingled with the others; its legacy of a system of planets remains, including a globe habitable by man.

Even in the long life of a star encounters of this kind must be extremely rare. The density of distribution of stars in space has been compared to that of twenty tennis balls roaming the whole interior of the earth. The accident that gave birth to the solar system may be compared to the casual approach of two of these balls within a few yards of one another. The data are too vague to give any definite estimate of the odds against this occurrence, but I should judge that perhaps not one in a hundred millions of stars can have undergone this experience in the right stage and conditions to result in the formation of a system of planets.

However doubtful this conclusion as to the rarity of solar systems may be, it is a useful corrective to the view too facilely adopted which looks upon every star as a likely minister to life. We know the prodigality of Nature. How many acorns are scattered for one that grows to an oak? And need she be more careful of her stars than of her acorns? If indeed she has no grander aim than to provide a home for her greatest experiment, Man, it would be just like her methods to scatter a million stars whereof one might haply achieve her purpose. . . .

. . . I do not think that the whole purpose of the Creation has been staked on the one planet where we live; and in the long run we cannot deem ourselves the only race that has been or will be gifted with the mystery of consciousness. But I feel inclined to claim that *at the present time* our race is supreme; and not one of the profusion of stars in their myriad clusters looks down on scenes comparable to those which are passing beneath the rays of the sun.

PROBLEMS

1. In what ways, aside from his conclusions, does Eddington's consideration of the problem of life on other worlds differ from the usual handling of the same question in popular magazines and in the magazine section of your Sunday newspaper? In answering this question consider the sources, kinds, and variety of evidence, the sureness or tentativeness of tone, and the purposes of the articles.
2. Note the frequency of such phrases as "fragmentary hints," "more practicable and commonplace purposes," "suggests a doubt," "at present we hesitate to draw so definite an inference," and "it may perhaps be inferred." Do you believe such a way of writing indicates an affectation of modesty, a device to protect Eddington from criticism, or certain characteristics of the scientific mind at work? If the last, which characteristics?
3. What known facts about Mars (climatology, existence of oxygen, and so forth) does Eddington use in considering the possibility of vegetable and animal life on Mars? in doubting its possibility?
4. What characteristic of the scientific method does Eddington reveal in his avoidance of the conclusion (from the formation of our own solar system) that *all* solar systems are formed in that way?

Hadley Cantril

After Eddington's cool reception of the people-on-other-planets view, it may be something of a shock to realize there were in the United States enough persons sufficiently convinced that people did live on other planets to create a real invasion-from-Mars panic in 1938. The immediate cause of the Mars scare was a slick, Halloween Eve broadcast, by Orson Welles' Mercury Theatre of the Air, of a totally imaginary invasion from Mars, the sort of cosmological fantasy that H. G. Wells and many other writers had been producing for years.

The present article is a social scientist's investigation into the thinking of those individuals who decided that interplanetary warfare had begun. That actual, man-made catastrophes of the 1940's—mass bombings, race exterminations, rockets, atomic bombs, and the prospect of the hydrogen bomb—have not turned men from the fascinating notion of superhuman horrors is indicated by a recent Mars-invasion scare in Peru, the cycle of "flying saucer" alarms, and the "discovery" of old and new monsters in oceans and lakes.

THE INVASION FROM MARS *

On the evening of October 30, 1938, thousands of Americans became panic-stricken by a broadcast purported to describe an invasion of Martians which threatened our whole civilization. Probably never before have so many people in all walks of life and in all parts of the country become so suddenly and so intensely disturbed as they did on this night.

Such rare occurrences provide opportunities for the social scientist to study mass behavior. They must be exploited when they come. Although the social scientist unfortunately cannot usually predict such situations and have his tools of investigation ready to analyze the phenomenon while it is still on the wing, he can begin his work before the effects of the crisis are over and memories are blurred. The situation created by the broadcast was one which shows us how the common man reacts in a time of stress and strain. It gives us insights into his intelligence, his anxieties, and his needs, which we could never get by tests or strictly experimental studies. The panic situation we have investigated had all the flavor of everyday life and, at the same time, provided a semi-experimental condition for reseach. In spite of the unique conditions giving rise to this

* Hadley Cantril, "The Invasion from Mars," from *Readings in Social Psychology* by Newcomb and Hartley. Copyright, 1947, by Henry Holt and Company, Inc.

particular panic, the writer has attempted to indicate throughout the study the pattern of the circumstances which, from a psychological point of view, might make this the prototype of any panic.

The fact that this panic was created as a result of a radio broadcast is today no mere circumstance. The importance of radio's role in current national and international affairs is too well known to be recounted here. By its very nature radio is the medium *par excellence* for informing all segments of a population of current happenings, for arousing in them a common sense of fear or joy, and for exciting them to similar reactions directed toward a single objective.

Because the social phenomenon in question was so complex, several methods were employed to seek out different answers and to compare results obtained by one method with those obtained by another. Much of our information was derived from detailed interviews of 135 persons. Over 100 of these persons were selected because they were known to have been upset by the broadcast.

Long before the broadcast had ended, people all over the United States were praying, crying, fleeing frantically to escape death from the Martians. Some ran to rescue loved ones. Others telephoned farewells or warnings, hurried to inform neighbors, sought information from newspapers or radio stations, summoned ambulances and police cars. At least six million people heard the broadcast. At least a million of them were frightened or disturbed.

For weeks after the broadcast, newspapers carried human-interest stories relating the shock and terror of local citizens. Men and women throughout the country could have described their feelings and reactions on that fateful evening. Our own interviewers and correspondents gathered hundreds of accounts. A few of these selected almost at random will give us a glimpse of the excitement. Let the people speak for themselves.

"I knew it was something terrible and I was frightened," said Mrs. Ferguson, a northern New Jersey housewife, to the inquiring interviewer. "But I didn't know just what it was. I couldn't make myself believe it was the end of the world. I've always heard that when the world would come to an end, it would come so fast nobody would know—so why should God get in touch with this announcer? When they told us what road to take and get up over the hills and the children began to cry, the family decided to go out.

We took blankets and my granddaughter wanted to take the cat and the canary. We were outside the garage when the neighbor's boy came back and told us it was a play."

From a small midwestern town came Joseph Hendley's report. "That Hallowe'en Boo sure had our family on its knees before the program was half over. God knows how we prayed to Him last Sunday. It was a lesson in more than one thing to us. My mother went out and looked for Mars. Dad was hard to convince or skeptical or sumpin', but he even got to believing it. Brother Joe, as usual, got more excited than he could show. Brother George wasn't home. Aunt Grace, a good Catholic, began to pray with Uncle Henry. Lily got sick to her stomach. I don't know what I did exactly but I know I prayed harder and more earnestly than ever before. Just as soon as we were convinced that this thing was real, how pretty all things on earth seemed; how soon we put our trust in God."

Archie Burbank, a filling-station operator in Newark, described his reactions. "My girl friend and I stayed in the car for awhile, just driving around. Then we followed the lead of a friend. All of us ran into a grocery store and asked the man if we could go into his cellar. He said, 'What's the matter? Are you trying to ruin my business?' So he chased us out. A crowd collected. We rushed to an apartment house and asked the man in the apartment to let us in his cellar. He said, 'I don't have any cellar! Get away!' Then people started to rush out of the apartment house all undressed. We got into the car and listened some more. Suddenly, the announcer was gassed, the station went dead so we tried another station but nothing would come on. Then we went to a gas station and filled up our tank in preparation for just riding as far as we could. The gas station man didn't know anything about it. Then one friend, male, decided he would call up the *Newark Evening News*. He found out it was a play. We listened to the rest of the play and then went dancing."

Mrs. Joslin, who lives in a poor section of a large eastern city and whose husband is a day laborer, said, "I was terribly frightened. I wanted to pack and take my child in my arms, gather up my friends, and get in the car and just go north as far as we could. But what I did was just set by one window, prayin', listenin', and scared stiff and my husband by the other snifflin' and lookin' out to see if people were runnin'. Then when the announcer said 'evacuate the city,' I ran and called my boarder and started with my child to rush down the stairs, not waitin' to ketch my hat or anything. When I got to the foot of the stairs, I just couldn't get out, I don't know why. Meantime my husband he tried other stations and found them still runnin'. He couldn't smell any gas or see people runnin', so he called me back and told me it was just a play. So I set down, still ready to go at any minute till I heard Orson Welles say, 'Folks, I hope we ain't alarmed you. This is just a play!' Then, I just set!"

If we are to explain the reaction, then, we must answer two basic questions: Why did this broadcast frighten some people when other fantastic broadcasts do not? And why did this broadcast frighten some people but not others? An answer to the first question must be sought in the characteristics of this particular program which aroused false standards of judgment in so many listeners.

No one reading the script can deny that the broadcast was so realistic for the first few minutes that it was almost credible to even relatively sophisticated and well-informed listeners. The sheer dramatic excellence of the broadcast must not be overlooked. This unusual realism of the performance may be attributed to the fact that the early parts of the broadcast fell within the existing standards of judgment of the listeners.

A large proportion of listeners, particularly those in the lower income and educational brackets, have grown to rely more on the radio than on the newspapers for their news. Almost all of the listeners, who had been frightened and who were interviewed, mentioned somewhere during the course of their retrospections the confidence they had in radio and their expectation that it would be used for such important announcements. A few of their comments indicate their attitudes:

"We have so much *faith in broadcasting*. In a crisis it has to reach all people. That's what radio is here for."

"The announcer would not say if it was not true. *They always quote if something is a play.*"

As in many situations where events and ideas are so complicated or far removed from one's own immediate everyday experience that only the expert can really understand them, here, too, the layman was forced to rely on the expert for his interpretation.

The logical "expert" in this instance was the astronomer. Those mentioned (all fictitious) were Professor Farrell of the Mount Jennings Observatory of Chicago, Professor Pierson of the Princeton Observatory, Professor Morse of MacMillan University in Toronto, Professor Indellkoffer of the California Astronomical Society and "astronomers and scientific bodies" in England, France, and Germany. Professor Richard Pierson (Orson Welles) was the chief character in the drama.

When the situation called for organized defense and action the expert was once more brought in. General Montgomery Smith, commander of the State Militia at Trenton, Mr. Harry McDonald, vice-president of the Red Cross, Captain Lansing of the Signal Corps, and finally the Secretary of the Interior described the situation, gave orders for evacuation and attack, or urged every man to do his duty.

This dramatic technique had its effect.

"I believed the broadcast *as soon as I heard the professor from Princeton* and the officials in Washington."

"I knew it was an awfully dangerous situation *when all those military men were there and the Secretary of State spoke.*"

The realistic nature of the broadcast was further enhanced by descriptions of particular occurrences that listeners could readily imagine. Liberal use was made of the colloquial expressions to be expected on such an occasion. The gas was "a sort of yellowish-green"; the cop warned, "One side, there. Keep back, I tell you"; a voice shouts, "The darn thing's unscrewing." An example of the specificity of detail is the announcement of Brigadier General Montgomery Smith: "I have been requested by the Governor of New Jersey to place the counties of Mercer and Middlesex as far west as Princeton, and east to Jamesburg, under martial law. No one will be permitted to enter this area except by special pass issued by state or military authorities. Four companies of State Militia are proceeding from Trenton to Grovers Mill and will aid in the evacuation of homes within the range of military operations."

The events reported proceeded from the relatively credible to the highly incredible. The first announcements were more or less believable, although unusual to be sure. First there is an "atmospheric disturbance," then "explosions of incandescent gas." A scientist then reports that his seismograph has registered a shock of earthquake intensity. This is followed by the discovery of a meteorite that has splintered nearby trees in its fall. So far so good.

But as the less credible bits of the story begin to enter, the clever dramatist also indicates that he, too, has difficulty in believing what he sees. When we learn that the object is no meteorite but a metal casing, we are also told that the whole picture is "a strange scene like something out of a modern Arabian Nights," "fantastic," that the "more daring souls are venturing near." Before we are informed that the end of the casing is beginning to unscrew, we experience the announcer's own astonishment: "Ladies and gentlemen, this is terrific!" When the top is off he says, "This is the most terrifying thing I have ever witnessed. . . . This is the most extraordinary experience. I can't find words. . . ."

The bewilderment of the listener is shared by the eye-witness. When the scientist is himself puzzled, the layman recognizes the extraordinary intelligence of the strange creatures. No explanation of the event can be provided. The resignation and hopelessness of the Secretary of the Interior, counseling us to "place our faith in God," provide no effective guide for action.

In spite of the realism of the broadcast, it would seem highly unlikely that any listener would take it seriously had he heard the announcements that were clearly made at the beginning of the hour. He might then have been excited, even frightened. But it would be an excitement based on the dramatic realism of the program. There would not be the intense feeling of personal involvement. He would know that the events were happening "out there" in the studio, not "right here" in his own state or his own county. In one instance a "correct" (esthetically detached or dramatic) standard of judgment would be used by the listener to interpret events, in another instance a "false" (realistic or news) standard of judgment would be employed. Tuning in late was a very essential condition for the arousal of a false standard of judgment. To be sure, many people recognized the broadcast as a play even though they tuned in late. It is important to raise and to answer the question of how anyone who tuned in at the beginning could have mistaken the clearly introduced play for a news broadcast. Analysis of these cases reveals two main reasons why such a misinterpretation arose. In the first place, many people who tuned in to hear a play by the Mercury Theatre thought the regular dramatic program had been interrupted to give special news bulletins. The technique was not a new one after their experience with radio reporting of the war crisis in September 1938. The other major reason for the misunderstanding is the widespread habit of not paying attention to the first announcements of a program. Some people do not listen attentively to their radios until they are aware that something of particular interest is being broadcast.

Tuning in late was very decisive in determining whether or not the listener would follow the program as a play or as a news report. For the story of the Martian invasion was so realistic that misinterpretation was apt to arise without proper warning signals.

In spite of the fact that many persons tuned in late to hear this very realistic broadcast, by no means all of them believed it was news. And not all of those who thought the invasion was upon them behaved the same way in the face of danger. Before we can understand the reasons for the varying behavior, the reactions must be arranged in some significant grouping. Otherwise no fruitful conceptualization is possible.

CLASSIFYING THE LISTENERS

1. Those who checked the internal evidence of the broadcast. The persons in this category were those who did not remain frightened throughout the whole broadcast because they were able to discern that the program was fictitious. Some realized that the reports must be false because they sounded so much like certain fiction literature they were accustomed to.

"At first I was very interested in the fall of the meteor. It isn't often that they find a big one just when it falls. But *when it started to unscrew and monsters came out, I said to myself, 'They've taken one of those Amazing Stories and are acting it out.'* It just couldn't be real. It was just like some of the stories I read in *Amazing Stories* but it was even more exciting."

2. Those who checked the broadcast against other information and learned that it was a play. These listeners tried to orient themselves for the same reasons as those in the first group—they were suspicious of the "news" they were getting. Some simply thought the reports were too fantastic to believe; others detected the incredible speeds revealed; while a few listeners checked the program just because it seemed the reasonable thing to do. Their method of verifying their hunches was to compare the news on the program to some other information.

"I tuned in and heard that a meteor had fallen. Then when they talked about monsters, I thought something was wrong. *So I looked in the newspaper* to see what program was supposed to be on and discovered it was only a play."

3. *Those who tried to check the program against other information but who, for various reasons, continued to believe the broadcast was an authentic news report.* Two characteristic differences separated the people in this group from those who made successful checks. In the first place, it was difficult to determine from the interviews just why these people wanted to check anyway. They did not seem to be seeking evidence to test the authenticity of the reports. They appeared, rather, to be frightened souls trying to find out whether or not they were yet in any personal danger. In the second place, the type of checking behavior they used was singularly ineffective and unreliable. The most frequent method employed by almost two thirds of the group, was to look out the windows or go outdoors. Several of them telephoned their friends or ran to consult their neighbors.

There are several reasons why the checks made by these persons were ineffectual. For some of them, the new information obtained only verified the interpretation which their already fixed standard of judgment provided.

"I looked out of the window and everything looked the same as usual *so I thought it hadn't reached our section yet.*"

"We looked out of the window and Wyoming Avenue was black with cars. *People were rushing away, I figured.*"

"No cars came down my street. *'Traffic is jammed on account of the roads being destroyed,' I thought.*"

4. *Those who made no attempt to check the broadcast or the event.* It is usually more difficult to discover why a person did *not* do something than why he did. Consequently it is more difficult for us to explain why people in this group did not attempt to verify the news or look for signs of the Martians in their vicinity than it was to determine why those who attempted unsuccessful checks displayed their aimless behavior. Over half of the people in this group were so frightened that they either stopped listening, ran

around in a frenzy, or exhibited behavior that can only be described as paralyzed.

Some of them reported that they were so frightened they never thought of checking.

"We were so intent upon listening that we didn't have enough sense to try other hook-ups—*we were just so frightened.*"

Others adopted an attitude of complete resignation. For them any attempt to check up, like any other behavior, appeared senseless.

"I was writing a history theme. The girl from upstairs came and made me go up to her place. Everybody was so excited I felt as if I was going crazy and kept on saying, 'what can we do, *what difference does it make* whether we die sooner or later?' We were holding each other. Everything seemed unimportant in the face of death. I was afraid to die, just kept on listening."

Some felt that in view of the crisis situation, action was demanded. A few prepared immediately for their escape or for death.

"I couldn't stand it so I turned it off. I don't remember when, but everything was coming closer. My husband wanted to put it back on but I told him *we'd better do something instead of just listen, so we started to pack.*"

Some listeners interpreted the situation in such a way that they were not interested in making a check-up. In a few instances the individual tuned in so late that he missed the most incredible parts of the program and was only aware of the fact that some kind of conflict was being waged.

"I was in my drugstore and my brother phoned and said, 'Turn the radio on, a meteor has just fallen.' We did and heard gas was coming up South Street. There were a few customers and *we all began wondering where it could come from.* I was worried about the gas, it was spreading so rapidly but I was puzzled as to what was actually happening, when I heard airplanes I thought another country was attacking us." . . .

PROBLEMS

1. What is the connection between simply not knowing enough facts and the "suggestibility" which leads to a panic reaction? For example, what would be the difference between the reaction of the

man who had designed a theater building to the cry of "Fire!" in that theater and the reaction of a movie patron? between the reaction of a lifeguard to the sight of a small child being tumbled by an ocean wave and the reaction of the child's mother?

2. If we define, rather crudely, two main kinds of thinking as *inductive* (moving from a set of particular observations to a general conclusion) and *deductive* (moving from a general assumption to a particular conclusion), can you classify the kinds of thinking indulged in by the four classes of listeners discussed by Cantril? Don't oversimplify here: some of these people may be thinking both ways.

3. What is the connection between the reliance of some of the listeners on "experts" in this episode and the reliance of the textile mill management on the efficiency engineers in "The First Inquiry"? How sound would the general inference, "You can't trust the experts," be? When do "experts" cease to be expert? Drawing on your own firsthand experience with an "upset" in athletics or politics, write a brief report in which you show how the upset led to the general conclusion, "You can't trust the experts." Then show by a thoughtful analysis why this conclusion might well have been unsound.

4. Re-read the passage describing the behavior of "those who tried to check the program against other information but who, for various reasons, continued to believe the broadcast was an authentic news report." What scientific procedures were they overlooking?

Bergen Evans

In this chapter from his sprightly book of debunking, *The Natural History of Nonsense,* Evans (author of "Skeptic's Corner" in the *American Mercury* and Professor of English at Northwestern University) suggests that the will to believe what we want to, even without facts, is so strong in human thinking that even outstanding scientists may fall victim to their wishes. Elsewhere in his book Evans has fun pointing out the unscientific thinking behind such conclusions as these: snakes have a hypnotic stare, dogs sense "instinctively" the death of a master who may at that moment be far away, female birds are passionately devoted to their own eggs, and hairiness (especially on the chest) is a sure sign of masculine strength and virility. Similar interesting exposés are found in David Jacobson's *The Affairs of Dame Rumor* and Osmond P. Breland's *Animal Facts and Fallacies.*

WOLF! WOLF! *

An interesting footnote to folk zoology is supplied by stories of children being reared by animals, stories that have been repeated among all peoples of all periods. And it is not without significance that this myth has reappeared in our own time and has been given wider credence, under more dignified auspices, than ever before in its long history.

Many legendary heroes were reared by animals. Zeus and Tarzan both had the benefit of such an association, and history is spotted with lesser figures who derive their whole importance from their feral foster mothers. Ireland had a sheep-boy, and at Salzburg there was a swine-girl who ate acorns and sat cross-legged in a sty to the admiration of all beholders. In 1403 a fish-woman with "sea-mosse that did stick about her" was washed through the dykes at Edam and lived for the next seventeen years in Haarlem, where she "learned to spinne and perform other pettie offices of women" though she was never able to master Dutch. She adored the cross and so impressed the local clergy that more than forty of them are said to have testified to her authenticity.

There seems to be something about these unhappy beings, in fact, that leads divines to vouch for them. Thus it is on the authority of Archbishop Matheson of Winnipeg that Ernest Thompson Seton tells the "true story" of little Harry Service's being adopted by a badger. In this instance, it is pleasant to relate, there was a reciprocation of unnatural affection and the badger herself was adopted by Harry's family, though it proved a trial, for an unfortunate rivalry for the boy's love developed between his real and his foster mothers. . . .

But the story of animal adoptions that reduces all the others to insignificance is that of the "wolf-reared waifs of Midnapore," which made its first full-dress appearance in *Harper's Magazine* in January 1941. This was not its first time in print, however. It had been run in the *Westminster Gazette* and had been reprinted in the

* Reprinted from *The Natural History of Nonsense* by Bergen Evans, by permission of Alfred A. Knopf, Inc. Copyright, 1946, by Bergen Evans. In the interest of brevity the editors have reluctantly omitted the frequently witty footnotes with which Mr. Evans salts his text.

New York Times as early as 1926. It had played peek-a-boo in various learned publications for a dozen years, and in 1939 it had filled a spread in the *American Weekly,* illustrated with those vivid sketches by which that lively journal seeks to assist such of its subscribers as find reading difficult. But the sponsorship of *Harper's* and the renown of its new narrator, Dr. Arnold Gesell, Director of Yale's Clinic of Child Development, raised it to a new dignity, while the singular style in which it was presented gave it an added grace and freshness.

Dr. Gesell's narrative can be briefly summarized. In the autumn of 1912, he says, an Indian she-wolf, "her teats gorged, her eyes . . . preternaturally mild" and her whole being "warmed by the chemistry of maternal hormones," adopted a Hindu baby girl. Nourished by "mammalian milk" (which Dr. Gesell asserts is "chemically very like" other milk), the child made "a remarkably effective adaptation to wolf mores." It was not easy: "Furniture there was none"; "Books, rugs, dishes" and "true table manners" were "conspicuously lacking."

But the little girl overcame all obstacles and made "a successful adjustment to the onerous demands of the wolf den." She got on without furniture and books, slept on the floor, ate directly with her mouth, politely overlooked the lack of good manners, and "rubbed her haunches over the ground for cleanliness." She developed "a deep and mysterious sense of community with the pack"—a "palship," Dr. Gesell would call it—scrambled after them on their forays, became adept at shooing buzzards off a dead hog, and added her treble wail to that "weird nocturne" which every night, at ten, one, and three, the wolves sent up to the shivering stars.

Her physical adaptation to what Dr. Gesell calls "wolverine" culture was in some ways more remarkable still. Her spine modified to suit "bi-patellar locomotion," a glow "emanated" from her eyes at night, her canine teeth grew long and pointed, and she ceased to perspire, tending rather "to pant and to extrude her tongue in the sun."

In 1919, "of all unpredictable wonders," the mother wolf adopted another child, also a girl. In 1920 the wolf was killed and the children, now doubly orphaned, were placed in the care of the Reverend J. A. L. Singh, of Midnapore, who discreetly kept their history a secret for six years lest it should "prejudice their chances of marriage." One would have thought that the younger girl's death and the older girl's strange habits would, in themselves, have been sufficient to discourage the most ardent suitor, but the good man's solicitude is none the less touching.

The death of the younger child occurred in 1921, but the older, who had been named Kamala, lived until 1929, slowly readapting herself to human ways. She continued the "traditional wolf howl" at ten, one, and three, but a human note was observed in 1922 when she addressed Mrs. Singh as "Ma." In time she "toileted in the bathroom," to use Dr. Gesell's chaste phrase, though this must have been one of her latest accomplishments, for in 1926 the Reverend Mr. Singh, in a letter to Paul C. Squires, stated that she didn't, and from the general gloom of his statement we are led to suspect that she continued her strange and strenuous abstersions. By 1927 she had "so far transcended wolf ways" as to be regular and devout in church attendance, in which she showed marked superiority to the Sikandra boy, who had interrupted divine service by shouting "Dham, dham!"—a proceeding which Dr. Gesell says indicated "a low idiot plateau of mentality."

By 1927 also "her behavior had become conventional" and she talked "with the full sense of the words used." But this advantage over her biographers was not long maintained, for she was taken ill "and gave up the ghost on the 14th morning at 4 A.M. in the month of November, 1929."

For his detailed account of life in the den, Dr. Gesell confessed that he drew heavily upon "imagination and . . . conjectures." For his knowledge of the later years in the orphanage he acknowledged his indebtedness to a "diary record" kept by the Reverend Mr. Singh and entrusted by him for publication to Professor Zingg who, despite Lukas's defalcation, continued a friend to feral man.

While this more scholarly work was in preparation, however, Dr. Gesell soothed the impatience of the public by publishing *Wolf Child and Human Child*, a fuller account of the episode, embellished with some retouched snapshots, a pen drawing of "the mother wolf," and "a quaint woodcut" of Romulus and Remus which he was forced to use, he admits, for lack of a suitable photograph. This volume added no new information, though a discussion entitled "Can Wolf Ways be Humanized?" was not without interest. *Time,* no shunner of issues, which had taken up the wolf-children with its customary vigor, answered definitely that they could not: "A wolf, or even an ape," the editors stoutly maintained, "reared in the Rev. Singh's orphanage would not attain a human personality."

The facts upon which this ringing enunciation was based were drawn (like Dr. Gesell's narrative, and the *Scientific American's*, *Coronet's*, the *American Weekly's*, and the *Saturday Home Magazine's*—for the story had wide circulation) from the Reverend Mr. Singh's diary and from the interpretation put upon it, in various learned articles, by Professor Zingg. Dr. Gesell was sure that Professor Zingg had "carefully checked the essential authenticity" of the whole business; but "carefully checked," like "wolverine," must have had here some meaning not commonly attributed to it, for Professor Zingg had said, only a few months before, that he had "unfortunately been unable to get in touch with scientists in India to check and recheck the cases." He had, however, he hastened to add, talked with at least two people who had traveled in India, one of whom referred him to the *Illustrated Weekly of India* for an account of another wolf-child "exhibited at the Gwalior Baby Week"; and later, when under fire, he insisted that he had spent three years "checking through voluminous correspondence with numerous persons." This activity apparently left no time for consulting an atlas, for he seems to have been under the impression that Midnapore was among the "the tiger-infested Jungles of north-west India"; whereas Dr. Gesell, who it would seem doubted the "essential authenticity" of at least *that* fact, strung along with Rand McNally and located it seventy miles southwest of Calcutta.

Before the diary could be published, however, skepticism, with "extraordinary license," had reared its ugly head and it was felt necessary to silence "irresponsible" doubters once and for all. To this end the diary, when it finally appeared in 1942, was prefaced with a formidable battery of testimonials. Unfortunately for their effect upon the skeptic, however, none of them happened to be by any of that "good number of men . . . of a sportive nature" in whose company the Reverend Mr. Singh went to preach the gospel and professed to have first seen the children living as wolves among wolves. Professor Zingg says boldly that five such persons "are on record," but he fails to make it clear that the record is the Reverend

Mr. Singh's and no one else's, that it consists entirely of the latter's say-so. That at least one of the five could not have been included among the "numerous persons" addicted to "voluminous correspondence" is regrettable.

In their place, however, Professor Zingg offered five character witnesses for the Reverend Mr. Singh—three professors, a judge, and a bishop.

Of these the professors did not profess to have seen either the Reverend Mr. Singh or his wolf-children, so that the only characters illuminated by their testimony were their own. The judge, a resident of Midnapore, testified that he believed the story and that he had actually "spoken to several people who saw the elder of the two girls" while she was living at the orphanage. The brunt of affirmation was thus thrown upon the bishop, the Right Reverend H. Pakenham-Walsh, who definitely stated that he saw the elder of the two girls four years after her rescue. He does not claim to have been personally acquainted with the mother wolf, yet he is able to assure us that she was "well pleased with her experiment." From his examination of the child he concluded that wolves have "no sense of humor" and "no interest except in raw meat." He was happy, though, to be able to announce that the wolf-parents had not taught their charges "anything bad," a fact that he felt has "a very pertinent bearing on the consideration of what we mean by 'Original Sin.'"

Fascinating though such reflections are, however, the severe logician must dismiss them as irrelevant. Professor Zingg's correspondents, Professor Gesell's prose, the judge's affidavit, the bishop's meditations, and the attending physician's uroscopy of the dying Kamala—all have an interest, even a charm, of their own; but they add nothing whatever to prove that the children were adopted and reared by wolves.

For this our sole evidence is that "diary of observation" which we are innocently told in a foreword "was nearing completion" in 1933, though the last of the children had died in 1929; and this diary, for all the eager promises of "internal evidence," fails to carry conviction. Though it professes to be a day-by-day record of the discovery of the children among the wolves and their subsequent behavior at the orphanage, it is actually a meager collection of entries, few and irregular, not arranged chronologically, and interspersed with reflections concerning the "divine" nature of the event that are, to say the least, unscientific. And the "proof" is further vitiated by the fact that the Reverend Mr. Singh had been convinced that the children were wolf-children even before he unearthed them.

That he reared a strange child in his orphanage is as incontestable as that he was probably the worst photographer that ever lived. That he found the child in the woods in the vicinity of wolves is at least possible, though that great scientific authority, the *Illustrated Weekly of India*, says that there are no wolves in this particular region. Furthermore, there are discrepancies in his earlier and later accounts of the findings, and his failure to secure testimonials from those who he says were with him at the time, while going to such trouble to get testimonials from others, adds to the growing doubt.

Of course even if he had found the children, exactly as he said he did, living in an ant-mound from which wolves had been seen to run, it would not have been positive proof that they had been reared by those or any other wolves. They may have fled into the den in fear. Or they may even have lived there independently. It would have been a strange situation, but nowhere nearly so strange as the one alleged.

That they curled up in a ball—which for some reason is thought to be irrefutable proof of their previous lupinity—merely proves that their backbones were flexible. It is not an uncommon condition in children and may be observed—as Dr. Gesell ought to know—in scores of nurseries that have known no other wolf than Red Riding Hood's.

But the most damning point of all, the thing that makes the whole story untenable, is the effort—which occupies the major portion of every version—to show that the children must have been reared by wolves because they later *behaved* like wolves. But the wolves they behaved like were not ordinary, four-footed wolves, or even a particular species of ordinary wolves, *Canis pallipes* (for Dr. Gesell is very learned on this detail), but were genuine funny-paper wolves, *Lupus vulgus fantasticus,* running in packs, howling by the clock, and emitting a "weird light" from their eyes.

Such is the basis for what one of the foremost publishers of the day regards as an "absorbing and invaluable human study" and which "testifies anew" (in the opinion of one of the highest-paid

savants of Yale University) "to the stamina of the human spirit."
Another artless pundit, crying that the story served admirably "to
introduce us to some of the basic matters with which sociology
deals"—as no doubt it does—proceeded in haste to revise his textbook, building the whole fabric of his new thought upon these
shifty sands. Others followed suit, until today the waifs, like God,
would have to be invented if they did not exist; they serve so many
purposes. Half a dozen college textbooks have been rewritten
to include them as "authenticated" facts. Two complete volumes
have been written about them. And practically every leading
journal and news organ has had an article on them in which the
veracity of the narrative was never questioned.

Sometimes one wonders why any self-respecting wolf would
want to adopt a human being.

PROBLEMS

1. Can incomplete collections of possibly irrelevant facts be as dangerous to clear thinking as having no facts at all? As Evans wryly suggests, the Reverend Singh, Professor Zingg, and Dr. Gesell had
   some facts, but how did their disregarding the *limited significance*
   of those facts make their inductive reasoning faulty? (Consider the
   actual number of sources, the first- or secondhandedness of the
   accounts, the reliability of the observers, the distinction between
   fact and opinion.) Also, what errors did they commit in drawing
   inferences from the facts?
2. Can you see how persons who criticize the scientific method of
   thinking as "just grubbing with facts" and people who like it because
   "it's pure facts" are misunderstanding the position of facts in scientific thinking? Are the man who scorns the findings of all fact-
   gatherers (economists, social investigators, "education testers," and
   so forth) and the man who has profound faith in their findings
   (simply because they involve "lots of figures") thus falling into the
   same error?

GENERAL PROBLEMS: *Reasoning Inductively*

1. An essential part of the scientific method of thinking (induction) is the posing of the problem to be solved. One method of putting the problem into sharp focus is to raise all the relevant questions which one attempting to solve this problem must face.

   Below are listed five practical problems from everyday life. Select *one*. Then write out all the relevant questions you would have to ask and answer in order to have a reasonable chance to solve the problem.

   Suggested procedure: First, make a list of *all* the questions that seem to you to have any bearing on the problem. (This should be a very full list containing a great many questions.) Second, edit this list, eliminating duplications, weeding out irrelevant and trivial questions. Third, arrange the remaining questions in some logical pattern. You might discover, for example, that you have 30 questions that fall into five main lines of inquiry of four to six questions each. Finally, arrange these main lines of inquiry into paragraph-clusters of questions. Your final paper, therefore, might well appear as five paragraphs—each paragraph a cluster of related questions.

   Note: You are not to attempt answers to these questions. Merely raise them.

   a. You are trying to determine the chances of establishing a successful amateur theatrical society in a semi-rural community of 10,000 people where such an experiment has never been tried before.

   b. As an officer of your high school student body, you have been asked by the principal to assist him in discovering the reasons for an epidemic of petty thefts in your school, the character of whose student body has recently been altered by the enrollment of a large number of migrant workers' children.

   c. Although you are about to begin your junior year in college and have successfully completed the first two years of work in your major, chemistry, you have been so impressed by a sociology course you took last year that you are seriously considering changing your major to Social Studies. We will assume that the transfer can be made without loss of credits, but only if it is made at this time.

   d. In an idle moment you boasted to your roommates that "any intelligent person could win one of those slogan contests that food companies are always running." Your friends have goaded you into proving your statement and have even given you attractive odds of 10 to 1 in a friendly wager. The agreement is that you are to enter a contest sponsored by a cooky company for the best 25-word statement as to "Why I Prefer X Cookies to All Others." It is further agreed that if you win any one of the 50 prizes offered, you will win the wager. How would you go about improving your chances of winning?

e. You own a small neighborhood grocery store. During the past two months your sales have been showing a definite decline. How would you set about determining the cause (or causes) of that decline?

2. The following problems are of a practical kind, but somewhat more complex than those in group 1. Your written answers to these might need to be even more detailed.

a. You are looking for your first teaching job, but until now, mid-July, have failed to find one. Suddenly you have two offers at once. There is little choice between them as to salary. Both schools are situated in towns which are just points on the map to you.

In choosing between the two teaching posts, what specific questions would you consider, and how would you go about obtaining the necessary information on each significant question?

b. You live in a thriving tourist town close to a seaport. Rats from ships that dock at this seaport have come ashore in your area. Carriers of bubonic plague, they have infected the ground squirrels of the region. The combination of infected rats and squirrels has resulted in the spread of the disease to human beings, with ten verified cases, including two fatalities, having been reported by your city's health officers.

Some townspeople have determined that an active campaign must be waged against this menace, a campaign involving, necessarily, widespread publicity. Some other townspeople have determined to hush up the matter.

You are an influential member of the community and your advice will carry weight. You are also a hotelkeeper, dependent for much of your annual income on the summer tourist trade. What must you consider in arriving at your decision?

c. You are an influential citizen of a city situated in an arid area where water supply is a critical problem. The War Assets Administration is about to put up for sale a large dam built by army engineers during the war to service a nearby military camp. The issue before the townspeople is whether they should throw their support to those who urge that the county purchase and operate the dam or to those who feel that the U. S. Bureau of Reclamation is the only agency equipped to handle the problem.

As a rational person you are attempting to discount all emotional arguments turning on such slogans as "home control" on the one hand, and "one-horse methods" on the other. Moreover, you have no personal or political ax to grind. You are interested solely in seeing that the dam is soundly financed and efficiently operated for the long-time benefit of the citizens of your town. What factors should you take into account in arriving at your decision? (Note: you are not asked to indicate what your decision is; instead, you are to focus on the *means* employed to reach a decision.)

d. The parents of a child come to the conclusion that "the X—— school is spending too much time on 'monkey-business' and not enough time on having the kids learn worth-while things."

The parents have based their conclusion on the following evidence:

(1) Mary sings children's game-songs she has learned in her classes.

(2) Mary talks more about the music and games and the various other activities that she apparently regards as games than she talks about assignments the parents can recognize as "regular class assignments." They have, for example, found that one day the arithmetic lesson consisted of "playing store"—"buying and selling" groceries and keeping simple accounts. The parents hear from Mary about "explorations" (e.g., trips to the county court house, a locomotive roundhouse, a ranch), movies, occasional plays. She brings home examples of her finger-painting.

(3) Mary's spelling is considerably below the standard the parents remember being held to at her age. It is also poorer than the spelling of the neighbor's children, who are about her age.

(4) A radio commentator, who talks about a variety of fields in the news (economics, politics, education, military strategy, and so forth) and to whose broadcasts the parents regularly listen, tells his radio audience that "progressive education" is "ruining the schools" by doing away with the emphasis on "mental disciplines."

Now, in what ways is their conclusion, no matter whether it be right or wrong for other reasons, not justified by the evidence which the parents now possess?

What questions still need to be asked and answered?

3. Here are two series of remarks of a type frequently heard during the past decade. Choose *one* for analysis.

a. "Look here! I ought to know what I'm talking about when I say those Arabs have no sense of morals. I was a whole year with the

Army over there in North Africa during the war, and we were always being robbed of our supplies by those Arabs. And when we went to their bazaars to look for stuff to send home to the girl friend—why, they'd ask us twenty times more than what the junk was really worth. And are they *dirty!*"

(1) Indicate all weaknesses you find in this generalization.

(2) What indications of prejudiced thinking (rather than observation and inductive reasoning) are apparent in the statement? (The man's believing that Arabs are immoral is not *in itself* a sign of prejudice. What characteristics of his statement suggest that he *came* to his conclusions by way of prejudice rather than by observation and objective analysis?)

b. "I had heard a lot about 'San Francisco hospitality'—but I had an overdose of it when I was in the Navy during the war and had shore leave there a couple of times. Every time I put my foot on its beautiful asphalt I lost my shirt—paid sky-high prices for everything I bought along Market Street, had to fork over a king's ransom for a meal, got royally robbed in night clubs, found the allegedly smiling cops not so smiling. 'San Francisco hospitality'? In the vernacular, 'There ain't no such animal.' "

(1) In what specific ways is the ex-sailor's statement a weak generalization?

Reasoning Deductively

Attention: students of political science

Do you conclude that because some powerful lobbies have influenced American legislators to pass measures detrimental to the welfare of a majority of people that lobbying should be prohibited by law?

Attention: students of journalism

Do you conclude that because propaganda has been one of the most effective weapons of totalitarian states it has no proper place in a democratic society?

Attention: students of agriculture

Do you conclude that courses dealing with soils, farm machinery, animal husbandry, feeds and feeding, and other technical matters are, *by their very nature,* more "practical" than courses in history, language, philosophy?

Attention: students of engineering

Do you conclude that in a technological society the solution to our difficulties is "more engineers in government"?

Attention: students of religion and ethics

Do you conclude that all books which make free use of certain four-letter words considered lewd in polite society should be barred from distribution through the mails as are certain kinds of pornography?

Attention: students of statistics

Do you conclude from the fact that the gross income of people in the United States is the greatest in the world that Americans enjoy the world's highest living standards?

Attention: students of psychology

Do you conclude because psychiatrists are in general agreement about the large percentage of people today who exhibit symptoms of neurosis that people are growing increasingly neurotic in our modern, high-speed, high-tension society?

Attention: students of education

Do you conclude because of the enormous influence of the movies, radio, television, magazines, and newspapers on the behavior of people in America today that American cultural values are being steadily debased and vulgarized?

If, when not put on your guard, you draw any or all of these conclusions, you are eminently eligible for a study of your own deductive reasoning processes. Not that a study of deduction is a guaranteed cure-all for crooked thinking. Far from it. In fact, we believe that the importance of a study of deductive logic has frequently been exaggerated out of all proportion to its usefulness as an instrument of straight thinking. Deduction, with its syllogisms, its fallacies, its appealing formal pattern, can became a gadget, used primarily to show off the "intelligence" of its proprietor. Used more wisely, however, it can be *one*, somewhat *limited*, means of spotting flaws in our own thinking and writing and in the thinking and writing of those who consciously, or unconsciously, influence our behavior.

The first selection, by Buckle, serves as a useful bridge between induction and deduction, revealing briefly the similarities and differences between the two. The second selection, by Marks, acquaints the student with as much of the paraphernalia of deductive logic as he is apt to need in order to apply its principles to his everyday thinking. Marks, it seems to us, shows considerable restraint in knowing where to stop. Koestler provides some sprightly examples of all the deductive fallacies explained by Marks, in a political context that may annoy some kinds of liberals and cause some kinds of conservatives to gloat. Such liberals and conservatives will be missing the point and will find themselves in the somewhat ridiculous position of making errors in deduction in the very process of studying it. The selection by Reves is at once a criticism of one set of deductions, which Reves feels are no longer useful, and the advocacy of a new set of deductions which, he argues, should supplant them. The section is rounded off by briefer examples of faulty deduction—some rollicking, some rather grim—provided by the editors of *The Nation*.

Henry Thomas Buckle

In this brief passage the nineteenth-century Bristish historian
Buckle draws a rough distinction between the inductive and deductive methods of thinking. Perhaps this distinction is too
rough to provide full, practical understanding, but it serves as a
good general introduction to the method of deduction, which
is developed in greater detail and with more accuracy in the
following selections. The point made by Buckle can serve as a
safeguard against the tendency to learn about one thing and
then about another and then about a third, without analyzing
similarities and differences—that is, how the several things fit
into the whole picture.

Buckle (1821-1862), in his *History of Civilization in England,*
departed from the methods of many historians of his day by
investigating the physical conditions (soil, climate, and so forth)
of a country and their relation to its history.

TWO PATHS TO AN IDEA *

The scientific inquirer, properly so called, that is, he whose
object is merely truth, has only two ways of attaining his result.
He may proceed from the external world to the internal; or he
may begin with the internal and proceed to the external. In the
former case he studies the facts presented to his senses, in order
to arrive at a true idea of them; in the latter case he studies the
ideas already in his mind, in order to explain the facts of which
his senses are cognizant. If he begin with the facts his method is inductive; if he begin with the ideas it is deductive. The inductive
philosopher collects phenomena either by observation or by experiment, and from them rises to the general principle or law which explains and covers them. The deductive philosopher draws the principle from ideas already existing in his mind, and explains the
phenomena by descending on them, instead of rising from them.
Several eminent thinkers have asserted that every idea is the result of induction, and that the axioms of geometry, for instance,

* From Henry Thomas Buckle, *The Influence of Women.*

are the product of early and unconscious induction. In the same way Mr. Mill, in his great work on *Logic,* affirms that all reasoning is in reality from particular to particular, and that the major premise of every syllogism is merely a record and register of knowledge previously obtained. Whether this be true, or whether, as another school of thinkers asserts, we have ideas antecedent to experience, is a question which has been hotly disputed, but which I do not believe the actual resources of our knowledge can answer, and certainly I have no intention at present of making the attempt. It is enough to say that we call geometry a deductive science, because, even if its axioms are arrived at inductively, the inductive process is extremely small, and we are unconscious of it; while the deductive reasonings form the great mass and difficulty of the science.

To bring the distinction home to you, I will illustrate it by a specimen of deductive and inductive investigation of the same subject. Suppose a writer on what is termed social science, wishes to estimate the influence of different habits of thought on the average duration of life, and taking as an instance the opposite pursuits of poets and mathematicians, asks which of them live longest. How is he to solve this? If he proceeds inductively he will first collect the facts, that is, he will ransack the biographies of poets and mathematicians in different ages, different climates, and different states of society, so as to eliminate perturbations arising from circumstances not connected with his subject. He will then throw the results into the statistical form of tables of mortality, and on comparing them will find, that notwithstanding the immense variety of circumstances which he has investigated, there is a general average which constitutes an empirical law, and proves that mathematicians, as a body, are longer lived than poets. This is the inductive method. On the other hand, the deductive inquirer will arrive at precisely the same conclusion by a totally different method. He will argue thus: poetry appeals to the imagination, mathematics to the understanding. To work the imagination is more exciting than to work the understanding, and what is habitually exciting is usually unhealthy. But what is usually unhealthy will tend to shorten life; therefore poetry tends more than mathematics to shorten life; therefore on the whole poets will die sooner than mathematicians.

PROBLEMS

1. One who studies the various errors (called "fallacies") that are possible in the deductive thinking process and then checks these errors against the everyday thinking of himself and his associates is bound, if he is observant, to be impressed by how frequently the error lies in the general assumption (called the "major premise") with which deductive thinking invariably begins. That is, he becomes increasingly aware of how few generalizations (major premises) can withstand the test of close analysis. How many such generalizations— truths that are universally accepted and that apply to *all* cases—are you prepared to defend? The classic example is, "All men are mortal." How far can you go from there?

2. If, as we suspect, you did not find very many generalizations which admit of no exceptions, what cautious inference might you draw, at least tentatively, as to the relative usefulness of *deductive* and *inductive* thinking? Keep your answer in mind as you thread your way through the next four selections; then reappraise it in the light of this experience with deductive thinking and your experience with induction already acquired from the immediately preceding section of this book.

3. Can you contribute any examples, similar to the one suggested here by Buckle, of persons arriving at the same conclusion even though one followed the inductive method, the other the deductive? You might consider the conclusion, arrived at deductively by certain U. S. policy makers during the late war with Japan, that attempts to break down by rational methods such deeply-rooted emotional attitudes as emperor-worship actually strengthen a people's morale. Alexander Leighton, one of the men who are making a true science of "social science," was frankly skeptical of this deductive conclusion, but proved its reliability for himself by careful inductive procedures, i.e., by trying it. (For a full account of this interesting experiment, see Leighton's *Human Relations in a Changing World.*)

Percy Marks

Deductive logic can be, and frequently has been, described in a highly complex, diagrammatic, elaborate manner. When thus presented it may easily lose its connection with the deductive thinking we actually do about personal daily problems and social issues. In the following selection, Percy Marks, a teacher of English and the author of a number of novels, tries to make clear the basic nature, main forms, and greatest difficulties of deductive logic.

LOGIC *

THE MAJOR PREMISE

The simplest form of logic is the syllogism, a scheme of deductive reasoning composed of a major premise, a minor premise, and a conclusion. The major premise is a general truth that we can, and do, accept, or a general statement that the writer believes to be the truth. The minor premise, on the contrary, is particular, a definite statement. The conclusion is derived from the two premises.

Let us suppose, for example, that we want to prove that a trout is a vertebrate. Our syllogism will take this form:

MAJOR PREMISE: All fish are vertebrates.
MINOR PREMISE: A trout is a fish.
CONCLUSION: Therefore a trout is a vertebrate.

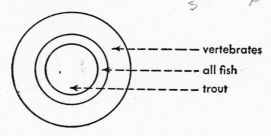

Expressed differently, we can state the syllogism this way: Since a trout is a fish, and since all fish are vertebrates, it follows necessarily that a trout is a vertebrate. Note, however, that if either premise is not entirely true, the conclusion does not necessarily follow. If a trout is not a fish, or if not *all* fish are vertebrates, a trout is not necessarily a vertebrate. It *may* be, but we shall not have proved that it is.

Let us consider another syllogism:

> MAJOR PREMISE: All men are mortal.
> MINOR PREMISE: Smith is a man.
> CONCLUSION: Therefore Smith is mortal.

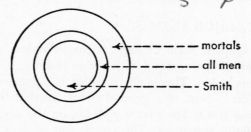

Everyone will accept the truth of both premises. Since Smith is a man, and since all men are mortal, it follows logically that Smith is mortal.

These syllogisms illustrate the uses of logic in its simplest form. We shall not go into the truly complex forms, but we shall consider some of the easier methods, especially those which reveal the most obvious faults in reasoning. First, let us reduce a plain statement to a syllogism and consider it: "Peter Hunkins was a hero because he died in the World War." As a syllogism that statement becomes:

MAJOR PREMISE: Every man who died in the World War was a hero.
MINOR PREMISE: Peter Hunkins died in the World War.
CONCLUSION: Therefore Peter Hunkins was a hero.

It must be obvious at once that the conclusion does not necessarily follow, since the truth of the major premise is very dubious. Certainly, most thinking people will not accept it as a general truth. Some of the men who died in the World War were heroes, and some of them were cowards. . . . We have to know *how* Peter Hunkins died before we will dub him a hero. He may have been a hero of heroes, but the argument offered proves nothing about his heroism because the major premise is weak.

Let us consider another syllogism of the same type:

> MAJOR PREMISE: Any physical ailment is a tragedy.
> MINOR PREMISE: A split finger is a physical ailment.
> CONCLUSION: Therefore a split finger is a tragedy.

At first glance, most people would accept the truth of the major premise without question. They would not notice how general it is, how much it includes. The minor premise promptly makes it ridiculous, however, and we therefore reject the conclusion.

Now for another syllogism based on the same major premise:

> MAJOR PREMISE: Any physical ailment is a tragedy.
> MINOR PREMISE: Blindness is a physical ailment.
> CONCLUSION: Therefore blindness is a tragedy

Is this a sound syllogism? Is the conclusion inevitable? Not at all. The syllogism is just as weak as the one preceding. The fact that the conclusion *happens* to be sound does not make the syllogism itself sound. *So long as we have any doubt about the truth of the major premise, the conclusion cannot be trusted.* The preceding syllogism offered plain evidence that the major premise is not true. If blindness is a tragedy because it is a physical ailment, and every physical ailment is a tragedy, then a split finger is a tragedy for exactly the same reason. Though one conclusion is sound and the other false, both arguments, *as arguments,* are either both sound or both false.

Here are three more syllogisms of the same type. Are they sound?

> MAJOR PREMISE: All children love candy.
> MINOR PREMISE: Jimmie Meridith is a child
> CONCLUSION: Therefore Jimmie Meridith loves candy.

> MAJOR PREMISE: All mammals live on land.
> MINOR PREMISE: A whale is a mammal.
> CONCLUSION: Therefore a whale lives on land.

> MAJOR PREMISE: All mammals suckle their young.
> MINOR PREMISE: A whale is a mammal.
> CONCLUSION: Therefore a whale suckles its young.

It must be evident that no syllogism is worth anything unless the major premise is completely acceptable. It is possible to reduce every argument to a syllogism, and it is possible to reduce every reason offered in support of an argument to a syllogism. Our reasoning is always stretched on this frame: If this is true, and that is true, then such and such must follow. If we write, "Peter Hunkins was a hero because he died in the World War," we are implying the syllogism we have earlier condemned. If we write, "Jimmie will always be small because he smokes cigarettes," we are basing our conclusion on this syllogism:

MAJOR PREMISE: Boys who smoke cigarettes never grow tall.
MINOR PREMISE: Jimmie smokes cigarettes.
CONCLUSION: Jimmie will never grow tall.

To those who accept the major premise as true, the argument will be valid. To all others, it will be false.

Brief and superficial as this study has been so far, it indicates at least the imperative need to analyze one's major premises. They are always present, sometimes implied, sometimes stated. The writer reasons *from* something. That something is his major premise. Whether he states it definitely in his theme or not, he should always state it definitely to himself. Surprisingly often, he will discover that it is either only sometimes true or that it is untenable.

THE GREATEST SIN IN LOGIC

The most common fault students make is to argue from a *particular* major premise to a *general conclusion*. There is no greater sin in logic. Cigarette smoking will again furnish a convenient example. Let us suppose that a theme writer disapproves of cigarette smoking. He is more than likely to make a statement of this kind: "I once knew a fellow who began smoking cigarettes when he was seven years old. His fingers and teeth were stained and his breath was bad. When he was eighteen, he was only five feet tall. A year later he died of consumption. It is certainly playing with fire to smoke cigarettes."

Lifted out of its context for examination, that argument seems ridiculous, as, of course, it is; but every instructor receives scores and scores of themes based on arguments of exactly the same type. *One can never draw a general conclusion from a particular premise.*

EXAMPLES AS EVIDENCE

What good, then, the student may ask, are examples? They are particular. Just so, but an example is not an argument and should not be offered as such. It should be offered as *evidence* of the truth of an argument. In other words, we have to establish our premises. Occasionally, their truth can be taken for granted. If we say that men are mortal, that all fish are vertebrates, that whales are mammals, or that stars are suns, no one is going to object. Accepted scientific truths have been established and do not need to be established again. But if there is any doubt of the truth of the premises, the writer must offer evidence to establish it. Examples are one kind of evidence; the opinions of authorities are another kind; and even comparisons may serve. If the student wants to write a theme arguing that the current world conflict (1944) is only a transient disturbance and will pass, he will necessarily base his argument on the premise that world disturbances, even global wars, do pass. The mere statement of that premise is not enough. It is not a proved truth. Furthermore, he can't prove it; but he can make it acceptable as a working major premise by demonstrating by comparison with earlier great conflicts that this one is not unique. Once he has compared the present conditions with the conditions evident in earlier wars and has shown the similarity between them, he can argue with considerable plausibility that since world upheavals have passed, this one will pass too. He can, of course, just as easily reverse his subject and seek his evidence in contrasts. Under those circumstances, his purpose will be to demonstrate that the present world war *is* unique in so many important respects that the past wars offer no evidence that this one will not last forever.

So much, then, for the major premises. *They must either be generalizations so universally accepted as true that no informed person denies their truth, or they must be established as acceptable bases for discussion and argument by evidence which is itself acceptable to informed persons.* One must say *informed* persons because there are always some cranks who deny premises which most of us accept without hesitation. We are willing to accept the generalization that the world is round as a premise, but every Sunday there are speakers in Hyde Park, London, arguing passionately that the earth is flat. Incidentally, if one accepts their major premises, one is forced by the power of their logic to accept their conclusions. They always say, as most debaters do, "It stands to reason." So it would if their major premises were not in direct contradiction to every known fact of science.

THE MINOR PREMISE

If the minor premise is not sound, the conclusion cannot be accepted as sound.

MAJOR PREMISE: Deciduous trees are bare of leaves in winter.
MINOR PREMISE: A fir tree is deciduous.
CONCLUSION: Therefore a fir tree is bare of leaves in winter.

Everyone will accept the major premise, but no one who ever saw a fir tree in winter will accept the minor premise. The statement is false, and so the conclusion is false.

MAJOR PREMISE: Poisonous snakes are a menace to human safety.
MINOR PREMISE: Garter snakes are poisonous.
CONCLUSION: Therefore garter snakes are a menace to human safety.

The minor premise in this syllogism is obviously untrue; the logical conclusion is also untrue. It is needless to labor the point that the minor premise must be true if the conclusion is to be tenable, but it is almost impossible to overstate the importance of the lesson taught by the minor premise, and that lesson is this: *Be sure of your facts.* Our study of the major premise demonstrated that the generalization on which the writer bases his argument must be acceptable if his conclusion is to be acceptable; and this brief study of the minor premise is meant to demonstrate that the facts offered must also be acceptable if the conclusion is to be acceptable. A weakness in either the major premise or the minor premise will invalidate the entire argument.

ESTABLISHING A HYPOTHESIS

We do not always reason with facts or generalizations as our major premise. Sometimes we set up a hypothesis—a supposition—and then reason logically from that to a conclusion that is also sound if the supposition can be proved sound. Scientists depend very largely on this method. When Walter Reed set out to conquer yellow fever, he argued in this fashion: "If, as I believe, yellow fever is carried solely by a certain mosquito, Stegomyia, the destruction of the Stegomyia will result in the prevention of epidemics of yellow fever."

He did not reason as we now reason: Since the Stegomyia is the sole carrier of yellow fever, the destruction of the Stegomyia prevents epidemics of yellow fever. We argue from an established fact, but Major Reed had no established fact; he had only a supposition. His major premise was based on an "if," and it was only sound if he could prove it sound beyond any doubt. He did prove it sound in a series of dramatic and thrilling experiments.

It is permissible to reason in exactly the same way in a theme. Let us suppose for purposes of illustration that a student plans to write a theme on "The Economic Benefits of a College Education." Let us further presume that he has come to college because he believes the possession of a degree will help him to make money. If he merely makes the assertion, the reader can nullify the entire theme by merely asserting that the possession of a college degree is not an aid toward making money. True, the reader has proved nothing; but, then, neither has the student.

With the aid of examples, however, the student can make his hypothesis into at least a working theory. If his examples are pertinent, his comparisons and contrasts sharp and clear, he can establish that theory as an acceptable major premise, which might be stated in this way: "Given two people of equal ability, the one who has a college degree will have much greater opportunities to earn money than the one who lacks the degree." Once he has justified his premise, he is in a position to justify his reason for coming to college. If the reader objects that one can prove quite as easily that the premise is false, one can only reply that the premise is not subject to absolute proof, whether it is stated in the positive or in the negative. Like a great many premises, it cannot be proved; it can only be made persuasive. If that by no means easy task is satisfactorily done, and if the deductions from the premises are logically made, the reader will usually accept the argument as sound. Few opinions are subject to absolute proof, because the premises on which they are based can seldom be established as undeniable truths. Very largely, we govern our lives on theories that we believe to be truths but which cannot be established as such.

UNWARRANTED CONCLUSIONS

There is a type of reasoning that must be watched very carefully because it leads the unwary easily into error. Students write this sort of statement often: "Since Tony is an Italian, you may be sure he is fond of music." The syllogism implied is this:

MAJOR PREMISE: All Italians are fond of music.
MINOR PREMISE: Tony is an Italian.
CONCLUSION: Therefore Tony is fond of music.

No one will accept the major premise without reservations. We will accept, however, the major premise in the following syllogism:

MAJOR PREMISE: Some Italians are fond of music.
MINOR PREMISE: Tony is an Italian.
CONCLUSION: Tony is fond of music.

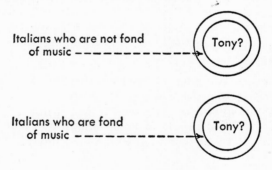

Italians who are not fond
of music – – – – – – – – – – – →   Tony?

Italians who are fond
of music – – – – – – – – – – – →   Tony?

It immediately becomes obvious that the conclusion does not necessarily follow from the premises. Since some Italians are fond of music, it follows that some are *not* fond of it, and it is entirely possible that Tony is an Italian of the second class. Even if we make the major premise "Most Italians are fond of music," the conclusion will not necessarily follow, because Tony may belong to the small minority to whom music is noise.

Still another type of argument that must be carefully avoided is the following:

MAJOR PREMISE: Italians are fond of music.
MINOR PREMISE: Tony is fond of music.
CONCLUSION: Therefore Tony is an Italian.

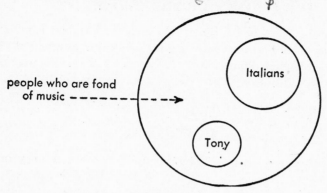

Even if we accept both the major and the minor premises as entirely true, the conclusion will not follow. A picture will make the fallacy immediately apparent.

Tony is in the class of people who are fond of music but not necessarily in the class of those who are also Italians.

Note another syllogism that is fundamentally of the same type as the foregoing:

MAJOR PREMISE: All men are mortal.
MINOR PREMISE: A deer is mortal.
CONCLUSION: Therefore a deer is a man.

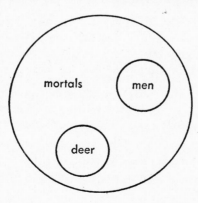

The major premise is entirely true; so is the minor premise; but the conclusion does not follow. . . .

THE FALLACY OF THE UNDISTRIBUTED MIDDLE TERM

This fallacy occurs constantly, especially in conversation. People use two general premises to argue to a general conclusion and never notice that the second premise is entirely outside the confines of the first. A person will declare righteously that all men are sinners and that all women are sinners—and then wave his hand to indicate that the conclusion is obvious. He doesn't at all realize that this is his syllogism:

> All men are sinners.
> All women are sinners.
> *Therefore*   All men are women.

In such a syllogism the middle term is said to be undistributed because nothing whatever is told about every sinner. In logic a term is said to be distributed when it is so used that it conveys information about every member of the class which it names. The proposition "All men are mortal," for example, distributes the term "man" but does not distribute "mortal." Note, though, that the syllogism becomes logically sound if the middle term is defined.

> All men are sinners.
> All sinners are weaklings.
> *Therefore*   All men are weaklings.

It is obvious, surely, that if all men are sinners and that all sinners in turn are weaklings that all men must likewise be weaklings, too. In the foregoing syllogism the middle term is distributed, but if it isn't, the following syllogism results:

> All men are sinners.
> All weaklings are sinners.
> *Therefore*   All men are weaklings.

The conclusion does not follow, though at first glance it seems to, since we think of weaklings as being men. If we use terms which carry no such implications, the falsity of the logic becomes at once evident:

All birds are <u>vertebrates.</u>
All fish are <u>vertebrates.</u>
Therefore   All birds are fish. . . .

What the fallacy of the undistributed middle term comes down to, of course, is that one cannot reason from parallel generalizations. Both generalizations may be perfectly true in themselves, but the truth of each does not warrant drawing a conclusion. The middle term, the term common to both generalizations, must be distributed; then if both premises are true, the conclusion will be true too.

There are other types of fallacies, other ways one can go astray in arguing from premises to a conclusion, but these will suffice to make the student aware of his methods of reasoning and suspicious of them. . . .

If the student learns to guard against arguing from a particular premise to a general conclusion, he will not write themes justifying a belief in superstitions because he once slipped on a banana peel after walking under a ladder. Nor will he argue, like a student who argued, that superstitions are absurd because Friday was his lucky day! He will not insist that churches are deplorable because two ministers in his home town falsified their accounts; nor will he argue that churches are prospering because a revivalist doubled the congregation in a single church. He will learn that *some* never justifies him in asserting *all*, although *most* may justify him in asserting *possibly all*. He will learn, in other words, to study his evidence, to analyze it; and as a result of his study and analysis, he will learn to distinguish between true evidence which is pertinent and a parallelism which may or may not be pertinent. He will discover that an example which he thought he was offering, and should be offering, as evidence, he is actually offering as a premise, and as a particular premise at that. If he is like most of us, he will discover that he is inclined to think in a careless, haphazard fashion, often permitting an emotional bias to take the place of sound reason, and even more often, perhaps, permitting unsound reason to justify an emotional bias.

PROBLEMS

1. What is the *starting* point of any *deduction?* How does the nature of that starting point indicate the importance of sound *inductive* thinking?
2. Why would a generalization about 75 per cent, or 99 per cent, of a certain category (elections, Americans, wars, depressions, small towns) be relatively useless as a major premise?
3. How may the reduction of deductive reasoning to *syllogisms* reveal weaknesses in one's deductive thinking? What, according to Marks, are the main kinds of errors in the deductive process? Now try your hand at reducing the following remarks to syllogisms, and then indicate the exact nature of the deductive error in each. (*Note*: the conclusion may be right or wrong, but in each the method of reaching that conclusion has a serious flaw.)

   a. My neighbor, Mrs. Swift, must be a very intelligent woman. She certainly reads a lot.

   b. Although X—— doesn't say much, I bet he's really very smart. Still waters run deep.

   c. Academic freedom is certainly going to disappear at —— College. Why, they've put in a military career-man as president.

   d. So our Peggy has been asked to go to a dance tomorrow night with a sailor? No, we've got to tell her she can't go. Sailors are dangerous.

   e. I'd never hire an ex-convict, no matter how good his prison record was. You can't teach an old dog new tricks.

   f. Jones is a good enough fellow now, but just wait until he comes into his father's fortune, and you'll find him a snob, just like the others.

   g. You say my blind date goes to art school? Well, then, I guess I'm not interested. Artists are too temperamental. Get somebody else to take her along.

   h. I won't need a course in accounting because it is far out of my field, farm machinery.

   i. They don't have any real two-party government in England any more, for the Laborites and Tories are in pretty general agreement on foreign policy.

   j. I didn't expect Ann to slap me, but she did. You never can tell what a woman will do.

   k. Did you see in yesterday's paper that two officers of Union Local 470 admitted in court that they held Communist Party cards?

That proves that the Communist Party is the real power behind the labor agitation in this country.

l. Be safe! Ride on good tires! Buy Sturdibilt Tires!

m. America doesn't have to worry about its chances in any new war. Our scientists and engineers have outdistanced those of any other country, and the big thing in war in modern times is technological supremacy.

n. Vote against the proposition to give the city control of the water-works! In Communist Russia the government owns the water-works, too.

o. This clock has streamlining, just like a locomotive. So, you see, this clock has true "functional design."

p. How can there be any question about this Board of Regents' choosing Dr. Z—— for the presidency of the State University? He's one of the greatest living physicists, and we, as a Board, have declared that what we need in education is more of the scientific spirit.

4. Once students learn what syllogisms are, they frequently find considerable amusement solving them. How might "playing with syllogisms" become an end in itself instead of a means to an end? What would you think of a college course which allotted an entire semester to the study of all the possible variations in the deductive pattern worked out by Aristotle?

5. How can a sound major premise obscure a weakness in the minor premise? Consider, for example, an advertisement which has as its banner line, "All Doctors Agree That Children Need a Correct Diet," followed by a plug for "Mighties," a breakfast cereal "indispensable to *your* child's diet." Now consider a major premise with which most of us concur: "Any democratic country must be vigilant to preserve its civil liberties." What misleading minor premise could easily follow this? Can you supply further examples?

6. What error in reasoning do the following statements have in common:

a. "There's —— fouling again. These Siwash teams certainly play dirty."

b. "Did you see that drape suit? Filipinos certainly go for gaudy clothes."

c. "Platitudes, platitudes, platitudes! What more can you expect from a politician?"

d. "I told you you'd be bored. It's a foreign film, isn't it?"

7. Once you have mastered the syllogistic formula it's relatively easy to pick out the fallacies. The real trick is to spot faulty deduction when it comes to you, as it usually does, with no syllogistic trappings

but in everyday language masquerading as "common sense." Take the following statements, picked up by the editors here and there, and reduce them to syllogisms. Do they make "sense"?

a. ". . . today, the 27 million Americans who read *Peer* [a picture magazine] each week could pick either Mr. Truman or Mr. Dewey out of a crowd. . . .

   "None of *Peer's* readers will vote for a stranger. . . ."

b. "The citizens have long desired a place where the climate would be a perfect antidote to malarial influences; this has been found: not a case of malarial fever ever known on the Island."

c. "We are going into logarithms today. Most of you fellows have had logs before. This work will be easy for you."

d. "The guy who stands around while another person struggles with a load, or the guy who for no reason at all will not donate a dollar to the student charity fund, is far from what can be termed a normal human being."

e. "After reading about Henry Wallace's hostile reception in the South . . . I'm further convinced of something I've thought all along—that Henry Wallace is the greatest American since Abraham Lincoln."

Arthur Koestler

The term "Babbittry," derived from the central character of Sinclair Lewis' novel *Babbitt,* has become a synonym for unthinking conformity, for reliance on unexamined assumptions about oneself and one's own society; it has been most commonly used in criticism of smug conservatism in political, economic, and religious thinking.

In this article, a composite of several talks he delivered while on a tour of this country, Koestler applies the term to the thinking *not* of such conservatives but of a certain kind of "liberal." He finds that some so-called "liberal" thinking is based on *the same kind* of fallacious deductive logic as that of some "conservative" thinking. Here Koestler is using a very helpful test of a way of thinking: By merely switching the terms he tries to find out whether the kinds of errors made by thinkers to whom one may be opposed are really the kinds of errors which also occur in one's own thinking.

Koestler, a news correspondent in the Near East and Europe during the 1920's, joined the Communist Party about 1930, fought against Franco in Spain, was imprisoned and condemned to die, and was released through British intervention. Becoming disillusioned with the methods and results of Communism, he left the Communist Party. He attacked Communism in the novel *Darkness at Noon,* a brilliant study of the mind of a man who has come to believe that the end justifies any means. Imprisoned by the French Government at the outbreak of World War II, Koestler escaped to England, where he joined the British Army. In his recent talks and writing he has urged the elimination from liberal thinking of logical flaws which he believes some liberals share with extreme radicals and extreme conservatives.

BABBITTS OF THE LEFT *

Before I started out on this my first visit to the U. S., my friends in Europe warned me: "You won't find a common language with the Americans. They live in the moon."

The first few days over here convinced me that this is not true. I do feel a growing awareness of the threat over Europe in this country. The only question is whether it is growing rapidly enough to catch up with the speed of the drift to catastrophe in Europe.

For the war hysteria of which a considerable number of people seem to suffer here is, of course, not a sign of mature awareness. Nor is the mentality of appeasement. I shan't waste your time and mine proving that appeasement doesn't lead to peace but to war; if you haven't found that out yet, I suggest you reread the arguments against the tactic of appeasement in the old 1933 to 1939 files of liberal and radical magazines—from the *New Republic* to *The New Statesman and Nation.* You will find there explained with a brilliant logic that appeasement of an aggressive, expanding power creates a fog in which neither of the two partners knows where he is; the aggressor, having grabbed positions A, B, and C, hopes to get away with grabbing D—and why shouldn't he hope so with all the encouragement that he receives from the appeasers in the opponents' camp? But unfortunately position D—Poland in 1939 and

* Arthur Koestler, "Babbitts of the Left," *Life,* May 3, 1948. Reprinted by permission of the International Rescue Committee.

maybe Italy today—has meanwhile come to be regarded by the defensive partner as a *casus belli,* and so the world slides into war— I didn't say it goes to war, I said it slides into war—without either of the two partners wanting it. In other words, appeasement means playing poker; a firm, clearly outlined, principled policy means playing chess.

These are platitudes, the type of platitude which every reader of the *New Republic* or *The New Statesman and Nation* knew by heart in the 1930s. Today they have forgotten it, and arguing against them means regressing to the kindergarten level. I hope that in this meeting we shall remain at least on the level of the primary school. So I shall take it, henceforth, for granted that war hysteria and appeasement are two equally deadly dangers, like Scylla and Charybdis, and that the liberals' extremely precarious task today is to navigate like Ulysses between the two.

Unfortunately our liberal Ulysses of today hardly deserves the title "nimble-witted" which Homer bestowed upon his hero. When the sorceress calls from the East and her fellow travelers are turned into pigs, he can hardly resist the temptation of sharing their fate. For it is not easy to be a liberal today. It is not easy to navigate between the Scylla of the Hearst press, of war hysteria and of Red-baiting, and the Charybdis of the Munich *cum* Pearl Harbor which Mr. Chamberlain—sorry, I mean Mr. Wallace—would prepare for us.

Allow me as an aid for this perilous task of navigation to point out some of the logical fallacies and emotional eddies in which liberals and leftists frequently get shipwrecked. I have listed for myself eight of them—the eight main fallacies of what you may allow me to call left Babbittism. Here they are:

First is the *confusion of Left and East.* Some sections of the reactionary press are unable or unwilling to distinguish between liberals, New Dealers, Social Democrats and Stalinites; they are all damned Reds. Naturally we are indignant at this poisonous imbecility. But don't forget that the Left itself is partly responsible for this confusion. The left Babbitt assumes that there is a continuous spectrum stretching from pale pink liberals to deeper red socialists and so on to purple Communists of the extreme left. His idea is based on the confusion of the political direction "left" with the geographical direction "east." It is time that he got it into his head that Moscow is not to his left but to his east. The Soviet Union is not a socialist country, and Cominform policy is not socialist policy. In 1939-41, for instance, French Socialists fought the Nazis on the battlefield and underground, while the Communists in France and here collaborated with the Germans against us.

So let us bear in mind that "East is east and Left is left" and if the twain sometimes still meet, the meeting is purely coincidental. The tragic decline of the Social Democratic movements in France, Italy and the rest of Europe is first and foremost caused by their failure to denounce Stalinism as a movement which discredits socialism—as the rule of the Borgias discredited Christianity. That is why liberals and social democrats in Europe are being swept away like straw in a hurricane.

The second fallacy of the Babbitt of the Left is what we may call the *soul-searching fallacy*. The other day there was a press conference where I mentioned that the people on the Continent, the frightened people in Italy and France, look upon you Americans as their only hope of salvation, salvation from the economic point of view through ERP; salvation from the military point of view in case of an open or disguised Russian aggression on the Czech pattern. Thereupon one of the journalists present said, "Do you really believe that we can help Europe with our dirty hands?" I said, "What do you mean by 'dirty hands'?" He said, "Well, I mean our policy in Greece and in Palestine and backing up Franco and the way we treat Negroes and Jews. We are dirty all over, and if we pose as defenders of democracy it is just hypocrisy."

The answer to this fallacy is to project the argument back to 1938. Then it would run as follows: "We have no right to fight Hitler's plan of sending six million Jews to the gas chambers so long as there are restricted hotels in America and so long as Negroes do not have absolute equality here. Our hands are dirty—so instead of using them to fight racial persecution let us first wash them clean and polish our nails. Once American democracy has become a perfect democracy, then and then only shall we have a right to defend what remains of Europe. And if Europe goes to the dogs before we have finished putting our own house in order, that's just too bad and cannot be helped."

Third and closely related to the soul-searching fallacy is the *fallacy of the false equation*. Its European version is "Soviet totalitarianism is bad. American imperialism is equally bad. There is nothing to choose between them, so let us stay in no man's land and found another 100% purist soul-searching sectarian little magazine until we are drowned in the deluge." To prove that the American system is "just as bad" as the Russian system, to make the two sides of the equation balance, your left purist has recourse to subconscious little subterfuges. He equates the Hollywood purges with the Moscow purges. The physical assassination of thousands of the elite of the Russian Revolution and the dismissal from their jobs of nine film script writers constitutes for him a perfect equation. Variations of this attitude are equally frequent in this country. The American fellow traveler has never lived under a totalitarian regime, so when he draws comparisons he mostly doesn't know what he is talking about. His conscience is in revolt against the "black belt" of Chicago, the appalling slums in which the workers of the packing industry live like rats. I spent only a few hours in Chicago, but most of them I spent in the "black belt" and at the local headquarters of the packing-house workers on strike. I was appalled by what I saw and heard and smelled. So don't think I am a naive tourist, a romantic admirer of your system. But now compare your treatment of racial minorities at its worst with the Soviet treatment of the minorities of the Crimean Republic, the Chechen Republic, the Volga-German Republic, whose total populations, men, women and children, were deported to the Arctic because they had proved, as the official Soviet communiqué about the Crimeans stated, "unreliable during the war"—even the babes in their cradles were unreliable and had to go to Siberia. In Chicago I saw men on strike and sympathized with them. In Russia strikes, or incitement to strike, are qualified as high treason and punished by the maximum penalty. In American elections political machines may distort the people's will. In Russian elections 99½% vote for the one official list—the remaining ½% presumably being in bed with influenza. Thus the fallacy of the false equation equates an imperfect democracy with a perfect totalitarian regime; its philosophy boils down to the simple maxim that there is nothing to choose between measles and leprosy.

Fallacy number four is the *anti-anti attitude*. It runs as follows: "I am not a Communist. In fact, I dislike Stalinist politics, but I don't want to be identified with anti-Communist Red-baiting, with the Hollywood purges and the Hearst press. Hence I am neither a Communist nor an anti-Communist, but an anti-anti-Communist." If W. R. Hearst says that twice two is four, I shall automatically hold that twice two is five or at least $4\frac{1}{2}$. The $2 \times 2 = 4\frac{1}{2}$ mathematicians are usually Wallace voters.

Don't laugh, for the roots of this fallacy are very deep in all of us, myself included. I remember how painful it was when an old dodderer in a London club walked up to me and said with a friendly tap on my shoulder, "Well, well, young man, I am glad that at last you have come around to see reason. I myself knew 25 years ago what Bolshevism means, and it's never too late to repent."

You can't help this sort of thing; you can't help people being right for the wrong reasons. In the last war we fought in the name of democracy in an alliance with Dictator Metaxas of Greece, Dictator Chiang Kai-shek and Dictator Stalin. And rightly so, because at that time Nazism was the main menace to the world, and politics is based on forming alliances. But there is a fundamental difference between a wartime alliance and political identification with one's allies. Being allied to Chiang didn't mean that we accepted the Chinese regime in England or America. Being against our will in one camp with the Hearst press against the totalitarian menace from the East doesn't mean that we identify ourselves with Mr. Hearst's ideology. This fear of being in bad company is not an expression of political purity; it is an expression of a lack of self-confidence. If you are sure of yourself—politically and ideologically—you will no longer be frightened to say that twice two makes four even if Colonel McCormick says the same.

Fallacy number five is the *sentimental fallacy.* For years we were allied to Communists in the antifascist struggle, and now when we have to part company some roots of past loyalty, of a sentimental conservatism remain in us which are very difficult to eradicate. Our bedfellows of yesterday do not, of course, share this emotional squeamishness. Over the slightest disagreement they will denounce us as fascists, spies and traitors. These emotional ties are one-way ties and it is essential to bear in mind that they are entirely irrational and conservative in nature.

Fallacy number six may be called the fallacy of *Caligary logics. The Cabinet of Dr. Caligary* was the first film which might be called surrealistic, made about 25 years ago. The fellow traveler, the fellow traveler's fellow traveler, the cryptofellow traveler and so on, live in a world of surrealistic logic where all facts are seen reflected in curved distorting mirrors. Example: The fellow traveler will tell you, "You criticized the Stalinist regime, but in Stalingrad the heroic Red Army defeated the Germans and thereby proved the superiority of the Stalinist regime over every other regime."

You answer, "If the military defeat of the Germans by the Russians in 1943 is to be regarded in itself as a proof of the superiority of the Stalinist regime, then the military defeat of the French by the Russians in 1812 must be regarded as a proof of the superiority of the czarist regime and of the system of serfdom over the ideology of the French Revolution."

The Caligary logician will thereupon answer you indignantly, "It is typical of your perverted mind to compare Stalin with the czar."

Fallacy number seven is the fallacy of the *perfect cause*. It is related to number two, the soul-searching fallacy. Only absolutely clean hands have a right to reach out to protect and save what remains of Europe. Only an absolutely perfect cause is worth fighting for. And the search for the perfect cause becomes an excuse for inactivity, for staying put in the homeless radical's no man's land.

History knows no perfect causes, no situation of white against black. Eastern totalitarianism is black; its victory would mean the end of our civilization. American democracy is not white but gray. To live, even to die for a perfect cause is a luxury permitted to few. In 1942 or '43 I published an article which began with the words, "In this war we are fighting a total lie in the name of a half-truth." The total lie was Hitler's New Order. The half-truth was our democracy. Today we face a similar emergency and a similar predicament. Once more the choice before us is merely that between a gray twilight and total darkness. But ask the refugees who manage to escape, at the risk of their lives, from behind the iron curtain into our gray democracy, whether this choice is worth fighting for. They know. You don't.

The last fallacy, number eight, is the *confusion between short-term and long-term aims*. It is the most dangerous of all. By long-term aims I mean the age-old struggle for reform, for social justice, for a more equitable system of government. By short-term aims I mean the necessity of fighting an immediate emergency. The danger of confusion is twofold. Your leftist Babbitt may refuse to fight against the short-term emergency until he has finished the job of creating a perfect government in his country, in 100 years or so. The opposite danger is to become so obsessed with the immediate emergency, that all principles of the long-term struggle are thrown overboard. Ex-Communists and disappointed radicals are in a particular danger of toppling over to the other extreme. It is essential that we should keep in mind that there are two distinct levels involved in our struggle; that to defend our system against a deadly threat does not imply acceptance of everything in this system, does not imply the giving up of the long-term fight to improve it; and vice versa, that our criticism of the shortcomings of this system does not free us from the obligation of defending it, despite its ambiguous grayness, against the total corruption of the humanitarian ideal.

This talk was mainly addressed to the Left. I may have been harsh to the left Babbitt; it was a brotherly harshness. To the Babbitt of the Right I have nothing to say; we have no language in common.

The power-vacuum which two world wars have created in Central and Western Europe, has inescapably linked your fate with that of the European continent. I feel the enormous burden which is falling on your shoulders. For there will either be a Pax Americana in the world or there will be no pax. Never has such a burden and such a responsibility been borne by any single nation in history. It is the more unfair to you as yours is an adolescent civilization, with adolescent enthusiasms and adolescent pimples. The task of the progressive intelligentsia of your country is to help the rest of the nation to face its enormous responsibilities. The time for sectarian quarrels in the cosy no man's land of abstract radicalism is past. It is time for the American radical to grow up.

PROBLEMS

1. Koestler analyzes the deductive fallacies of some present-day "liberal" thinking, but he does not reduce those ideas quite to the bare bones of a syllogism. Can you take that step in each of the eight cases? As a starter, consider this as an illustration of the *confusion of Left and East:* Liberals deplore the totalitarian administration of General Franco in Spain; there is no more vigorous opponent of Franco Spain than Russia; therefore, it must be apparent to liberals that their cause and that of Soviet Russia are the same. Or this illustration of the *soul-searching fallacy:* Only people and nations who are themselves free from all moral taint have a right to attempt to improve society; America's treatment of certain minority race groups is not free from this moral taint; therefore, Americans were in no position to condemn German persecution of the Jews. Now go ahead on your own.

2. A very good corrective in one's deductive thinking is to change the terms. This indicates whether you really can think logically or whether you are just moved emotionally by a writer's conclusions. Can you, on the basis of what you have read and heard, and the information that Koestler presents, indicate the form that each of these fallacies may take in the thinking of political and economic *conservatives* today? Change the terms in the major and minor premises and see what happens. For instance, conservatives sometimes, as Koestler points out, argue this way: many liberals support a program of government health insurance; Communists also support such a program; therefore, those liberals are really Communists. How does this tune sound when we play it this way: "The conservative press is openly hostile to Tito; Russian Communists hate Tito; therefore, the conservative press is really sympathetic with Russian Communism"? Now try some of these variations on the themes by Koestler.

3. Can you find examples of each of the fallacies that Koestler deals with in your own or your friends' thinking? For instance, have you ever voted for a student-body presidential candidate because you admired his athletic ability? The syllogism: Fine athletes are superior fellows; Johnny —— is a fine athlete; therefore, he'd make a fine student-body president—the one I'll vote for. Isn't that the same deduction as the one Koestler terms "the fallacy of Caligary logics," with "fine athletes" substituted for "heroism in war," and "Johnny ——" for "Russians"?

4. How does Koestler agree, in his analysis of the second and seventh fallacies, with Overstreet's criticism of "monistic thinking"?

Emery Reves

In the sixteenth century Copernicus challenged the accepted Ptolemaic doctrine that the world was the center of the universe and suggested the hypothesis that the world, together with the other planets, revolved around the sun. This new way of looking at the universe called for a drastic modification of many other set ideas about the world and its place in the universe. It marked a revolution in men's thinking, for it scrapped the major premise of many of their favorite deductions. Reves considers just such a revolution in our *social thinking* necessary today.

Reves, an Englishman who was educated in three distinguished European universities, came to this country in 1941. He presently operates a press syndicate in New York City which gathers and prepares for distribution to subscribers the views of statesmen and writers of all nationalities on questions of international interest. In the first chapter of his book, *The Anatomy of Peace,* Reves suggests how Americans, Englishmen, Frenchmen, Germans, and Russians are all incapable of understanding the present international conflicts ("cold" and "hot" wars) because they all cling to the worn-out formula of national sovereignty, the right of each nation to determine its own policies without reference to the interests of other nations. This state of affairs he compares to the inadequacy of outworn astronomical premises for solving problems in "a Copernican world." In the remainder of his book Reves presents a broad plan for world government.

NEW PREMISES *

Our political and social thinking today is passing through a revolutionary era very much the same as were astronomy and abstract science during the Renaissance.

For more than fourteen centuries, the geocentric theory of the universe, formulated and laid down by Ptolemy in the second century A.D. in Alexandria, was paramount in the scientific world. According to this theory—as explained in Ptolemy's famous *Al-*

* Emery Reves, *The Anatomy of Peace,* Harper & Brothers. Copyright, 1945, by Emery Reves.

magest, the culmination of Greek astronomy—the earth was the center of the universe around which revolved the sun, the moon and all the stars.

No matter how primitive such a conception of the universe appears to us today, it remained unchallenged and unchallengeable for fourteen hundred years. All possible experimentation and observation before the sixteenth century A.D. confirmed the Ptolemaic system as a rock of indisputable scientific truth.

Strangely enough, Greek scientists several centuries before Ptolemy had a concept of the universe far more advanced and nearer to our modern knowledge. As far back as the sixth century B.C., Pythagoras visualized the earth and the universe as being spherical in shape. One of his later disciples, Aristarchus of Samos, in the third century B.C., in his hypothesis deposed the earth as the center of the universe, and declared it to be a "planet," like the many other celestial bodies. This system, called the Pythagorean system, plainly anticipated the Copernican hypothesis nineteen centuries later. It was probably not completely developed by Pythagoras himself, but it had been known several hundred years before Ptolemy.

Yet for almost two thousand years following the first insight into the real construction and functioning of the universe, people were convinced that all the celestial bodies revolved around the earth, which was the fixed center of the universe.

The geocentric system worked perfectly as long as it could solve all the problems which presented themselves under the then existing methods of observation. Ptolemy himself appears to have sensed and suspected the transitory character of his system, as in his *Syntaxis* he laid down the general principle that in seeking to explain phenomena, we should adopt the simplest possible hypothesis, *provided it is not contradicted in any important respect by observation.*

The geocentric theory of Ptolemy was perfectly in harmony with the religious dogma concerning the story of the creation of the universe as told in the Bible and it became the doctrine approved by the Church.

But in fifteenth century Italy, under the light of new learning and observation and under the impetus of the revolt against the dictatorship of accepted philosophical and scientific doctrines, there came a radical change. Several thinkers, particularly one Dominico Maria Novara, denounced the Ptolemaic system and began spreading "Pythagorean opinions"—as they were called—about the universe. Around 1500, these old, yet revolutionary, ideas attracted and deeply interested young Copernicus while he was studying at the universities of Bologna and Padua.

So new circumstances, new methods of observation, new needs, led to the birth of the Copernican system, one of the most gigantic steps of scientific progress in human history.

Through the Copernican system, man's outlook on the universe changed fundamentally. In this new concept, the earth itself rotated. It was no longer a stable point. Our globe, just like the other planets, revolved in space around the sun and the new theory of planetary movement was founded on the principle of relativity of motion.

This heliocentric theory of Copernicus was by no means perfect. It solved many problems the Ptolemaic system could not solve, but certain outstanding anomalies compromised its harmonious working. It is also well known that for thirty-five years Copernicus did not dare publicly proclaim his discovery. When he finally decided to publish it (in the year of his death) he called his theory "Hypothesis" to forestall the wrath of the Church and public opinion.

The later experience of Galileo proved how justified were the fears of Copernicus. The heliocentric theory was not only condemned by the church authorities as heresy; it was rejected by the greatest astronomers and other scientists of the time. Indeed, it was impossible to prove Copernicus' hypothesis by the then existing methods of observation. Only later, through the work of Kepler and Galileo, was the heliocentric theory put on a solid scientific foundation.

At its inception, the Copernican system was nothing more than a daring speculation. But it opened a new world, pointed out the road to science and prompted new and more refined methods of observation which finally led to general acceptance of the revolutionary but correct outlook on the universe.

During the first half of the twentieth century, in so far as our political, social and economic thinking is concerned, we find ourselves in the same dead-end road as Copernicus during the Jubilee of 1500.

We are living in a geocentric world of nation-states. We look upon economic, social and political problems as "national" problems. No matter in which country we live, the center of our political universe is our own nation. In our outlook, the immovable point around which all other nations, all the problems and events outside our nation, the rest of the world, supposedly rotate, is—our nation.

This is our basic and fundamental dogma.

According to this nation-centric conception of world affairs, we can solve political, economic and social problems within our nation, the fixed, immutable center, in one way—through law and government. And in the circumambient world around us, in our relations with the peoples of other nations, these same problems should be treated by other means—by "policy" and "diplomacy."

According to this nation-centric conception of world affairs, the political, social and economic relations between man and man living within a sovereign national unit, and these very same relationships between man and man living in separate sovereign national units are qualitatively different and require two qualitatively different methods of handling.

For many centuries such an approach was unchallenged and unchallengeable. It served to solve current problems in a satisfactory way and the existing methods of production, distribution, of communications and of interchange among the nations did not necessitate nor justify the formulation and acceptance of a different outlook. But the scientific and technological developments achieved by the industrial revolution in one century have brought about in our political outlook and in our approach to political and social phenomena a change as inevitable and imperative as the Renaissance brought about in our philosophical outlook.

The developments creating that need are revolutionary and without parallel in human history. In one century, the population of this earth has been more than trebled. Since the very beginning of recorded history, for ten thousand years, communication was based on animal power. During the American and French revolutions, transportation was scarcely faster than it had been under the Pharaohs, at the time of Buddha or of the Incas. And then, after a static aeon of ten thousand years, transportation changed within a single short century from animal power to the steam and electric railroad, the internal combustion automobile and the six hundred-mile-per-hour jet propulsion plane.

After thousands of years of primitive, rural existence in which all human beings, with few exceptions, were exhausted from producing with their own hands just enough food, clothing and shelter for sheer survival, in less than one century the population of the entire Western world has become consumers of mass-production commodities.

The change created by industrialism is so revolutionary, so profound, that it is without parallel in the history of any civilization. Despite Spengler, it is unique.

In this new and as yet unexplored era we find ourselves completely helpless, equipped with the inadequate, primitive political and social notions inherited from the pre-industrialized world. Slowly we are coming to realize that none of our accepted theories is satisfactory to cope with the disturbing and complex problems of today.

We realize that although we can have all the machinery we need, we cannot solve the problems of production. We realize that in spite of the far-flung and tremendous scope of transportation, we cannot prevent famine and starvation in many places, while there is abundance elsewhere on the earth. We realize that although hundreds of millions are desperately in need of food and industrial products, we cannot prevent mass unemployment. We realize that even though we have mined more gold than ever before, we cannot stabilize currency. We realize that while every modern country needs raw materials that other countries have, and produces goods which other countries need, we have been unable to organize a satisfactory method of exchange. We realize that although the overwhelming majority of all people hate violence and long to live in peace, we cannot prevent recurrent and increasingly devastating world wars. We knew that armaments must lead to wars between nations, but we have learned the bitter truth that disarmament also leads to war.

In this confusion and chaos in which civilized nations are struggling with utter helplessness, we are bound to arrive at the inevitable conclusion that the cause of this hopelessness and helplessness lies not in the outer world but in ourselves. Not in the problems we have to solve but in the hypotheses with which we approach their solutions.

Our political and social conceptions are Ptolemaic.

The world in which we live is Copernican.

Our Ptolemaic political conceptions in a Copernican industrial world are bankrupt. Latest observations on ever-changing conditions have made our Ptolemaic approach utterly ridiculous and out-of-date. We still believe, in each one of the seventy or eighty sovereign states, that our "nation" is the immovable center around which the whole world revolves.

There is not the slightest hope that we can possibly solve any of the vital problems of our generation until we rise above dogmatic nation-centric conceptions and realize that, in order to understand the political, economic and social problems of this highly integrated and industrialized world, we have to shift our standpoint and see all the nations and national matters in motion, in their interrelated functions, rotating according to the same laws without any fixed points created by our own imagination for our own convenience.

PROBLEMS

1. Reves demonstrates how men starting from different premises as to the nature of the universe (here the "Ptolemaic" and the "Copernican") arrive at quite different answers to such specific problems as determining the nature of gravity, the nature of the stars and the other stellar systems, the evolution of the earth and the other planets. Indicate orally or in writing, as your instructor prefers, the different kinds of conclusions that would be drawn about the following problems by persons starting with these very different premises:

   a. *The problem:* How can we prevent cheating in school examinations?

   Premise 1— Cheating results from improperly supervised examinations.

   Premise 2— Cheating is the result of improperly devised examinations, i.e., those with easily copied answers.

   Premise 3— Cheating is generated by an atmosphere of hostile suspicion on the part of teachers and administrators.

   Premise 4— Cheating is the result of an artificial learning situation which puts a premium on "right answers," rather than on the ability to find independent answers, supportable by cited evidence.

Premise 5— Chronic problems admit of no single, simple answers.

b. The problem: What can we do about "tramps" in today's society?

Premise 1— Tramps are naturally shiftless men who, to avoid work, move from place to place, getting "handouts" from people who will give only once.

Premise 2— Tramps are destitute men, suffering from a variety of personal and social maladjustments, who move from place to place to avoid arrest under our vagrancy laws.

(In connection with this last problem, the student is advised to read George Orwell's *Down and Out in Paris and London,* a remarkable example of how close observation dispels social myths. The fact that Orwell was *not* a reformer makes his report all the more convincing.)

2. According to Reves, how did Ptolemy's followers, in using his hypothesis as a major premise, overlook Ptolemy's own note of scientific caution?

3. Reves implies that the idea of one's own nation as the center of the world, and, therefore, "a law unto itself," worked fairly well as a major premise in solving economic and political problems one or two hundred years ago. On the basis of your knowledge of history, can you see some justification for this view? Reves also implies that the nationalistic premise does *not* work well in solving economic and political problems today because the world has changed in certain ways. Can you see the specific differences between today's world and that of the eighteenth and nineteenth centuries which support Reves' contention that the "nation-centered" principle is no longer workable?

4. Write a paper employing the same analysis of outmoded premises to *one* of the following:

   a. In many American frontier communities the citizens set up "vigilante" law, taking it on themselves to judge and punish. Today, law-abiding citizens in those same communities frown on "vigilante justice." They regard such vigilante principles as "kill or be killed," "every man for himself," "the law of the jungle," as both inadequate and dangerous. What changes in conditions made these "principles" no longer valid?

   b. During a man's boyhood he may get into numerous playground scraps without particularly disastrous results, but when he becomes a man the same kind of brawling may have quite different results. What has changed to make his old "answer" no longer adequate?

c. Men in northern Europe evolved, over hundred of years, a kind of house—with steep roofs, thick walls, and small windows—adapted to building materials and climatic conditions in northern Europe. When Americans now build the same kind of Norman, English, or Dutch houses in Florida or Southern California, in what ways is at least one of the premises on which they are continuing to work no longer adequate?

d. How is mass flight for exits in a theater at the cry of "Fire!" an illustration of an almost automatic deduction that perhaps was once adequate to existing conditions but is not so in a crowded modern theater?

5. The law is a rich field in general principles from which deductions, in the form of legal decisions, are made. What major changes in some principles governing the relations of men have been made to accommodate changed conditions in the following instances:

a. The relationship of employer to employee, where the legal principles originally invoked were those based on the master-servant relationship?

b. The relationship of man and the state in America, where the legal principles originally invoked were based on "the divine right of kings"?

(*Special note:* As this goes to the printer, the Idaho Supreme Court has just voided a sentence of one to fourteen years imposed by a state judge on four Indian boys for carrying off a sheep worth twelve dollars during an alcoholic joy ride. The sentence was based on a law going back to frontier days which makes the theft of a domestic animal grand larceny.)

"The Nation"

The following pieces were selected from columns, variously titled "In the Wind" and "No Comment," appearing in *The Nation,* whose editors rather regularly put on exhibit prize bits of fallacious reasoning from American life and thought and in so doing contradict the frequently held notion that "liberals and reformers have no sense of humor." For obvious reasons no "problems" follow these selections.

HOW'S THAT AGAIN? *

I

"May I call your attention to the remarks of Anthony B. Meany, lecturer and author? Mr. Meany tells us 'the . . . radio arrived in 1928: the following year . . . business collapsed.' Now then, he asks, is television 'a Frankenstein' which will promote 'industrial suicide'?"

II

In the Phillips Brooks House at Harvard University . . . there is a small bronze plaque under the bust of old Phillips himself which reads: "This House is Dedicated to Piety, Charity, and Hospitality." Directly under the plaque is tacked a white card with this message prominently inscribed thereon: "No Trespassing. Unauthorized Persons Are Not Allowed in This Building."

III

Editorial from the Seattle *Times* for January 30, 1948:
"The several reports of President Truman's commission on higher education contain recommendations which constitute a constructive contribution to American educational thought . . . but many will find it difficult to follow the commission in some of its . . . reasoning.
" 'All too often,' one report says, 'the benefits of education have been sought and used for personal and private profit, to the neglect of public and social service. . . . Teaching and learning must be invested with public purpose.' Here is a philosophy that has a familiar ring. . . . So, in this newer education, the opportunities and aspirations of the individual must be subordinated to 'public purpose.' Not the individual good, but the good of the state, must be served. The old order changeth, yielding place to new. But we remain old-fashioned. Though it was promulgated by a Presidential Commission, this is no American program. It has a European accent."

* From various issues of *The Nation*, 1948-1949.

IV

"This group . . . included men from many walks of life and members of all political faiths, both Democrats and Republicans." —From a statement by Governor William Tuck of Virginia supporting the recommendations of a state commission on suffrage amendments.

V

"The fact is that in too many American labor unions the notion of class conflict has taken deep root. We mean the belief tracing back to Karl Marx and the other brainstorm troopers in the gray dawn of the machine age, that the interests of employers and workers are directly opposed and can never be reconciled. . . . It is nothing but tripe, and never was anything else—though it is a fact that there were many more employers with slave-driver mentalities a couple of generations ago than there are today."—From an editorial in the New York *Sunday News,* Sept. 18, 1949.

VI

From the *Daily Worker* for March 3, 1948: "In Czechoslovakia the world is witnessing one of those magnificent leaps in human history. Men are sloughing off a slave mentality and simultaneously embalming the would-be enslavers."

VII

Testimony of Dr. Frederick J. Carpenter against a proposed Massachusetts birth-control bill, as delivered in the Boston State House on April 6 and reported in the Boston *Globe:* "If this law had been in effect prior to my birth, I might be standing here today without a mother."

GENERAL PROBLEMS: *Reasoning Deductively*

In studying deductive reasoning the trick is to master the process and not be mastered by it. Too often teacher and student become so enamored of the syllogistic process and the various "fallacies" that the study of deduction becomes merely a kind of intellectual parlor game with all the emphasis placed on forms and rules. The product of such a method has frequently been a student who can demonstrate considerable skill at solving a variety of syllogistic puzzles, but who shows a deplorable inability to spot the faulty deduction heard over the radio or the back fence. This failure to make deductive reasoning a more immediately useful skill, then, would appear to stem from the almost exclusive emphasis on the syllogistic pattern; whereas, in everyday life such a pattern almost never presents itself. To be able to put this training to any practical use, one must have some practice in analyzing the informal language and thought of everyday action. Only when he can spot faulty assumptions used consciously or unconsciously as major premises, errors in fact used as minor premises, and conclusions which either do not follow from the premises or which are derived from faulty premises—only when he can spot these in the frequently blurred, half-buried forms in which they come to him in everyday conversation, can he be said to have learned something useful about deductive reasoning.

The three problems that follow are arranged with the simplest (the one with the most formal syllogistic pattern) first. The student who works his way thoughtfully through problem 1 should be prepared for the more interesting and practical problems that follow.

1. Below are four syllogisms illustrating some of the more common "fallacies" mentioned by Marks. What is the error in each? (Some may have more than one error.)

    a. Frontier life makes men more flexible in their thinking; Lincoln was raised in a frontier community; because of his frontier training, Lincoln was better able to adjust himself and his policies to changing times.

    b. Mateo is a Mexican; he is a fun-loving little rascal; just like all Mexicans.

    c. Savages are notoriously fond of shiny trinkets; John likes them too; he has a bit of the savage in him.

    d. Statistics are reliable forms of evidence; statistics show that traffic deaths in this state have declined 10 per cent since the raising of the speed limit from 50 to 60 miles an hour; raising the speed limit is responsible for the decline in fatalities.

2. Below are listed three comments growing out of three different situations. Read all three carefully, then answer the questions that follow them.

    a. "You'll never get good teachers to teach at those migrant schools down at N—— unless you give them a bonus."

    b. "Don't try to sell Congress on a low-rent housing program with humanitarian arguments; show them how support of the plan will get them votes in the next election."

c. "The only way you'll get merchants to support the March of Dimes in this community is to convince them that a substantial donation is good advertising."

Can you reduce the reasoning behind *each* of these statements to a syllogism? (Note: you must work with more than just the words and ideas in the statement itself; you must *go behind* the statement to reconstruct the assumption and the "reasoning" from that assumption which has led to the statement.)

Next, can you find the basic similarity which underlies all three of these seemingly different statements and construct *one* syllogism which will cover all three? (Here your major premise will be a very broad assumption that lies at the root of the thinking in all three statements.)

Finally, with these four syllogisms before you, can you point out the error in logic (the "fallacy") *common to them all?*

3. Before tackling the following two-part problem, re-read the brief introduction to this entire set of problems.

a. Here is a discussion between two citizens of a city which is building a civic center. They are watching the final touches being put on one of the two still unfinished buildings. The other three buildings have been completed; one, the public library, is already in use.

Write a careful analysis of the deductive processes carried on in this discussion, determining the several basic premises and the deductions drawn from them. You will find no neat, prefabricated syllogisms, but you will find a number of them implied. Also, perhaps, you can detect one major syllogism embodied in the entire discussion carried on by the first speaker.

A. Why did the city fathers go and put up a bunch of factory buildings in the middle of town and call it a "Civic Center"? That's all they are, Bob, just factory buildings, with all that glass and steel and that long wall of brick. Now take that Library building—did you ever see a library look like that before?

B. No, I never did.

A. Don't know when you're outside and when you're inside the doggone thing—you look over the magazine rack right into a garden. No statues of Homer or Shakespeare—no, uh, atmosphere—it's too light, not dim the way you expect a library to be—and it's got no class to it—it isn't impressive the way most libraries are.

B. But I know one of the librarians, Joe, and she says it's a lot easier to work in—more light and not all the drafts they had in the old Library—and she says the use of books has gone up 20 per cent in the two months since they moved in.

A. O.K., maybe it has, but that doesn't make it any more like a library or any less like a factory. And the same goes for these other things, that City Hall, set up on those concrete pillars with all that space underneath.

B. That's for parking, Joe.

A. I don't care *what* it's for, it looks silly, anyway. The old city fathers must be turning over in their graves. No marble steps; instead, you swoop up a ramp and there you are, right in front of a clerk. And there's nothing impressive out in front—no different than a factory. And that Hall of Justice doesn't look any more like a place of justice than I look like Judge McCarthy.

B. Judge McCarthy can fine you fifty dollars in the new one, just the way he did in the old one, Joe.

A. He better not try it again. But, as I was saying, some things just ought to be a certain way, and we know how a court-house should be.

B. Still, Joe, you've got to admit the Recreation Center Building is all right on that score. We've never had one before, so—

A. And *there* you've got a point, friend! We've never had one before, and we don't need one now. A lot of foolishness—a whole big building—good taxpayers' money—for a lot of kids to fool around in, playing basketball, swimming, shooting pool, making clay statues! When I was a kid we got along fine, just going swimming at Craig's Point.

B. They've got a dock there now, Joe.

A. We got along, I say, and so should these kids today. But kids are spoiled today and expect a lot of trimmings. And who pays for the trimmings, huh? We do, you and me. I'm a loyal citizen, and I'm willing to pay my share, but I don't like paying for *frills*. Essentials, yes, but it's wrong to foot the bills for a lot of frills. We got to have firemen and policemen and decent streets, but what do we need swimming coaches for? Answer me that!

B. Yes, but—

b. For this next discussion, *you* can name the time and place. You've heard it before, in smoking cars, on picnics, in your own living room, perhaps. But did you ever analyze it? Here's your chance.

A. Now get me straight, fellows, I'm not condemning a married woman for working if she has to, if she's a widow or her husband's sick, or something. All I'm objecting to is a woman's working when her husband's got a job. A woman's place is in the home.

B. But a home's a place for a lot of people. Why's a woman's place in the home any more than a man's is?

A. Because it's natural, that's why. You can't go changing people's natures. Women were meant to be mothers and homemakers, and men to be breadwinners.

B. I've known some women who were darned poor mothers, and I knew a woman riveter once who was a crackerjack.

A. Exceptions to the rule, that's all, and they don't disprove the rule that women just aren't able to do the things men can do.

B. Why not, if they're strong enough, and so on?

A. I'm not talking about muscle, I'm talking about their mental makeup. They haven't got the natural aggressiveness men have, or men's ability to organize. How many successful businesses are run by women? How many scientists or politicians are women?

B. Not many, that's true, but some. So how can we say they *naturally* aren't fit for those jobs? What about that woman who discovered radium, or for that matter, what about the lady head of the soap company right here in town?

A. Yes, but you have to look hard for them. And you can't find many of them even in the less masculine fields like writing and art and music. Compare the number of great women writers and painters and composers with the number of great men. And why this big difference, tell me that? *I'll* tell you why—because women just don't have the natural quality of leadership and organizing ability that men have. Sure, women can do jobs in labs and run departments in a business, but they don't get to the top because—

B. Some of them do.

A. They don't get to the top because they lack those basic necessary qualities, those important things that make all the difference. But when it comes to motherhood and homemaking, that calls for something different.

B. Why? A woman has to organize her own home, and some don't do it as well as others.

A. That's different. What's needed in being a wife and mother is not executive ability or a big brain but that inborn womanly touch, and she has it because that's what nature intended her for.

B. But you still haven't explained about the women who don't do so well at these things.

A. That's only because it hasn't been developed in them; too often they get ideas that are against their inner nature.

B. How do you or I know what any woman's inner nature is?

A. Why, simply by looking at what women have shown the most talent at—raising kids and baking and caring for the house. And there's the fact that they're biologically the mothers of the race.

B. Wait a minute—now you're talking about being mothers, and we were talking about making a home, and they're not the same thing.

A. All I'm saying is that women were meant to be homemakers, and you can bet your bottom dollar I wouldn't let *my* wife go to work. *I* don't want to depend on a woman, even partly.

B. Now you're talking about something else.

A. No, I'm not. I'm just for what's *natural*.

PART TWO

The Problem of Communication

I. UNDERSTANDING THE RELATION OF LANGUAGE TO THINKING

Recognizing Words as Symbols

HOW is a *word* like a catcher's signal, a stop light, a fire alarm, a national flag, a knock at the door, the · · · — of the Morse Code, a line on a map, a wave of the hand, your grade in last semester's chemistry class, a sorority pin?

"They're all symbols," calls a voice from the back row.

Right! You get an A (a symbol) and can go to the head of the class (another symbol). But can you stay there? If you will agree that MARY is not the girl you hope to take to the next prom but only the noise people make when they wish to address her, then are you ready to agree that, if all the people using certain symbols come to the same understanding, we could substitute RUSSIA for UNITED STATES, DECEMBER for JUNE (remember the old song hit, "It's June in January"?), CLEVER for STUPID, A for F, BUDDHIST for CHRISTIAN, NORTH POLE for SOUTH POLE, UP for DOWN?

"Wait a minute! You can't go turning the world upside down. You can't change certain *facts*."

Wait a minute yourself. Are we changing the *facts*? Does changing a *name* for a fact *change that fact*? Does the fact that an English-speaking dairy farmer calls a certain animal A COW while a French-speaking dairy farmer calls it UNE VACHE, mean that the one is drawing milk from a different species of animal than the other?

"Well, if that's all you mean, I'll go along. But isn't all this pretty obvious?"

Is it? If it is, why do millions of people feel quite different about SPIES and INTELLIGENCE OFFICERS, about a TRAITOR and A CONVERT TO OUR CAUSE, about a PROTECTIVE ASSOCIATION and a MONOPOLY, about a CEMETERY and a BONEYARD, about PUBLIC RELATIONS and PROPAGANDA? Why do many parents, without knowing how an "I.Q." is obtained, want to know what their child's I.Q. is, and then, when they have the quotient, crow or worry about it? Why do governments act as though they believe that forbidding the use of certain rebellious *words* will do away with the rebellious feelings that prompted them? Why do some men today lose their jobs when they are called REDS by irresponsible people even when they have succeeded in demonstrating to a court, jury, or investigating committee that they are not Communist sympathizers?

And here are one or two more questions to mull over. Do the words (symbols, don't forget) you speak and write and read without question always represent *something,* even to you? Do "justice," "immorality," "democracy," "common sense," "intelligence," "efficiency," "human nature," all words that are part of your working vocabulary, actually represent specific persons doing specific things under specific circumstances? Can you *point to* what they represent?

Is the connection between *language* and the *things it represents,* then, really so easy to grasp? The authors of the three selections in this section have not found it so. Kerfoot discovered that many people think "learning to read" is simply the ability to recognize the verbal symbols, the letters and words. He suggests that language, written or spoken, read or heard, has no meaning until the reader or listener brings the word down out of the air and attaches it to something in his own experience. Hayakawa, in a more systematic way, goes to the heart of the symbolic (representational) nature of language and suggests several practical ways to keep language-symbols in touch with reality. And Silone, in "The King of Diamonds," reminds us of the whole purpose of all symbols—playing-card kings, real kings, or words—and points up amusingly the difficulties men make for themselves when they start letting the symbols control them, instead of their controlling the symbols.

Are you ready to take the plunge (symbolically speaking)?

J. B. Kerfoot

Although the title of Kerfoot's essay may sound a little childish, we think you will agree that the problem of "learning to read" in Kerfoot's sense goes pretty deep into the nature of learning and thinking and, in fact, into the whole problem of using language tools to our advantage rather than to our disadvantage.

Do not allow yourselves to miss the point of this article because the movies Kerfoot saw are different from the ones you see.

LEARNING TO READ *

A few months ago I happened to be present at a dinner where a chance question led to an interesting talk. Some phase of primary education was under discussion; and in the course of it the host, turning to one of the guests, asked, "When did *you* learn to read?"

"At three," was the prompt reply, given with a touch of pride.

"And you?" said the host to the next guest.

"Oh, I don't know. About five, I suppose."

"And you?" to a lady beyond.

There was a moment's embarrassed hesitation. And then, with something about scarlet fever, came the confession that she had not learned her letters till she was nine. . . .

There was a cumulative inflection of finality in their declarations. It almost sounded as though, in dealing with the primary-school meaning of "learning to read," they felt that they had dealt with the whole meaning of that expression. And while it never entered my head at the moment that this was really true, the fact that it was somehow being made to appear true struck me as amusing. It struck me as amusing enough to call attention to. And so, presently, when the host asked me when I had learned to read, I answered with a smile that I was still learning.

And to my utter astonishment it developed, in the chaffing and

---

* J. B. Kerfoot, *How to Read,* reprinted by permission of and arrangement with Houghton Mifflin Company, the authorized publishers.

talk that followed, that no single member of that largely literary and more or less intellectual company had ever thought of the expression "learning to read" as *having* any other meaning than the technical, primary-school meaning; that, namely, of learning the alphabet, learning to recognize words made out of the alphabet, learning the dictionary meanings of more, and more, and still more words, and thus learning to *receive messages sent by print or handwriting*.

No one of them, it turned out, had ever asked himself what it is, exactly, that we do when we read. No one of them had ever watched himself in the act of reading. And all of them, in consequence, had retained intact the careless assumption that reading is essentially a *receptive* process. They all looked upon it, let us say, as though print were a sort of silent telephone, into one end of which an author delivers a message, and from the other end of which (by simply "knowing how to read") his audience receives it.

Now, as a matter of fact, and as we shall see presently, this is not true at all. It is not even an inadequate statement of the facts; it is a misstatement of them. And when I had pointed out something of this,—when I had, hurriedly, and to the poor best of my surprised unpreparedness, mobilized a few arguments and illustrations in defense of what I had regarded as a neutralized axiom,—we began, in the course of the give-and-take of the talk that followed, to make discoveries. And we continued, excitedly and joyously, to make them until 1 A.M.

We discovered that the common-school definition of "learning to read" is so universally accepted as the whole definition, that, while almost every newspaper and magazine publishes regular articles on *what* to read, none of them, so far as any of us knew, ever publishes articles on *how* to read. We discovered that, while there is a whole literature of books about books,—about what books it behooves us to read, and why it behooves us to read them, and what (according to the author) it behooves us to read into them,—there is little or nothing in the whole literature about literature that tells us anything at all about how we *have* to read books and what it is that we *have* to read into them. We discovered—But, enough! What we are here concerned with is the last discovery that we made; the discovery upon which, so to say,

the inquiry culminated and broke up; the discovery that I have
tried to summarize in a sentence on the title-page of this book.

We discovered that reading, so far from being a merely receptive act, is a creative process. That it is "creative," not simply
in the more or less cant-sodden "artistic" sense, but in a biologic
sense as well. That it is an active, largely automatic, purely
personal, constructive functioning. That it is, indeed, a species of
anabolism. In short, that it is *a form of living*. And as this last
expression will be found, as we proceed, progressively to absorb
and adequately to sum up the essence of our successive conclusions,
I will put it that it is this last "discovery"—the discovery of reading as a form of living—that I propose to examine and hope to
elucidate in the following pages.

And now, having said this much by way of introduction; having,
as it were, established a mental take-off; let us, like sensible
swimmers, dive at once into the deepest pool that our preliminary
subject affords.

II

Until ten or twelve years ago, no man who ever lived could tell
another man a story.

I am sorry to begin by making so obviously idiotic a statement.
But I have two excuses for doing so. One (which I merely mention
in passing) is that the statement is literally true. The other (upon
which I want to lay all possible emphasis) is that the trueness
of this truth is of the essence of our inquiry.

Allow me, therefore, to repeat the statement.

From the beginning of time, right down until about ten years
ago, no man ever lived who could tell another man a story. Moses
couldn't. Homer couldn't. Chaucer couldn't. The minstrels and
minnesingers couldn't. Dante couldn't. Dickens couldn't. Even
Conan Doyle couldn't.

The best that the very best of them ever succeeded in doing
was to trick, or to coax, or to compel their readers or their hearers
into *telling stories to themselves*.

"Pshaw!" you are very likely going to exclaim at this point.
"Here is a man pretending to explain one idiotic statement by
making another." And perhaps it does look that way. But, before
we continue the discussion, let us take a few minutes off and go
to the movies.

III

That stirring photo-play, "The Two Rattlesnakes," is on the bill. We scuttle down the darkened aisle and slip into some vacant seats near the front.

There is a little hissing splutter overhead. A flickering green frame, with *"Jim meets a rattler"* inside it, springs into view on the dim curtain. And a moment later the entire audience, and we with them, have settled down into an eager, yet perfectly passive, receptivity, and are looking (through a hole in the darkness) at the arid slope of an Arizona sheep-ranch, where a cowboy with a lamb in his arms and an old ewe at his heels is picking his way down the rocky and cactus-grown hillside. On he comes, twisting and turning; near enough now for us to see the litheness of his limbs and his cheery eyes. Then, suddenly, there is a blur of motion at his feet. A snaky something launches its length and strikes for a second at his knee. Bewilderment, horror, realization, chase each other across his face. We see him drop the lamb; snatch out a knife; rip away the cloth; slash the naked flesh; bend to suck the poison from the wound. We watch him make a tortion bandage from the kerchief at his neck. We watch him start, limping, down the hill. We watch him waver, and stumble, and stop to rest with his hand on a boulder. We watch him press on; and fall; and get up; and struggle on again. We see him fall, and fail to rise. We see him, with a last spurt of strength, pull his six-shooter from its holster; fire three slow shots in the air; and drop back into unconsciousness. And we see a little cloud of distant dust turn into the mounted figures of his friends; see them ride furiously up; leap to the ground; gather round him; examine his hurt; lift his inert body to a horse's back, and ride away—just as the hole in the darkness disappears and we find ourselves back again in the dim-lit, crowded hall.

Now it would be nice to sit out the show. To see how *"Mollie gets the News"*—Mollie in her Harlem flat; with her sleeves rolled up above her plump forearms; interrupted in the act of touching a moist finger to a hot iron by the coming of a telegram—"Jim bitten by a rattler. Come at once." To see her drag a chair to the corner cupboard; take down the old teapot; empty its contents on the ironing-board; stuff the money into her purse; put on her wraps and go. To see her, in the next reel, poring over time-tables in an emigrant sleeper; while the other rattlesnake—a human one—watches her from across the aisle. To see him scrape acquaintance with her; learn her story; get out maps; offer suggestions; finally send a telegram of his own—"Meet me at Dry Gulch with the buckboard." To see her whisked behind fast horses to the cattle-thieves' camp. To see the cowboy raid; the timely rescue; the ride to the ranch; the reunited lovers. To see the human rattler tied hand and foot and tossed (on the same hillside that Jim came down in the beginning) into the center of a grim-faced circle and within reach of a coiled something that writhes, and springs, and dashes obscene fangs against his contorted face.

But we haven't time for that. We must get back to our discussion. Let us slip out quietly while the hall is dark.

IV

Do you happen to know how the movies are made?

They begin, like any other piece of fiction, in the mind of a man who has *told himself a story.* Having done so, he undertakes, by means of a short piece of descriptive writing (called a scenario) to guide the imagination of his readers along the road his own imagination has followed. And this scenario is submitted to a movie-manager, who, if he likes it, buys it and turns it over to his producing department.

Now the producing department of a moving-picture concern is a remarkable establishment. It has a long list of actors at its beck and call. It has storehouses full of stage properties. It has clothes-presses full of costumes. It has a card index of "likely places." It has a corps of mechanics to do its bidding. And when the scenario of an author's story is turned over to the directing intelligence of this establishment, he chooses actors for it from his troupe. He supplies them with costumes from his cupboards. He draws stage properties from his stores. He selects scenes from his card index. He has his mechanics provide effects that are not in stock. And finally, before the recording eye of the camera, he proceeds—well or ill according to his ability and his resources— to *re-tell the author's story in the concrete terms of his own equipment.*

And for us who sit in the audience his re-telling—his reading of the story—is final. *You* may know a hillside far more picturesque than the one *Jim* comes down. But you cannot substitute it, in your mind, for the movieman's hillside. *I* may know a girl a dozen times more Molly-ish than the *Mollie* of the film. But I cannot cast her for Mollie's part in "The Two Rattlesnakes." The movieman is reading the author's story, not we. For the moment he stands, like St. Peter, at the gates of our imaginations. What he chooses is chosen. What he puts in is in. What he leaves out is out.

He is the first man who has told another man a story since the world began.

"But," you are perhaps exclaiming, "how then about the others? How about Virgil? And Cervantes? And Balzac? And—Marie Corelli?"

Every one of them, from the least to the greatest, has but written for the movies.

Not for the movies of the photo-theater, but for the movies of our minds.

For a novel is nothing but an elaborate scenario. And each of us is a moving-picture concern.

When we examine a book at a bookstore; when we look at the opening sentences, and read a snatch of conversation on page 247, and turn back to the last page to see how it all ends,—a scenario has been submitted to the manager. When we pay down our $1.35 or present our library card to be stamped,—we have purchased the local rights in it. And when we switch on our electric reading-lamp, and stretch out in our favorite chair, and open the book at the first chapter,—we turn the tale over to our producing department.

And the producing department of a human moving-picture concern is also a remarkable establishment.

All the people we have ever known, plus thousands we have spoken to, or crossed eyes with in a crowd, or watched in public places, or merely glimpsed in passing, are actors at its beck and call. And it can, moreover, pick and choose, not only among these actors, but among their attributes. It can, and that in the twinkling of an eye, take a chance expression on the face of one's best friend, the body of a blacksmith seen years since at a country crossroad, the mustache of yesterday's organ-grinder, and the eyes of last year's cotillion leader, and cast the composite of them (together with the composite suggestion of personality that results) as the villain of a piece.

It, too, has memory storehouses full of stage properties; mental cupboards crammed with costumes; a brain-cell index of likely places. It, too, has a marvelous mechanic, called Imagination, that contrives effects that are not in stock out of odds and ends of raw material.

And when a story-teller's scenario is submitted to it, the directing mind of this establishment—contriving, as they are needed, actors from this troupe; stage properties from these stores; costumes from these cupboards; scenes from this cell catalogue—proceeds, paragraph by paragraph and page by page, before the estimating eye of our intelligence, and well or ill according to its ability and its resources, to *re-tell the author's story in the recollective and imaginative and emotional terms of its own equipment.*

V

Do you, by any chance, doubt this?

If so, I have a confession to make. I have, deliberately and with malice aforethought, deceived you. The photo-play performance of "The Two Rattlesnakes" never took place. *There never has been such a photo-play.*

I made that all up "as I went along," as the children say. And I placed before you, not a story, but only the skeleton of a story— the merest dry bones of a half-finished scenario.

Yet I'll warrant that in reading it you pictured to yourself a *Jim* of your own fancying, walking down a hillside of your own invention. That you contrived a *Mollie* to your own liking and placed her in a flat of your own furnishing. That at the last you invested the horrid death of the villain with emotions dictated by your own temperament. That you either exulted in a punishment that so poetically fitted the crime, or shuddered to see men, made in God's image, capable of such horrors.

Is it not so?

Moreover, when you stop to consider it, you will see that this cannot be otherwise.

The terms of one's own equipment are the only terms in which a story *can* reach us.

For the heroine that the author imagined is forever invisible to us, no matter how minutely he describes her. And though his scene for the moment be Chicago, and though we chance to live there, it is in *our* Chicago, and not in his, that we stage that chapter of his tale. Indeed, if he describes a character *too* minutely,— if he keeps our minds too long from imagining their own protagonists in the effort to imagine his,—our minds end by shrugging their shoulders, going on strike, and refusing to imagine *any*. And it is for the same reason that we so often skip elaborate descriptions of scenery, and that meticulously word-painted landscapes commonly prove invisible to the eyes of our imaginations.

Nor is it alone to the things of the senses that this inexorable law applies. It is the same with less tangible stage properties. When we are called upon to "register" horror, we have only our own brands of that emotion to register. When a mental attitude is asked of us, we can but place our own minds, like lay figures, in, or somewhere near, the posture demanded. And if the specifications of our author's scenario include a spiritual reaction, we must either supply it, or a substitute for it, from the laboratory of our own spirit, or else pass on, saying in effect (as the motion-picture man would say in the vernacular), "Kill that soul stuff!"

VI

But let us go back for a moment to that beginning which we have skipped. Let us go back to the nursery and to our own "learning to read."

Let us suppose that you have just mastered your letters (or, if you happen to belong to the later order, that you have not mastered them) and that you are about to receive your first lesson in reading.

A book is placed before you, open at the first page.

On this page is the woodcut of an animal. And below that are the mystic hieroglyphics, *See the Cat.*

Do you see what has happened?

Do you perceive the significance—the practical symbolism—of this performance? Do you see that at the very threshold of "learning to read," even in the restricted, common-school sense of learning to interpret an arbitrary code of black marks on white paper, there has been placed before you, as a symbol of what you are to do, *the moving picture reduced to its simplest form?* Do you see that in effect, and by the silent pantomime of that juxtaposition, they are saying to you, "Visualize, darn you!"?

But perhaps you will balk at this interpretation.

Let us, therefore, suppose again.

Let us suppose that there is no house cat in your home.

Let us suppose that the weeks have gone by and that you have learned to read many pages in your picture primer; and that one fine morning, on a pictureless page in another book, you come across again those now familiar characters, *See the Cat.*

What happens now?

Why, instantly and inevitably you *visualize the woodcut.*

Why? Because it is the only cat you have in stock; and so, willy-nilly, you cast it for the hero of the sentence. You have, in short, on a ridiculously inadequate capital, begun your career as a moving-picture concern.

Let us pursue the inquiry.

Let us suppose that you go for a few weeks' visit to some cousins in the country, and that one of them has a Maltese kitten.

And let us suppose that on your return, fearing perhaps that you had forgotten your lessons, they put that old primer in your hand, open at the first page.

What happens this time?

Do you accept the woodcut?

Not you. As you take in the words *See the Cat,* your mind presents you, unasked, the picture of a blue-gray kitten, the extreme tip of its tail twitching back and forth above the grass and one curved paw tapping a red apple just fallen in the orchard. And with this picture comes a swift sense of soft winds; and just a taste of cider.

You have, you see, increased the capital of your moving-picture establishment and are already exercising your prerogatives as a producing manager. You have just rejected with scorn the illustrator's offer to supply your equipment. You are *telling the author's story yourself.*

VII

And now I think that we are ready to sum up.

Or, shall we put it that we have now acquired the equipment necessary to read what follows? For that, after all, is what we really mean.

We read, then, quite literally, with our own experience. We read with what we have seen and heard and smelled and tasted and felt. We read with the emotions we have had—with the love we have loved, the fear we have feared, the hate we have hated. We read with the observations we have made and the deductions we have drawn from them; with the ideas we have evolved and the ideals we have built into them; with the sympathies we have developed and the prejudices we have failed to rid ourselves of.

"Learning to read" in the common-school sense—learning, let us put it, to *read print* and learning to *read handwriting*—has exactly as much (and exactly as little) to do with our reading of a novel as it has with Forbes-Robertson's "reading" of Shakespeare.

Learning to read, in the real sense, means enlarging our equipment, and learning, creatively, to use it.

We *receive* in reading; but we receive, not directly by what the author tells us, but indirectly, by the new uses that he stimulates us into putting our experience to.

For reading consists of our making—with the aid of the pattern and the hints supplied by the author, but out of *our* mental stock, which we have produced by living—something that never existed before; something that only exists at all in so far as we make it; something that can never be duplicated by any other reader; something that we ourselves can never wholly reproduce.

Reading is a copartnership. What we receive from it is in the nature of dividends on a joint investment. . . .

X

When you began this chapter, you quite definitely didn't have in your head several ideas that are now there.

You didn't, for instance, have in your head the idea that authors do not tell us stories; that they only issue instructions to us for telling ourselves stories; that they only write "scenarios" for us to "produce."

How, then, did this idea get into your head?

Not, certainly, by my putting it there.

If you are inclined, for the moment, to think that I did this, you have only to turn back to section II of this chapter in order to see how you felt toward *it,* and what you thought of *me,* when I pretended to think that I *could* put this idea into your head.

No. I didn't put it there. I couldn't.

All that I could do was to furnish you, in the proper order, the various formulae needed for distilling it; to see that you were supplied, on occasion, with certain necessary raw materials; and to stimulate you, from time to time, to make certain combinations out of these ingredients.

I knew, for instance, that you were going to need the idea that there were two meanings to the expression "learning to read"; and I was afraid that you might not have this idea in stock. So I suggested that you take a number of ideas that I knew you *could* supply from stock—the ideas of an inquisitorial host; of a series of guests, each of whom thought in his own way that he had learned to read, once for all, when he was a child; and of one guest who thought that he hadn't—I suggested that you take these simple ideas and mix them in a certain way. And you did as I suggested and got the desired result—the more complex idea.

And I took pains to "stimulate you into making this new combination of ideas that were already on hand."

That was a part of my job as author.

I did it, in this case, by inducing you to dramatize the ideas; by inducing you to imagine people holding these ideas, or enacting them. In fine, I did it by *inventing this dinner party;* which, like the photo-play of "The Two Rattlesnakes," never took place.

But the dinner party and the photo-play were invented for entirely different reasons. In the latter case I knew that you were going to need the idea that *we read in terms of our own equipment and not in terms of the author's equipment;* and I was also afraid that you did not have this idea in stock.

But this is an idea that is not easily derivable from the mixing of other, simpler ideas. This is an idea that we get best first-hand, from experience—by actually doing the thing and watching ourselves do it. It is practically one of those realization-ideas, like the idea that fire is hot. Its extreme complexity is due to the extreme complexity of the experience itself.

So I took measures to supply you with the experience.

I wrote a scenario and I tricked you into "producing" it.

And then, while the experience was fresh in your mind, I called your attention to what you had done.

PROBLEMS

1. How does the popular notion of what "learning to read" means illustrate a failure to think inductively?
2. How does Kerfoot get us to use the inductive method to demonstrate the validity of his proposition, that reading is a "creative art" which we are continually learning?
3. After reading Kerfoot, can you see why, later in his book, he argues that the man with the greatest number of experiences is the "best reader"? How is this suggestion related to the scientific thinker's contention that one can arrive at sound generalizations only after a consideration of a great many relevant particulars?
4. In what ways is all reading a performance involving the constant use of symbols? How does a great variety of firsthand experiences, then, serve to prevent a man's becoming confused and misled by reading? (In this connection consider that individual without whom many a college faculty—or student body—would seem incomplete, the "learned fool.")
5. Kerfoot is mainly concerned with the *reading* of words. But what picture does his analysis of reading give of all the other roles of language? Is spoken language any less symbolic and, therefore, any less open to confusion than written language?

S. I. Hayakawa

In a matter-of-fact manner Hayakawa makes suggestions that may startle (and possibly insult) some readers, for he suggests that many of us react to various symbols the way an ape reacts to a green light, and that most people, to some degree, confuse symbols with the things those symbols were invented to represent.

Indeed, he says elsewhere in his book, *Language in Thought and Action*, that people who do this are "linguistically naïve." We suspect, on the basis of our experience as word-users and as teachers of word-use, that few, if any, of us do *not* do those things. This would mean, then, that some, if not all, of us are linguistically naïve.

Angry? Or interested?

SYMBOLS *

THE SYMBOLIC PROCESS

Animals struggle with each other for food or for leadership, but they do not, like human beings, struggle with each other for things that *stand for* food or leadership: such things as our paper symbols of wealth (money, bonds, titles), badges of rank to wear on our clothes, or low-number license plates, supposed by some people to stand for social precedence. For animals, the relationship in which one thing *stands for* something else does not appear to exist except in very rudimentary form.

The process by means of which human beings can arbitrarily make certain things *stand for* other things may be called the *symbolic process*. Whenever two or more human beings can communicate with each other, they can, by agreement, make anything stand for anything. For example, here are two symbols:

X   Y

We can agree to let X stand for buttons and Y stand for bows; then we can freely change our agreement and let X stand for the Chicago White Sox and Y for the Cincinnati Reds; or let X stand for Chaucer and Y for Shakespeare, X for the CIO and Y for the AFL. *We are, as human beings, uniquely free to manufacture and manipulate and assign values to our symbols as we please.* Indeed, we can go further by making symbols that stand for symbols. If necessary we can, for instance, let the symbol M stand for all the X's in the above example (buttons, White Sox, Chaucer, CIO) and let N stand for all the Y's (bows, Cincinnati Reds, Shakespeare, AFL). Then we can make another symbol, T, stand for M and N, which would be an instance of a symbol of symbols of symbols. This freedom to create symbols of *any* assigned value and to create *symbols that stand for symbols* is essential to what we call the symbolic process.

Everywhere we turn, we see the symbolic process at work. Feathers worn on the head or stripes on the sleeve can be made

---

* From *Language in Thought and Action,* by S. I. Hayakawa, copyright, 1941, 1949, by Harcourt, Brace and Company, Inc.

to stand for military leadership; cowrie shells or rings of brass or pieces of paper can stand for wealth; crossed sticks can stand for a set of religious beliefs; buttons, elks' teeth, ribbons, special styles of ornamental haircutting or tattooing, can stand for social affiliations. The symbolic process permeates human life at the most primitive as well as at the most civilized levels. Warriors, medicine men, policemen, doormen, telegraph boys, cardinals, and kings wear costumes that symbolizes their occupations. Savages collect scalps, college students collect membership keys in honorary societies, to symbolize victories in their respective fields. There are few things that men do or want to do, possess or want to possess, that have not, in addition to their mechanical or biological value, a symbolic value.

All fashionable clothes, as Thorstein Veblen has pointed out in his *Theory of the Leisure Class* are highly symbolic: materials, cut, and ornament are dictated only to a slight degree by considerations of warmth, comfort, or practicability. The more we dress up in fine clothes, the more we restrict our freedom of action. But by means of delicate embroideries, easily soiled fabrics, starched shirts, high heels, long and pointed fingernails, and other such sacrifices of comfort, the wealthy classes manage to symbolize, among other things, the fact that they don't have to work for a living. The not-so-wealthy, on the other hand, by imitating these symbols of wealth, symbolize their conviction that, even if they do work for a living, they are just as good as anybody else. Again, we select our furniture to serve as visible symbols of our taste, wealth, and social position; we trade in perfectly good cars for later models, not always to get better transportation, but to give evidence to the community that we can afford such luxuries. We often choose our residences on the basis of a feeling that it "looks well" to have a "good address." We like to put expensive food on our tables, not always because it tastes better than cheap food, but because it tells our guests that we wish to do them honor.

Such complicated and apparently unnecessary behavior leads philosophers, both amateur and professional, to ask over and over again, "Why can't human beings live simply and naturally?" Often the complexity of human life makes us look enviously at the relative simplicity of lives such as dogs and cats lead. But the symbolic process, which makes possible the absurdities of human conduct, also makes possible language and therefore all the human achievements dependent upon language. The fact that more things can go wrong with motorcars than with wheelbarrows is no reason for going back to wheelbarrows. Similarly, the fact that the symbolic process makes complicated follies possible is no reason for wanting to return to a cat-and-dog existence. A better solution is to understand the symbolic process so that instead of being its slaves we become, to some degree at least, its masters.

LANGUAGE AS SYMBOLISM

Of all forms of symbolism, language is the most highly developed, most subtle, and most complicated. It has been pointed out that human beings, by agreement, can make anything stand for anything. Now, human beings have agreed, in the course of centuries of mutual dependency, to let the various noises that they can produce with their lungs, throats, tongues, teeth, and lips systematically stand for specified happenings in their nervous systems. We call that system of agreements *language*. For example, we who speak English have been so trained that, when our nervous systems register the presence of a certain kind of animal, we may make the following noise: "There's a cat." Anyone hearing us expects to find that, by looking in the same direction, he will experience a similar event in his nervous system—one that will lead him to make an almost identical noise. Again, we have been so trained that when we are conscious of wanting food, we make the noise, "I'm hungry."

There is, as has been said, *no necessary connection between the symbol and that which is symbolized.* Just as men can wear yachting costumes without ever having been near a yacht, so they can make the noise, "I'm hungry," without being hungry. Furthermore, just as social rank can be symbolized by feathers in the hair, by tattooing on the breast, by gold ornaments on the watch chain, or by a thousand different devices according to the culture we live in, so the fact of being hungry can be symbolized by a thousand different noises according to the culture we live in: "J'ai faim," or "Es hungert mich," or "Ho appetito," or "Hara ga hetta," and so on.

However obvious these facts may appear at first glance, they are actually not so obvious as they seem except when we take special pains to think about the subject. Symbols and things symbolized are independent of each other; nevertheless, we all have a way of feeling as if, and sometimes acting as if, there were necessary connections. For example, there is the vague sense we all have that foreign languages are inherently absurd: foreigners have such funny names for things, and why can't they call things by their right names? This feeling exhibits itself most strongly in those English and American tourists who seem to believe that they can make the natives of any country understand English if they shout loud enough. Like the little boy who was reported to have said, "Pigs are called pigs because they are such dirty animals," they feel that the symbol is inherently connected in some way with the things symbolized. Then there are the people who feel that since snakes are "nasty, slimy creatures" (incidentally, snakes are *not* slimy), the word "snake" is a *nasty, slimy word.*

THE PITFALLS OF DRAMA

Naïveté regarding the symbolic process extends to symbols other than words, of course. In the case of drama (stage, movies, radio), there appear to be people in almost every audience who never quite fully realize that a play is a set of fictional, symbolic representations. An actor is one who *symbolizes* other people, real or imagined: Fredric March may, in a given play, enact the role of (symbolize) a drunkard. The fact that Mr. March can do so with extraordinary realism proves nothing about his drinking habits, if any. Nevertheless, there are movie-goers who, instead of admiring Mr. March's skill in acting, begin to feel sorry for Mrs. March who is, alas, married to such a heavy drinker! Lewis Stone, who often plays the part of a judge, often gets letters from fans asking for legal advice. James Cagney, who plays "tough guy" roles, is often challenged to fight by men who say to him, "Think you're tough, do you? Lemme show you!" It was said some years ago that when Edward G. Robinson, who plays gangster roles with extraordinary vividness, visited Chicago, local hoodlums telephoned him at his hotel to pay their professional respects.

One is reminded of the story of the actor, playing the part of a villain in a traveling theatrical troupe, who, at a particularly tense moment in the play, was shot by an overexcited cowpuncher in the audience. The cowpuncher of this story, however, is no more ridiculous than those thousands of people today, many of them adults, who write fan letters to a ventriloquist's dummy, or those goodhearted but impressionable people who send presents to the broadcasting station when two characters in a radio serial get married, or those astonishing patriots who rushed to recruiting offices to help defend the nation when, on October 30, 1938, the United States was "invaded" by an "army from Mars" in a radio dramatization.

An extreme case of this kind is that of a woman who had a baby on the same day a fictitious baby was born to the heroine in her favorite soap-opera. She named her baby "Margaret" because the soap-opera "baby" was given that name. Some time later, the soap-opera "baby" "died." Thereupon the woman went into a state of inconsolable grief, being convinced that *her own baby* was dead. When her friends tried to convince her that *that* was her own baby, alive and howling right there beside her, she would not be consoled. "You can't fool me," she said. "Margaret is dead. I heard it on the radio." The woman was, of course, placed in a mental hospital— this was probably only one of many such misevaluations she was in the habit of making. Whatever else was wrong with her, one way of describing this particular misevaluation is to say that the words (in this case of the soap-opera) not only possessed for her the characteristics of reality, but *became a substitute reality completely shutting out the facts.*

THE WORD IS NOT THE THING

The above, however, are only the more striking examples of confused attitudes toward words and symbols. There would be little point in mentioning them if we were *uniformly and permanently aware* of the independence of symbols from things symbolized, as all human beings, in the writer's opinion, *can be* and *should be.* But we are not. Most of us have, in some area or other of our thinking, improper habits of evaluation. For this, society itself is often to blame: most societies systematically encourage, concerning certain topics, the habitual confusion of symbols with things symbolized. For example, if a Japanese schoolhouse caught on fire, it used to be obligatory in the days of emperor-worship to try to rescue the emperor's *picture* (there was one in every schoolhouse), even at the risk of one's life. (If you got burned to death, you were posthumously ennobled.) In our society, we are encouraged to go into debt in order that we may display, as symbols of prosperity, shiny new automobiles. Strangely enough, the possession of shiny automobiles even under these conditions makes their "owners" *feel* prosperous. In all civilized societies (and probably in many primitive ones as well), the symbols of piety, of civic virtue, or of patriotism are often prized above actual piety, civic virtue, or patriotism. In one way or another, we are all like the brilliant student who cheats in his exams in order to make Phi Beta Kappa: it is so much more important to have the symbol than the things it stands for.

The habitual confusion of symbols with things symbolized, whether on the part of individuals or societies, is serious enough at all levels of culture to provide a perennial human problem. But with the rise of modern communications systems, there arises with peculiar urgency the problem of confusion of verbal symbols with realities. We are constantly being talked at, by teachers, preachers, salesmen, public relations counsels, governmental agencies, and moving-picture sound tracks. The cries of the hawkers of soft drinks, soap chips, and laxatives pursue us into our homes, thanks to the radio—and in some houses the radio is never turned off from morning to night. The mailman brings direct mail advertising. Billboards confront us on the highway, and we even take portable radios with us to the seashore.

We live in an environment shaped and largely created by hitherto unparalleled semantic influences: mass circulation newspapers and magazines which are given to reflecting, in a shocking number of cases, the weird prejudices and obsessions of their publishers and owners; radio programs, both local and network, almost completely dominated by commercial motives; public relations counsels, who are simply highly paid craftsmen in the art of manipulating and reshaping our semantic environment in ways favorable to their clients. It is an exciting environment, but fraught with danger: it is only a slight exaggeration to say that Hitler conquered Austria by radio.

Citizens of a modern society need, therefore, more than ordinary "common sense"—which was recently defined by Stuart Chase as that which tells you that the world is flat. They need to be scientifically aware of the powers and limitations of symbols, especially words, if they are to guard against being driven into complete bewilderment by the complexity of their semantic environment. The first of the principles governing symbols is this: The symbol is NOT the thing symbolized; the word is NOT the thing; the map is NOT the territory it stands for.

MAPS AND TERRITORIES

There is a sense in which we all live in two worlds. First, we live in the world of happenings about us which we know at first hand. But this is an extremely small world, consisting only of that continuum of the things that we have actually seen, felt, or heard—the flow of events constantly passing before our senses. So far as this world of personal experience is concerned, Africa, South America, Asia, Washington, New York, or Los Angeles do not exist if we have never been to these places. Chiang Kai-shek is only a name if we have never seen him. When we ask ourselves how much we know at first hand, we discover that we know very little indeed.

Most of our knowledge, acquired from parents, friends, schools, newspapers, books, conversation, speeches, and radio, is received *verbally.* All our knowledge of history, for example, comes to us only in words. The only proof we have that the Battle of Waterloo ever took place is that we have had reports to that effect. These reports are not given us by people who saw it happen, but are based on other reports: reports of reports of reports, which go back ultimately to the first-hand reports given by people who did see it happening. It is through reports, then, and through reports of reports, that we receive most knowledge: about government, about what is happening in China, about what picture is showing at the downtown theater—in fact, about anything which we do not know through direct experience.

Let us call this world that comes to us through words the *verbal world,* as opposed to the world we know or are capable of knowing through our own experience, which we shall call the *extensional world.* . . . The human being, like any other creature, begins to make his acquaintance with the extensional world from infancy.

Unlike other creatures, however, he begins to receive, as soon as he can learn to understand, reports, reports of reports, reports of reports of reports. In addition he receives inferences made from reports, inferences made from other inferences, and so on. By the time a child is a few years old, has gone to school and to Sunday school, and has made a few friends, he has accumulated a considerable amount of second- and third-hand information about morals, geography, history, nature, people, games—all of which information together constitutes his verbal world.

Now this verbal world ought to stand in relation to the extensional world as a *map* does to the *territory* it is supposed to represent. If a child grows to adulthood with a verbal world in his head which corresponds fairly closely to the extensional world that he finds around him in his widening experience, he is in relatively small danger of being shocked or hurt by what he finds, because his verbal world has told him what, more or less, to expect. He is prepared for life. If, however, he grows up with a false map in his head—that is, with a head crammed with false knowledge and superstition—he will constantly be running into trouble, wasting his efforts, and acting like a fool. He will not be adjusted to the world as it is; he may, if the lack of adjustment is serious, end up in a mental hospital.

Some of the follies we commit because of false maps in our heads are so commonplace that we do not even think of them as remarkable. There are those who protect themselves from accidents by carrying a rabbit's foot in the pocket. Some refuse to sleep on the thirteenth floor of hotels—this is so common that most big hotels, even in the capitals of our scientific culture, skip "13" in numbering their floors. Some plan their lives on the basis of astrological predictions. Some play fifty-to-one shots on the basis of dream books. Some hope to make their teeth whiter by changing their brand of tooth paste. All such people are living in verbal worlds that bear little, if any, resemblance to the extensional world.

Now, no matter how beautiful a map may be, it is useless to a traveler unless it accurately shows the relationship of places to each other, the structure of the territory. If we draw, for example, a big dent in the outline of a lake for, let us say, artistic reasons, the map is worthless. But if we are just drawing maps for fun without paying any attention to the structure of the region, there is nothing in the world to prevent us from putting in all the extra curlicues and twists we want in the lakes, rivers, and roads. No harm will be done *unless someone tries to plan a trip by such a map.*

Similarly, by means of imaginary or false reports, or by false inferences from good reports, or by mere rhetorical exercises, we can manufacture at will, with language, "maps" which have no reference to the extensional world. Here again no harm will be done unless someone makes the mistake of regarding such "maps" as representing real territories.

PROBLEMS

1. By all odds the most important of the propositions advanced by Hayakawa is the one citing the disposition of people to confuse the symbol with the thing the symbol stands for. Despite the number and variety of Hayakawa's examples, you cannot be sure you really understand this pitfall in your thinking unless you can supply further examples of your own. Cite examples of this confusion:
   a. In which one might identify a uniform with the thing for which it stands.
   b. In which one mistakes a symbol for proof of patriotism.
   c. In which one mistakes a symbol for proof of his neighbor's prosperity (or his health).
   d. In which one mistakes a symbol for proof of modesty (or immodesty).
   e. In which one mistakes a symbol for proof of genuine friendliness.
   f. In which one mistakes a symbol for proof of progress in education in a community.
   g. In which one mistakes a symbol for proof of someone's piety.
   h. In which one mistakes a symbol for proof of a nation's wealth (or power).
2. Practice in recognizing sources of confusion between non-verbal symbols and what they stand for should sharpen one's awareness of the similar confusion between *verbal* symbols and the objects, experiences, or attitudes they stand for. Try your hand at these examples.
   a. A few years ago, Representative Charles Eaton of New Jersey, then Chairman of the Foreign Affairs Committee of the United States House of Representatives, declared in a public statement: "Neither the Russians nor their tyrants understand the meaning of democracy. They are Slavs, which means captives or slaves."

b. Overheard in a college corridor: "Why does Professor A—— talk so much about taxes and prices and tariffs in History 203? After all, it's a course in American *history,* not *economics.*"

c. An argument has been raging recently before the Merchant Marine and Fisheries Committee of the U. S. House of Representatives. It was prompted by a House bill to protect the bald eagle, symbol of the United States, from hunters in Alaska. At the present time, by Federal law, anyone who kills a bald eagle in any of the 48 states is subject to a $500 fine or six months in jail. But in Alaska anyone can collect a $2 bounty for a set of bald eagle talons. The proposed bill to extend Federal protection of the eagle to Alaska prompted the following statements, as reported in the San Francisco *Chronicle* for February 19, 1950.

   (1) Mrs. Rosalie Edge, chairman of the Emergency Conservation Committee: "The American eagle is a sight to stir the patriotism of every loyal American."

   (2) Republican Representative Edward T. Miller of Maryland: "The unicorn and the lion have for centuries inspired British patriotism. The American bald eagle serves equally well. Long may she wave!"

d. The following is reproduced from the pages of the San Francisco *Chronicle,* October 1, 1950:

   Un-American River—It was the closing night of the Redwood Empire Association's annual convention among the pines at Hoberg's. The meeting had been routine, producing nothing more newsworthy than election of the same executive board again. And the delegates were yawning behind their fists.

   Then a member of the executive board hopped up. "Gentlemen," he said, "we are at war. As loyal Americans we oppose efforts of the Russian government to expand its ideas throughout the world." The convention, he said, should pass a resolution suggesting to the Board of Supervisors in Sonoma, Humboldt, and Mendocino counties that the name of the Russian River be changed to the Redwood River. . . .

   All but one of the convention delegates agreed, and the resolution was duly approved. But it failed to impress the Sonoma County Board of Supervisors last week. Such a thing would be "ridiculous," Supervisor Richard C. Miller said, after the millions of dollars spent on advertising the popular resort stream under the name Russian River.

   Supervisor Victor H. Anderson delivered the *coup de grâce.*

"So we change it to Redwood River," he snorted. "What about that first syllable?"

e. On a college campus where only a few years ago students were forbidden to live in off-campus social clubs because of some "incidents" which had brought complaints from townspeople, a movement to introduce Greek-letter fraternities has been started. Because of the physical limitations of the campus, such fraternities will have to be housed in the city away from the campus. When reminded of the fate of the "clubs," proponents of the fraternity movement reply: "This is different. Greek-letter fraternities are national organizations with respectability and prestige. There will be no repetition of the unwise 'incidents.' " *Query:* Can you detect confusion between *symbol* and *referent* (the thing the symbol stands for) here?

3. Do you agree with Shakespeare that ". . . a rose by any other name would smell as sweet"? What do you think, then, of the charge of blasphemy leveled against the student who argued that another name for God would have done just as well? What obvious evidence is there, indeed, that another name for God has done as well?

4. What is the connection between this tendency to identify word and thing and the long-established literary practice of "humor names," e.g., Dickens' *Scrooge, Dick Swiveller,* and *Rogue Riderhood,* Trollope's *Dr. Proudie* and *Mrs. Bold,* Hawthorne's *Ethan Brand* and *Roger Chillingworth,* to say nothing of the popular juvenile heroes, *Frank Merriwell, Tom Swift,* and *Joe Palooka,* who, between them, span four or five generations of hero-worshipers? A more subtle indication of our tendency to identify word with thing is the little shock of horror we receive from Faulkner when he gives the name *Jesus* to the sullen, potential murderer in his memorable story, "That Evening Sun."

5. A friend of one of the editors was recently offered a valuable collie by a dog fancier who was switching breeds and was looking for a good home for his animal. The friend wanted the dog, a gentle animal with a fine disposition, as a pet for his children. He was not interested at all in the dog's pedigree or the "papers" that proved it. Because he inadvertently revealed this, the dog fancier indignantly refused to give him the dog, exclaiming, "I won't give up this dog to anyone who cannot appreciate his fine qualities." Explain specifically the nature of the dog fancier's confusion.

6. In what way do the varying connotations of the following words and phrases and their effects on us reveal confusion between word and referent?

a. Room 12, Room 13
b. Polack, Pole
c. social security, relief
d. teacher, professor
e. a work stoppage, a work holiday, a strike
f. most people in this country, the average American
g. Mr. A——, Dr. ——; Andrew Mull, Sir Andrew Mull
h. boss, foreman, supervisor, member of the managerial staff
i. a bureaucrat, a government official
j. poetry, verse
k. saloon, cocktail bar
l. mystic, religious person, devout person
m. literature, books, reading matter

7. You wish, for various reasons, that you had read more "good literature." A publishing firm advertises a "Best Books" arrangement by which they will send you one of the "best books of the month" every month of the year. Without considering the nature of the books in the advertisement or those books previously advertised for distribution by the same company, you send them your money. You want to read the "best books" rather than wade through second-rate things. Now, in what way have you mistaken the word for the referent? been guilty of unscientific thinking?

Ignazio Silone

> This short selection is from Ignazio Silone's novel, *Bread and Wine,* which portrays primitive South Italian peasant life and its relation to the world conflicts of the twentieth century. The scene centers around an argument over the nature of a symbol, in this case a visual, not verbal, symbol.
>
> Silone is generally considered one of present-day Italy's most distinguished novelists.

THE KING OF DIAMONDS *

Four youths playing settemezzo had started a quarrel about the king of diamonds. In settemezzo the king of diamonds is the

* Ignazio Silone, *Bread and Wine,* Harper & Brothers, New York, and Jonathan Cape Ltd., London. Copyright, 1936, by Ignazio Silone. Used with the permission of the publishers.

most important card. Matalena only had two packs of cards, and in both the king of diamonds was so worn and easily recognizable that it was impossible for the game to be fair. Daniele Maglietta made a proposal to avoid disputes.

"Since the king of diamonds is recognizable, let us substitute, say, the three of spades, for it. The king of diamonds which is recognizable, will count as the three of spades, and the three of spades, which is indistinguishable from the rest, will count as the king of diamonds."

"That's impossible," Michele Mascolo objected. "It would be impossible, even if we all agreed to it."

"Why?"

"It's obvious," said Mascolo. "The king of diamonds is always the king of diamonds. He may be filthy, or marked, or have holes in him, but he's still the king of diamonds. This, for example, is a pipe. You ask me why. It's obvious. It is a pipe because it is a pipe. In the same way the Pope is the Pope. Why? Because he is the Pope. The king of diamonds is the king of diamonds in the same way. That's what he is and that's what he remains."

"It doesn't matter if we all agree," said Daniele. "If we all agree, it will be perfectly all right. And it will be a better game, because no one will know in advance who has the king of diamonds."

Mascolo remained unconvinced.

"You say it won't matter if we all agree?" he said. "I say it will matter. You say that the game would be the same? Perhaps it would, but it would be a false game. It would be like a wife committing adultery with her husband's consent. Isn't that a sin? It's a double sin, even if everybody agreed."

Sciatàp, who was sitting at the other table, the old man's table, had overheard the argument.

"You must ask Don Paolo," he said.

Don Paolo came down from his room once more and the arguments were repeated for his benefit.

"Tell us who is right," Sciatàp asked him.

The priest held up the king of diamonds.

"Do you think this card has any value in itself or that its value was given to it?" he asked Michele Mascolo.

"It's worth more than the others, because it's the king of diamonds," said Mascolo.

"Where do cards come from?" the priest asked.

"From the printer's," several voices answered.

"What was this card before it was printed?" the priest asked Mascolo.

"A piece of paper, like all the rest of the pack," various voices answered again.

"So its value was given it by the printer," the priest went on. "It had no value in itself, but its value was given to it. And that's not all. Is its value constant or does it vary? Does the king of diamonds have the same value at all games, at tresette, briscola, and scopa, for instance?"

"It has different values in different games," said Mascolo.

"And who invented the games?" the priest went on.

Nobody answered.

"Don't you think the games were invented by the players?" the priest suggested.

Everybody agreed, including Mascolo. The game had been invented by the players, and the value of the cards was different in different games and was therefore fixed by the players.

"So if this card has a value," the priest concluded, "not in itself, but because a value was attributed to it, if it has a value which differs according to the players' whim and fancy, it means that you can do what you like with it."

Enthusiasm for the priest broke out again. "Hurrah!" they shouted. "Bravo! Bravissimo! Never has there been such a wise man of God in our part of the world!"

Don Paolo turned to Sciatàp and said:

"Once upon a time there was a man here, at Pietrasecca, named Carlo Campanella, and now there's a man in New York named Mr. Charles Little-Bell, Ice and Coal. But are Carlo Campanella and Mr. Charles Little-Bell, Ice and Coal, one man or two?"

"They're the same man!" a number of voices replied.

"Sha-tap!" Sciatàp shouted. "It's I who ought to answer that question!"

He answered it.

"They are the same man under a changed name," he said.

"If a man can change his name, why can't a card?" the priest asked.

"A king is always a king," Mascolo replied.

"A king is only a king as long as he reigns," said Don Paolo. "A king who no longer reigns is no longer a king, but an ex-king. There is a country, a big country, in the direction the sun comes from, which used to have a king. Let us call him a big king of hearts. He used to rule over millions of peasants, but from the moment the millions of peasants stopped obeying him, he no longer reigned, and so he wasn't a king any longer. Not far away, in the direction in which the sun sets, there is another country where there used to be a king. Let us call him the king of diamonds. But from the moment his subjects ceased obeying him he ceased to reign. He ceased to be a king and became an ex-king, and now he is a political exile, which is a thing that even a peasant can be. So go on playing at settemezzo how you like, and good-night!"

Don Paolo handed the cards back to Daniele, once more said good-night to everybody and went up to his room, followed by acclamations.

"As you're worn and filthy, from this moment you cease to reign and are not king any longer. You're barely even an ex-king," said Daniele to the king of diamonds.

Then he addressed the three of spades.

"From now on you take the place of the king of diamonds at settemezzo," he said. "Don't get filthy or marked, or you'll lose your crown to another card!"

PROBLEMS

1. The quaintness and remoteness of Silone's setting may strengthen a tendency in some readers to feel that they are too sophisticated to make Mascolo's mistake. Can you recall, however, certain *verbal symbols* used in your college or community that have come to be regarded as important in themselves and whose original meaning has been almost forgotten or entirely lost? Consider, for instance, the password of a fraternity or lodge, or such statements as Socrates' "Know Thyself," occasionally inscribed on the walls or arches of college buildings, or the combination of drawing and text that frequently makes up the seal used on college letterheads.

2. Mascolo reasons that "it is a pipe because it is a pipe." Apparently, Mascolo would reject a bowl-shaped smoking instrument with a stem, called a *shrdlu*. Before you smile patronizingly, consider: Do you buy

aspirin by the name aspirin alone, or do you ask for this commodity by some highly advertised trade name? When you are asked to list the greatest musical composers, do you list those whose music you have *experienced* (Duke Ellington, say), or do you list the *names* of "the masters" whose music you have always been told was "great"? Does your heart leap up when your school hires an "All-American" as football coach even when you know absolutely nothing about his coaching ability? Have you stopped laughing at Mascolo?

3. What has Mascolo permitted to happen to some of the symbols—the king of diamonds and the title of king—which he uses? How does this reduce the usefulness of these symbols to him while playing cards? while playing politics?

GENERAL PROBLEMS:
Recognizing Words as Symbols

1. It is difficult to exaggerate the influence of symbols on our everyday thinking and behavior. Symbols may take verbal or non-verbal forms. To acquire skill in the recognition of *verbal* symbols, our main task, we should probably begin by learning to recognize *non-verbal* symbols.

   a. Start by making a collection of cartoons: cartoons rely heavily on symbols to convey their messages. Look for answers to these questions. What is the symbol for *the* politician? *the* big businessman? *the* farmer? *the* laborer? *the* taxpayer? *the* U. S. citizen? *the* American boy? *the* lobbyist? *the* army officer? *the* college professor? *the* housewife? *the* doctor? *the* poet? *the* social worker? *the* motion picture director? *the* immigrant? *the* vacationer? *the* communist? *the* capitalist? *the* reformer?

   b. Select three or four of the symbols that represent types of people with whom you are best acquainted. Make a careful inductive appraisal of as many *individuals* as possible who, because of their vocation, sex, interests, or environment, fall into the categories you have selected. How closely does each *individual* fit the symbolic pattern? how far does each *individual* deviate from the pattern? How, then, can such symbols lead to confusion in our thinking?

2. Advertising uses symbols nearly as frequently as cartoons do. Moreover, advertising makes use of both *non-verbal* and *verbal* symbols. Advertising, therefore, provides an excellent means of understanding

the transition from the non-verbal symbol to the more complex verbal one.

a. First make a collection of ads from several national magazines (*The Saturday Evening Post, Collier's, Life, The Ladies' Home Journal,* or *Cosmopolitan* will do), ads in which the main idea is got over by means of a non-verbal symbol. To help you get started, these examples are listed: an ad for a motor oil which its makers claim will give your car more power may feature the picture of a tiger ready to spring; a paint guaranteed to "stick to any surface" may be advertised by a picture showing a cowboy "staying on" a bucking bronco; a cast iron pipe alleged to have a high "bursting strength" may be represented by the picture of a trumpet player, with cheeks distended, blowing for all he's worth on his horn.

b. We are now ready to make the transition to verbal symbols. One of the chief purposes of much advertising is to create in us *automatic reactions* to certain brand names. We are expected to act as if we believe the name (the verbal symbol) *is* the thing. So we are urged not to ask for a package of cigarettes, but for "Raffles"; not to ask for a toothbrush, but for "Dr. Tusks"; not to bathe with soap but with "Flux." Make a second collection, this time looking for ads which seek to set up in each of us an automatic reaction to a *word,* a verbal symbol.

c. Still another means employed by advertising is to work through the power of *association.* This can be done by both words and pictures, but in each instance the symbolic process is at work. For example, men are urged to join the most *exclusive* club in the world, a club of *discriminating* men who use "Slicko" after-shaving lotion; and a picture of a well-known athlete or movie star is attached. The implication is, of course, that if you use Slicko you are discriminating, athletic, and ought to be in the movies. And a public that has been awed by the magic of vitamins may be expected to appreciate the value of a "vitaminized" breakfast food like "Beefies," especially when "distinguished scientists" (invariably white-coated men of 60 with Vandyke beards) "attest to the need for vitamins in our daily diet." Your third collection of ads, then, should feature those in which "glamorous words" are relied on to sell the product. (The magic words may or may not be accompanied by pictures; the main indication of such an ad is that it seeks by means of *words* to *associate* the product with something generally assumed to be desirable.)

d. Operating on the highest level of verbal abstraction is the editorial commentary in the form of an ad. Although making frequent use of all the symbolic devices noted above, this masked editorial relies chiefly on very abstract words with powerful emotional connotations. A little girl counting pennies counsels the reader on the necessity for thrift and "sound investment"; a steamfitter, a dirt farmer, a housewife, and a cab driver look up from their work long enough to let us know that "plain folks" like them are the real owners of a great corporation whose management is directly responsible to them for company policies; or a businessman and a mechanic compare, in parallel columns, the American standard of living with the living standards of other countries. The thoughtful reader of "editorial advertising," like the alert reader of all editorial expressions of social, political, and economic views, keeps in mind the *real* speaker and his probable reasons for bringing these views to public attention. Make a collection of this kind of ad.

e. Finally, make a careful analysis of the techniques common to all four kinds of ads. Do you see how the symbolic process links them all? Do you begin to have some real awareness of the symbolic role of words? Do you see how *words* (just words, divorced from any reality except the vaguest kind of association) condition the behavior of us all as consumers? Can you see how this verbal symbol, which affects you dramatically as a consumer, might also be playing a larger part than you previously suspected in your behavior as student, son, daughter, friend, club-member, newspaper-reader, radio-listener, movie-goer, voter (actual or potential), employee (or possibly employer), church-goer (or non-church-goer), traveler, American citizen?

3. Having acquired some knowledge of the easy confusion between word (symbol) and thing (referent) from this little survey of advertising, you should be better equipped to recognize, understand, and guard against this sort of confusion when you see it in other forms of communication.

a. Review swiftly the examples of this sort of confusion set forth in Problems 2 to 6, immediately following Hayakawa's essay, "Symbols," earlier in this section. Now read (1) and (2) below. Point out very specifically the nature of the confused thinking of both the committee of educators and the clergyman.

(1) Recently a state legislature employed a committee of educators to analyze and report on higher education in that state. One of the committee's purposes was to assist the legislature to see that the state university and various of the state colleges did not needlessly duplicate services and functions. As a result, the committee recommended that the architecture department of one of the state colleges delete the word "Design"

from its catalogue description because, said the committee, the function of the *university's* architecture department is "Design, Research, Development" and that of the *college* architecture department is "Planning, Production, Maintenance." So the word "Planning" replaced the word "Design" in keeping with the committee's directive. Members of the *college* architecture department later disclosed that their curriculum, courses, and methods remain precisely as they were before the *word* "Planning" replaced the *word* "Design."

(2) "The Divine is rightly so called." (Clergyman's sermon)

—From Walpole, *Semantics*

b. Now tackle this more difficult example.

A few years ago, a well-known radio commentator and columnist enunciated this doctrine on radio's "Town Hall Meeting of the Air." She committed the future of civilization to the "English-speaking world," arguing that whereas "the German world of Hitler thinks that man is determined by his blood," the English-speaking world "holds the idea that man is determined by his speech, by his mind, and by his soul." She pointed out that it is the Anglo-Saxon tradition that has given mankind the *words* "freedom," "congress," "suffrage," and "rule of the people," and concluded that "the English language instead of being the great separator of men has been the great uniter of men."

Armed with a knowledge of how people confuse the *word* with the *thing,* can you dissect this proposition and expose the nature of the confusion implicit in it? Is this commentator's theory essentially different in its *implications* and *applications* from the Hitlerian philosophy of racism which she was attacking?

4. It is perhaps understandable, if not altogether excusable, that students exposed to this and other kinds of crooked thinking for the first time may occasionally slip into that easy refuge of the tired mind, "Yes, but what's the use of knowing all this? What good is it going to do me now?"

One very immediate and specific "good" that recognition of the pitfalls of verbal symbolism can produce *right now* is the writing of far better papers in all your college classes. If you think the writing of better papers is desirable, give this experiment an honest try. Compare any of your recent themes with *one* of the following pieces of writing: the care and maintenance manual issued to the purchaser of a new car; the safety regulations posted over a campus fire extinguisher; the school manual explaining how to use the library catalogue; any description of a community in any of the forty-eight State

Guidebooks which came out of the Federal Writers' Project (these are found in almost all college libraries). Notice which is the more *factual*, employs the greater number of *relevant details*, says *more in fewer words*, is *better organized*, is *clearer*, and is, therefore, *more interesting*. Now recall the following cryptic notes constantly appearing on the margins of your papers, notes equally familiar to composition instructors and students: "Stick to the point," "More details needed," "Eliminate irrelevancies," "Your subject is too broad, too vague; narrow it," "Be specific," "Boil it down," "Poorly organized," "Not clear," "This idea [sentence, paragraph] doesn't follow logically from the preceding one," "This doesn't say anything," "Make every word count." Then ask yourself this one question: If the *words* I use in my themes had definite, clear, concrete *referents* to something real in the everyday world, how many of these adverse criticisms could I avoid?

To see if you really understand this, study the following list of "typical theme subjects." About which subjects would you have a good chance of writing factually, concretely? Which might lead you into a jungle of verbal abstractions?

a. Communism vs. democracy
b. One specific way (or several related ways) in which inflation has affected me
c. The necessary connection between horsepower and brainpower
d. My reaction to cheating in examinations
e. A change I intend to make (in study habits, in performing some routine task, in budgeting my time)
f. Why I like (dislike) student newspapers
g. When a goal is gained, much is lost
h. Professionalism in college athletics
i. How to construct an inexpensive bookshelf
j. Three ways of making the Army (or Navy) more appealing to enlistees

Now, prove your understanding by selecting wisely and then writing a paper in which every word has a clear, definite, unmistakable referent.

Defining Your Terms

DID you ever ride a verbal merry-go-round and never get the gold ring? Let's watch Susie take such a ride. We may as well seat her on a unicorn, too; it's appropriate that Susie ride a mythical animal in pursuit of a mythical "meaning."

"Gee, that Gregory Peck movie down at the Apollo is terrific!"
"What do you mean, terrific, Susie?"
"What do I mean, terrific? Why, it's out of this world!"
"What does out of this world mean, Susie?"
"Dreamy, stupid, dreamy."
"What does dreamy mean, Susie?"
"Say, what's the matter with you, anyway?"

Silly? Maybe. But do *you* know what Susie means? Does she like Gregory Peck's smile? Or does she like the gowns "created by Estelle" for the heroine? Or did she unconsciously substitute herself for the heroine in the romantic scenes? Or does Susie just like movies?

Probably you can't take Susie seriously (although you'd be making a serious mistake if you thought Susie didn't take herself seriously). All right, then, let's watch a staid lexicographer ride the same verbal merry-go-round.

"How do you define liberty, professor?"
"Liberty is freedom, freedom from a variety of external forces like arbitrary government, foreign rule, captivity, et cetera."
"And how do you define freedom?"
"Freedom is independence as opposed to subjection to arbitrary control."
"And how do you define independence?"
"As freedom from external controls. The terms are really synonymous."
"Thank you, professor."

Are you now in a position to understand what Stuart Chase had in mind when he said that a dictionary definition has about as much relation to the study of semantics (you're studying semantics now) as a windshield wiper has to the second law of thermodynamics?

If these two whirls on the verbal merry-go-round have made you a little less confident that you know what a word *means* when you can substitute another *word* for it, or that all you have to do to find out what a word *means* is to "look it up in the dictionary," you are now in a position to take a long, hard look at the method of definition suggested and illustrated in this section on "Defining Your Terms." The first two essays, by Thouless and Philbrick, will acquaint you with this method. The next three will test your ability to understand and apply this method to a cluster of abstract words very frequently used today, very powerful, and very confusing: the terms Communism, Socialism, Fascism, and Democracy. In selecting these difficult ones to cut your teeth on, we have been governed by two considerations. First, these words have all the characteristics of most hard-to-define words: a high degree of abstractness, the existence of many other abstractions which can be used to "define" them, a powerful emotional impact, and the power to excite rather than to illuminate, to confuse rather than to clarify. Second, if your wrestling with these slippery words leads to *even a little more understanding* of the social forces and conflicts they symbolize, then you may well feel confident that you can pin down other bothersome abstractions.

Robert Thouless

Thouless, a leading English psychologist who has perceived clearly the close connection between language and thinking, here suggests that there is more to the "definition" of our terms than what we find in a dictionary, and he does not recommend "just using simple language" as an easy way out. In fact, he holds that many of our "simplest" words, e.g., "love," "beauty," "loyalty," "freedom," "good," and "bad," may cover up very complex situations and very puzzling problems.

VAGUENESS AND RELATED EVILS *

Definition was intended as a safeguard against all the crookedness in thought which results from either the speaker or the listener in a discussion being uncertain as to the exact meaning with which words are being used, or from a similar uncertainty existing (as it well may) in the mind of an individual thinker even when he is not engaged in discussion with any one else. However convinced we may be that the reckless use of definition has its own dangers, we must still concern ourselves with freeing thought and discussion from these perils. Vagueness in thought and speech is not to be tolerated. Used in moderation and in conjunction with other methods of making thought clear, the method of definition will be found to be a valuable weapon in the overcoming of vagueness.

The most useful kind of definition will, it is true, not generally be the formal definition of the textbooks of logic. When the things we are talking about are not sharply distinguished in fact from related things, we cannot usefully or properly try to cut them off sharply in thought. To devise a definition of "religion," for example, which would satisfy textbook requirements would be a waste of ingenuity. But that does not excuse us from the necessity of being prepared to say as clearly and as precisely as we can what we mean by the word.

The most obvious piece of crooked thinking which results from an absence of clear meanings is that in which a word is used in different senses in different parts of the same argument. A popular writer on "crowd psychology," for example, begins by pointing out the cruelty, irresponsibility, and lack of intelligence of a crowd (that is, of an actual gathering in street or market-place of people with a common interest). He then points out that cruelty, irresponsibility, and lack of intelligence are necessary faults of democratic government, because democracy is government by the crowd. Here, however, he has obviously changed the meaning of the word "crowd,"

* Robert Thouless, *How to Think Straight*. Reprinted by permission of Simon and Schuster, publishers. Copyright, 1939, by Simon and Schuster, Inc.

using it first in its literal sense and secondly in a vague metaphorical sense.

Similarly, in popular discussion of industrial relationships, the terms "labor" and "capital" are used both with their strict economic meaning of work and accumulated wealth, and also as meaning "laborer" and "capitalist" (which is, for example, the meaning implied in the common conclusion that "capital and labor are complementary to one another"). The meanings of the terms may shift from one to the other of these in the course of a single argument so that the words are used in one sense in the premises and in the other in the conclusion.

This habit of using words with two meanings not distinguished is "ambiguity." Bad as this fault is, it is only a minor degree of vagueness. If a word is used with no particular meaning or meanings but only with a general tendency in some direction, we have a more extreme form of the disease which makes accurate thought and reasonable discussion impossible.

In order to be vague it is not necessary that a statement should also be obscure. It often is, and more or less deliberate obscurity is often a cloak for vagueness. But the simplest statement or thought may be vague if it does not embody a clear meaning in the mind of the person making it. This is particularly liable to happen with abstract words. Such words, for example, as "principle," "wealth," "mind," "spiritual" have meanings which can never be carried by a mental image of an outside object or action or of a relation between outside objects or actions. Their proper meaning is a kind of summary or abstraction of many different outside things.

We all of us hear many such words which at the beginning carry no meaning for us at all, and we are quite likely to take them over into our vocabulary before they have a clear meaning. To obtain clear meanings for any but the common names of outside things requires a certain amount of mental effort, and idleness leads us to be content with taking many words into our speech and thought without making this mental effort.

Let us first consider how to get rid of vagueness from our own minds before we consider how we can combat our opponent's vagueness in argument. We can begin by consulting definitions. Habitual recourse to the dictionary whenever we meet with a new word before taking it into our vocabulary is a useful rule which helps against the development of words without clear meanings in our vocabularies.

While the use of dictionary definition should save us from using words with shifting and variable meanings, it does not do everything that is necessary to make them a serviceable part of our mental equipment for straight thinking. In order to provide an example of the further difficulties which must be overcome, let us consider a fairly new technical word in medical psychology which has escaped into popular speech, where it is misused as badly as is possible. This is the word "complex."

Let us turn to a definition of this word and see whether it provides us with complete safeguards against its improper use. We shall not find it in dictionaries, but in the glossary of a recent psychological textbook I find a definition which I have slightly shortened as follows: "COMPLEX: A group of ideas linked together because they form a chain in some potential instinctive reaction. A complex is always unconscious or, at least, owes its importance to elements in it which remain unconscious."

If we understand all parts of this definition and the rather unusual sense in which the author is using the words "idea" and "unconscious," we should have a fairly clear notion of the way to describe a complex, and we should be certain that a number of ways of using the word were not what is intended by the definition. We should not, however, have any confidence that we knew how to use the word in practice or what kinds of facts in human nature ought to be labeled by it, any more than from having read an accurate description in words of a deep-sea fish, we should be able to draw the fish or even to recognize it if we saw it.

We may thus know in words what "complex" means and yet find that it does not for us serve the purpose of indicating anything whatever. For us it remains, in a sense, meaningless. Probably the vocabulary of most people contains some words which are thus meaningless. Even if they can say in other words what they mean, they cannot make use of them in understanding the external facts they are meant to deal with. Any mental activity they carry out by means of such words hardly deserves the name of thinking. It is rather a kind of mental game carried out with word habits. The game may amuse the player, but it cannot guide him to sound conclusions which he can apply to the world outside him.

Something more must be done after we have read and mastered the definition of "complex." We must ask also for an example or examples of what is meant. Let us suppose that someone who undertakes to explain the word to us goes on to describe the mental origins of the so-called "nervous" disorders, such as a long-forgotten fright in childhood from an oncoming train producing in later life a persistent terror of going more than a few hundred yards from home, or forgotten childish resentment against one's father producing a later passionate hatred of kings, judges, policemen, and all in authority. After having heard these illustrations, we may be able to say: "Now I see what you mean by 'complex.'"

The word "complex" now arouses in our minds ideas of the sources of peculiarities in emotion and behavior which we have actually experienced. It has a usable meaning. The definition alone may have connected it up with nothing but a set of other words which in combination had no clear meaning for us.

Of course the two examples of complexes given are by themselves not a sufficient system of ideas to have attached to the word to make it a serviceable part of our mental equipment. Under their guidance, however, we should soon gain enough experience of our own and other people's complexes to enrich the system of ideas connected with the word; the definition also playing a useful part in this process by enabling us to decide which of the curious phenomena of behavior we are to attribute to complexes and which not. So, by the combined use of the method of definition and the method of illustration, we have gained a clear and useful meaning to the word and are saved from the danger of using it vaguely and also from the danger of using it without reference to anything real in the world around us. . . .

PROBLEMS

1. Thouless distinguishes between two kinds of crooked thinking growing out of the misunderstanding and misuse of words. Suppose you were asked, "What are these two kinds?" Those of you with a fair degree of verbal skill and rote memory ability might respond, "ambiguity" and "meaninglessness." Would these "correct" answers indicate that you necessarily understood what Thouless was talking

about? Are you assuming that because you can supply the right *words* you necessarily understand what the words refer to? Both "ambiguity" and "meaninglessness" are themselves highly abstract words. Can you give a concrete illustration of either or both as Thouless defined and illustrated them? If not, they are "meaningless" to you.

2. Thousands of students and teachers mistake for intelligence the ability to verbalize. This confusion is well illustrated in those examinations where the student gives back to the teacher the *words* he guesses are in the teacher's mind. Study some examples of your examinations. What is being tested—your ability to *apply* an idea or your ability to *recall* the "right word"?

3. Many of you brought up by mass production educational methods— "objective tests," drills and exercises, textbook memorization—are baffled and even resentful when you are confronted by a course in which you are exposed to doubt and uncertainty, in which, as you yourselves put it, you "have to think." Re-appraise such a course and ask yourself to what extent the difficulties you rebel against are the result of your being seldom required in the past to find the exact *referent* (a concrete act in the real world) for all the vague and abstract words you customarily use so loosely.

4. One of the most unfair jokes ever played on unsuspecting college students was the publication a few years ago of a series of little volumes called "College Boners." The volumes consisted of examples of word-errors made by students in their compositions and examinations. An example: "Lincoln *emaciated* [instead of emancipated] the slaves." These were greeted by many editors, publishers, reviewers, and the reading public in general as "howlers." The conclusion of most of these people was that anyone who couldn't use these *words* correctly was "dumb," and "what are our colleges coming to, anyway?" In the light of Thouless' essay and the foregoing questions, can you point out a fundamental error in their thinking? Digging a little deeper, what was probably wrong with the training of the student who wrote, "Lincoln emaciated the slaves"? What part did rote memory probably play in his "learning" about this historical event? Cite other examples of this kind of "learning."

5. Course descriptions in college catalogues are almost always brief. They seldom mention the *means* or *methods* employed in the course. Why could this omission be a serious defect? What are some of the reasons, do you suppose, for such omissions? Remembering the use to which a college catalogue is usually put, do you think such omissions are justified?

Consider this description:

Art in Everyday Living. A course designed to add to the student's understanding and enjoyment of the visual arts. The basic principles of artistic expression will be approached through a study of their application in architecture, landscaping, sculpture, painting, photography, motion pictures, and such applied arts as ceramics, metal work, and weaving. The course will stress the role of the visual arts in everyday living. Much use will be made of prints, slides, and other visual aids, and field trips will be arranged to acquaint the student with the ways in which art enters into the life of an American community.

Knowing some of the common "definitions" of "art," can you determine why this description is so detailed? At what common assumptions about "art" is it aimed? To whom is it designed to appeal? Whom is it designed to warn away, perhaps?

F. A. Philbrick .

This brief excerpt from *Understanding English* by Frederick A. Philbrick, who deals with language problems at St. Paul's School in Concord, New Hampshire, will serve as an introduction to the three selections which follow it. Philbrick's "On Definition" and the succeeding three selections tackle one of the most fought-over and significant terms of the twentieth century: "democracy." None of these writers leans hard on the dictionary, for all find themselves wrestling with a problem not so much of *language* as of observing and thinking inductively. As you read these selections you will, if you follow the writers' meanings, find yourself looking at your own and your neighbors' actions, at your classroom activities, your family life, your dormitory living, the way your community voted yesterday, the strike in a certain industry. None of these writers comes up with a pat, one-sentence "definition" of "democracy"; rather, they all focus on many contemporary facts which, to one attempting to discover a workable definition of democracy, might prove more useful in the long run than high-sounding phrases.

You might find it helpful to try out the same method of definition on abstract terms which, although significant to our thinking, are somewhat less immediately "world-shaking" in their effects, for instance: "school spirit," "cheating," "friendliness," "good health," "co-operation," "intelligence," "realism," "efficiency," "leadership."

ON DEFINITION *

WHAT IS A DEFINITION?

There are two ways of defining a word. One is to look up a synonym in the dictionary, that is, another word with a similar reference. Even though exact synonyms do not exist, this resort to the dictionary is often useful, but it is obviously one link in an endless chain, because all we do is to define one word in terms of another word, and so on, with no reference at any stage to things. As a device for learning about the relations between *"Things, Notions, and Words"* (as John Wilkins calls them), this cyclic process is therefore of very little help.

To explain the second way of defining words, let us suppose that the person who is going to do the defining, Mr. D, is alone in some remote spot, perhaps a desert island, with the inquirer, Mr. E. The island must be provided with all the objects that have to be defined, but Mr. D and Mr. E do not speak any common language, and there are no dictionaries. In these surroundings recourse must be had to the methods used in certain schools of language instruction—namely, pointing and pantomime.

This is a useful beginning, but it is not sufficient to cover all the words; some of them have to be defined by the use of metaphor. Words will now be classified according to whether they can be defined by one or another of these three ways—pointing, pantomime, or metaphor. This classification is for the most part independent of parts of speech, such as nouns, verbs, adjectives, and so on.

DEFINITION BY POINTING

Some words can be defined by pointing to the referent. To define *goat*, Dr. D procures a goat and points to it. Things which can be defined in this way may be called *picturable*. This convenient word is not perfectly adapted to its present use, because there are some things that can be pointed to but cannot be pictured—for instance, oxygen (a colorless, transparent, invisible gas). But with a very

* F. A. Philbrick, *Understanding English.* Copyright 1942 by The Macmillan Company, and used with their permission.

few exceptions picturable things can be defined by pointing. Some qualities also can be defined by pointing—*red* and *reddish*, for example, as well as *redness*. To define *red*, Mr. D has only to collect a number of red things of different sorts, and to show them as a group to Mr. E. It is quite true that Mr. E might think at first that the word *red* meant "same-colored" or "homogeneous," but continued experience would convince him of his error, because he would see that other words were given for collections of green, blue, and yellow objects. This defining of words by pointing to their referents must not lead the unwary to suppose that there is a direct connection between word and referent, an error which has serious results if it occurs when words are being defined in more elaborate ways.

DEFINITION BY PANTOMIME

To define by pantomime is to do something to show what the word means. *To dig* and *to run* are defined by the acts of digging and running. But not only verbs are thus defined; *yard, acid, energy,* and *ampere* can be defined by pantomime, or by *operational definitions,* as they are called by scientists. To define *yard*, Mr. D takes a stick a yard long, or with two marks on it a yard apart, and lays it along several things as if to measure them. A yard is not a picturable thing (the stick, in particular, is not a yard), and it is not a class of things, like *fruit* or *ore*, nor can it be defined by pointing. It has to be defined by doing something, in this example by making a measurement. *Ampere* is likewise incapable of definition by pointing and has to be defined by doing something—namely, by measuring the increase in weight of a silver wire immersed in a certain solution and connected in a certain way to a circuit in which the current flows for one second. (There are several alternative definitions, of which this is one.) Among the adjectives which have to be defined by operations are *soft, elastic, poisonous, combustible.*

For discussions of language . . . the difference between definition by pointing and definition by pantomime is not of great importance. *Spade,* for example, may equally well be defined by pointing to a collection of spades or by using the spades in turn for digging. But the distinction between definition by pointing or pantomime on the one hand, and definition by metaphor on the other, is of great importance both in language and science, as will soon be apparent.

DEFINITION BY METAPHOR

Words that cannot be defined by pointing or pantomime will be called *abstractions,* using a word borrowed from *Language in General Education,* where it is used with a somewhat similar reference. Abstractions are defined by metaphors. These metaphors often involve other abstractions, which in turn must be defined by metaphor, and for elaborate abstractions the chain may be a long one; but ultimately the metaphors reached can be made to include only words definable by pointing or by pantomime. *Beauty* and *goodness* are complicated abstractions of this sort, and the discussion of what metaphors are most suitable for defining them forms a large part of the subject matter of aesthetics and ethics. Because such discussions are beyond the range of this book we shall choose simpler abstractions as examples. In some words, which are used as symbols both for abtractions and for things definable by the other two methods, it is easy to detect the metaphor by which the abstract use can be defined. For instance the relation of *bitter* feelings to the feeling part of a man resembles the relation of a *bitter* taste to the tasting part of him. Other examples of such words are gravity, fortitude, lowliness. But for some other words the task of finding an appropriate metaphor is less easy. The word *war* is a comparatively simple abstraction and may be defined by the metaphor, "One group of people wars with another group as one man fights another man." In this metaphor the vehicle is "One man fights another man" (a relation between two groups). In the metaphor, *group, people,* and *man* can be defined by pointing; fights, by pantomime.

Navigation, navigator, and *to navigate* are other examples of abstractions. "As a man finds the way on the ground, so a navigator finds the way in a ship or aircraft." *To find the way* can be defined by pantomime; *ground, ship,* and *aircraft* by pointing.

The abstractions of greatest practical interest are usually those whose definition requires the longest chain of metaphors, and also those used in the greatest number of senses. As an illustration, suitable by reason of its practical importance and theoretical interest, it may be profitable to examine the many elements of meaning in the word *democracy*.

DEFINING THE WORD *DEMOCRACY*

An abstraction of this type is best considered as a collection of many different words. *Democracy* has different references for different people, and different references when presented in different settings to the same person, or even when used by him in different settings. There is no "correct" definition or set of definitions, and all that can be done is to study the settings in which the word is used. Here is a list of some of the ideas which people are likely to have in mind when they use the word *democracy* or *democratic:*

1. The leaders or rulers are to be chosen from the people in general, and not from any privileged class.
2. They are to be chosen by the majority of the people.
3. They are to be responsible to the people for their acts and may be dismissed by the people.
4. They are to govern for the benefit of the people.
5. The actions of the government are to be directed to securing the greatest happiness of the greatest number.
6. No privileges are to be given simply because of birth, wealth or race.
7. There are to be no forms suggesting such privileges: no titles, for instance, or elaborate social codes, or special forms of speech, such as a socially acceptable accent.
8. Every citizen is to have equal opportunities.
9. Every citizen may speak freely (freedom of speech).
10. Every citizen may write freely (freedom of the press).
11. No one shall interfere with religious opinions or ceremonies (freedom of worship).

More debatable, though certainly considered by some to be included in this word, are the ideas:

12. Women should have the same opportunities as men.
13. Private enterprise should be encouraged and public enterprise discouraged or forbidden. This view is popular with the members of some business associations. The National Association of Manufacturers, for instance, pays for billboard advertising in which private enterprise is connected with less

controversial notions such as 2 (representative government) or 11 (freedom of worship).

These thirteen statements include many abstractions, themselves in need of definition. Each of these could ultimately be reduced by metaphor to words definable by pointing or pantomime, but the task would be a very long one. That it is necessary to distinguish between the various meanings of *democracy* is shown by the frequent confusion between meanings 1 to 4 and meanings 8 to 12, that is, by the belief that individual liberty is necessarily connected with a democratic way of choosing the government. History proves that individuals and minorities can be oppressed quite as savagely in democratic states (meanings 1 to 4) as in autocratic ones.

PROBLEMS

All of us use, read, and hear many abstract terms which mean—refer to—a number of things. This multiplicity of meaning leads to vague, unconcrete thinking and to misunderstanding. Both you and I may approve of "loyalty," but we may be thinking of loyalty to different things: to one's own conscience, one's family, the boys at the club, the union, an employers' association, the Army or Navy, the nation, a political party, a social ideal that crosses national boundaries. For instance, I may feel that loyalty to one's nation is the fundamental, most important kind of loyalty and so may urge that everyone take a "loyalty oath." Approving of something called "loyalty," too, you approve of such an oath, or at least do not actively oppose it. Too late you discover that my kind of "loyalty" (my country, right or wrong) clashes with your loyalty to your own conscience or to your union (which may be fighting certain things of which the government has approved) or to your religious faith (whose demands may clash with the demands of the nation). Maybe I purposely misled you; maybe I didn't know we meant different things. In either case, the misunderstanding got you into a very real difficulty.

We can never entirely escape the use of abstract, general language; we have to generalize and so have to use generalizing terms. Hence, we can never entirely avoid the kind of communication trouble mentioned above. But we can *reduce* its frequency and dangers by:

One, using concrete words (words having definite referents) whenever possible, and

Two, qualifying our abstractions when we use them, e.g., "loyalty to the federal laws," "loyalty to one's economic class," "loyalty to a certain party," "loyalty to a certain religious faith"—not just "loyalty."

These precautions might seem to bury us under a load of words. Sometimes we *do* have to be long-winded in order to make ourselves clear. But, before you get discouraged, consider the following points:

One, a scientist's account of a flower, an animal, a machine, or a process is usually in very concrete, definite language and is full of qualifications, and, hence, is probably quite accurate and quite lengthy—in contrast to the non-scientist's simple, inaccurate generalization. You may find the scientist's report tiring—but contrast the advances made in the physical sciences in the past hundred years with the confusion that still exists in almost all man's other activities.

Two, the use of qualifications and concrete terms frequently saves time. Debaters, rushing into an argument over the merits of Communism or liberal education or public ownership or free enterprise, without taking time to define what these terms mean to them, usually end where they started; and everybody goes away mumbling, "What was it all about?" Or they may leave feeling they know what it was about when they really don't.

1. Here is a list of statements based on frequently used and very potent abstract words. After each statement are questions which, if answered, will lead to a clearer understanding of the issue under consideration and of the writer's view of it. After answering such questions one can then tackle more surely the problem under debate.

    a. Any female schoolteacher who smokes should be fired; women who smoke are not *respectable.*

    Respect for what? (Conformity, timidity, intellectual ability, self-restraint, self-sacrifice, human warmth, social grace, ability to do the job?)

    Respect of whom? (The town's bar set? most of the parents? the more tolerant parents? the less tolerant parents? the school board? the principal? the principal's wife? a certain religious sect? the children?)

    b. A college education should be *practical:* therefore, a man's time should not be taken up with such courses as music, history, economics, philosophy, literature, and psychology.

    Practical in what sense? (Immediately applicable? Applicable to the whole of a man's life and requiring further specialized training, for which it is a necessary basis?)

    Practical to whom? (Poor, middle-income, or rich students? Men, women, or both? Future mechanics, farmers, engineers, scientists, businessmen, medical men, lawyers—or persons whose future work is still uncertain?)

Practical for what? (To give a man certain skills and knowledge by which he can gain a livelihood? To give him methods and habits of thought which he can apply in later specialization? To make him a responsible, thoughtful, as well as skillful, citizen? To help him develop a fuller, richer way of life? To give him certain facts and degrees which would make him acceptable to certain groups? To help him develop a personal philosophy?)

On the answer to these questions depends one's agreement or disagreement with the conclusion in the statement given above.

c. The union shop is unjust because it interferes with every wage-earner's *right to work.*

Whose right to work? (The *right to work* of the wage-earner who is willing to accept any wages and conditions the employer will offer him? Or the *right to work* of the wage-earner who will work only for what he considers a living wage and under what he considers healthful conditions, and who has joined a union to obtain these basic requisites?) Now, if an employer offers less and the first wage-earner accepts, does not *his* right to work cancel out the union man's right to work? The union man may feel that his job (his right to work) is protected by the union which restricts other men's right to work. Do we have here a clash of rights of different groups analogous to that which may occur when a government, by guaranteeing prices on a producer's product, to protect his right to a certain standard of living, raises costs to foreign consumers and thus infringes on the right of those consumers to a certain living standard? Having perceived that there are two kinds of *right to work,* we are now better equipped to go into the question, "Is the union shop unjust because of its interference with the *right to work* of a certain group of wage-earners?"

d. *The American home* is the safeguard of our American way of life.

Of course, we first have to explain what we mean by "our American way of life," but once we think we know the writer really means something by it and are pretty sure of what he means, we still have to face the phrase, *The American home.*

What kind of American home? (The slum home or the well-to-do man's home? The Southern, New England, Middle Western, or Far Western home? The Negro home or Italian home or Mexican home or *Mayflower*-ancestor home? Big-family home or small-family home? Broken or happy home? Religious, or non-religious home? Father-dominated, mother-dominated, or nobody-dominated home?

If we find there is a home most typical of America (dominant in America and not dominant elsewhere), what are its characteristics or qualities? We are now ready to ask: Are these qualities peculiar to the home and not found in other American institutions such as fraternal organizations, churches, and schools?

Now, maybe, we are ready to consider the question: "Do these qualities of the American home safeguard our American way of life?"

With these several examples as a guide, consider the following statements. Each statement contains one or more potent abstract terms; these terms are italicized. What questions would you have to raise and answer in order to obtain any very clear idea of the "meaning" of these abstractions?

a. It should be apparent to any *thinking* man that a college education is *indispensable*.
b. The French are an *immoral* people.
c. What our schools need above everything else today are *superior* teachers.
d. The *American people* will never surrender their *liberties*.
e. The problem of the Navajo Indian is unsolvable: you can't do anything with a *backward* people.
f. Wartime strikes are *un-American*.
g. Greenfield is a more *religious* community than Overhill.
h. The practices of some corporations are downright *fascistic*.
i. The tax proposals of the Democratic Party shake the *confidence* of *business*.

2. What abstractions used by Philbrick in the thirteen "definitions" of democracy *themselves need defining*?
3. What sensible, but not simple, procedure does this vain substituting of one abstraction for another compel you to adopt eventually if you are to come to grips with the *processes* (certain people acting in certain ways under certain circumstances) that the word "democracy" has come to symbolize? (The selection called "Democracy and Despotism" in this section will be especially helpful to you here.)

Carl L. Becker

Becker (1873-1945), a distinguished professor of history at Cornell and one of America's best-informed thinkers about contemporary political philosophies, was primarily concerned with discovering the ends and means of democracy. This task, of course, compelled him to look at the fundamental problems of society and at the various types of social organization, including democracy, that man has evolved in the attempt to solve them. Can you define a vertebrate without also defining an invertebrate? define a growing plant without also considering the earth and air by means of which it grows?

As a historical analyst, Becker always tried to get beneath the labels of periods and events, to determine the trends of events, and to find what help they may give us in our efforts to understand, and usefully label, today's history-in-the-making. His writings include *The Declaration of Independence, Freedom and Responsibility, Everyman His Own Historian,* and *Modern Democracy.*

SOCIALISM, COMMUNISM, FASCISM *

That the defects of the capitalist system are inherent is the contention of those ideologies known as Socialism and Communism. Socialism and Communism, taken in the generic sense of the words, are at least as old as Plato; but in their modern forms they derive from the doctrines formulated by Karl Marx in the middle of the last century.

Marxian Socialism, inspired by the failure of democratic institutions to effect an equitable distribution of wealth, was essentially a reinterpretation of the modern doctrine of progress, and as such it comprised a social theory and a philosophy of history. As a social theory it maintained that the social structure at any time is fundamentally determined by the methods of production and distribution of wealth, and that the prevailing institutions and ideas are those best adapted to maintain the interests of the class which, by ownership and control of the chief forms of wealth, dominates the social structure in its own interest. As a philosophy of history it maintained that social change, or progress, is the result, not of a conflict of ideas, but of economic forces, a conflict between the economic interests of the ruling and the dispossessed classes. Not by the persuasive force of ideas, but only by the impersonal pressure of economic conditions, could the ruling class ever be dispossessed, or the

* Carl L. Becker, *Modern Democracy,* Yale University Press, 1941.

institutions and ideas through which its power operates ever be transformed.

Applying this theory to European history, Marx found that the liberal-democratic revolution was the result of the conflict between the economic interests of the landed aristocracy and the rising capitalist class. So far from reflecting the triumph of true over false ideas, it reflected the triumph of capital over land as the pre dominant factor in production; and the superstructure of liberal democratic ideas and institutions, so far from having a universal validity, had merely the relative and temporary value of being suited to the functioning of the capitalist system and the interests of the ruling bourgeois class. The liberal-democratic revolution could not, therefore, be regarded as the final term in the historic process. On the contrary, the capitalist system once established there necessarily developed within it a new conflict between the interests of the ruling bourgeois class and the dispossessed proletariat which would inevitably issue in another social revolution.

The coming social revolution was inevitable, according to Marx because the capitalist system, like the landed aristocratic system before it, contained within it the defects that would transform it— defects inherent in the institution of private property and the competitive system. The ruthless competition for profits would necessarily result in an increasing concentration of wealth in the hands of those who proved most able in the ruthless competition for profits thereby reducing the laborers and the defeated capitalists to the level of a bare subsistence; and when this process reached a certain stage the system would collapse for the simple reason that there would be no profit in producing commodities when the underlying proletarian population was no longer able to purchase them at a price that would yield a profit. When this state was reached, the proletariat, made class conscious by their misery, instructed in the dialectic of social change by their leaders, and united for the defense of their class interests, would by revolutionary action abolish private property in land and capital, and through a democratic government based upon a classless society, organize the production and distribution of wealth for the common good.

The Marxian doctrine provided a new and persuasive ideology for the oppressed working classes whose hopes were persistently defeated by liberal-democracy as a going concern. Its analysis of the capitalist system justified their grievances against their employ-ers, while its philosophy of history promised them that all would be made right in the future, and assured them that in defending their class interests they could not fail since they were supported by the indefeasible forces that shaped the destiny of mankind.

Inspired by the Marxian faith, the industrial workers formed new political parties, for the most part called Socialist, and for the most part accepting the Marxian doctrine of the social revolution. But meantime, while waiting for the coming revolution, and as a prepa-ration for it, the Socialist parties adopted a program of social legis-lation designed to benefit the masses at the expense of the classes. Attracted by this practical program, lower middle-class people, mostly timid folk who abhorred the idea of violence, voted in in-creasing numbers for Socialist candidates in the hope of benefiting from the legislation which the Socialist parties promised to support. One result of this trend in practical politics was that the Socialist parties derived their chief support from voters who were not Marxian socialists; another was that the leaders of the Socialist parties, in order to win and hold non-Marxian voters, found it neces-sary to soft-pedal the doctrine of imminent, catastrophic revolution. In the decade before the Great War the dominant Socialist parties had therefore virtually abandoned the Marxian conception of the revolution as a violent upheaval, and conceived of it as a slow and peaceful process in which the masses, by established political meth-ods, would gain control of the government and by normal legis-lative procedure within the existing democratic regime would abol-ish private property in land and capital and socialize the produc-tion and distribution of wealth.

During the Great War the influence of Socialism naturally de-clined, but the orthodox Marxian tradition, barely kept alive by minority groups within and without the dominant Socialist parties, was given a dramatic and world-wide significance by the Russian Revolution. As reinterpreted by Lenin and realized in the Soviet regime, neo-Marxianism took the name of Communism, and must be clearly distinguished from Socialism as understood by such pre-war Socialists as Bernheim and Kautsky, and such present-day Socialists as Norman Thomas. Present-day Socialism and neo-Marx-ian Communism agree in one thing only—the necessity of abolish-ing private property in the means of production. In respect to the means for accomplishing this desired end they disagree radically. Socialism maintains that it can be accomplished by peaceful political methods within the framework of the existing democratic regime; Communism maintains that it can be accomplished only by violent revolutionary expropriation of the capitalist class, carried through for the masses by the dictatorship of a disciplined Communist party.

It was also an essential part of Communist theory that the establishment of Communism in one country would be the prelude to an international Communist revolution. So far, the prediction has not been realized. Revolutions there have been, in Italy, in Germany, in many European countries. But these revolutions, stimulated in part by the fear of Communism rather than by devotion to it, have taken the name of Fascist; and until recently at all events Communism and Fascism have been commonly regarded, especially by the Communists and Fascists themselves, as being fundamentally opposed to each other.

In respect to political theory there are certain differences between Communism and Fascism. In theory Communism maintains that the dictatorship, a drastic technique essential to the revolution but ending with it, will be replaced by a democratic government of free and equal individuals, while Fascism rejects the democratic ideal altogether in favor of the permanent dictatorship. In theory Communism professes to be international, while Fascism frankly accepts the doctrine of racial superiority and national egoism. In theory Communism recognizes the value of reason and science, while Fascism is essentially anti-intellectual in its subordination of reason to will.

In theory, yes; but the Soviet regime in Russia has failed, even more conspicuously than existing democratic societies, to harmonize theory and practice. Although the revolution has long since ended, the classless society has not emerged. The dictatorship is now more firmly established, the prospect for a democratic government is now more remote, than in the time of Lenin. The Stalin regime is no less nationalist and no more international than the regime of Hitler, and its regimentation of opinion and scholarship no less effectively subordinates reason to the will of the dictator. The revolution in Russia, as Trotsky said, has been betrayed; but it has been betrayed less by men and circumstances than by a radical contradiction in

Communist theory. The rational and humane values proclaimed in Communist theory are frankly divorced from the means by which they can be realized; they are regarded as ideal ends projected into the future, but incapable of being attained except by the temporary resort to antirational and inhumane means. So far at least the result of this radical contradiction between ends and means has been, and as I think must under any circumstances have been, that the ideal ends were defeated by the very means employed to attain them.

It is in this fundamental discord between ends and means that Communism and Fascism, as they actually function, are alike—alike in the methods they employ and in the assumptions by which the methods are justified. The Communist and the Fascist revolutions were carried through by the same political technique and the same resort to naked force. The personal power of Mussolini and Hitler is no more arbitrary, more complete, or more ruthlessly employed than that of Stalin. Both Communism and Fascism assume that the welfare of the community and the progress of mankind are in some mystical fashion identified with an abstract entity, called in the one case the dialectic of history and in the other the totalitarian state. Both assume that this abstract entity is realized in the person of an inspired leader to whom the truth has been revealed and the direction of affairs committed. Both assume that the individual, in comparison with the state or the dialectic process, has no significance except as an instrument to be used, with whatever degree of brutality may be necessary, for realizing ends which the leader judges to be good. Both do in effect, whatever they may proclaim in theory, subordinate reason to will, identify right with naked force as an instrument of will, and accord value to the disinterested search for truth only in so far as the leader judges it to be temporarily useful for the attainment of immediate political ends.

Communism and Fascism claim to be theoretical formulations of a "new order" in the world. But as revealed in their works they are no more than the recurrence of old political forms, that is to say, the recurrence in practice of what is variously known as tyranny, dictatorship, absolute monarchy; the recurrence in theory of what is known as divine right. As such they are alike, and alike at war with the fundamental values and assumptions which liberal-democracy, if it is to retain any significance, must preserve.

PROBLEMS

1. Probably the most significant point made by Becker in this excerpt is that the *means* used to accomplish any action ultimately determine the *ends* or purposes of that action, even when some men try to keep the two divorced in their heads. How does this relationship of means to ends explain the shifts in the policies of Socialists? Do the policy shifts change the definition of Socialism for one who defines abstractions in terms of "operations" (i.e., actual things that actual men do)? for one who defines an abstraction by substituting another abstraction for it? Is the confusion of many people today as to the "meaning" of Socialism explained by their failure to distinguish between *means* and *ends?* between "operational" definitions and purely verbal definitions?
2. Drawing on Becker's essay, make up a careful list of the *theoretical* differences between Communism and Fascism. Now draw up a list of the *actual* similarities between the two. How does this help to explain how the means determine the ends? How does this illustrate further the need for "operational" definitions when we are attempting to make useful distinctions between political philosophies?
3. Does the Marxian "dialectic of history" (social change is the result of economic forces only; these forces are immutable and impersonal, not subject to influence by the pressure of ideas; social revolution is, therefore, inevitable) seem to you to be a result of inductive thinking or deductive thinking? Explain.
4. Re-read paragraph five of Becker's essay. How does this passage illustrate the confusion in some people's minds between Marxism as a *symbol* of a social theory and Marxism as a *referent* (that which is actually taking place in the real world)? Are Koestler's "Babbitts of the Left" among those confused? Are the "Babbitts of the Right" confused? Is there a basic similarity in the confusion of these two opposing groups?

John Dewey

Although now over 90 years of age, John Dewey continues to stir up controversy with his contributions to philosophy, political and economic thinking, and educational theory. For a half-century since the death of William James, Dewey has been America's leading spokesman for pragmatic thinking. Since to the pragmatic thinker the only reality is human experience, which keeps changing and developing, the pragmatist believes that the "truth" of an idea, instead of being abstract, absolute, and eternal, lies in its usefulness to man in the solution of his specific problems. It is quite natural that a man with such a philosophy would not be content with philosophical *theory*, and Dewey was not. Through his writings, his teaching at the University of Chicago and later at Columbia University, and his experimental school at Chicago, he pioneered the way for a kind of education, tagged "progressive," which focused on the child rather than on the subject matter and which tried to help the child understand his present complex physical and social environment. Dewey has also been in the forefront of battles for free speech, experimentation in art, development of the social sciences, and application of the scientific method to all social problems. It is not surprising to find a pragamatist like Dewey, who holds that the only real knowledge is functional and concrete rather than theoretical and abstract, striving to find useful "operational" definitions for such abstractions as "Democracy"— definitions in terms of *what people do*. Notice the emphasis on experience, action, and the here-and-now in these Dewey book-titles: *Experience and Education, Experience and Nature, Human Nature and Conduct, Art as Experience, Liberalism and Social Action, Logic, the Theory of Inquiry.* (For a good sampling of Dewey's thinking see *Intelligence in the Modern World,* edited by Joseph Ratner.)

DEMOCRACY *

Democracy is much broader than a special political form, a method of conducting government, of making laws and carrying on governmental administration by means of popular suffrage and elected officers. It is that, of course. But it is something broader and deeper than that. The political and governmental phase of democracy is a means, the best means so far found, for realizing ends that lie in the wide domain of human relationships and the development of human personality. It is, as we often say, though perhaps

---

* From an address by John Dewey before The National Education Association, 1937, published in *School and Society*, April, 1937, under the title "Democracy and Educational Administration."

without appreciating all that is involved in the saying, a way of life, social and individual. The key-note of democracy as a way of life may be expressed, it seems to me, as the necessity for the participation of every mature human being in formation of the values that regulate the living of men together: which is necessary from the standpoint of both the general social welfare and the full development of human beings as individuals.

Universal suffrage, recurring elections, responsibility of those who are in political power to the voters, and the other factors of democratic government are means that have been found expedient for realizing democracy as the truly human way of living. They are not a final end and a final value. They are to be judged on the basis of their contribution to end. It is a form of idolatry to erect means into the end which they serve. Democratic political forms are simply the best means that human wit has devised up to a special time in history. But they rest back upon the idea that no man or limited set of men is wise enough or good enough to rule others without their consent; the positive meaning of this statement is that all those who are affected by social institutions must have a share in producing and managing them. The two facts that each one is influenced in what he does and enjoys and in what he becomes by the institutions under which he lives, and that therefore he shall have, in a democracy, a voice in shaping them, are the passive and active sides of the same fact.

The development of political democracy came about through substitution of the method of mutual consultation and voluntary agreement for the method of subordination of the many to the few enforced from above. Social arrangements which involve fixed subordination are maintained by coercion. The coercion need not be physical. There have existed, for short periods, benevolent despotisms. But coercion of some sort there has been; perhaps economic, certainly psychological and moral. The very fact of exclusion from participation is a subtle form of suppression. It gives individuals no opportunity to reflect and decide upon what is good for them. Others who are supposed to be wiser and who in any case have more power decide the question for them and also decide the methods and means by which subjects may arrive at the enjoyment of what is good for them. This form of coercion and suppression is more subtle and more effective than is overt intimidation and restraint. When it is habitual and embodied in social institutions, it seems the normal and natural state of affairs. The mass usually become unaware that they have a claim to a development of their own powers. Their experience is so restricted that they are not conscious of restriction. It is part of the democratic conception that they as individuals are not the only sufferers, but that the whole social body is deprived of the potential resources that should be at its service. The individuals of the submerged mass may not be very wise. But there is one thing they are wiser about than anybody else can be, and that is where the shoe pinches, the troubles they suffer from.

The foundation of democracy is faith in the capacities of human nature; faith in human intelligence and in the power of pooled and and cooperative experience. It is not belief that these things are complete but that if given a show they will grow and be able to generate progressively the knowledge and wisdom needed to guide collective action. Every autocratic and authoritarian scheme of social action rests on a belief that the needed intelligence is confined to a superior few, who because of inherent natural gifts are endowed with the ability and the right to control the conduct of others; laying down principles and rules and directing the ways in which they are carried out. It would be foolish to deny that much can be said for this point of view. It is that which controlled human relations in social groups for much the greater part of human history. The democratic faith has emerged very, very recently in the history of mankind. Even where democracies now exist, men's minds and feelings are still permeated with ideas about leadership imposed from above, ideas that developed in the long early history of mankind. After democratic political institutions were nominally established, beliefs and ways of looking at life and of acting that originated when men and women were externally controlled and subjected to arbitrary power, persisted in the family, the church, business and the school, and experience shows that as long as they persist there, political democracy is not secure.

Belief in equality is an element of the democratic credo. It is not, however, belief in equality of natural endowments. Those who proclaimed the idea of equality did not suppose they were enunciating a psychological doctrine, but a legal and political one. All individuals are entitled to equality of treatment by law and in its administration. Each one is affected equally in quality if not in quantity by the institutions under which he lives and has an equal right to express his judgment, although the weight of his judgment may not be equal in amount when it enters into the pooled result to that of others. In short, each one is equally an individual and entitled to equal opportunity of development of his own capacities, be they large or small in range. Moreover, each has needs of his own, as significant to him as those of others are to them. The very fact of natural and psychological inequality is all the more reason for establishment by law of equality of opportunity, since otherwise the former becomes a means of oppression of the less gifted.

While what we call intelligence may be distributed in unequal amounts, it is the democratic faith that it is sufficiently general so that each individual has something to contribute, whose value can be assessed only as it enters into the final pooled intelligence constituted by the contributions of all. Every authoritarian scheme, on the contrary, assumes that its value may be assessed by some *prior* principle, if not of family and birth or race and color or possession of material wealth, then by the position and rank a person occupies in the existing social scheme. The democratic faith in equality is the faith that each individual shall have the chance and opportunity to contribute whatever he is capable of contributing and that the value of his contribution be decided by its place and function in the organized total of similar contributions, not on the basis of prior status of any kind whatever.

I have emphasized in what precedes the importance of the effective release of intelligence in connection with personal experience in the democratic way of living. I have done so purposely because democracy is so often and so naturally associated in our minds with freedom of *action,* forgetting the importance of freed intelligence which is necessary to direct and to warrant freedom of action. Unless freedom of individual action has intelligence and informed conviction back of it, its manifestation is almost sure to result in confusion and disorder. The democratic idea of freedom is not the right of each individual to *do* as he pleases, even if it be qualified by adding "provided he does not interfere with the same freedom on the part of others." While the idea is not always, not often enough, expressed in words, the basic freedom is that of freedom of *mind* and of whatever degree of freedom of action and experience is necessary to produce freedom of intelligence. The modes of freedom guaranteed in the Bill of Rights are all of this nature; Freedom of belief and conscience, of expression of opinion, of assembly for discussion and conference, of the press as an organ of communication. They are guaranteed because without them individuals are not free to develop and society is deprived of what they might contribute. . . .

PROBLEMS

1. Throughout this essay, but especially in the first two paragraphs, Dewey is contrasting two definitions of democracy. What are they? Are either or both of these definitions spelled out in terms of specific "operations"? Which definition focuses exclusively on means? which on a combination of definitely stated ends and implied means?

2. In the final paragraph Dewey distinguishes between three kinds of freedom. What are they?

3. Dewey obviously believes that only the third kind of freedom is consistent with democratic behavior. Why? In the light of his definition of freedom, how do you suppose he would interpret the conduct of an employer of hundreds of men who sincerely believes that the right to hire and fire should remain exclusively his? of a school superintendent who feels that his faculty should have no hand in determining school policy? of a librarian who, acting with the best intentions, refuses to buy certain books which she regards as "undesirable"? of a clergyman who forbids his congregation to see a certain movie he regards as "unwholesome"? Any one of these four would doubtless be very indignant if told his conduct was undemocratic. Which of the two definitions of democracy discussed here would the indignant person be thinking in terms of?

4. What is the connection between the conduct of the four people in question 3 and "the subtle form of coercion" discussed by Dewey in his third paragraph? What is the nature of the loss to a social group when group participation and decision-making is subordinated to the will of the few? In answering this question consider first the loss to the whole group, next the loss to the subordinated individuals, finally, and most importantly, because it is most frequently overlooked, the loss to the dominating individual.

5. In the essay by Becker we saw how the means can determine, even alter and subvert, the ends. The converse can, of course, also be

true: the ends can determine the means, *if the ends are commonly understood and agreed to.* What changes in the *means* employed in such of our modern American institutions as the home, the school, the church, industries, unions, farm organizations, social clubs, political parties, would take place if an overwhelming majority of Americans clearly understood and agreed to apply Dewey's definition of democracy?

6. John Dewey has been called America's greatest living philosopher. It is apparent that such a man's views on democracy would have influence. To claim that his theory of democracy as outlined briefly here has been widely understood and accepted would be to reveal ignorance of both the theory and contemporary American society, but it may be an illuminating experience to look at some men and organizations in American society whose conduct indicates their acceptance of Dewey's principles. Make a list of as many men and organizations as you know whose words and acts exemplify Dewey's principles. Such an exercise will serve you in two ways: it will test your ability to recognize an important theory in terms of its "operations," i.e., to determine what people and groups are actually *doing* the things Dewey urges; and it will test your ability to exclude all moral judgments ("good" or "bad," "right" or "wrong") and simply recognize substantiating evidence wherever you find it. Remember, then, that the test is not, Do I agree or disagree, like or dislike, support or oppose, but, Do these men and groups, for better or for worse, behave in a manner consistent with Dewey's concepts?

Encyclopaedia Britannica Films

The twin films "Democracy" and "Despotism" produced by Encyclopaedia Britannica Films use the operational method of definition in a medium of pictures-with-words. The editors have found these films very suggestive in teaching students to translate abstract ideas and words into terms of "what is done." The following selection, the scripts of the films, gives a clear picture of the steps taken toward forming a useful working definition of "democracy" along with "despotism" or "non-democracy."

The two motion pictures were produced with the assistance of Harold D. Lasswell, a social scientist who has pioneered in the field of propaganda-analysis.

DEMOCRACY AND DESPOTISM *

NOTES ON THE FILM

The film *Democracy* and its companion film *Despotism* are primarily definitional in purpose. These films are intended to give students a common basis for discussing and further investigating problems of democracy and despotism.

This film has been built around subject matter on which there is a substantial body of general agreement. Out of the wealth of material available, four major concepts have been chosen. These are defined in the film as simply as possible.

FOUR FACTORS

The four factors which have been selected for definition and illustration in *Democracy* fall into two groups:

a. The definitional factors: *Shared Respect* and *Shared Power*
b. The conditional factors: *Economic Balance* and *Enlightenment*

The four factors which have been selected for definition and illustration in *Despotism* fall into two groups:

a. The definitional factors: *Restricted Respect* and *Concentrated Power*
b. The conditional factors: *Slanted Economic Distribution* and *Controlled Information*

Ways in which these factors show themselves in a community— that is to say the indexes of these factors—have been selected as far as possible out of experiences that members of the average school audience can be largely assumed to have in common.

* *Teacher's Handbook* for the instructional films "Democracy" and "Despotism," Encyclopaedia Britannica Films Inc., Wilmette, Illinois.

VERBAL TOOLS

Both *Democracy* and *Despotism* give students a kit of verbal tools with which to work. As the Social Observer points out in *Democracy*, one must choose one's words carefully, use them consistently, and have one's definitions clear before one can look intelligently at a community. The terminology has been carefully selected to avoid words that have emotional overtones. The aim is to present students with a model of calm and dispassionate observation and analysis.

The two films present as simply as possible what may be called a distillation of social scientific observation and analysis over a period of more than two thousand years. There are scores of partisan films in this area which have already been made and scores which can still be made. The two films are not dogmatic. They do not represent the point of view of a single "school" or a single "ideology."

This approach represents a radical departure from the typical materials in this area which are usually full of exhortation rather than exposition. A deliberate and conscientious effort has been made to avoid propaganda in these films. The tone of the narration has been made calm and conversational. The narrator is not pleading a cause. He is expounding. His tempo is slow and almost deliberate. A sense of hurry and urgency has been avoided.

COMPLEMENTARY FILMS

The two films are complementary. As far as treatment goes, *Democracy* is the less complex of the two. The definitions are simple in nature and are restricted to the subject of democracy alone without reference to any alternative system. In *Despotism* the treatment is somewhat more elaborate and by use of the scale technique the students are led to think in comparative rather than in absolute terms. Experience will probably show that a class should see and discuss *Democracy* first before it sees and discusses *Despotism*.

DEMOCRACY

continuity of the film

Scenes	*Commentary*

Leader
Main Title

SEQUENCE A: ORIENTATION

1. Legislature Voting	Democracy has been defined in many ways. We would all agree that democracy includes government by majority. Let's see if we . . .
2. Speaker	can, each of us, sharpen up our own ideas of democracy.
3. Constitutional Document	We know that democratic words and forms have been written into laws. But it is the way people *practice* democracy . . .
4. Social Observer	that really counts. Let's ask this man about defining democracy. He studies . . .
5. Desk Top	communities, and the way people live in them. He goes about his job scientifically: Observing . . . Recording . . . Analyzing . . . and . . . Reporting.
6. Social Observer	SOCIAL OBSERVER: Well . . .
7. Stepping Over to Bookcase	I'll tell you one thing:
8. Indicating Books	Students of society have been reporting their observations . . .
9. Social Science Books	and analyses for a good many centuries. And as yet there is no single definition of democracy that they would all accept. There is one point, however . . .
10. Social Observer at Bookcase	they would all agree on . . .

Scenes	Commentary
11. Stressing Need for Careful Definitions	and this is it: In thinking seriously of democracy, one must define his words carefully, and use them consistently. When you have your own definitions clear, you know exactly what to look for in a community.

SEQUENCE B: SHARED RESPECT

Scenes	Commentary
12. Signs of Democracy: Shared Respect	NARRATOR: Many students agree that two important signs of democracy are . . . shared respect . . . and shared power.
13. Town Hall Audience Assembling	Let's take shared respect first. Sharing respect means that each shares the respect of all . . . not because . . .
14. Executive and Workman	of his wealth . . .
15. Rabbi with Housewife	or his religion . . .
16. Negro and Clubwoman	or his color.
17. Hown Hall Audience	But because each is a human being and makes his own contribution to the community . . .
18. Physician	from healing its sick . . .
19 Garbage Collector	to collecting its garbage . . .
20. Railroad Executive	from managing its railroads . . .
21. Locomotive	to running its trains.
22. High School	One sign of shared respect in a community is that everybody . . .
23. Chemistry Laboratory	is given a fair chance . . .
24. Chinese Student	to *develop* useful skills . . .
25. Chinese Inventor	and the chance to put these skills to effective *use*.

Scenes	*Commentary*
26. Riverside Church	And, there is shared respect . . .
27. Rural Church	if various groups in the community . . .
28. Catholic Church	recognize each other's right . . .
29. Synagogue	to hold different . . .
30. Suburban Church	faiths and opinions.

SEQUENCE C: SHARED POWER

31. Signs of Democracy: Shared Power	And now let's see how we spot the second of the two signs of democracy: shared power.
32. Election Poster	Most observers agree that there is true democracy in a community only if there is shared power . . .
33. Counting Ballots	that is to say, only if many people have a share in making decisions . . .
34. Traffic Light	that the community will support . . .
35. Policeman	with force, if necessary.
36. Exterior of Polling Place	More specifically, you can say that power is shared wherever regular popular elections . . .
37. Employer and Employee Receiving Ballots	are authorized, and are actually held. There is shared power wherever people actually . . .
38. Entering Booths	get out voluntarily and vote,
39. Employer Voting	and if they can vote without interference . . .
40. Employee Voting	or pressure from anybody.
41. Rear View of Legislature	There is shared power if officeholders are drawn from representative groups in society. If they . . .

Scenes	Commentary
42. Farmer in Legislature	include men . . .
43. Farmer on Tractor	from the farms . . .
44. Lawyer in Legislature	men . . .
45. Lawyer Pleading	from the law courts . . .
46 Grocer in Legislature	men
47. Grocer in Store	from the stores . . .
48. Mechanic in Legislature	men . . .
49. Mechanic at Lathe	from the factories: officeholders . . .
50. Front View of Legislature	who are drawn from representative groups of the community. In a democratic legislature, shared power shows itself in a strong opposition.—Listen:
51. Administration Speaker	ADMINISTRATION SPEAKER: And that is why I am confident the governor will have the support of the House on this bill.
52. Opposition Speaker	OPPOSITION SPEAKER: Mr. Speaker . . . As usual, the honorable gentleman is quite wrong. He and the governor he serves so dutifully . . .
53. Front View of Assembly	can expect no support for their policy from this House. The happiness of the people . . . (FADE OUT)
54. Political Party System	NARRATOR: A strong opposition is made possible by an effective political party system.
55. Town Hall Audience Assembling	The two most important signs of democracy, then, are SHARED RESPECT . . .

Scenes	Commentary
56. Ballot Count	and SHARED POWER. They, in turn, depend on many conditions.

SEQUENCE D: ECONOMIC BALANCE

Scenes	Commentary
57. Conditions for Democracy: Economic Balance	Let's consider two of these conditions: economic balance . . . and enlightenment. Economic balance means that the community contains a large middle-income group.
58. Social Observer at Bookcase	SOCIAL SCIENTIST: A relationship between economic balance and democracy has been noted and reported for . . .
59. Picture of Aristotle	centuries by students of society.
60. Social Observer with Books	Aristotle said that a government made up of middle-income people has the best chance to be democratic. That was two thousand years ago in Greece. And well over a century ago in America, James Madison warned that extremes of riches and poverty set group against group.
61. Feudal Disintegration	NARRATOR: In past centuries, economic balance was improved when large feudal estates were gradually reorganized into independent farms as one part of the development of democracy. This creation of better economic balance aided the further growth of democracy.
62. Growth of Middle-Income Group	The social observers of our time have also noted that the development of democracy usually goes hand in hand with the growth of large middle-income groups. In today's world of giant technology one of democracy's serious problems is how to maintain flourishing middle-income groups.

Scenes   *Commentary*

SEQUENCE E: ENLIGHTENMENT

63. Conditions for Democracy: Enlightenment — Another important condition for democracy is enlightenment:

64. Radio Speaker — making information . . .

65. Printing Press — available to citizens . . .

66. Library Reading Room — and giving them the skill . . .

67. Motion Picture Cameraman — with which to judge it.

68. High School — As public education increases, democracy grows.

69. Teacher at Blackboard — In checking a community for democracy we must . . .

70. Questioning Class — find out whether it provides schools adjusted . . .

71. Teacher Writing Newspaper Checks — to the needs of its young people.

72. Student Reading Funnies — But just being able to get books and newspapers is no guarantee of democracy.

73. Teacher Completing Third Check — The newspapers of a real democracy meet these tests:

74. Three Newspaper Checks — Balanced presentation of news . . .
Disclosure of source . . .
Competence of the staff . . .

75. Front View of Class — In applying these tests to newspapers . . .

76. Boy and Girl — we find out . . .

77. Reading Newspaper — first of all . . .

78. Front Page — if they report both sides. See if the news pages . . .

Scenes	*Commentary*
79. News and Opinion	contain news only, and if opinion is kept . . .
80. Editorial Page	for the editorial page. Next we see if the paper says plainly who publishes and edits it, so we know which side they're on.
81. Newspaper Editor	Newspapers in a real democracy meet a third test: competence of staff. This test requires newspapermen . . .
82. Bluepencilling Copy	to value accuracy and impartiality and to interpret the news skillfully for the public . . .
83. Editor Telephoning	The competence test also requires newspapermen . . .
84. Specialist Listening	to use the services of experts.
85. Editor Phoning	EDITOR: I want five hundred words on freedom of the press for our anniversary edition. How about it?
86. Specialist Listening	But, Professor . . . you know more about the history of freedom of the press than probably any other man in the country.
87. Editor Completing Conversation	Yes . . . that's right. I mean the *responsibility* of a free press—and other forms of communication like the radio and the movies—to enlighten the public in a democracy.

SEQUENCE F: INTEGRATION

88. Large City	NARRATOR: When we examine any democratic community, large, or small, or just . . .
89. Average Community	average we find that we can separate out two distinct signs of democracy:
90. Dynamically Related Factors	shared respect, and shared power. They in turn, depend on at least two conditions in the community: economic balance, and enlightenment. There is no standing still: the more economic balance and enlightenment, the more shared respect and shared power.

Scenes	Commentary

Democracy's something that's never finished. It wanes with neglect, and it grows with care. If a community works to balance its economy and if it works to enlighten its citizens, such a community can achieve shared respect; and it can achieve shared power. By working hard at it, the citizens of any community can achieve democracy.

End Title
Trailer

END

DESPOTISM

continuity of the film

Scenes	Commentary

Leader
Main Title

SEQUENCE A: ORIENTATION

1. Democracy-Despotism Scale

You can roughly locate any country in the world somewhere along a scale running all the way from democracy to despotism.

One community may be near the democracy end; another, somewhere in the middle; and a third may be near the despotism end.

2. Social Observer at Map

Let's find out about despotism. This man makes it his job to study these things. SOCIAL OBSERVER: Well, for one thing,

3. Social Observer Turning to Map

avoid the comfortable idea that the mere form of government can of itself safeguard a nation against despotism.

4. Pre-1933 Germany

Germany under Hindenburg was a republic . . .

Scenes	Commentary
5. Swastika	and yet, in this republic an aggressive despotism took root and flourished under Adolf Hitler.
6. Social Observer Turning Back from Map	When a competent observer looks for signs of despotism . . .
7. Flag Pledge	in a community, he looks beyond fine words and noble phrases. CHORUS: (Fades In) ". . . Republic for which it stands; One nation indivisible,
8. Lynching	". . . . with liberty and justice for all."

SEQUENCE B: RESPECT, SHARED OR RESTRICTED?

9. Social Observer Indicating Chart	SOCIAL OBSERVER: Many observers have found that two workable yardsticks help in discovering how near a community is to despotism: The Respect Scale and the Power Scale.
10. Respect Scale	NARRATOR: A careful observer can use a respect scale to find out how many citizens get an even break. As a community moves towards despotism, respect is *restricted* to fewer people.
11. Party Officials Approaching	A community is low on a respect scale if common courtesy
12. Party Officials Jostling Old Lady	is withheld from large groups . . .
13. Party Officials Proceeding	of people on account of their political attitudes. . . .
14. Employer Entering	If people are rude to others because . . .
15. Snubbing Employees	they think their wealth . . .

Scenes	Commentary
16. Rebuffed Secretary	gives them that right; or because . . .
17. Camp Gentilhomme Folder	they don't like a man's race . . .
18. Application Blank	or his religion.
19. Junior College	Equal opportunity for all citizens to *develop* useful skills is one basis for rating a community on the respect scale.
20. Graduate Being Photographed	The opportunity to *develop* useful skills is important, but not enough.
21. Graduate Posing	The equally important opportunity . . .
22. Graduate as Jobseeker	to put skills to use . . .
23. Employment Agency Line	is a further test on a respect scale.

SEQUENCE C: POWER, SHARED OR CONCENTRATED?

24. Power Scale	A Power Scale is another important yardstick of despotism. It gauges the citizens' share in making the community's decisions.
	Communities which concentrate decision-making in a few hands rate low on a power scale, and are moving towards despotism.
25. Louis XIV Statue	Like France under the Bourbon Kings, one of whom said, "The State?—I am the State!"
26. City Hall	Today, democracy can ebb away in communities whose citizens allow power to become concentrated . . .
27. Political Boss: Press Conference	in the hands of bosses.
	BOSS: What I say, goes—see?
28. Conference Ending	I am the law around here! Ha! Ha!
	NARRATOR: The test of despotic power . . .

Scenes	Commentary
29. Declaration of Independence	is that it can disregard the will of the people; it rules without the "consent of the governed."
30. Plebiscite Polling Place	Look beyond the legal formalities . . .
31. First Party Official	of an election . . .
32. Voter Entering Booth	in measuring a community on a power scale, to see if the ballot is really free.
33. Voter Leaving Booth	If the citizens can vote only the way they're told . . .
34. Second Party Official	a community approaches despotism.
35. Hitler Addressing Reichstag	When legislatures become ceremonial assemblies only, and have no real control . . .
36. Reichstag Audience	over law-making, their community rates low
37. Applauding Hitler	on a power scale
38. Audience Heiling	EFFECT: Sieg Heil! Sieg Heil!
39. Concentration Camp Sign	In a downright despotism, opposition is dangerous . . .
40. Executioner Tightening Noose	whether the despotism is official . . .
41. Ku Klux Klan	or whether it is unofficial.

SEQUENCE D: ECONOMIC DISTRIBUTION, BALANCED OR SLANTED?

42. Social Observer Indicating Chart	SOCIAL OBSERVER: The spread of respect and power in a community is influenced by certain conditions which many observers measure by means of the Economic Distribution and Information Scales.

Scenes	Commentary
43. Economic Distribution Scale	NARRATOR: If a community's economic distribution becomes slanted, its middle income groups grow smaller, and despotism stands a better chance to gain a foot-hold.
44. Land Concentration in Township	Where land is privately owned, one sign of a poorly balanced economy is the concentration of land ownership in the hands of a very small number of people.
45. Farmer and Wife	When farmers lose their farms, they lose their independence.
46. Notice of Foreclosure	This one can stay on—
47. Farmer and Wife	but not as his own boss any more.
48. Land Concentration in Nation	To the extent that this condition exists throughout a nation, the likelihood of despotism is increased.
49. Single Factory Town	It is also a sign of poor economic balance in a community if it depends almost entirely on a single company—a factory or a mine.
50. National Liquid Wealth Concentration	If this condition exists over the nation as a whole so that the control of jobs and business opportunities is in a few hands, despotism stands a better chance.
51. Heavy Tax Burden on - Poor	Another sign of a poorly balanced economy is a taxation system that presses heaviest on those least able to pay.
52. Sales Tax	A larger part of a small income is spent on necessities such as food. Sales taxes on such necessities hit the small income harder.
53. Tax Collector and Peasants	In the days of the salt tax, feudal despotisms . . .
54. Close-up. Tax Collector	were partly sustained by this . . .

Scenes	Commentary
55. Tax Collector and Peasants	and other forms . . .
56. Close-up: Tax Collector	of sales tax.

SEQUENCE E: INFORMATION, UNCONTROLLED OR CONTROLLED?

57. Information Scale	A community rates low on an information scale when the press, radio, and other channels of communication are controlled by only a few people; and when citizens have to accept what they are told. In communities of this kind despotism stands a good chance.
58. Teacher Training Class	See how such a community trains its teachers.
59. Professor Lecturing	PROFESSOR: Bear this in mind: young people cannot be trusted to form their own opinions. This business about openmindedness is nonsense.
60. Student Taking Notes	It's a waste of time trying to teach students to think for themselves. It's our jobs to tell 'em!
61. Same Student as Classroom Teacher	NARRATOR: And when teachers put such training into practice, despotism grows rapidly.
62. Boy Rising with Question	These children are being taught to accept uncritically whatever they are told. Questions . . .
63. Teacher Noticing Him	are not encouraged.
64. Boy and Teacher	TEACHER: How can you ask such a question? Have you got a textbook? PUPIL: Yes, Ma'am. TEACHER: Doesn't it say here that our law courts . . .

Scenes	Commentary
65. Rebuked Boy Sitting Down	are always just? PUPIL: Yes, Ma'am. TEACHER: Then how dare you question the fact? Sit down!
66. Same Boy at Home	NARRATOR: And so we aren't surprised when BOY: But it must be true; I saw it in this book, right here!
67. Propaganda Ministry	NARRATOR: And if books, the newspapers and the radio . . .
68. Internal Censorship Office	are efficiently controlled the people will read . . .
69. Censor at Desk	*and* accept, exactly what the few . . .
70. Censorship Stamp	in control want them to. Government censorship is one form of control.
71. Suspending a Newspaper	A newspaper which breaks a government censorship rule . . .
72. Suspension Notice	can be suspended.
73. Newspaper Editor Leaving Office	It is also possible for newspapers and other forms of communication . . .
74. Editor Entering Advertising Manager's Office	to be controlled by *private interests*.
75. Editor Quitting	ADVERTISING MANAGER: I thought I told you to kill this story. It'll cost us a lot of advertising. EDITOR: If this story goes, I quit! ADVERTISING MANAGER: All right!
76. Average Community	What sort of community do you live in? Where would you place it on a Democracy-Despotism Scale? To find out . . .
77. The Four Factors	you can rate it on a Respect Scale, and a Power Scale. And to find out what way it is

Scenes   *Commentary*

likely to go in the future, you can rate it
on Economic Distribution and Information
Scales. The lower your community rates on
Economic Distribution and Information
Scales the lower it is likely to rate on Re-
spect and Power Scales . . .

78. Democracy-   and thus to approach despotism.
    Despotism
    Scale

79. From Com-   What happens in a single community is the
    munity to   problem of its own citizens.
    Nation   But it is *also* the problem of us *all* . . . be-
                      cause as communities go, so goes the nation.

End Title
Trailer

END

PROBLEMS

These two educational films have supplied you with some useful
"yardsticks" by means of which you should be able to detect democratic
or despotic tendencies in a variety of everyday situations.

1. Which of the following situations, all having to do with the publishing
   business, show democratic tendencies? despotic tendencies? Defend
   your answers in terms of either one or both of the yardsticks—*shared
   respect* and *shared power* or their opposites, *restricted respect* and
   concentrated power—with which you have been supplied. (The editors do not mean to imply that these problems are all capable of
   categorical "either-or" answers.)

   a. The publication of lists of "undesirable" books by such groups as
      anti-vice societies
   b. Government censorship in peacetime; in wartime
   c. The restrictions placed on publishers by libel laws
   d. Cornering of the paper-pulp market by a small number of firms
   e. Motion picture subsidies for books suitable for movies
   f. Easy accessibility for all to the published findings of government-
      sponsored research agencies
   g. Book-of-the-month clubs

h. High publishing costs which force many small-scale publishers out of business

i. The free circulation through the mails of unsolicited "literature" from unidentified sources

j. In journalism:

    (1) Chain ownership of newspapers

    (2) Only one paper in a city

    (3) Strong unions for printers, linotype operators, news reporters

    (4) Dependence of a newspaper on a small number of big advertisers for its income

    (5) A large number of small-town and rural newspapers

    (6) Dependence of a rural press on large amounts of "boilerplate," i.e., editorials, commentary, and news furnished by syndicated press services

    (7) A considerable number and variety of "special interest" papers (farm, labor, trade, professional)

    (8) Two papers published in a town, but one offering merely token competition

    (9) Two papers published in a town, with a broad, general difference in social attitude

    (10) Appearance of the same syndicated columns in many papers

    (11) Appearance of many syndicated columns expressing a wide-ranging variety of opinions and attitudes in one paper

    (12) Regular appearance of paid-for editorials in the form of advertisements

2. Now try your hand in much the same way with these educational institutions or situations:

a. Private schools and colleges with relatively steep tuition fees

b. State colleges and universities

    (1) Appointment of policy makers (board of regents) by governor

    (2) Limiting of offerings of state university to academic type mainly suited for professional training

    (3) A state university whose standards tend to govern the programs of high schools and other colleges (through accreditation, entrance examinations, and so forth)

c. A large variety of subject offerings in school or college

d. A strong fraternity and sorority system

e. Large gifts to a college by just a few individuals, families, or groups

f. An active and vigorous *remedial* program (in such skills as arithmetic, reading, spelling, and speech) playing an important part in the school or college curriculum

g. Closed school-board sessions

    h. Informal community pressures on administrators and teachers

    i. A system of electives

    j. Hiring, firing, and promotion policies largely formulated by representatives of the faculty

    k. Keeping the position of superintendent of schools as an elective office

3. Finally, consider in the same fashion some phases of community life:

    a. A single dominant moral code in the community

    b. One movie house

    c. Several movie houses all under one management (local)

    d. Several movie houses all under one management (chain)

    e. Several movie houses under different management

    f. Appointment of city mayor by council

    g. City manager (appointive)

    h. Election of judges

    i. Many independently owned banks

    j. Only one secure lending agency

    k. Work opportunities in town centered in just a few types of work

    l. Lending libraries

    m. Community concert series

        (1) Dependence of concert series upon New York booking agencies

    n. Unofficial agreements among property owners to limit property ownership on the basis of race

    o. A big difference between desirable and undesirable residential districts in a town

    p. Large public parks

    q. Large private recreation areas (beaches, game preserves)

    r. Toll bridges

    s. A great variety and number of churches

    t. Much absentee ownership of property

    u. Good attendance at meetings (especially business meetings) of an organization

    v. One major veterans' organization only

    w. A system of "instructed" convention delegates

    x. A uniform system of medical fees charged by all doctors in town

    y. A scarcity of accessible and available meeting places for social and political organizations

    z. Many "competing" charitable and philanthropic organizations

GENERAL PROBLEMS: *Defining Your Terms*

1. Professor Arthur Meier Schlesinger, an American historian, has provided a definition of the term "radical" in his book, *New Viewpoints of American History*. Basing his definition on an analysis of the activities of certain kinds of men throughout the entire course of American history, he says, "It should be clear, then, that the radical is a person who, in contrast to the conservative, favors a larger participation of the people in the control of government and society and in the benefits accruing from such control."

   Digest that definition for a moment, then consider this problem. As you are walking through Pershing Square in Los Angeles with a friend, you both observe four men, one on each corner, each standing on a soapbox haranguing a crowd. Your companion turns to you and says, "Look at those crazy *radicals.*"

   Upon investigation, you learn that one man is attempting to arouse in his audience a hatred toward members of a minority group, a second man is selling "snake oil" alleged to cure various physical ailments, a third man is trying to obtain signatures to a petition asking that *all* city employees be included in a retirement plan that now benefits only those who have served for five years and are drawing salaries over $3,500 a year, and the fourth man is warning his hearers that the day of judgment is to be July 4, 1954, and that they had better repent their sins now.

   Write a thoughful analysis of the word "radical," pointing out specifically: (1) what all four men had in common that prompted your friend to identfy them all as "radicals"; (2) the man (or men) to whom the label could be correctly applied if we were using Schlesinger's definition; (3) the man (or men) to whom the term "conservative" could be applied if we were using Schlesinger's definition; (4) the relative usefulness of these very different definitions (your friend's and Schlesinger's) to one who is attempting to impart a clear and definite meaning to a slippery word.

2. In your community, a public park and playground is badly needed. Some members of the city council favor a bond issue to finance its construction. A bond issue, which must be passed on by the voters of the community, will eventually be paid for out of monies acquired through taxes. Other members of the council are in favor of appealing to the generosity of the town's wealthiest citizen, an old man who is known to be looking for some suitable means of leaving a memorial

to his name. The problem is further complicated by the known opposition of many property owners to the levying of any further property taxes, which, they argue, place a heavier burden on them than on non-property owners. The Commissioner of Recreation has argued, however, that the public park and playground, by reducing juvenile delinquency and crime, will in the long run save the taxpayers money now spent on law enforcement and penal institutions.

Guided by the definitions of "democracy" and "despotism" agreed on by Dewey, by Lasswell (in the film scripts), and, at least by implication, by Becker, write an analysis in which you indicate which policy tends to be the more democratic, which the more despotic. Do not permit yourself to be governed by your emotions, but concentrate entirely on the problem of applying to these particular circumstances the "operational" definition with which you have been supplied.

3. You are to write a brief paper in three parts. Part 1 will involve an analysis of situation A below, part 2, an analysis of situation B; part 3 will test your ability to see underlying relationships between the two situations.

Situation A. Your town has recently adopted by popular vote a city zoning ordinance. The ordinance calls for the dividing of the city into various well-defined residential, commercial, and industrial districts "to promote health and safety, insure property values, avoid congestion, and increase the beauty of the community." The ordinance is to be administered by a City Planning Commission of five members to be appointed by the mayor. These men are sworn to act "in the best interests of the entire community."

The mayor appoints to the Commission the town banker, a leading insurance man, an outstanding lawyer, a noted surgeon, and the manager of the town's largest industrial concern, all men of unquestioned ability in their own fields and men who have repeatedly demonstrated an interest in civic affairs.

Has the mayor unwittingly failed to recognize and solve a problem of definition, a problem which, if unrecognized, might lead to an inequitable enforcement of the plan? Explain.

Situation B. One commonly agreed-upon yardstick of a democratic state is that its legislators be "drawn from representative groups in society."

Assuming that the legislature of your state maintains a nearly equal balance between representatives of important industries and businesses, organized labor, and the well-established farm organizations (Farm Bureau and Grange), has it met the requirements of the definition outlined above? Discuss.

Now, what is the basic similarity between situations A and B?

4. As a stable, successful, and respected businessman in your home town, and as a member of the local chapter of a national veterans' organization, you have been asked to head the "Americanism Committee" of your chapter. The avowed purpose of the committee is "to assist in safeguarding *the American way of life*" in your town.

Discuss in detail how a knowledge of the importance of defining terms would assist you in performing this task skillfully, wisely, and fairly. What are some of the pitfalls you would have to guard against?

5. Sometimes we discover, through inquiry, how complex are the realities behind a simple word we have been using all along as if it had only one clear, valid meaning. More often, we are shaken into an awareness of this multiplicity and variability by events.

Here are a few words on which men recently leaned as if each term stood for a single easily determined, taken-for-granted referent. They took it for granted that each of these words represented one thing and that it was unnecessary to consider seriously what that one thing or referent was. But events of the past two decades have shaken our confidence in the unqualified use of these terms. These words, used as if they had a single, obvious meaning, no longer seem to work as well as they once did; they now seem to confuse instead of enlighten. Write a careful paper revealing how recent events have made us aware of the complex realities behind any *one* of the following words, and what different referents these events have brought to our attention:

a. isolation

b. national safety

c. neutrality

d. appeasement

e. loyalty

Controlling Emotional Language

POLITICS

Sixty needles and sixty pins,
Sixty dirty Republikins.

Sixty rats and sixty cats,
And sixty dirty Democrats.

HAVE you ever noticed what happens when someone, choosing his words carefully, says "unmarried woman" instead of "old maid," "homeless unemployed" instead of "skid row bum," "union official" instead of "labor boss," "a student experiencing some difficulty with language" instead of "illiterate"? For one thing, a certain amount of tension is relieved, isn't it? For another, you get a clearer picture of the person under discussion, don't you?

How did this diminished tension and added clarity come about? Wasn't it because certain words rather heavily charged with emotion were replaced by others carrying a lesser emotional load? This is what is meant by controlling emotional language. You wouldn't point a loaded gun at anyone if you knew better. Why point "loaded words" at anyone? You won't if you learn to appreciate the danger to others, and to yourself, of playing carelessly with verbal firearms.

Of course, *real control* only comes with the skill acquired from thorough familiarization with the weapons, whether guns or words. We would all concede that a loaded gun in the hands of an experienced hunter is more "controlled" than a loaded gun in a rack on the wall of a hunting lodge. Not only is it out of reach of the inexperienced, but it can be used to perform the real job for which it is designed. So with words. "Control" implies more than leaving dangerous "loaded words" alone; it also implies using words honestly and exactly, and therefore efficiently, when the need for them arises. This matter of using words honestly raises a rather tricky

question. Are you "controlling" emotional language when you shy
away from reality to refer to a "debt" as an "obligation," to "fat"
as "avoirdupois," to "blindness" as "permanent night," to "death" as
"passing on"? Or are you being controlled by language and emotion to the point where you sacrifice clarity to timid evasion? In
short, have you, in your anxiety not to use this weapon recklessly,
rendered it incapable of being used effectively?

To pursue our metaphor one step further, have you noticed
how the person inexperienced in the use of firearms reveals much
more about himself than about either the gun or the purpose for
which it was designed when he is turned loose on the range, the
skeet course, or in the shooting gallery? Our attention is diverted
from the target to the reckless, or timid, or clumsy marksman.
Doesn't the same thing apply to words? When someone lets fly
with such wildly-aimed verbal buckshot as "red" (for anyone he
doesn't agree with), "merchant of death" (for any industrialist with
munitions contracts from the government), "traitor" (for anyone
critical of our national policies), about whom do we learn more,
the speaker or the persons he is referring to? Isn't it clear, then,
that a word can do more than let us know about something? It
can also let us know how someone feels about it—and perhaps
make us feel the same way, too!

The selections which follow are designed to point up the whole
problem of the emotional quality of language and to suggest ways
in which that emotional quality may be kept under control. Ward,
in the first selection, reveals how language, useful as a tool for
understanding and problem-solving, can become so emotionally
charged that it leads to misunderstanding and the creation of new
problems. Sergeant Tacitus finds the emotional impact of language
one of the hazards of wartime reporting. (You can easily see
how the reporter covering a Congressional debate, a local newsman
describing the progress of a trial, and your college sportswriter
extolling the merits of the college backfield may run into the same
hazards.) Sargent's "Stereotypes and the Newspapers," warns us
that the words which bombard us daily in the press may help
to create emotional "sets" or automatic responses to a problem,
"sets" which may persist quite apart from, even in spite of, the facts
of the problem. And Lee's "How Does It Strike You?" tops it off

with a peppering of anecdotes revealing how people who consider themselves "hardheaded" may really be more sensitive to word vibrations than to solid facts.

F. Earl Ward

As most English teachers are becoming increasingly aware, the emphasis in the teaching of rhetoric is shifting from the old concept of rhetoric as a badge of gentility to rhetoric as a tool of communication. F. Earl Ward, Chairman of the Department of English at Macalester College, reveals in this excerpt from his recent book, *English for Communication,* that he is sensitive to the emotional power of language and aware of the necessity for carefully controlling this "double-edged tool."

EMOTIONAL LANGUAGE *

Every word has an essential meaning, called its denotation, and a strategic meaning, called its connotation. Both are important, the first because it names what we are talking about, the second because it expresses our feelings or attitude and invites the reader or hearer to respond by sharing our feeling or attitude. Words cut two ways, and we should be careful in using them not to wound ourselves or others by using them ignorantly or clumsily.

1. *The strategic value of synonyms.* Words that stand for essentially the same thing but express a different feeling or attitude toward it are called synonyms. In a certain context, for example, *capitalist* and *business man* might refer to the same person and express his customary behavior yet suggest a quite different feeling about him. The first suggests that he is idle and predatory, the second that he is active and productive. By choosing one word rather than the other, we turn the meaning toward the reader in the way we want him to take hold of it. Or if we are not sensitive to the connotations of words, we turn the meaning the wrong way

* F. Earl Ward, *English for Communication.* Copyright 1949 by The Macmillan Company, and used with their permission.

and fail to get the desired response. The following list of synonyms shows some of the possibilities of strategic choice and bungling:

> go to bed, retire, hit the sack
> Phoebus, the sun, the old haymaker
> food, victuals, grub, eats, chow
> impasse, quandary, fix, pickle, plight
> fired, dismissed, kicked out, canned
> legs, limbs, pedal extremities, gams
> story, fable, fabrication, lie, untruth
> money, cash, finances, filthy lucre, dough
> die, decease, pass on, go west, croak, kick the bucket
> drunk, intoxicated, inebriated, pie-eyed, fried
> weary, tired, fagged out, pooped out, exhausted.
> understand, comprehend, grasp, savvy
> nudity, nakedness, indecent exposure, Adamitism

In general, the connotations of words suggest approval, disapproval, or neutrality. These are the attitudes upon which all our feelings are based. Approval may range from mere acceptance, a shade above tolerance, to passionate devotion. Disapproval may range from mild dislike to terror or abhorrence. Neutrality suggests the impartial attitude of the scientist or the broad sympathy of the socially adjusted person. When our feelings are engaged, it is hard to be neutral. A teacher, observing one of his students, may speak of him as conscientious, because he approves of students who work. A fellow student may speak of him as a grind or a plodder. One student, speaking of his teacher, may call him a fine scholar who expects thorough and accurate work. Another student, speaking of the same instructor, may call him a hard taskmaster or a slavedriver. One person, speaking of some one who is careful about spending his money, may praise his thrift; another may blame him for being an old tightwad. A connoisseur may speak of Limburger as "a robust cheese," but to many people it just stinks.

2. *Genuine neutrality and verbal evasion.* Scientific language is chosen for its neutrality. Its connotations are those of neatness, impartiality, and precision. Many of the words are long, derived from foreign language, and seldom met with outside the classroom and the laboratory. Particularly in biology and sociology, scientific words are useful in making possible the bland discussion of matters

pertaining to sex, reproduction, elimination, and degeneracy. Most popular words used to convey these meanings are too freighted with emotions and social disapproval to be used in mixed company or even in polite conversation among persons of the same sex. Neutral scientific words eliminate the leer and the blush from biological discussion; they also eliminate the lifted eyebrow from sociological discussion. In sociology, where a neutral attitude toward unfortunate members of society is desirable, the language must reflect this attitude. Hence people with sociological training, speak of mental patients rather than of lunatics and of itinerant workers rather than of tramps. All these choices are made with understandable purpose, to cool off the atmosphere surrounding highly electrified meanings and make possible the sharing of information. The connotations of these words are said to be informative.

On the other hand, many people habitually choose words with what they think of as neutral connotations simply to avoid acknowledging unpleasant reality. They go through life with verbal gloves on. In trying to be genteel they seek out soft, evasive words to put in place of plain, downright expressions of hushed up or disagreeable meanings. The choice of words to soften vulgar or ugly meanings is called euphemism. In part, the use of euphemisms is the result of social pressure. If everyone we respect avoids certain words, we avoid them in order to be respected in turn. Our grandmothers avoided words like *leg* and *breast,* substituting the euphemisms *limb* and *bosom.* They even avoided these words when they served chicken, and spoke instead of "dark meat" and "white meat." We are more downright in speaking of these formerly unacknowledged parts of the body. But there are limits beyond which most of us do not ordinarily go.

In part, the use of euphemisms comes from our desire to escape the thought of unpleasant reality. Death is such a reality. We don't like to mention it to friends and relatives of a person who has recently died. Hence, persons who have much to do with death—lawyers, ministers, and undertakers—have invented numerous euphemisms. Lawyers speak of a person as deceased. Ministers speak of him as having gone to his reward, or passed on. Undertakers, realizing the poor advertising value of the plain words for their trade, have substituted *mortician* for *undertaker, funeral car* for *hearse,* and *memorial park* for *burying ground.* Collecting money is an unpleasant process. Business men avoid direct reference to it by sending statements instead of bills, and by expecting a remittance instead of cash. Drunkenness is an unpleasant sight. We avoid the word *drunk* and refer to people as intoxicated, inebriated, or "under the influence." Or we laugh off the matter by using one of a dozen slang expressions. The behavior of one's children is sometimes an unpleasant matter. The doting mother therefore refers to her mule-bird as "serious" and to her hell-child as "so active." When euphemisms are not the result of social pressure, they are the result of over-fastidiousness, timidity, or downright dishonesty.

3. *Loaded words and slanting.* Dishonest statements often depend entirely upon connotation. A deliberate choice of words to pile up connotations of approval or disapproval and thereby to distort the truth is called slanting, and words that are heavy with favorable or unfavorable connotations are called loaded words. Without telling an outright lie—that is, without using words whose denotations are contrary to fact—a clever writer can, for example, dress up a calamity in loaded words to make it look like a triumph. An Axis writer could describe a battle as follows: "The enemy's violent effort to hamper the Axis disengagement and interrupt our systematic advance to the rear was successfully repelled." According to the loaded words in this statement, the enemy was violently attempting to do something and failing, and the Axis was successfully making a systematic advance. The connotation of these words are so favorable that they almost obscure the fact that the advance was to the rear. Few Axis readers with hope in their hearts would realize that they were reading about a retreat. On the basis of the same events, Allied writers could make the following statement: "Axis retreat rapidly becoming rout under determined Allied pounding." Few Allied readers with hope in their hearts would realize that they were reading about a retreat; the word *becoming* would entirely escape them and they would take the rout as an accomplished fact. Of course, neither side would have been taken in by the other's propaganda; slanting is effective only when it confirms what is already inside our heads.

When we take sides we approve whatever is on our side, disapprove whatever is on the other side. And what we approve we believe. Wars and political crises promote the use of loaded words to bolster morale and foster hatred for the other side. Between wars and political crises, when the lines are not so publicly drawn, loaded words are used to divide people on the basis of their desires, fears, and prejudices. A writer with something to sell, whether soap, perfume, cigarettes, automobiles, or intolerance, chooses words loaded with favorable or unfavorable connotations. Soap and perfume advertising does not describe the soap or perfume; it merely promises more and better dates to the person using it and social ostracism to those who don't. Cigarette advertising shows a girl on the end of each cigarette, and automobile advertising shows a girl in every car. When the product is intolerance, the appeal is to race or class snobbery, or the reverence we feel for the land and faith of our fathers.

4. *We must be aware of both denotation and connotation in context.* Of course, there is nothing dishonest in making people feel pride in what they are or reverence for what they hold good. All words have connotations that tug at our feelings. Even neutral words give us the feeling of precision and impartiality. The dishonesty in slanting comes from the purpose of the writer or speaker to direct attention away from what exists in the world of reality and toward the desires, fears, and prejudice already in our heads. Since our heads since childhood have been filled with ideas about our own race, religion, country, and class, it is easy for dishonest people to concentrate our attention upon these ideas and our fears for their preservation, while they insinuate facts from the outside world. The technique is exactly that of the magician who distracts his audience by false motions and a line of chatter while he gets the rabbit ready to pull out of the hat.

The way to see through tricks of either sort is to watch not what you are intended to see but what is really going on. Think of what the words mean in the particular setting where they are used. When a business man talks about free enterprise, don't think, as you are intended to do, "We Americans are a free and enterprising people." Ignore the chatter and find out what this particular business man wishes he could do to his competitors that the law won't let him do now. When a politician calls another politician "tinged with Communism" don't think, as you are intended to do, "Wouldn't it be awful if the Communists got control of our country?" Ask what it is the second politician wants to do that the first politician doesn't like. It may be as innocent as to raise the minimum wage or keep the streetcar fare at seven cents. What a man does or wants to do is the important consideration, not what he calls himself or other people.

PROBLEMS

1. A parlor game recently popular in this country illustrates rather neatly Ward's point about the "strategic value of synonyms." The game consists of labeling yourself with a descriptive word or phrase indicating approval, a friend who is present with a word or phrase indicating only mild disapproval, and a third person who is absent with a third word or phrase indicating strong disapproval. Thus: "I am *articulate;* you are *talkative;* he is *a wind-bag.*" Can you supply similar examples? You might begin with such self-congratulatory words as *dignified, clever, well-dressed,* and *reserved.* Warning: don't play for keeps.

2. What are some of the verbal labels in present-day America that one should exercise particular care not to apply unjustly to others (or permit to be applied unjustly to oneself) because of their "cutting edge"? What serious, ever-present weakness in our thinking gives such dangerous power to mere words? (Here you should recall Hayakawa's discussion of words as symbols.)

3. *For the ladies:* Can you recall examples of the very different words used to describe precisely the same hair-do or dress style when it was in fashion and, again, when it was not?

4. Ward distinguishes between "genuine neutrality" and "verbal evasion" (euphemism). This distinction will not always be easy to draw if we look only at the *words* used. For instance, is one being "neutral" or "evasive" when he uses the word "limb" instead of "leg"? What method must we use *to get behind the words* to the writer's meaning? In what respects is this method similar to the one used to determine a useful definition of an abstract word? Similar to the method used by Neuberger and Oliver to discover what a politician is? Do you see once more the necessity for keeping one's eye on the "operations" (what men are actually doing under very specific conditions and circumstances) rather than on verbal symbols? How does this relate, in turn, to what Ward calls being "aware of both denotation and connotation *in context*"?

5. Test your own stature as a "socially adjusted person" by listing spontaneously and honestly the words that spring to mind when you read or hear the following names and terms:

atheist	C.I.O.	taxes
umpire	Pearl Harbor	capitalist
picketing	syphilis	Hiroshima
Stalin	N.A.M.	reformer

How many of *the words with which you responded* might fairly be classified as neutral? How many suggest approval or disapproval? Do you see why the scientist frequently feels that he must become emancipated from words?

6. To illustrate how almost any word can assume emotional overtones under certain circumstances, consider the special attention we bestow on a person whom we have met, even if only in the pages of a book, if that person bears *our* name. Consider also the things people think about when they are selecting a name for a newborn child. Have you known people to change their names because of the unfortunate effect of the name on other people's opinion of them?

Sergeant Tacitus

Did you ever read Caesar's *Commentaries* on his military campaigns in a high-school Latin text, or perhaps in an English translation? Or have you read any recent military histories by such men as Douglas Freeman (the American Civil War) or Samuel Eliot Morison (the Navy's part in World War II)? If so, you must have been struck by the difference in tone and manner of these books and that of the "reports" of present-day war correspondents which you can read almost any day. Why are the former so matter-of-fact, the latter so highly colored?

Sergeant Tacitus, really Dave Dempsey, a former Marine Corps combat correspondent, explains this puzzler and, incidentally, reveals still another aspect of emotional language.

THE SEMANTICS OF WAR
CORRESPONDENCE *

To a war correspondent a well run battle is, professionally, a bit of hard luck. Tarawa, one of the most disorderly battles of all times, was a reporter's field day. No correspondent, of course, wants a Tarawa at the price that must be paid in lives. But the public, he will tell you, wanted its battles presented on a Tarawa-like scale; your correspondent had to dip his typewriter in blood and riddle his copy with bullets or go back to the copy desk. The semantics of war reporting became a highly developed science, based on the premise that all battles must be made to sound like battles.

Being an ex-reporter myself, I can sympathize with the problem. Almost four years of war reporting put heavy demands on the correspondent's stock of colorful adjectives and verbs, and with each successive campaign he had to find new ways to describe the age-old drama of physical conflict. Yet the divergencies between his picture of battle and the realities of fighting are only too apparent to the millions who read about the war while fighting it too.

The war correspondent should not be blamed too severely for this. For a long time he wasn't allowed near the battlefield. Perhaps that is why he had trouble with words. He had to take the official communiqué, which was about as undramatic as a bank statement, add his behind-the-lines observations, and turn out "good copy."

In his choice of words the reporter—let us, for the sake of argument, call him Hector Ronson—will no doubt defend himself, like Pooh-Bah, on the grounds of artistic verisimilitude. He does not mean to falsify the picture, but to dramatize it. Yet the final impression frequently is false. For he is not one to disabuse his public of the idea that land warfare has become less adventurous since the days of Ivanhoe. Out of the necessity to make warfare continuously dramatic, he has developed a battle lexicon of his own. Happily, words, like wounded men, can be given a blood transfusion. It is this, quite frankly, that has saved Hector's life too.

* Sergeant Tacitus, "The Semantics of War Correspondence," from *The Combat Forces Journal*, formerly *The Infantry Journal*, December, 1945.

The first time I saw Hector was in a landing boat in the Marshall Islands. When we hit the beach he headed for the command post, where most of the newspapermen had congregated. I advanced inland with my company. The battle was short, the atoll was taken, and we returned to our base. You can hardly imagine the surprise with which I read the first clippings of Hector's report on our operation. He had turned a fairly routine operation into such a bloody battle that I shuddered to think I had been in it.

We "stormed ashore" he wrote (actually we had taken our time, as there was a good deal of ammunition and equipment in our boat to be unloaded) while "bullets whizzed around us." (True, but they were strays from another part of the island, well over our heads.) Our men advanced "in the face of desperate rifle and machine-gun fire." Pillboxes and blockhouses blocked our way and had to be "blasted." Snipers were a constant menace.

Outside of the fact that none of these things happened to Hector, there is an element of truth in them. What is not true is that the battle fitted into the neat verbal clichés in which Hector chose to describe it.

There are a great many battles that are not very bloody. They are usually lacking in "color." Casualties are likely to be light, the men will get eight hours' sleep and take time out to eat three meals a day. (Such fighting is usually described as "dogged.") War, as someone has written, is 95 per cent housekeeping and 5 per cent combat. To the correspondents, the percentages are likely to be reversed. Who would buy the daily newspapers to learn that our forces in the battle of X Island consumed 50,000 K rations, set up a water purifying plant, and opened a post office?

A selected list of key words in the correspondent's lexicon, to which cling the heaviest aura of gore and glory, is translated below. The reader should bear in mind that it is not without the realm of possibility that the apparent meaning of the word is sometimes the correct one. But he should be skeptical. All too often the word will be disguising a tactically sound, if less dramatic, incident.

"Troops *splashed* ashore." There is something rugged about the word splash. It connotes the unexpected, as though the men supposed they were to be landed high and dry in unwrinkled khaki. Amphibious troops are trained to make the last 25 yards to shore under their own steam if necessary. Amphibian tractors, preceding them with troops that were landed high and dry, help protect their landing. Hector Ronson wrote: "This is where they separate the men from the boys." Nonsense. Can you imagine a first-class fighting organization waiting until D-day for that? For splash read *walked carefully* or *waded*. Amphibious troops are especially careful to keep their weapons dry, hence do little splashing.

"Savage, *hand-to-hand* fighting." Naturally, if it is hand to hand it will be savage but your chances of such an encounter are about one in 10,000 and I can say flatly that Hector Ronson has seen more hand-to-hand fighting in his favorite New York bar than he ever saw on the battlefield. Most close combat occurred when some patrol was ambushed, or a lone sentry was surprised at night, far from Hector's foxhole.

"Troops *stormed* a blockhouse." Troops did no such thing. A blockhouse is a formidable obstacle, loaded with machine guns and antitank guns. The picture of their reduction frequently drawn by correspondents, who wisely stay as far away from them as possible, leaves a false, if terrifyingly brave, image in the public mind. A blockhouse is usually reduced by (a) tank and/or artillery; (b) high explosives; (c) siege. None of these methods envisages mass infantry attack, which would be suicidal. A more accurate description would be to say that troops, infiltrating toward the blockhouse, managed to fire into the open gun ports and thus cover the advance of a few men with demolitions. Assuming that this is successful, and one wall of the blockhouse is blown away, the troops will then very cautiously creep in for the kill, getting close enough to lob grenades into the blasted opening. In general, this technique applies to any heavily armored position. For stormed read *crept up to.*

"*Bitter* fighting." A word resorted to when the fighting is characterless and refuses to lend itself to a more precise, colorful term. It is frequently followed by the phrase "although casualties were light." A stalemate is often described as "bitter." As both sides tend to regroup for a new offensive at this point, a better word would be *indifferent.*

"*Plunged* forward." In the same category as stormed, smashed, assaulted. If soldiers fought as our reporters sometimes describe them, most of the plunging would be on their faces. It is sometimes necessary to take a position by frontal assault—a costly method—but the usual procedure is to direct mortar and machine-gun fire on it first, rendering it as ineffective as possible before the Infantry, usually by a flank attack and seldom in a plunging manner, closes in. For plunged it is better to read *deployed.*

"*In the face of murderous machine-gun fire.*" Not if the boys can help it. A better way is to work your way around to the sides or rear. Precisely because machine-gun fire is murderous no one is going to advance frontally if a flank attack is possible. If our men had been as foolhardily brave as they were sometimes depicted, it would have been a short war.

"*Patrol activity.*" An ambiguous phrase usually resorted to when there was a lull in the fighting. Patrols are either reconnaissance or combat forces, sent out to get information about the enemy. They are usually lightly armed and instructed not to fight unless necessary to avoid capture. A colleague of Hector's on the Italian front wrote that "artillery rolled back" two German patrols. Either the Infantry was on leave or what was advancing was not a patrol but a large number of assault troops prepared to do business. When the reader is told that "action was limited to patrol activity" he may safely assume, 99 times out of a hundred, that there was virtually no fighting. He will also be right in assuming that the correspondent wouldn't admit that there are times when there is really nothing to write about. . . .

Is it not possible to write war stories that follow the action faithfully? Hector Ronson's dispatch might then have read something like this:

"United States troops, treading their way ashore, took the island of Goona Goona today. A two-day aerial and naval bombardment had virtually paralyzed enemy opposition.

"I came ashore several hours after the initial landing with the general and his staff and proceeded immediately to the command post where juleps, flavored with native mint, were waiting for us. From where I am watching the battle about the only danger is from falling coconuts. It is a strange sight to see more than half of our men unloading supplies, setting up tents, and so forth, while others, darting about cautiously, advance inland against the enemy. From reports that reach us they have crept up to several pillboxes and destroyed them.

"As the enemy regrouped his remaining forces for a final stand the fighting became quite indifferent and our men stopped for lunch. Later they resumed their forward movement and deployed around a number of machine-gun nests, wiping them out at a distance of about 25 yards.

"During the night, while our men slept, the artillery shelled enemy positions with moderately effective results. Following this, while patrols scouted for information, the fighting stopped. Early this morning the enemy counterattacked but was frustrated and our own units . . . went forward again. Most of the enemy was killed by machine-gun, mortar, and rifle fire. After the battle, as the Quartermaster Corps moved up to look for souvenirs, several frightened opposition soldiers came out from hiding places to surrender, although a few were indiscreet enough to take some shots at our men."

Please don't blame Hector too much. Who wants to read about *that* kind of war?

The editors won't like it, but I'll tell you right now it was a hell of a good way to *fight* a war.

PROBLEMS

1. Hector Ronson, says Sergeant Tacitus, "does not mean to falsify the picture, but to dramatize it." Does this sound to you like one of Ward's synonyms which "turn the meaning toward the reader in the way we want him to take hold of it"?

2. Sergeant Tacitus tells us not to blame Hector Ronson too much, for "who wants to read about *that* kind of war" (the actual events, the way they really happened)? Can you think of some recently published, highly factual accounts of war or a scientific experiment or an investigation of a social problem which throw some doubt on this common assumption that the public wants "dressed-up fiction," not facts? In this connection, how do you account for the steadily increasing popularity of documentary and semi-documentary films?

3. Do you see any connection between this assumption, repeated by Sergeant Tacitus, and your deep-rooted belief, and that of thousands of other composition students, that strictly factual themes about homely, everyday affairs "can't possibly be interesting to anybody"? To test the validity of this belief, ask at least three experienced com-

position instructors, men who have read many hundreds of freshman themes, whether they prefer your detailed accounts of observed facts or your themes about "big, important problems" like "race prejudice," "the international situation today," or "my religion."

4. Can you see any danger to the reading public in the desire on the part of foreign correspondents to "dramatize" the news? Consider the reporting of such episodes as the disappearance of a U. S. Navy plane on a flight over the Baltic Sea. (You would do well to read in this connection the chapter entitled "Antepenultimatum," from A. J. Liebling's *The Wayward Pressman.*) How much of the war jitters of recent years might be attributed to this tendency to "dramatize" the news? Compare the treatment of the latest international incident in your local newspaper with that in *The Christian Science Monitor*, which you can find in almost any college library.

5. If this dramatizing of international, especially "cold war," news continues to the point of making the average reader cynical—and there is already some evidence that this attitude of "You can't believe what you read in the newspapers" is widespread—can you see the very real danger to a nation's preparedness that might follow? Here the old fable of the boy who cried "Wolf!" takes on meaning.

S. *Stansfeld Sargent*

The following selection, like "The Invasion from Mars," is a report of a scientific survey. This survey covers the reactions of a representative group of Americans to certain words. Sargent, who teaches psychology at Columbia University, is especially interested in the analysis of propaganda and public opinion.

STEREOTYPES AND THE NEWSPAPERS *

This study deals with propaganda as shown in the effects of emotional stereotypes on newspaper readers, not with the motives which prompt the use of such terms.

Forty terms were selected from the news columns of the *Chicago Tribune.* Twenty of these had been used frequently by the *Tribune*

* S. Stansfeld Sargent, "Stereotypes and the Newspapers," from *Readings in Social Psychology* by Newcomb and Hartley. Copyright, 1947, by Henry Holt and Company, Inc.

referring to policies that it does not support. The other twenty terms referred to approved policies. (See the two columns in Chart 1.) Ten neutral terms were added to the list, and the fifty items arranged in mixed order.

Six groups of adults were used, totaling 231 subjects: a large P.T.A. meeting, a high school alumni fraternity, beginning and advanced college students, a workers' forum, and a middle-class community forum.

Procedure was as follows: Each subject was given a mimeographed sheet and told that the purpose of the experiment was to get his immediate emotional reactions to various words and phrases. As the experimenter read the terms one at a time, the subject checked L (Like), D (Dislike) or ? (No feeling about it). Two sample words were given before the experiment began. Intervals of about six seconds only were allowed between the words to insure an immediate emotional reaction. Source of the term was not indicated.

Results were tabulated for each group, and for the total of 231 subjects in all the groups thrown together. A stereotype score was calculated for each term by subtracting the number of D from the number of L responses, dividing this by the number of persons in the group and multiplying the decimal by 100. The question mark responses are omitted from the formula, but they affect the results by diminishing the size of the numerator and thus reducing the score. Hence the term that arouses the most consistent or standardized emotional response is considered the most stereotyped. (See examples at top of each column in Chart 1.) How far down the list may we go and still speak of the term as stereotyped? Plus or minus 50 is suggested as a good point of demarcation, but the differences exist, of course, in all degrees.

Marked similarity of reactions exists among the different groups. Rank order correlations ran from .81 to .96 between all groups except the workers' forum. The correlations between its responses and the other groups averaged close to .40. The members of this workers' forum showed their atypicality by registering strong favorable reactions to "collectivist economy," "spending program," "radical," "economic innovations" and "assault on business." Their strong negative reactions included *"Tribune,"* "tax-payer," "conservative," "capitalism," "private enterprise" and "businessmen." A

Chart 1

REACTIONS OF 231 SUBJECTS (MEMBERS OF SIX DIFFERENT
ADULT GROUPS) TO FORTY TERMS SELECTED FROM THE
COLUMNS OF THE *CHICAGO TRIBUNE*

A		B	
Terms referring to New Deal policies and practices and to organized labor (especially industrial unionism)		Terms used to refer to Republican policies and practices, nonstrikers, etc.	
	Score [1]		Score [1]
Czarism	−84	Cooperation	95
Dictatorship	−84	Freedom	92
Monopolistic practices	−82	Reemployment	88
Domination	−79	Recovery	79
Repressive measures	−65	Right to work	77
Regimentation	−64	Industry	77
Agitator	−63	Business	68
Assault on business	−59	Private initiative	66
Espionage	−57	Loyal workers	59
Court packing	−52	Business community	58
Communist	−49	Free competition	57
Inquisitor	−46	Constitutional principles	53
Radical	−37	Private enterprises	52
CIO partisan	−36	Businessmen	52
Brain Trust	−30	Investment capital	34
Alien	−27	Constitution defender	30
Spending program	−08	Conservative	28
Political regulation	−04	Taxpayer	27
Collectivist economy	03	Capitalism	−01
Economic innovations	12	Resolute Democrat	−22

$$^1 \text{ Score} = \frac{100 \text{ (number checking L minus number checking D)}}{\text{Total number of subjects}}$$

forum group can hardly represent a good cross section of labor
attitudes. Nevertheless the contrast with all other groups (which
were essentially middle class in character) suggests that class differences in emotional stereotypes deserve further study.

Another interpretation concerns the number of question mark responses found in the various groups. The fewest, an average of 6.85
per subject, was found in the P.T.A. group. The greatest number of
question marks was found among the college students, especially

the advanced class, which averaged over sixteen per subject. The difference amounts to almost ten responses, having a critical ratio of 6.0. Apparently fathers and mothers are more susceptible to emotion-arousing terms than college students; but this generalization must be discounted somewhat as the environment of the two groups is not identical.

Because the word *"Tribune"* was one of the so-called neutral terms added to the forty chosen items, the reactions of all subjects who marked L for *"Tribune"* (68 in number) were compared with the reactions of those who marked D (105 in number). As might be expected, the former group showed greater dislike for the term "radical," "agitator," "brain trust," "court packing," and "assault on business." Likewise it showed greater liking for "business," "private enterprise," and "the Constitution." The most striking contrast between these *Tribune* likers and *Tribune* dislikers, however, concerns the degree of emotional reaction. Out of a possible twenty unfavorable stereotypes, the group of subjects liking the *Tribune* showed a significant score (minus 50 or more) on seventeen, while the other showed significant scores on only seven. Similarly, out of a possible twenty favorable stereotypes, the Like *Tribune* group showed a significant score on seventeen, and the other group on only six. Furthermore, the Like *Tribune* group shows only 7.70 question mark responses per list, compared with 12.02 for those who dislike the paper. The critical ratio of the difference is 3.63 (d/σ_d). It would seem that those who like the *Chicago Tribune* also have pronounced likes and dislikes in political and economic matters.

Another step was taken to obtain a more direct check on the use of emotionalized terms. Twelve terms having possible emotional value were chosen from the *Tribune* news columns, and twelve parallel terms used in the same connection were taken from the *New York Times*. (See Chart 2.) These twenty-four items, in mixed order, along with twenty-six other terms were submitted to sixty college students. The results are shown in Chart 2. The median difference in stereotype score for these pairs of items is considerable—57.5 points. In each case the *Tribune* term is found to influence subjects in a direction consonant with the political and economic policies of that paper.

Chart 2

COMPARISON OF EMOTIONAL REACTIONS OF SIXTY COLLEGE
STUDENTS TO VARIOUS *CHICAGO TRIBUNE* TERMS AND TO
OTHER TERMS USED IN THE SAME CONNECTION BY THE
NEW YORK TIMES

Paper	Word or phrase	Score	Difference
CT	Radical	−53	
NYT	Progressive	92	145
CT	Government witch hunting	−38	
NYT	Senate investigation	57	95
CT	Regimentation	−53	
NYT	Regulation	32	85
CT	Communist CIO leader	−68	
NYT	Maritime leader	10	78
CT	Labor agitator	−63	
NYT	Labor organizer	12	75
CT	The dole	−35	
NYT	Home relief	27	62
CT	Farm dictatorship	−55	
NYT	Crop control	−02	53
CT	Loyal workers	60	
NYT	Nonstrikers	08	52
CT	Inquisitor	−22	
NYT	Investigator	23	45
CT	CIO dictator	−72	
NYT	CIO chieftain	−33	39
CT	Alien	−35	
NYT	Foreign	0	35
CT	Mass picketing	−55	
NYT	Picketing	−50	5

PROBLEMS

1. Sargent suggests, rather tentatively, to be sure, and with one important qualification, that college students appear to be less susceptible to emotion-arousing terms than do mothers and fathers, because the college students responded to more words with a question mark, indicating no feeling about them. Both students and teachers might very understandably be eager to accept this conclusion as correct. But, if this book has been to any purpose, students who have studied its contents so far ought to be able to suggest several reasons why this conclusion *may* be invalid. What are these reasons?

2. What are some possible inferences about both the newspaper and its readers that might be drawn from the fact that those readers who liked the *Tribune* had the most positive likes and dislikes in political and economic affairs?

3. Chart 2 is made up of a list of twelve *pairs* of words. The two different words in each pair stand for the same thing. What point made by Ward about the "strategic value of synonyms" does this illustrate?

4. The New York *Times* has a national reputation for fairness. The words it employs to discuss some people, institutions, and ideas of which it does not always approve resulted in this test in *favorable* responses to those *words*. What does this suggest about the basis for the *Times's* reputation?

5. The Chicago *Tribune,* on the other hand, is considered by a vast majority of thoughtful observers to be conspicuously slanted. The *Tribune* claims some 944,133 daily readers. Faced with this fact, many observers have been inclined to discount the *Tribune's* influence, arguing that people read this paper for its comics, sports, and other non-reporting features. Do Sargent's concluding remarks in this essay and your own analysis of Chart 2 give support to this viewpoint? Would your study in this book of the influence of words on behavior lead you to share this viewpoint?

Irving J. Lee

Irving Lee, of the School of Speech at Northwestern University, has concerned himself with the main problems of human communication, and so, in his book, *Language Habits in Human Affairs,* he quite naturally devotes much attention to ways in which people may be more deeply affected by words than by facts.

HOW DOES IT STRIKE YOU? *

A friend of mine, the owner of a department store, sought to test the intentionality of customers by a practical experiment. One morning he set out at different ends of a counter piles of men's handkerchiefs. On the one he placed a sign reading "Soft-Textured, Genuine Irish Linen Handkerchiefs, Special 3 for 50¢."

---

* Irving J. Lee, *Language Habits in Human Affairs,* Harper & Brothers, 1941.

On the other the sign read "Nose Rags, three for a quarter." During an eight-hour period, twenty-six different persons examined and eleven bought from the "Irish Linen" stock, while but six examined and only two bought the "Nose Rags." The point of this experiment should by now have been guessed: both piles contained the same kind of handkerchiefs. The salesgirl's comment is more than a little in point, "The people just didn't look at the merchandise."

Poffenberger tested this phenomenon by giving to fifty-seven men copies of the following advertisement of a well-known razor company:

A new triumph of American inventive genius of startling interest to every man with a beard to shave . . . for the first time in any razor micrometric control of the blade position made possible by the fulcrum shoulder, overhanging cap, and channeled guard. [A diagram showed] how the blade is biflexed between overhanging cap and fulcrum shoulder. It is flexed once into the inside curve of the cap. This is the minor flexure—the curve for easy gliding action and play of the wrist in shaving. It is flexed a second time—more sharply and in a shorter radius—by the grip of the overhanging cap the whole length of the fulcrum shoulder.

After they had read and studied the copy, he asked a list of seven questions to learn to what extent they believed and understood what they read. This is what he reported:

The answers to these questions showed that all the students agreed that the new razor was better than the old one, and that they would rather pay $5 for the new one than $1 or $2 for the old one. In supporting their belief they were allowed to consult the advertisement as much as they wished. They quoted the "fulcrum shoulder," which made possible "micrometric control of the blade position," but not one of them could explain how the micrometric control was obtained or what advantage there would be in having such a micrometric control. They believed that the "channeled guard" was an improvement although they could not tell why it was an improvement. As to the importance of major and minor flexures they were entirely ignorant.

In 1935 Sherif investigated the existence of aesthetic stereotypes. He first found the preferences of his subjects for certain English and American writers, including Barrie, Conrad, Cooper, Dickens, Poe, etc. Several weeks after receiving their rank-order votes on these sixteen authors, he gave sixteen prose passages, *all written by*

Stevenson, but after each passage was written the name of one of the authors in the original list. The subjects were asked to rank the writings in terms of their literary merit. As far as was known, no one of the subjects realized the deception.

Some of the subjects said they had ignored the names appended. As a result, their correlation between the preference for the writers and the preference for the merit of the writing was zero. However, for the remaining nearly two hundred subjects, the average correlation was $+.46$. Passages attributed to highly rated writers were considered "good," while passages attributed to lowly rated writers were thought to be "bad."

One conclusion is inevitable. Since the passages were all from Stevenson, the rating of the passages in terms of favored and unfavored authors' *names* indicated that the responses were to the names and not to the passages. . . .

Bernays tells of responses to words even in moments of crisis.

In Great Britain, during the war, the evacuation hospitals came in for a considerable amount of criticism because of the summary way in which they handled their wounded. It was assumed by the public that a hospital gives prolonged and conscientious attention to its patients. When the name was changed to evacuation posts, the critical reaction vanished. No one expected more than an adequate emergency treatment from an institution so named. The cliché hospital was indelibly associated in the public mind with a certain picture.

. . . The consequences of such automatic reaction to words cannot be underestimated if we see how the failure to observe the order of facts first produces misevaluation. Readers might ponder the effects of such orientation on the quality of our larger political and social decisions. When individuals are so oriented that their acts of judgment in connection with simple and unimportant matters are rendered impractical and useless as guides to proper evaluation, we should be little surprised (though greatly worried) if their judgments are equally distorted and unfounded in more significant matters.

PROBLEMS

1. Which of the great variety of weaknesses in our thinking is illustrated by the "handkerchief—nose rag" story?

2. It is told that a well-known professor of philosophy at the University of Chicago once delivered a short talk to a group of college students during which he deliberately avoided making a single meaningful statement. Instead, he relied on a careful selection of rhetorical devices and high-sounding words to create the impression of meaningfulness. It is said that several minutes passed before many of his listeners were fully aware of the hoax. What error did the professor's listeners and Poffenberger's readers have in common? How do you account for the relative success of each of these hoaxes? What are the underlying similarities between the professor's hoax and the Sherif investigation?

3. Have you noticed a small child's awe of some high-sounding name for a minor physical ailment? Of course, the child's response may vary all the way from increased terror and imagined heightening of the pain to a curious pride which carries with it its own solace. What is the basic similarity between the child's reactions to these medical terms and that of the public in Lee's story to the "evacuation hospitals"?

4. What evidence is there that motion picture producers understand the importance of titles? Can you recall any instances of movie titles that were misleading? Any instances in which a movie title succeeded in selling an otherwise "unsaleable" product? Any instances in which a studio's choice of a movie title backfired? Check also the changes in titles made in the 25-cent reprint novels (the law says the original title must appear, but you may, nevertheless, have to hunt for it). Why are such changes made?

GENERAL PROBLEMS:
Controlling Emotional Language

1. Semanticists employ different terms to designate those words whose primary function is to convey information and those words whose primary function is to convey or arouse emotion. One pair of useful terms is *informative* for the first, *emotive* for the second. Arrange

each of the following words in a context which will illustrate its *informative* function and its *emotive* function. (Example: "The Pilgrims prayed for *divine* guidance." "Your Easter hat is simply *divine!*") The first five words are adjectives, the second five are nouns:

sharp	scab
shady	barbarian
cracked	tool
flashy	G.I.
oily	cat

2. Now distinguish the *informative* from the *emotive* terms in the following advertisements:

a. "Today's tasty citrus juices, with all of their health-giving goodness, are scientifically squeezed from tree-ripened, whole-bodied fruit by unique XYZ Juice Extractors. To capture the delicate natural flavor and freshness, dexterous cup-shaped metal fingers quickly, but gently, compress each fruit, separating clean, pure sun-sweetened juice from pulp and other unappetizing fruit substances. . . . These novel machines, employing a patented extraction principle, produce millions of gallons of luscious high-quality juices to satisfy the nation's favorite daily diet."

b. "WHERE YOUR WILL HAS ITS WAY

"Once you gun the Bearcat heart of this gorgeous motorcar and see how the hills bow down before you . . .

Once you transmit your travel thoughts through the magic of Easyflow Drive and find them turned instantly and smoothly to reality . . .

Then you begin to discover how much of your will and your wishes find response in any model of the Jukes Travelmaster."

EDITORS' NOTE: Don't say, "Yes, yes, we know how advertising is, so why spend time analyzing it?" How often have you heard (or made) reference to the "master bedroom" in a modest two- or three-bedroom house? How many times have you spoken with studied casualness of your "deluxe model" car, refrigerator, or vacuum cleaner? Does the term "high quality" set up a familiar echo in the corridors of your mind? Where do you suppose you picked up such ways of speaking—and thinking?

3. Compare your language as to its degree of emotion-expression in three fields about which you may commonly think and speak or write (e.g., cooking recipes, raising garden vegetables, and fixing your car—or religion, politics, and morality). On the basis of this comparison, do you find that in some fields you use language that is much less emo-

tional than the language you use in other fields? If you find such a difference, how can you explain it? Do you feel that you are more successful in meeting the problems in one field than those in another? Does the language you use have something to do with your success or failure to meet the problems you encounter in these different fields? How is the kind of language you use related to the kind of thinking you do in these different fields?

4. In the light of the very considerable body of evidence presented to you so far in this book, in both the essays and the problems, what conclusions are you prepared to draw about the following:

   a. The extent of verbal confusion in your own mind

   b. The extent of verbal confusion in the minds of those people you know best

   c. The kinds of folly, injustice, and "blindness" into which this sort of confusion can easily lead you

   d. The areas of communication and the kinds of occupations and professions where this sort of confusion is most likely to be encountered; least likely

   e. The importance of an awareness of this kind of confusion to you right now as a student in a college composition course; the importance to your teacher

   f. The best means of recognizing, guarding against, and overcoming this kind of confusion

   g. The relationship of the *inductive* method of thinking to these means; the *deductive* method

   h. The relationship of an adequate method of arriving at "operational" definitions to both of these methods of thinking

II. UNDERSTANDING THE MEANS AND ENDS OF PROPAGANDA IN MASS COMMUNICATION

Analyzing Propaganda

WHAT do you do when a rough-looking, big-fanged, loud-barking dog in your neighborhood comes charging down at you? Turn away in flight, either dignified or undignified? Stand your ground and observe him cautiously? Attempt, physically or psychologically, to bring him down to size? Regardless of what you actually do, which of these possible alternatives seems most desirable?

Granted that most analogies are dangerous, we suggest, nevertheless, that the most common attitude toward propaganda today, at least in this country, is much like that of the people who never stop long enough to observe and hence, possibly, to control the dog's behavior. This reaction is understandable, for in recent years propagandists have helped men bury facts, create myths of national, racial, and class superiority and inferiority, set up tyrannies, imprison, torture, and kill millions of their fellow men, and wage world-wide wars of aggression. But is this turning away in fear or disgust rational? Can we assume that propaganda will always "bite" until we have really observed it?

Of course, just looking at dogs or propaganda doesn't help much unless one knows what he is looking for. This raises some questions. With what kinds of people and causes do you associate propaganda? Do you generally disapprove of them? What specific methods did these people use to work on other people's minds? Were some of the methods they used similar to methods which, used under other circumstances, you feel quite different about? If so, then what made you consider the methods wrong in one case and quite all right, even laudable, in another? Are you confusing methods (means) with causes (ends)? Can you see how this "making fish of one, flesh of another" might make the man who "hates propaganda" an easy victim of some kinds of propaganda? Do you find in certain kinds of propaganda any possibilities for constructive use? On the basis of what you have discovered about the problems of thought and language from reading this book, can you see how you can keep yourself from being victimized by propaganda of all kinds, including even that of which you approve?

In the selection from *Mein Kampf,* Adolf Hitler describes the main methods he used to get certain beliefs accepted. (When you concentrate your attention on his methods rather than his beliefs, which are doubtless loathsome to you, do you find that many of these methods have been used to get you to accept other beliefs of which you strongly approve?) The second selection, from *Consumer Reports,* and the third, "How to Lie with Statistics," unlike the Hitler selection, are concerned with protecting the propagandee from the propagandist. Hummel and Huntress, in their "Propaganda and the Mass Media of Communication," suggest the problems of the reader-listener as he will meet them today; they also indicate ways in which the intelligent citizen may find his way toward information rather than misinformation, toward a comparison of representative views rather than toward a collection of unexamined dogma.

When you finish this section, if you have done your job well, you should be able to bring this particular "dog" to heel, if not make him roll over and play dead.

Adolf Hitler

To learn how something is done, one may try doing it himself, observe an expert doing it, or study the findings of men who have studied the techniques of the experts. Here we will start with the advice of an expert in the art of propaganda.

There can be no doubt that Hitler was a master of propaganda. His use of this instrument of mass persuasion was at least partially responsible for the welding of the Germans into a fanatic working-fighting unit, for the creation of a state of mind that could lead seemingly civilized men to organize the slaughter of whole races, for the rearing of a generation of German youth to venerate their own leader and their own "race." Hitler's understanding of other matters, such as moral issues, world geography, and military strategy, may have been meager, but his mastery of propaganda methods was proved by results.

Remember that, in looking into the suggestions of Hitler and others, we are doing so not as apprentices in the craft of propaganda but as members of the propagandists' public. We want to be, so far as possible, masters of our own fates; therefore, it will be necessary for us to be able to recognize the propaganda techniques of men who use those techniques to make themselves masters of our fates.

ADVICE FROM AN EXPERT *

To whom should propaganda be addressed? To the scientifically trained intelligentsia or to the less educated masses?

It must be addressed always and exclusively to the masses.

What the intelligentsia—or those who today unfortunately often go by that name—what they need is not propaganda but scientific instruction. The content of propaganda is not science any more than the object represented in a poster is art. The art of the poster lies in the designer's ability to attract the attention of the crowd by form and color. A poster advertising an art exhibit must direct the attention of the public to the art being exhibited; the better it succeeds in this, the greater is the art of the poster itself. The poster should give the masses an idea of the significance of the exhibition, it should not be a substitute for the art on display. Anyone who wants to concern himself with the art itself must do more than study the poster; and it will not be enough for him just to saunter

* This selection from Adolf Hitler, *Mein Kampf* (translated by Ralph Manheim), is reprinted by permission of and arrangement with Houghton Mifflin Company, the authorized publishers.

through the exhibition. We may expect him to examine and immerse himself in the individual works, and thus little by little form a fair opinion.

A similar situation prevails with what we today call propaganda.

The function of propaganda does not lie in the scientific training of the individual, but in calling the masses' attention to certain facts, processes, necessities, etc., whose significance is thus for the first time placed within their field of vision.

The whole art consists in doing this so skillfully that everyone will be convinced that the fact is real, the process necessary, the necessity correct, etc. But since propaganda is not and cannot be the necessity in itself, since its function, like the poster, consists in attracting the attention of the crowd, and not in educating those who are already educated or who are striving after education and knowledge, its effect for the most part must be aimed at the emotions and only to a very limited degree at the so-called intellect.

All propaganda must be popular and its intellectual level must be adjusted to the most limited intelligence among those it is addressed to. Consequently, the greater the mass it is intended to reach, the lower its purely intellectual level will have to be. But if, as in propaganda for sticking out a war, the aim is to influence a whole people, we must avoid excessive intellectual demands on our public, and too much caution cannot be exerted in this direction.

The more modest its intellectual ballast, the more exclusively it takes into consideration the emotions of the masses, the more effective it will be. And this is the best proof of the soundness or unsoundness of a propaganda campaign, and not success in pleasing a few scholars or young aesthetes.

The art of propaganda lies in understanding the emotional ideas of the great masses and finding, through a psychologically correct form, the way to the attention and thence to the heart of the broad masses. The fact that our bright boys do not understand this merely shows how mentally lazy and conceited they are.

Once we understand how necessary it is for propaganda to be adjusted to the broad mass, the following rule results:

It is a mistake to make propaganda many-sided, like scientific instruction, for instance.

The receptivity of the great masses is very limited, their intelligence is small, but their power of forgetting is enormous. In consequence of these facts, all effective propaganda must be limited to a very few points and must harp on these in slogans until the last member of the public understands what you want him to understand by your slogan. As soon as you sacrifice this slogan and try to be many-sided, the effect will piddle away, for the crowd can neither digest nor retain the material offered. In this way the result is weakened and in the end entirely cancelled out.

PROBLEMS

1. On what basic premise about human intelligence (a premise which you will recall Dunham examined) are Hitler's recommendations to propagandists based? Is it a sufficiently self-evident and sound generalization to serve as a major premise? If not, what limited truths may it contain? In what specific ways may these observations be helpful to the person who wants to read and listen intelligently?
2. Hitler distinguishes carefully between the formula for successful propaganda and that for "scientific instruction." What is the basic distinction he sees? Which method of reasoning, inductive or deductive, does he want his audience to use? Does this mean that propaganda cannot be studied scientifically?

"Consumer Reports"

No one today questions the fact that advertising, a relatively new propaganda invention of the past 200 years, exercises a powerful influence on public behavior. It is precisely because of this influence that advertising has been subjected to thoughtful criticism. Adverse criticism has been directed chiefly at two aspects of advertising: the stimulation of irrational responses to *words* and other *symbols* (the "snob appeal" of much advertising is a conspicuous example); and the use of various artifices, chiefly word-combinations, which may mislead the prospective purchaser.

Just as the semanticist has been largely concerned with the former abuse, so have various federal agencies, and, more recently, consumer groups, been concerned with the latter. Perhaps the most powerful, and certainly the most articulate, of these consumer groups has been Consumers Union, "a nonprofit organization chartered under the Membership Corporation laws of New York State," which, by means of its monthly publication, *Consumer Reports,* conducts an interesting and effective campaign to see that the consumer "gets his money's worth." The present excerpt from *Consumer Reports* is doubly interesting because it represents the views of the United States Supreme Court and the National Better Business Bureau as well as those of Consumers Union on the subject of misleading advertising.

"PEOPLE HAVE A RIGHT . . ." *

COURT DECISION SETS ADVERTISING STANDARDS FOR CONSUMER PROTECTION

Back in 1945, the Postmaster General issued a fraud order to stop a "$10,000 First Prize Puzzle Contest," put on by Publishers Service Company for Read Magazine, Inc., and Facts Magazine. The Supreme Court has now upheld the Postmaster General—and, in the process, handed down a Magna Carta for consumers upholding their right to honesty in advertising. The Supreme Court's decision in the case goes much further than any previous pronouncement in defending the consumer's right to have the truth, the whole truth, and nothing but the truth, free of "fraudulent traps and stratagems," and clear enough to be understood by "ordinary and trusting minds."

First, the Court held that contestants reading the advertisement for the contest with ordinary care might be falsely led to believe that they might be eligible to win prizes on payment of $3 in connection with their contest entry, whereas, in fact, the minimum payment required was $9, and, as it later developed, contestants were finally called upon to pay as much as $42 to be eligible for maximum prizes.

Second, the contest was advertised as a "puzzle contest," although the prizes would actually be awarded on the basis of "tie-breaking letter-essays" among those successfully solving the puzzles; and the

* From *Consumer Reports,* August, 1948, published by Consumers Union of U. S., Inc.

Publishers Service Company (which had repeatedly run similar contests to promote newspaper circulation) well knew from its past experience that winners would in the end be selected on the basis not of puzzles but of essays.

Justices Burton and Douglas thought the contest not fraudulent because, by carefully reading the rules embodied in the advertisement in fine six-point type, a prospective contestant could have unearthed the facts. Even the Postmaster General, they pointed out, did not allege that a single sentence in the advertisement was by itself untrue. But the court majority, speaking through Justice Black, defended the right of consumers not to be misled:

> Advertisements as a whole may be completely misleading although every sentence separately considered is literally true. This may be because things are omitted that should be said, or because advertisements are composed or purposely printed in such a way as to mislead. . . . That exceptionally acute and sophisticated readers might have been able by penetrating analysis to have deciphered the true nature of the contest's terms is not sufficient to bar findings of fraud by a fact-finding tribunal. Questions of fraud may be determined in the light of the effect advertisements would most probably produce on ordinary minds. . . . People have a right to assume that fraudulent advertising traps will not be laid to ensnare them. "Laws are made to protect the trusting as well as the suspicious."

The National Better Business Bureau, in a service bulletin for members, states with admirable clarity the five "lessons for advertisers" which the decision lays down:

> Advertising as a whole must not create a misleading impression even though every statement separately considered is literally truthful.
>
> Advertising must be written for the probable effect it produces on ordinary and trusting minds, as well as for those intellectually capable of penetrating analysis.
>
> Advertising must not obscure or conceal material facts.
>
> Advertising must not be artfully contrived to distract and divert readers' attention from the true nature of the terms and conditions of an offer.
>
> Advertising must be free of fraudulent traps and stratagems which induce action which would not result from a forthright disclosure of the true nature of an offer.

PROBLEMS

1. The writers of this article seem to be most concerned here not with the outright falsehood but with the literally true statement that can lead one to a false conclusion. Analyze half-a-dozen advertisements in newspapers or magazines. Determine: (a) the impression which most readers, in a quick, unanalytical reading, would be likely to get; (b) the presence—or absence—of any of the five stratagems which the National Better Business Bureau urges advertisers not to use.
2. One might make the mistake of concluding that this kind of crooked thinking is confined to the advertising of commodities. If you share this opinion, recall ads in recent political elections, or your own efforts to persuade school authorities to give you certain doubtful transfer credits for courses taken at another school. With these suggestions in mind, draw up a list of four or five other situations about which you have firsthand knowledge where you or others misled someone else or were misled by a literally true statement that resulted in the drawing of a false conclusion. Indicate in what specific ways it was possible for these statements to mislead.

Darrell Huff

Huff's article might be subtitled, "Or How to Make Statistics Lie Down." If in your study of the inductive method of thinking you avoided jumping to the oversimple conclusion that the inductive method is simply "getting facts," then you will not take Huff's article as an attack on "statistics"; you will have no trouble in seeing Huff's main point, for you will already understand how the *interpretation* of facts is as essential a part of inductive thinking as is the initial fact-gathering. In this connection, Huff's analysis of some types of statistical manipulation may make clear how much of the propagandist's effectiveness depends on the propagandee's neglecting to inspect closely whatever "facts" the propagandist lets him have.

Huff is a free-lance writer. His awareness of the importance of the correct interpretation of statistics began in a college course in statistics.

HOW TO LIE WITH STATISTICS *

"The average Yaleman, Class of '24," *Time* magazine reported last year after reading something in the New York *Sun,* a newspaper published in those days, "makes $25,111 a year."

Well, good for him!

But, come to think of it, what does this improbably precise and salubrious figure mean? Is it, as it appears to be, evidence that if you send your boy to Yale you won't have to work in your old age and neither will he? Is this average a mean or is it a median? What kind of sample is it based on? You could lump one Texas oilman with two hundred hungry free-lance writers and report *their* average income as $25,000-odd a year. The arithmetic is impeccable, the figure is convincingly precise, and the amount of meaning there is in it you could put in your eye.

In just such ways is the secret language of statistics, so appealing in a fact-minded culture, being used to sensationalize, inflate, confuse, and oversimplify. Statistical terms are necessary in reporting the mass data of social and economic trends, business conditions, "opinion" polls, this year's census. But without writers who use the words with honesty and understanding and readers who know what they mean, the result can only be semantic nonsense.

In popular writing on scientific research, the abused statistic is almost crowding out the picture of the white-jacketed hero laboring overtime without time-and-a-half in an ill-lit laboratory. Like the "little dash of powder, little pot of paint," statistics are making many an important fact "look like what she ain't." Here are some of the ways it is done.

The sample with the built-in bias. Our Yale men—or Yalemen, as they say in the Time-Life building—belong to this flourishing group. The exaggerated estimate of their income is not based on all members of the class nor on a random or representative sample of them. At least two interesting categories of 1924-model Yale men have been excluded.

First there are those whose present addresses are unknown to

* Darrell Huff in *Harper's Magazine,* August, 1950. Copyright, 1950, by Harper & Brothers.

their classmates. Wouldn't you bet that these lost sheep are earning less than the boys from prominent families and the others who can be handily reached from a Wall Street office?

There are those who chucked the questionnaire into the nearest wastebasket. Maybe they didn't answer because they were not making enough money to brag about. Like the fellow who found a note clipped to his first pay check suggesting that he consider the amount of his salary confidential: "Don't worry," he told the boss. "I'm just as ashamed of it as you are."

Omitted from our sample then are just the two groups most likely to depress the average. The $25,111 figure is beginning to account for itself. It may indeed be a true figure for those of the Class of '24 whose addresses are known and who are willing to stand up and tell how much they earn. But even that requires a possibly dangerous assumption that the gentlemen are telling the truth.

To be dependable to any useful degree at all, a sampling study must use a representative sample (which can lead to trouble too) or a truly random one. If *all* the Class of '24 is included, that's all right. If every tenth name on a complete list is used, that is all right too, and so is drawing an adequate number of names out of a hat. The test is this: Does every name in the group have an equal chance to be in the sample?

You'll recall that ignoring this requirement was what produced the *Literary Digest's* famed fiasco. When names for polling were taken only from telephone books and subscription lists, people who did not have telephones or *Literary Digest* subscriptions had no chance to be in the sample. They possibly did not mind this underprivilege a bit, but their absence was in the end very hard on the magazine that relied on the figures.

This leads to a moral: You can prove about anything you want to by letting your sample bias itself. As a consumer of statistical data—a reader, for example, of a news magazine—remember that no statistical conclusion can rise above the quality of the sample it is based upon. In the absence of information about the procedures behind it, you are not warranted in giving any credence at all to the result.

The truncated, or gee-whiz, graph. If you want to show some statistical information quickly and clearly, draw a picture of it. Graphic presentation is the thing today. If you don't mind misleading the hasty looker, or if you quite clearly *want* to deceive him, you can save some space by chopping the bottom off many kinds of graph.

Suppose you are showing the upward trend of national income month by month for a year. The total rise, as in one recent year, is 7 per cent. It looks like this:

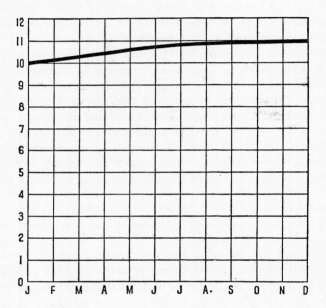

That is clear enough. Anybody can see that the trend is slightly upward. You are showing a 7 per cent increase and that is exactly what it looks like.

But it lacks schmaltz. So you chop off the bottom, this way:

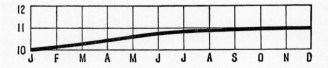

The figures are the same. It is the same graph and nothing has been falsified—except the impression that it gives. Anyone looking at it can just feel prosperity throbbing in the arteries of the country.

It is a subtler equivalent of editing "National income rose 7 per cent" into ". . . climbed a whopping 7 per cent."

It is vastly more effective, however, because of that illusion of objectivity.

The souped-up graph. Sometimes truncating is not enough. The trifling rise in something or other still looks almost as insignificant as it is. You can make that 7 per cent look livelier than 100 per cent ordinarily does. Simply change the proportion between the ordinate and the abscissa. There's no rule against it, and it does give your graph a prettier shape.

But it exaggerates, to say the least, something awful:

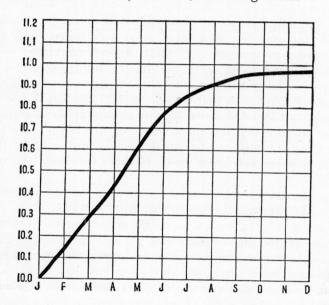

The well-chosen average. I live near a country neighborhood for which I can report an average income of $15,000. I could also report it as $3,500.

If I should want to sell real estate hereabouts to people having a high snobbery content, the first figure would be handy. The second figure, however, is the one to use in an argument against raising taxes, or the local bus fare.

Both are legitimate averages, legally arrived at. Yet it is obvious that at least one of them must be as misleading as an out-and-out lie. The $15,000-figure is a mean, the arithmetic average of the incomes of all the families in the community. The smaller figure is a median; it might be called the income of the average family in the group. It indicates that half the families have less than $3,500 a year and half have more.

Here is where some of the confusion about averages comes from. Many human characteristics have the grace to fall into what is called the "normal" distribution. If you draw a picture of it, you get a curve that is shaped like a bell. Mean and median fall at about the same point, so it doesn't make very much difference which you use.

But some things refuse to follow this neat curve. Income is one of them. Incomes for most large areas will range from under $1,000 a year to upward of $50,000. Almost everybody will be under $10,000, way over on the left-hand side of that curve.

One of the things that made the income figure for the "average Yaleman" meaningless is that we are not told whether it is a mean or a median. It is not that one type of average is invariably better than the other; it depends upon what you are talking about. But neither gives you any real information—and either may be highly misleading—unless you know which of those two kinds of average it is.

In the country neighborhood I mentioned, almost everyone has less than the average—the mean, that is—of $10,500. These people are all small farmers, except for a trio of millionaire week-enders who bring up the mean enormously.

You can be pretty sure that when an income average is given in the form of a mean nearly everybody has less than that.

The insignificant difference or the elusive error. Your two children Peter and Linda (we might as well give them modish names while we're about it) take intelligence tests. Peter's IQ, you learn, is 98 and Linda's is 101. Aha! Linda is your brighter child.

Is she? An intelligence test is, or purports to be, a sampling of intellect. An IQ, like other products of sampling, is a figure with a statistical error, which expresses the precision or reliability of the figure. The size of this probable error can be calculated. For their test the makers of the much-used Revised Stanford-Binet have found it to be about 3 per cent. So Peter's indicated IQ of 98 really means only that there is an even chance that it falls between 95 and 101. There is an equal probability that it falls somewhere else—below 95 or above 101. Similarly, Linda's has no better than a fifty-fifty chance of being within the fairly sizeable range of 98 to 104.

You can work out some comparisons from that. One is that there is rather better than one chance in four that Peter, with his lower IQ rating, is really at least three points smarter than Linda. A statistician doesn't like to consider a difference significant unless you can hand him odds a lot longer than that.

Ignoring the error in a sampling study leads to all kinds of silly conclusions. There are magazine editors to whom readership surveys are gospel; with a 40 per cent readership reported for one article and a 35 per cent for another, they demand more like the first. I've seen even smaller differences given tremendous weight, because statistics are a mystery and numbers are impressive. The same thing goes for market surveys and so-called public-opinion polls. The rule is that you cannot make a valid comparison between two such figures unless you know the deviations. And unless the difference between the figures is many times greater than the probable error of each, you have only a guess that the one appearing greater really is.

Otherwise you are like the man choosing a camp site from a report of mean temperature alone. One place in California with a mean annual temperature of 61 is San Nicolas Island on the south coast, where it always stays in the comfortable range between 47 and 87. Another with a mean of 61 is in the inland desert, where the thermometer hops around from 15 to 104. The deviation from the mean marks the difference, and you can freeze or roast if you ignore it.

The one-dimensional picture. Suppose you have just two or three figures to compare—say the average weekly wage of carpenters in the United States and another country. The sums might be $60 and $30. An ordinary bar chart makes the difference graphic. [See next page.] That is an honest picture. It looks good for American carpenters, but perhaps it does not have quite the oomph you are after. Can't you make that difference appear overwhelming and at the same time give it what I am afraid is known as eye-appeal? Of course you can. Following tradition, you represent these sums

by pictures of money bags. If the $30 bag is one inch high, you draw the $60 bag two inches high. That's in proportion, isn't it?

The catch is, of course, that the American's money bag, being twice as tall as that of the $30 man, covers an area on your page four times as great. And since your two-dimensional picture represents an object that would in fact have three dimensions, the money bags actually would differ much more than that. The volumes of any two similar solids vary as the cubes of their heights. If the unfortunate foreigner's bag holds $30 worth of dimes, the American's would hold not $60 but a neat $240.

You didn't say that, though, did you? And you can't be blamed, you're only doing it the way practically everybody else does.

The ever-impressive decimal. For a spurious air of precision that will lend all kinds of weight to the most disreputable statistics, consider the decimal.

Ask a hundred citizens how many hours they slept last night. Come out with a total of, say, 7.813. Your data are far from precise to begin with. Most people will miss their guess by fifteen minutes or more and some will recall five sleepless minutes as half a night of tossing insomnia.

But go ahead, do your arithmetic, announce that people sleep an average of 7.813 hours a night. You will sound as if you knew precisely what you are talking about. If you were foolish enough to say 7.8 (or "almost 8") hours it would sound like what it was—an approximation.

The semi-attached figure. If you can't prove what you want to prove, demonstrate something else and pretend that they are the same thing. In the daze that follows the collision of statistics with the human mind, hardly anybody will notice the difference. The semi-attached figure is a durable device guaranteed to stand you in good stead. It always has.

If you can't prove that your nostrum cures colds, publish a sworn laboratory report that the stuff killed 31,108 germs in a test tube in eleven seconds. There may be no connection at all between assorted germs in a test tube and the whatever-it-is that produces colds, but people aren't going to reason that sharply, especially while sniffling.

Maybe that one is too obvious and people are beginning to catch on. Here is a trickier version.

Let us say that in a period when race prejudice is growing it is to your advantage to "prove" otherwise. You will not find it a difficult assignment.

Ask that usual cross section of the population if they think Negroes have as good a chance as white people to get jobs. Ask again a few months later. As Princeton's Office of Public Opinion Research has found out, people who are most unsympathetic to Negroes are the ones most likely to answer yes to this question.

As prejudice increases in a country, the percentage of affirmative answers you will get to this question will become larger. What looks on the face of it like growing opportunity for Negroes actually is mounting prejudice and nothing else. You have achieved something rather remarkable: the worse things get, the better your survey makes them look.

The unwarranted assumption, or post hoc *rides again.* The interrelation of cause and effect, so often obscure anyway, can be most neatly hidden in statistical data.

Somebody once went to a good deal of trouble to find out if cigarette smokers make lower college grades than non-smokers. They did. This naturally pleased many people, and they made much of it.

The unwarranted assumption, of course, was that smoking had produced dull minds. It seemed vaguely reasonable on the face of it, so it was quite widely accepted. But it really proved nothing of the sort, any more than it proved that poor grades drive students to the solace of tobacco. Maybe the relationship worked in one direction, maybe in the other. And maybe all this is only an indication that the sociable sort of fellow who is likely to take his books less than seriously is also likely to sit around and smoke many cigarettes.

Permitting statistical treatment to befog causal relationships is little better than superstition. It is like the conviction among the people of the Hebrides that body lice produce good health. Observation over the centuries had taught them that people in good health had lice and sick people often did not. *Ergo,* lice made a man healthy. Everybody should have them.

Scantier evidence, treated statistically at the expense of common sense, has made many a medical fortune and many a medical article in magazines, including professional ones. More sophisticated observers finally got things straightened out in the Hebrides. As it turned out, almost everybody in those circles had lice most of the time. But when a man took a fever (quite possibly carried to him by those same lice) and his body became hot, the lice left.

Here you have cause and effect not only reversed, but intermingled.

There you have a primer in some ways to use statistics to deceive. A well-wrapped statistic is better than Hitler's "big lie": it misleads, yet it can't be pinned onto you.

Is this little list altogether too much like a manual for swindlers? Perhaps I can justify it in the manner of the retired burglar whose published reminiscences amounted to a graduate course in how to pick a lock and muffle a footfall: The crooks already know these tricks. Honest men must learn them in self-defense.

PROBLEMS

1. Huff suggests that "statistical terms," which impress people who do not "know what they mean," are examples of "semantic nonsense." What is the connection between this idea and the underlying theme of the sections "Recognizing Words as Symbols" and "Defining Your Terms" in this book?

2. Huff explains carefully in what way the sampling of "Yalemen" was faulty. In what specific ways are the following people making the same error: the summer tourist who concludes that Southwest Indians "live on" the tourist trade? the high school student who builds his picture of college undergraduates from the half-dozen undergraduates who came to his school to publicize "life at —— College"? the lecturer who concludes, largely on the grounds of his many meetings with club-women, that "American women are profoundly gregarious"? Supply still further instances which reveal that the sampling error is not limited to thinking which involves statistics or "figures."

3. What is the similarity between the individual who "makes a lot of" a few selected incidents to "prove" a point and the statistician who, consciously or unconsciously, gives the impression of a quick rise in wages, and so forth, by use of "truncated" and "souped-up" graphs?

4. In what respects would an "operational" definition, that is, defining a term by finding *how something is done,* prevent a reader's misunderstanding and falling for a "well-chosen average"?

5. In just what ways do Huff's discussions of the "insignificant difference or the elusive error" and the "ever-impressive decimal" deal with the same kind of faulty thinking pointed out in "Guarding Against Oversimplification" and again by Chase in his discussion of the danger of overlooking negative instances?

6. The reader's acceptance of the "semi-attached figure" as proof and his swallowing an "unwarranted assumption" are, of course, errors in deductive logic. Can you see how the reduction of such arguments to syllogistic form—finding their major and minor premises and their conclusions—can help one resist the appeal of this sort of "reasoning"?

William Hummel and Keith Huntress

> The following selection from Hummel and Huntress' book, *The Analysis of Propaganda,* is a brief but suggestive summary of the main characteristics of propaganda and of the present use of mass media for propaganda purposes. The authors teach English at Iowa State College, where considerable emphasis has been placed on the students' need for understanding how their own pictures of events are formed and for developing their ability to take care of themselves in the propaganda wars of contemporary society.

WHAT IS PROPAGANDA? *

"Propaganda" is a word of evil connotation. The average American, hearing it, is reminded of spies and secret police, of cynical reporters and biased magazines, of lobbies and special privilege and lies.

The reason for this is easy to understand. In wartime, when enemy nations report victories over our forces or publish news of terrifying new weapons, those reports are labeled in our newspapers and magazines as "propaganda." The implication is that such announcements are made in order to influence the people of this country to relax their efforts and that the claims are false. When we achieve victories or create atom bombs, our papers make much of such reports, and we call them "news." In general, we are inclined to call reports which favor our own interests true; reports from the opposition are called propaganda. And so the word has become a synonym for a lie. The creation of government bureaus of propaganda and of

* Reprinted with the permission of William Sloane Associates from *The Analysis of Propaganda* by William Hummel and Keith Huntress. Copyright, 1949, by William Hummel and Keith Huntress.

institutes for propaganda analysis, always with emphasis on slanted news and deceptive claims, has strengthened the prejudice against the word.

Let us take one example of "propaganda" and place it beside an example of "news." German newspapers reported the Battle of the Bulge as a Germany victory, cited tremendous Allied losses, and claimed that the front would be stabilized, that German arms would yet be victorious. American newspapers reported the Battle of the Bulge as a limited German success, headlined Allied heroism, and minimized the possibilities of further exploitation of the break-through. In the event the American newspapers were right, but you must note that the news stories of the two countries were trying to do exactly the same thing—inform readers about some important events and give them confidence in the armies of their countries. The American stories were the more accurate, but the purpose was the same.

As another example, let us suppose you have made a new acquaintance whom you rather like. He invites you to a public-meeting on a certain Tuesday; he has been to a number of such meetings, and they are always interesting. So you go. You sit and listen. The speaker criticizes your present way of life; he points out faults in the society around you and explains a system that will, he says, eliminate those faults, and that will make you a happier and better person. You are interested. But then you suddenly realize that his solution involves some difficulties, that you do not under-stand his new society. "But that's Communism," you whisper. "Sure it is," answers your friend. Later you make another acquaintance, who invites you to another meeting. The speaker criticizes your present way of life; he points out faults in the society around you and explains a system that will, he says, eliminate those faults, and that will make you a happier and better person. You are interested. "I think I'll join this church," you whisper to your friend. "I'm a member now," he says.

Yet again, advertisements are propaganda for products. They are attempts to sell large quantities of shampoos and baby food and automobiles, sheets and roofing and Zwieback. But the same methods are used to sell war bonds, to win support for the Red Cross, to obtain help for crippled children. The aims are different, but the methods are the same.

It is the contention of this book, therefore, that the idea that propaganda is always harmful, always false, is wrong. Propaganda can be used for a good cause as well as for a bad one. The motives and the ends are the important parts of any campaign; propaganda merely supplies the method of operation. In this book, propaganda means *any attempt to persuade anyone to a belief or to a form of action.* Any narrower definition will result in difficulties that must be avoided in the attempt to analyze this process.

Hence this book is not a warning against the "dangers of propaganda." The propaganda process is an essential feature of life in the modern world, no more evil because of its frequent misuse than drugs or dynamite, the characteristics of which it shares. We live our lives surrounded by propaganda; we create enormous amounts of it ourselves; and we form most or all of our cherished beliefs with its aid.

The sum of what we know through personal experience is small. In politics and economics, for example, where the facts are often not clear-cut and where rival authorities are common, all of us depend on sources outside ourselves for our opinions. Most Americans "know" their stands on Communism, big business, labor unions, and international relations. You have opinions on all these things. But do you know any Communists? Have you ever administered a big business? Are you a member of a labor union? A screen lies between each of us and the world of events, through which we allow certain kinds and amounts of information to filter, and our term "propaganda" describes the way in which that filtering occurs.

It follows that we cannot "guard against" propaganda; we should be lost without it. Most of us know that the earth moves round the sun because we have accepted the propaganda of mathematicians and astronomers, or that vaccination prevents smallpox because we believe the arguments of physicians and bacteriologists; but few laymen can produce adequate scientific evidence to support these propositions. So with most of our opinions and attitudes. We live in a reported universe, and our most essential information comes to us, at best, at second hand.

These remarks imply that anything may be labeled propaganda that attempts to make someone accept a fact or a point of view. On the basis of such a definition, a fish that imitates a rock in order to lure its luncheon a little closer is a propagandist, and so is a physicist who presents the results of his experiments to a group of his colleagues. And broadly speaking, both fish and physicists *are* propagandists.

But this book is to be concerned with propaganda as it reaches the citizens of the United States in the twentieth century, and for practical purposes we must limit our definition a little further. Most people sense an overtone in the word, an overtone that suggests *organized* attempts to persuade or systematic assaults on public beliefs. Thus we speak of the propaganda of the labor unions, or of the N.A.M., or of the Russians, Germans, or Chinese, and rarely of propaganda as something individual and personal. This qualification is useful, and dictionary definitions note the connotation of organized, group activity.

THE MEDIA OF PROPAGANDA

There are a number of channels of propaganda that are important to the average American. They are, in no special order, personal contacts, newspapers, magazines, radio programs, books, and visual media, such as motion pictures, the theater, and television. There is nothing final in this list. If you like, you may divide the propaganda that reaches you into the things you read, the things you hear, and the things you see. Every individual will have to make his own evaluation of the importance of these media. The man who gets most of his news through the radio and most of his entertainment from motion pictures lives in a different world from the man who reads carefully two or three newspapers a day and spends most of his evenings reading books and magazines of opinion. But everyone is affected by some of these channels of propaganda, and the more conscientiously one attempts to "keep up with things," the longer will grow the list of contenders for belief.

Most of the propaganda in our lives relates trivially to those lives—the small decisions, the tepid judgments that make up immensely the largest part of our days. Personal contacts are supreme in the field of such decisions. The attitudes of parents are often decisive in the lives of their children; teachers in their schools and ministers in their pulpits have moved all of us at one time or another. A few words from friends have changed most lives and much history, but it is impossible to assess such influences. They are with us always, like the poor and the air we breathe. The propaganda lines are as diverse as the speakers, and as numerous. Most strongly affective personal contacts are emotionally supercharged—one might be inclined to accept market tips from a dear friend even though the friend is on his way from filing petition in bankruptcy, for after all the old double room at college was a very pleasant place. Voting habits in America have a suspicious tendency to run in families. How many of your own most cherished beliefs are, by merest chance, those which you remember hearing around the family dinner table?

It might be worth while to analyze the influences that work upon us at such times, to scrutinize the gossip and the flung word, and tell exactly what they are and mean. But no one has time to question all his attitudes and decisions, and the purposes of this book restrict the analysis of propaganda to those things which affect other people, many other people. Chief among these media are newspapers, books and magazines, motion pictures, and radio and television.

THE MEDIA OF PROPAGANDA: NEWSPAPERS

The influence of newspapers is felt in almost every American home, and most of us form our first ideas of national and international problems from their pages, either directly or by hearing about them at second or twenty-second hand. During the last twenty years, we have had abundant proof that newspapers are less effective as propaganda agents than they once were or were thought to be. In five consecutive national elections the newspapers of the country have opposed the candidate who won and have been clearly defeated by such competing media as the radio or the personal-appearance tour or the record. Or, if you please, the newspapers of the country have so thoroughly lost touch with popular opinion on political issues that their views on these subjects are no longer of much importance. Whichever alternative you choose, it is an inescapable fact that for nearly twenty years the domestic political propaganda of most American newspapers has gone unheeded by most Americans.

But there are many other areas of opinion that the modern newspapers have claimed as their own. Your news of international affairs comes to you, if you are a reader of a daily of any pretensions at all, through one of the great wire services, such as A.P. or U.P. The odds are long that your local newspaper does not maintain a correspondent at any of the places mentioned in dispatches impressively headed Ankara, Moscow, or Aberystwyth, Wales; few dailies, and those only the largest, can afford the expense of a foreign staff. Americans dislike the word "censorship," but almost everything they read has been "censored" by correspondents and editors along a line that runs from the event to the newsstand and the breakfast table. There is an alternative. If you are a subscriber to a daily of no pretensions at all, you get no foreign news. . . .

There are dozens of good newspapers in the United States and scores of competent ones, but it is still difficult for many of us to hear the various sides of complicated issues. This situation has always existed to a certain extent, of course, but it is more true now than it used to be, and the difficulty is becoming greater every year. Time was when every sizable town had its newspaper or, frequently, newspapers. Now there are only a half-dozen cities in the United States that offer any real competition for the reader's interest. The usual pattern, even for a large city, is one morning and one evening newspaper, and they are frequently owned by the same company.

The difficulty is one of expense. Seventy-five years ago one good journeyman, a set of type, and a press made a newspaper. Now the establishment of a big-city paper that can hope to compete with other such journals is a matter for millionaires alone. Our newspapers are better than they have ever been in coverage, in features, in the offering of trained intelligence, but the average newspaper reader can hear only one tune played year after year.

For years it was the fashion to hint darkly at the advertisers as the greatest threat to the freedom of the press in this country. The theory was that since a newspaper lives by its advertising, it must necessarily be at the beck and call of the owners of department stores and grocery chains. But this situation is not often the true one. If the newspaper depends on advertising, so does the grocery chain, and in many cases the owner of the newspaper is probably as rich as the store owner and much more powerful. Publishers seldom take dictation from anyone. And yet it is a fact that most American newspapers are conservative in political tone, more conservative by a good deal than the people who read them, if we can believe the evidence of election returns. The reason is probably a simple one. Publishers are necessarily wealthy and powerful individuals, and they naturally associate chiefly with people like themselves, whose interests are their interests. People who are wealthy and powerful in any society tend to resist changes—for obvious reasons. Hence newspapers, which are, to a certain extent, extensions of the personalities of their owners, tend also to be conservative. This generalization admits of individual exceptions, but it is broadly true.

Considered as vehicles for propaganda, newspapers make an almost ideal medium. There is something in every issue for everybody, and a reader naturally moves from the item of his first interest to other items which may also affect his opinions and decisions. It has been established that more people read the weather report than anything else in newspapers, but they read other sections as well.

Probably the news should be considered first—the headlines and the front-page stories that come to us hot from life and the A.P. wires. The news is not supposed to be colored by propaganda, by any effort to persuade or convince. Ideally each news story should tell us what happened and where and to whom and how and why; but reporters are human beings with human biases, as their stories show. And then each story must be edited and assigned its place in the makeup of the paper, and prejudice may decide whether a story deserves a front-page spread or a soberer inside column. Sometimes there is overt use of news articles for propaganda purposes. The Chicago *Tribune* has found political capital in the drama and in baseball, at different times.

The editorial page is, of course, where the newspaper is supposed to do its persuading. The one great difficulty is that so few readers ever turn to the editorials. If you do read them, though, you should know where the newspaper stands on controversial questions, and that is valuable in assessing the "slanting" of its news.

The last half-century has seen the rise of the columnists. Limited at first to wisecracks, humorous verse, and gossip, the columnists have lately assumed the role of prophets and seers. One can buy solutions to most of the world's evils for a mere nickel. Like the writers of editorials, the columnists are supposed to persuade and convince, and like them, too, the columnists are keys to the leanings of the paper. One seldom finds a Westbrook Pegler in a newspaper friendly to labor or a Samuel Grafton in a conservative Republican journal.

There is little propaganda in weather reports or daily recipes, but the rest of any newspaper is fair game. Comic strips extol the virtues of true love and the innocence of childhood—though one strip did have a villain who was the spitting image of John L. Lewis—and Al Capp has frequently bruised the sensibilities of the United States Senate.

THE MEDIA OF PROPAGANDA: MAGAZINES AND BOOKS

Magazine and book circulation in the United States is, of course, not so large as newspaper circulation, yet for several reasons these media must be considered among the most important vehicles of written propaganda.

Magazines vary much more widely than newspapers, their contents ranging from the primitive appeals of the pulps and comic books to the serious and often scholarly articles in such quality periodicals as *Harper's* and *The Atlantic Monthly*. The great mass-circulation weeklies and monthlies, which reach millions with every issue, are carefully tailored to editorial formulas that have gained and held large readerships. Thus the women's magazines combine sweetness and light with the value of true love and a sprinkling of household hints; the immensely successful *Reader's Digest* sells self-help and minimum reading time; the big news weeklies are departmentalized newspapers with a week's perspective and no comic strips.

The biases of magazines are usually milder than those of newspapers. Sharp competition for huge audiences makes it dangerous for a journal seriously or consistently to offend any group of its readers. What may seem like a bold discussion of a controversial issue may really be nothing of the kind; it may be only a fiery restatement of what the magazine's readership already believes and wants to hear reiterated. Analysis of propaganda content and direction of a national magazine requires some familiarity with the publication over a period of several issues, and some notion of what audience is reached by it.

The propaganda effect of magazines on general attitudes is perhaps more noticeable than that on particular issues. The fiction in the big "slicks," for example, consistently reinforces a set of values which G. B. Shaw has unkindly dubbed "middle-class morality"— virtue triumphs, evil gets its deserts, and a white, middle-class hero is united with a white, middle-class heroine after a period of tribulation ranging from 2,500 to 30,000 words. Even the advertisements in these periodicals have an effect upon our general ideas about what is desirable for and typical of the American people. They have been as effective as the motion pictures and Sears-Roebuck in bringing about the end of hayseed rural America, and what many people think of as the typical American standard of living is probably the standard of the "typical" family which smiles at them from the beer and refrigerator ads.

Books are read by two groups—less than one per cent of the population, and students. The average American reads less than one book a year. *Gone with the Wind* has been the best-selling novel of our time, with six million copies sold. But *The Reader's Digest* sells more copies than that every month, and the New York *Daily News* sells the same number in a little over two days. Books are a luxury item with a limited market. Yet they are among the best media for propaganda, and to underestimate their importance is to ignore the very special groups that read books in large numbers. The people who control our government, our industries, our art, and our education are the readers of books, and their influence is out of all proportion to their numbers. *Mein Kampf* and *Das Kapital* and *The Origin of Species* have made our world, though *Life's* circulation for a year would cover all those who have read these books, with enough readers to spare for several digests.

THE MEDIA OF PROPAGANDA: MOTION PICTURES AND THEATRE

In general, motion pictures are made for profit. Since that is so, and since any "message" beyond the vaguest affirmatives is certain to offend some potential customer, motion pictures have tended to steer clear of controversial material. They have tried, successfully, to sell entertainment, with an occasional bow in favor of love and democracy. They are propaganda, but they are propaganda for the great myths of our time, because they must please Everyman.

The great box-office hits are likely to be literally out of this world: costume dramas like *Gone with the Wind* and the comic sagas of Crosby and Hope have nothing to do with our lives. Occasionally, though, a motion picture may have a real propaganda point—you will remember *The Grapes of Wrath, Mission to Moscow,* and *Gentleman's Agreement*—and these are likely to be more effective than any number of factual reports. A few documentary films like *The Plow That Broke the Plains* and *The River* have been successful, and they show what motion pictures can do when they turn their attention to overt propaganda. There are thousands of training and educational films that are persuasive in their purpose, but they are not easily available to the public. The same comment that we have already made about magazines may be made about motion pictures: They help to determine our values and social beliefs, and, in part, our behavior. But their influence is long-range and pervasive rather than immediate and particular.

The professional theater, except in the largest cities, is a dying art; yet it deserves to be mentioned because like books it has a wider influence than could be expected from the number of its patrons. There is direct influence through the fact that successful plays are often bought and produced as movies in Hollywood, and there is indirect influence through reviews and word of mouth. Nevertheless, few lives are changed by plays; they are an excellent propaganda medium, but they reach far too few people directly to be comparable to newspapers and magazines.

THE MEDIA OF PROPAGANDA: RADIO AND TELEVISION

Radio is dominated by networks like the National Broadcasting Company, the Columbia Broadcasting System, and the Mutual and American Broadcasting companies. These associations present the most popular shows and the best-known commentators. There are also hundreds of local radio stations which serve the news and advertising and home-talent needs of the smaller cities. As propaganda media, radio stations are most important because of two features—the news and advertising. In general, the news is a straight recital of events with only indirect editorial comment, and the advertising is straight selling, even by way of the soap opera. The only really complicated propaganda coming to us through radio is the work of commentators, who have a role similar to that of columnists in newspapers. Indeed, they are often the same people. With them, of course, every opinion or statement is only as valuable as the source. How much does the commentator know? Why should he be believed?

Any comments on television as a propaganda medium must be largely guesswork, since the greatest development of this visual broadcasting is obviously in the future. Yet we can surmise that it will combine some of the best and worst features of both motion pictures and radio: It will be comparatively inexpensive for the viewer; it will be almost universal in its coverage; it will be commercial in its motives; it may be artistically and intellectually timid. It may easily become, and that quickly, the most important of all mass-communication techniques; once broadcasting equipment is erected on a national scale and receivers are widely distributed, America may become a nation of viewers as she became in the nineteenth century a nation of newspaper readers. Television coverage of news events and entertainment will apparently be wide and expert, but most of the time will be subsidized by advertisers; and we should probably anticipate anguished cries from those who are aware of the immense potentialities of such a medium and who compare these possibilities with achievement. Increasing numbers of our most intelligent citizens never go to motion pictures and rarely turn on their radios, since these commercialized media are necessarily aimed at a fairly low common denominator, educationally and intellectually speaking. Television will certainly have these critics to answer and may answer as Hollywood and the radio have—by more or less systematically ignoring them.

FREEDOM FOR PROPAGANDA

As we have seen, outlets for propaganda are necessary in any society, and they are particularly necessary in a democracy. Our freedom of the press is really only a freedom to be propagandized, but it deserves to be defended on that ground. One of the great dangers of our time is the threat against freedom of speech and freedom of the press, two liberties that are unknown through a large part of our world.

And there is another freedom that is equally important—the freedom to hear all sides of a question, to be able to choose among alternative versions of the truth. The editors of *Pravda* and *Izvestia* are doubtless free to print the news as they see it. But they would not be editors of those newspapers if they did not see news in the proper light, Kremlinically speaking. The people of Russia have no freedom of choice, no alternative versions. They read the gospel according to *Pravda* and *Izvestia* or they do not read at all. Freedom of the press without freedom for more than one kind of press means nothing.

The average American has alternative sources of information now. His newspaper is likely to be the only one easily available in his town, and it is likely to have a definite bias, but he can subscribe to an outstanding paper like the New York *Times*, and he can dial a dozen radio stations with a turn of his hand. Some of them may present views that differ from those of his newspaper. He can go to motion pictures that may express views on economics or international affairs, though there are not many, and he can read magazines or books that advocate everything from aeronautics to yoga. And that is as it should be. If we can hear all sides of a question, then there is hope for an honest and intelligent choice among the alternatives that continually face us. But the tendency of the last three decades has been toward greater and greater control of the media of mass propaganda by fewer and fewer great owners and publishers. This tendency is dangerous beyond any doubt, as dangerous, perhaps, as a corresponding growth of government control would have been. It is a tendency on which the propaganda-conscious citizen should keep a very wary eye.

PROBLEMS

1. List the statements (measures, plans, ideas, and so forth) which have during the past few weeks become linked in your thinking with the term "propaganda."

    Now, going down that list, make a check beside each proposal to which *you* are opposed. What proportion of the ideas consists of ideas you oppose? If it is large, may that indicate that perhaps you have made propaganda synonymous with publicity for things you either dislike or distrust?

2. Why is such a definition of "propaganda" as "reports from the opposition" not a useful definition, that is, a definition which will help us understand the purpose and method of a particular news story or editorial? Why is a definition which could cover publicity both for and against "the other side" more useful?

    In these days of mass media (media through which ideas reach great masses of people almost at the same time), why is it useful to qualify our working definition of propaganda with "the connotation of organized, group activity"?

3. What evidence of propaganda on political, economic, educational, or religious questions have you observed in comic strips?

    If you have found it in such an unexpected source as this, why not look at the sports pages, movie gossip, and book reviews? What specific evidence of "propaganda" do you find in these departments of your newspaper?

4. Look at as many of these columnists as are available to you (preferably over the *same* period of several days): Westbrook Pegler, George Sokolsky, Walter Winchell, Dorothy Thompson, Drew Pearson, Walter Lippmann, and Thomas L. Stokes. Cite evidence of the following: (a) supporting generalizations with facts, and (b) dependence on facts and on clear, sound logic rather than on question-begging, folksiness, appeals to sentiment and special prejudices, appeals to group fears and hates, name-calling, or smart-aleck quips. It might be useful to compare Pegler with Lippmann, Sokolsky with Stokes.

5. Analyze the contents of several issues of *one* of the following mass-circulation magazines to determine what "set of values" it presents to its readers: *Reader's Digest, Saturday Evening Post, Woman's Home Companion, Good Housekeeping, Cosmopolitan, Collier's, American, Life, Time, Country Gentleman, Look.*

6. Have you recently seen a motion picture which contains overt propaganda (e.g., "The Great Dictator," "The Big Lift")? A picture that gives "long-range and pervasive" support to popular beliefs, attitudes, and customs (e.g., "Life with Father," "The Lou Gehrig Story," "G. I. Joe," "The Egg and I," and "Father of the Bride")? A picture that does both (e.g., "Gentleman's Agreement")? Do not stop with these examples but go on to supply your own.

7. To what extent do you believe you have "the freedom to hear all sides of a question, to be able to choose among alternative versions of the truth" in (a) your newspaper reading, (b) your magazine reading, (c) your radio listening, (d) your movie going, and (e) your book reading? On what observations do you base your conclusion? Do you notice that some of these media offer greater latitude than others?

GENERAL PROBLEMS: *Analyzing Propaganda*

1. Hitler believed in the importance of (a) emotional, non-factual appeal, and (b) simplicity in effective propaganda.

   Arrange a half-dozen editorials, advertisements, or syndicated columns on two scales: one an *emotion scale or yardstick* (from a predominantly emotional appeal all the way to a factual, reasoned appeal) and the other a *simplicity scale or yardstick* (from extreme simplicity of ideas and presentation, all the way to complexity of material and presentation). Do you find any correlation between them, that is, do you find that an increase in emotional over factual appeal goes along with an increase of simplicity in the ideas?

   Now, arrange these same editorials, advertisements, or columns on an *effectiveness* scale, from the one you believe would be *most likely* to influence people's behavior to the one which would have the least chance of influencing their behavior. (Try to keep your approval or disapproval of the ideas themselves from affecting their placement on the scale.) What were your specific reasons for arranging them in this order? Finally, is there any correlation between the effectiveness of these writings and their emotion-rousing qualities? between their effectiveness and their simplicity? If there is, how would you answer the question, "What makes some propaganda effective, and other propaganda ineffective?"

2. It is much easier to distinguish between valid and invalid arguments, between objective and slanted statements, between arguments that

face a problem and arguments that merely face an audience, *if* you have already got yourself set by (a) determining the speaker's probable purpose, (b) analyzing his audience (which includes you), and (c) determining the particular kinds of appeal that would be most likely to win over such an audience to his cause.

In the following question the first two steps have already been taken for you, that is, an effort has been made to find the speaker's probable purpose and to break up the audience into its component parts. Your job here is to take step 3: to work out, as if you were an alert member of the audience, the specific sorts of appeal you will be watching for so that you will be mentally prepared if the speaker elects to use propaganda unscrupulously to win over all sections of his audience.

a. You are attending a political rally which will be addressed by a candidate for state governor. His primary purpose in speaking tonight is to persuade more voters to vote for him in the coming election.

b. As a Senator from this state, the gubernatorial candidate has paid lip service to a state program for more and cheaper water, a program which is popular in this very dry area; he has done nothing tangible in promoting it. He has voted for bills favoring retention of high tariffs on grains. He has favored lowering income taxes; he has supported all anti-subversive measures, including several that his own party, generally in favor of such measures, decided were too extreme; he has voted against time-extension of rent controls, for further restrictions on labor unions, and against a reduction of railroad freight-rates (a measure which had wide support in this area). He has taken no very clear stand on government support of farm prices, and the opposition has made the most of his vagueness on this point. He is from a rural area of the state. All the people at this meeting live in a grain-producing region. About half of them are "small" farmers, many of them members of farm organizations that advocate lower freight rates and more and cheaper water. The rest are mainly business people (small store owners, garagemen, and so forth), with a light scattering of professional people (doctors, lawyers, teachers), and a few representatives of union labor.

Now take the next step.

3. Taking a *new* group situation which you know personally, write all three of the analyses indicated in Problem 2: (a) "size up" the speaker's probable purpose in speaking to this group; (b) analyze his audience; and (c) determine the specific kinds of appeal that would

most likely move the audience in the direction desired by the speaker.

4. What statistical surveys have you used or otherwise known about? Your opinions have very likely been affected by at least one such survey. Here are some examples: the United States census, the Gallup and Roper polls, the Hooper ratings (used by radio broadcasters as a basis for programming), the *Variety* polls (used by the motion picture industry), state and national crime surveys, sales surveys, a local newspaper's survey of townspeople's attitudes on a particular civic issue, the local health department's survey of sanitary facilities.

Now, choosing one such statistical survey, consider the main *types* of information that would be obtained and the main limitations of the survey, and on these bases *list the dangers of misinterpretation that one should guard against in interpreting the findings of such a survey.* (For instance, most hindsighters are agreed that one of the main oversights of the pollsters in their interpretation of their pre-election surveys in 1948, before Truman's victory contradicted their statistical prophecies, was their assuming that people's opinions in the summer could not change by November.)

Evaluating the Mass Media
of Communication

IN this book you have been given a chance to concentrate on one problem of practical thinking and communication at a time—to distinguish between fact and opinion, to spot oversimplification, to detect rationalization, to avoid the more common and dangerous pitfalls in inductive and deductive thinking, to look for the *things* which a word represents in a specific situation, to recognize ways in which words can confuse rather than clarify. Then you have been given the more complex job of applying all of these skills at once to propaganda. And, now, you face the most complex job of all, one that demands the most from you: to apply your understanding of all these problems of thought and language to the here-and-now, to human thinking and communication as you find them in the news and magazine article, the radio program, the Hollywood movie, the television broadcast.

Even though you may be able to see oversimplification in a particular argument when you are watching for it, or to separate facts from opinion, or sound from unsound reasoning when you are consciously trying to do just that one job, the real test of your ability to use all these skills comes when you do not know which skill or combination of skills is going to be required of you by a particular news article or a certain controversy going on in your school or town. But if, after working through this section, you find you can now read the daily papers or listen to the radio or read a magazine article with a new feeling of confidence, a new sense of being more than just a passive target, a feeling that you can find out more about a question than you formerly could, then you have profited from your reading of these selections and your wrestling with these problems. Moreover, not only will you have developed certain necessary *reading* skills, but also you will have developed certain *writing* skills—skills that should enable you to communicate to others precisely what you mean, because you will have come to understand something of the nature of *meaning*. In short, you will have begun to think before you write.

The following selections have been included not with a view of *completely* surveying all the mass media or raising *all* of the significant problems which they involve, but with the purpose of suggesting how an understanding of the thinking-communication processes may enable you to see more clearly the main aids and dangers to you as an individual in any language medium you may use. The three opening articles deal with the press. The first two are concerned primarily with the basic questions: Who controls this medium today, and what effect does such control have over the nature of the facts and ideas we can obtain through our newspapers? The writers of these two articles come up with different answers, but both writers attempt to see more than one side of a multi-sided problem. The third article examines very carefully one particular obstacle in the way of the reader who wants to get a clear picture of events today. "Digesting a Digest," the fourth selection, considers, in connection with magazines, the problem of "thought control" through the mass media. In the final article, Klein surveys the remaining mass media—movies, radio, and television—pointing out their common defects and suggesting ways in which they might come closer to realizing their nearly unlimited potentialities as instruments for promoting social well-being.

This is your final run around an indoor-track, because all books, no matter how hard they try to be otherwise, are a kind of shelter for the timid. But, throughout, we have tried to keep the doors and windows open so that you might become better acclimated to the rough winds from the outside world. If we have succeeded in our efforts to provide a climate as much like that of everyday life as possible, and if you have resisted the temptation to dive down to the locker-room and so escape this toughening-up process, you should be ready to step outdoors without any qualms.

Hold your hats, and good luck!

Arthur B. Tourtellot *   *Robert Lasch* *

"Freedom of the press" is no theoretical, academic matter. It has been, along with equality before the law and the right to elect one's own lawmakers, a primary concern of all who have taken part in the development of the democratic way of life during the past 300 years, and a free press has undoubtedly played a leading part in the struggle to free men from tyranny. People need to *know* the facts if they are to be able to rule themselves, and a free press has been the main channel through which they could come to know the *facts* and the conflicting *views* of the facts.

A free press, however, is hard to come by, and thoughtful men, especially during the past two decades, have come to feel that present social developments are making the preservation of a free press increasingly difficult. When they turn to examine the problem of maintaining such a press in today's society, such men are inevitably faced with the question of who is responsible for the preservation of this fundamental liberty of a free people. Some, like Tourtellot ("In Defense of the Press"), although aware of the abuses of which any press is capable, assign the final responsibility to the people themselves, pointing out that "We get about what we deserve." Others, like Lasch ("For a Free Press"), feel that this is an oversimplified explanation; that, indeed, it is essentially a rationalization of the press's failure to assume responsibility for its own conduct; that the rise of vast, privately owned newspaper chains, the decline in the number and independence of rural and small-town papers, the syndication of feature material, and the increasing difficulty of publishing a newspaper without great financial backing have immeasurably increased the complexity of the problem and removed papers too far from popular control. They feel that mere public demand is no longer an effective instrument by means of which the people can make the press a true expression of the varied points of view without which no society can remain truly democratic. But on one point these two writers agree: both indicate an awareness of the dangers inherent in any direct or indirect government control of the press.

* The two selections that follow, the one by Tourtellot (p. 421) and the one by Lasch (p. 430), are considered jointly. The problems covering these selections begin on p. 441.

In 1941 Lasch, a practicing news reporter and editorial writer, won a Nieman Fellowship to study the problems of modern journalism at Harvard University. "For a Free Press" won him first prize in *The Atlantic Monthly* 1944 competition for the best article on freedom of the press. Tourtellot, a runner up in the same contest, is an associate producer of *The March of Time*, and recently headed the editorial staff that worked on *Life's Picture History of World War II*.

IN DEFENSE OF THE PRESS *

Democracy is not merely a political system. It is the long, the patient, the informed, and the critical effort of a people to live together for a common good. In America that good has been held to be the liberation of the individual from any kind of oppression, whether it be political or religious or social or economic.

The framers of the Bill of Rights believed that the people should reserve certain rights permanently, largely because Jefferson was convinced that the people must achieve freedom for themselves, and that they could achieve freedom only if they were informed and capable of critical observation. Democracy, the art and the reality of self-government, was to Jefferson the product of a giant educational process. And he held that process and a free press to be interdependent. "Where the press is free," he wrote, "and every man able to read, all is safe." Jefferson knew that you could no more have an educated people without a free press than you could have a free press worth its salt without an educated people.

If the American people are constitutionally endowed with a free press, that press is *ipso facto* charged with certain functions. Those functions are, first, to inform the people, and second, to stimulate criticism by being critical itself. In the historical development of American journalism, the first function has come to be known as reporting the news; and the only standard for that is truth. The second function is fulfilled by editorials, by commentators' columns, and by other expressions of opinion; and the only standard for them is honesty. Without such truth and without such honesty, the press would not deserve any freedom at all. Moreover, far from aiding the people in their responsibility of governing and directing themselves intelligently, it would make efficient government and enlightened self-direction a virtual impossibility.

In a democracy, then, a free press vindicates the special right guaranteed it in direct proportion to the truth of its news and the honesty of its opinions. It would also follow that our journalism has been positive and good to the extent of its contribution to the achievement of the American goals, which are not only the preservation of such freedom as we may already have, but the constant exploration of new frontiers of freedom. Only on these grounds—on the fulfillment of its informative and critical functions—can the progress of a free press in America be judged. Only on these grounds can its future be weighed. That future is mere speculation, however, and the past experience only a series of accidents, if the press is unaware of its functions and without a spirit of inquiry about the degree to which those functions have been fulfilled—if, in short, it is without a conscience.

After the 1940 Presidential election, much was written to suggest that grave dangers imperiled the usefulness of the press as an instrument of democracy. Roughly 70 per cent of the nation's newspapers supported Mr. Willkie, even though such news stories as the Gallup reports in the same papers foretold the re-election of President Roosevelt, who had the support of only about a fourth of the papers. The post-election complaint was that the "power of the press" was at a vanishing point, and that the press either misrepresented public opinion or did not represent it at all. Mr. Harold Ickes felt sufficiently alarmed about this subject to assemble a symposium on it.

The storm was pretty much a tempest in a teapot, for the function of a press in a democracy is not to serve as a weathervane of public opinion. Nor is there anything healthful in a public opinion that serves as a weathervane of press opinion. It would have been alarming if, in 1940, the pro-Willkie papers had refused to carry stories indicating a Roosevelt victory, or if the electorate had veered blindly to the support of Mr. Willkie simply because the vast majority of the press advocated his election.

The first would have been a concealment of news, a withholding of information on the part of the press. The second would have meant an abrogation, on the part of the people, of that power to judge the press which Jefferson wisely held to be a duty of the citizens of a democracy. Nothing would be more dangerous to a democracy than a press of such power that the elections were merely an automatic, popular stamp of approval on its choices for public offices.

When we are worrying about the power of the press, it is well to remember that the kind of power which is able to swing elections increases only as the ability of the people to exercise critical judgment decreases. An enlightened people ought to make up its own mind. It is a far healthier symptom of the condition of a democracy that a people exposed to such an overwhelming urging of the election of one man should go out and elect another than it would be for the candidate who happened to have the most editors on his side to ride into office.

The power of the press, in short, should be a stimulative power and not a persuasive power, and the function of the press editorially should be to provoke criticism and to foster a critical attitude. Certainly that function is well fulfilled when the critical attitude of the people is sufficiently developed to enable them to criticize the critics!

Since journalism in America is a commercial enterprise, it is sometimes argued that the press must necessarily fall far short of ever achieving the ends for which it was guaranteed freedom. It is no more reasonable to condemn a newspaper because it is a product to be marketed than it is to condemn a book or a play for the same reason. Certainly book publishing and play producing are commercial enterprises, too. But, say these critics, newspaper publishers have to sell both their papers and advertising space in them, while book publishers and theatrical producers do not. And the advertiser is frequently accused either of dictating editorial policy under threats of pulling his advertising, or of choosing his advertising medium on the basis of that medium's editorial policy on public questions.

The evidence against the existence of any such conspiracy on the part of advertisers is much clearer than the grounds on which they are indicted. In the first place, the main purpose of the advertiser is to get the virtues of his product before as many people as possible. If there were any relationship between advertising and editorializing, then one would expect the advertiser to advertise in the paper with the most popular editorials. Hence, the pro-Roosevelt papers might have expected a huge increase in advertising in 1936, after the people had overwhelmingly rejected the rationalizing of the pro-Landon papers. But no such shift of advertising occurred.

The argument is frequently advanced that, though papers vary in editorial opinion, they all protect and further the interests of big business—in which category advertisers are lumped indiscriminately. The fact is that most American newspapers are supported, not by big businesses, but by small local businesses owned and operated by people in the middle economic group. Frequently the small town or country newspaper, supported almost exclusively by the very smallest businesses and by farmers, is the most conservative publication in the world; it may look upon the policies of a liberal metropolitan daily with horror. Again, in a typical large American city, where there are two or more dailies, the more liberal is likely to be the stronger newspaper, as the liberal *St. Louis Post-Dispatch* is stronger than the *Globe-Democrat*. All this suggests that there is no direct relation between a journal's editorial policy and the amount of its advertising revenue.

The general mores of American newspapers are the mores of a capitalistic democracy, for the obvious reason that the United States happens to be a capitalistic democracy, and the press is a part of it. If it is capitalistic democracy that limits the press, then the critic should condemn capitalistic democracy; he should not condemn the press for being commercial in structure in a society where it would be suicidal and unnatural for it to be anything else. There can be no legitimate quarrel with the press for operating under the capitalistic impetus when the rest of the nation does the same thing. If there is any quarrel, it should be about the capitalistic impetus as the springboard for any individual or group action.

These fallacies about the press are important today because they confuse the people, who are the ultimate judges of the press. It is wrong to indict the press, or to excuse its shortcomings, on grounds that merely make big business or advertisers the scapegoats and then dismiss the problem. While a free press has neither the obligation nor the right to sit in judgment on the people, the latter have both the right and the duty to sit in constant judgment over the press.

Such judgment is a condition of the press's freedom in a democracy, as Jefferson construed it when he wrote that "we have found it better to trust the public judgment, rather than the magistrate, with the discrimination between truth and falsehood." Historically, the people have demonstrated the will and the ability to suppress a paper more than once in America, as in 1865 when the people of Cleveland forced the suspension of the *Plain Dealer* for its disloyalty to the Union. It is only the intelligent exercise of such power on the part of the people that can keep the conscience of the press alive.

The concern of our democracy should be less with the organizational or commercial nature of the press than with its sense of moral responsibility to fulfill its functions. Judgment must come from the people as an integral part of the democratic process. If they sidestep this responsibility, then the whole democratic adventure has failed and not the press alone. Consequently, the press in America has advanced in quality with the ability of the people to judge it.

Nor can the press blame its shortcomings on the people. The press is always on probation, and when it violates that probation—when it suffers a lapse of conscience—then it is the press that is at fault. It is at fault when it ignores the people's judgment simply because it can get away with such a course. It is at fault always when it slants, or entirely omits, news that would enable the people to formulate a sound judgment. And these are sins that have not yet completely disappeared from American journalism, although they appear to be diminishing.

They are on the decline solely because Americans are better educated today than ever before—a fact of which the wise editors and publishers are well aware. Americans today demand more from their news organs than in the past. They are quick to detect the false or distorted. They want breadth of opinion, a variety of views, and thoroughness in reporting. The *Washington Star*, an extremely conservative paper, does not publish the columns of Dorothy Thompson and Lowell Mellett—both liberals—for nothing. The *Star* simply knows good journalism. There was a century and a quarter of journalism in America when nobody's opinions graced a paper except the editor's. Today, most great dailies carry several columns of opinions that differ radically from the editor's. The press in America today fulfills its critical function more thoroughly than in earlier days, simply because the diversity of opinions opens up competition of ideas.

In the days when personal journalism was at its height in the United States, a paper's personality was that of its editor. Not only to the readers of the old *New York Tribune,* but to the entire nation, Horace Greeley and the *Tribune* were synonymous. If you quoted the *Tribune,* you quoted Greeley; and if you said that the *Tribune* was guilty of a piece of folly, you meant that Greeley was off on a tangent again. . . .

Where once the personality of any newspaper was a rigid reflection of the views of its publisher, it is now a composite personality reflecting the minds of many editorial forces: the columnists, the Washington, foreign, and war correspondents, the news analysts, and the military and political commentators. This tendency towards a many-sided, broader personality, in place of the rigid, narrow view, better equips the journal to achieve its informative and critical ends, and the reader to judge the paper, to read it critically.

The editorial change has been accompanied by a considerable increase in both the scope and the accuracy of news coverage. Today the world-wide network of news sources covers every major spot on the globe. The California papers have access to as full and accurate reports of Washington events as the capital's own papers. The New York papers know as much of happenings in London as any Fleet Street office. The recent Supreme Court decision liberating the Associated Press services from monopolistic restrictions opens the way for even better news coverage by more papers. Indeed, there remains today no material or physical obstacle to the fulfillment by the press of its cardinal duty to get the facts and to give them to the people.

I have suggested so far that the health of a free press depends upon the ability of the people to act as its censor, but that it is futile for them to act as censors on any such general, ill-informed grounds as the belief that the press is now exclusively the organ of big business, or is dictated to by advertisers, or is losing what power it ever had anyway; that the capitalistic structure of the press cannot be condemned as such so long as it is a part of a capitalistic society and must operate within that society; and, finally, that the commercial growth of the press has brought with it a complex editorial nature and a breadth, completeness, and speed of news coverage which makes it far more able today to discharge its responsibilities to the people than it has ever been in all its history.

The question is: Does the press have sufficient conscience to avail itself of its own opportunities and to do all that it can, within its structure as part of a capitalistic democracy, to fulfill its obligations to the people? And if it hasn't such moral awareness or, having it, ignores it, then what is the remedy?

The history of the press during the years immediately preceding this war is a highly creditable one. During the most ostrich-like period of our whole national history, the press alone kept hurling at the people the tragic facts of the progress of fascism. While the intellectuals were still admiring the brilliant cynicism of Walter Millis's *The Road to War,* the foreign correspondents were pouring out the story of the rising threat of Hitler. But the foreign correspondents were not even worth a laugh or a satire then. They were simply ignored. Later it was amusing when Dorothy Thompson was thrown out of Germany, and when American correspondents were tossed right and left out of Berlin and Rome.

The Spanish civil war was the most completely reported foreign rebellion in the annals of the American press, and rightly so, but most readers got too much of it. There seemed to be better things to do than read about an irrelevant squabble in Spain. Later still, when the implications of the European war could escape no half-thorough reader of the papers in 1940, the nation was treated to a Presidential campaign in which both candidates found it desirable to close their eyes to the inescapable fact that America must actively intervene or go down with the rest.

The wire services and the daily papers, the free press, spent more and more money to bring the realities of the storm in Europe to the attention of the American people as the thirties drew to a close—long before the other democratic institutions of the United States even cared to face the task of thinking seriously about it. Never was any one group of people more justified in shouting "I told you so" than the men of the press on December 7, 1941.

And never was any people less justified in protesting that the facts had been withheld from them than the American nation. The newspapermen published the facts in their papers; they expanded them in books; they preached them in lectures. Whatever charges may be brought against the press, the fact is that the press, its reporters and its commentators, brought the meaning of world history straight to the people months and years before the people wanted to hear it. And the press as a whole was far ahead of the nation on the moral duty and the practical expediency of America's aiding the foes of fascism during the early years of the war.

It would seem that it was democracy itself, rather than the press, that suffered a lapse of conscience. The American people simply could not be told; they had to be shown. The answer, so far as the conscience of the press is concerned, is that it did have a very strong sense of moral responsibility all through the late thirties and it did not ignore that sense.

At the same time, the press does compromise with its conscience, and does rationalize questionable practices. There is, for example, the competitive foolishness of afternoon editions, when papers vie for attention by sacrificing all sense of value and proportion to sell copies on the strength of the sheer dimensions of the headlines. The afternoon press of any large city would lead an observer to believe that a decisive turn in the war is taken every single day just before each edition goes to press. As any newspaperman knows, it is better in such cases to be fast than to be right.

There is also the incompleteness of news on such controversial domestic subjects as labor and birth control. In both cases, there is either a largely one-sided story or a shameless pussyfooting. Industrialists must not be offended, and churches must not be offended. Otherwise, apparently, the people can have the news. Again, there is still the practice of editorializing the news. A paper should have no news policy except truth. But it frequently does, and that news policy is far more difficult for the reader to discover than is the editorial policy, which is often blatant and sometimes hysterical.

By headlining a strike in which a policeman is killed and six pickets badly hurt, with "Policeman Killed by Pickets," the press can turn many readers against the workers. Or by headlining it "One Killed, Six Injured as Police Battle Strikers," readers can be turned against the police. Such direction of emphasis and slanting of stories is not done because the newspapers are without a conscience. It is done as a temporary departure from that conscience for the sake of misconceived prudence. If every paper in this country began tomorrow morning to print impartial, unslanted news of labor, reserving its verdicts for opinion columns, those papers would not suffer a single bit. All the press needs is a voluntary compact to print all controversial news without doctoring it by omission or by emphasis.

These are all cases—and there are others—where the press is prepared to ignore its conscience, which amounts to a temporary and partial repudiation of its functions in a democracy. Such cases are undesirable. And because they are not easy to detect, they can be dangerous. But there is no possible way both to keep a free press and to require it to publish unslanted stories. You cannot legislate the press into a more consistent adherence to its conscience and still have a free press.

Some have suggested that removing the press from contact with advertisers will make it completely free, consistently truthful in its news stories, and thoroughly honest in its editorials. The answer to that is, "Look at *PM*." There is a paper immune from "pressure" from advertisers, and immune also from the necessity of paying its own way.[1] It certainly has no commitments to any special interests. It has on its staff many men of better than average ability. But it is a bad newspaper. It editoralizes all the news it prints; it omits a huge amount of news altogether; its sense of proportion in make-up is a total mystery to its most faithful readers; it is intemperate, hysterical, shrill, and easily as sensational on a high level as the *Graphic* ever was on a lower one. It proceeds on the principle that a man is guilty until proved innocent, and usually it dares anyone it has once convicted to try to be or do good.

There is probably no qualified observer who will question the essential rightness of the instincts of *PM*. But you cannot stop there. It is not enough that the purposes of *PM*, however confused they sometimes seem, are high and worth while. To be an effective part

[1 By refusing all advertising, *PM*, published in New York, sought to keep itself free from outside controls. *PM*, whose editorial policy was strongly pro-New Deal, ceased publication in 1949. Most students of the American press would today probably agree with Tourtellot that *PM*, although a courageous experiment, was no more objective and reliable in its news presentation than those papers whose influence it was designed to counteract.—EDITORS] of our society, our press must be not only in it but of it. To improve the press you must improve the society. The improvement must spring from the people. If the people are improved, then you will have an improved press, a press with a quickened conscience. Or as Bruce Bliven has put it, "We get about what we deserve."

The free press, to fulfill its functions more adequately, has but one crying need—more adequately educated readers. You cannot blame the *New York Times* because four million people read the *Daily News* while only a tenth of that number read the *Times*. The burden of a better press in a democracy, like the burden of a better government, rests with the education of the people. The better educated they are, then the more critical, the more demanding, the more discerning they will be. And then the press will have to improve to survive.

FOR A FREE PRESS *

Let us be frank about it. What the press in America needs is a constitutional revolution. It needs a measure of judicious abdication. It needs a transfer of power from publishers as kings to publishers and editors as prime ministers. It needs ownership that will give up the prerogatives of absolutism and function as a trustee recognizing direct responsibility to the people.

Freedom-of-the-press discussion is frequently barren and futile because it ignores two highly pertinent considerations: the historic social purpose of freedom, and the effects of economic development upon our freedom.

When these factors fall into perspective, the whole picture changes. Freedom is seen then not as something to be defended, but as something to be attained. The complacency and defensiveness that mark the traditional approach to the subject suddenly become pitifully inadequate. One realizes that instead of waging constant war against an imaginary enemy without, the newspapers would do well to take steps against the enemy within.

They would do well, too, to take warning from the widening

* Robert Lasch, "For a Free Press," copyright by *The Atlantic Monthly*, July 1944.

gulf that separates the conception of freedom held by themselves and that held by the people.

Nothing illustrates the divergence better than the government's antitrust suit against the Associated Press, now on appeal before the Supreme Court. Almost to a man, the publishers of America interpreted the filing of this action as a foul assault upon the First Amendment, and with frightening unanimity exerted all their power to impress upon the public that point of view.

"We see in this, not the end perhaps, but surely the gravest peril, to a free press in America," said the *Detroit News*. From the citadel of its monopoly position in a city of 600,000 the *Kansas City Star* cried: "This is the sort of thing that belongs in the totalitarian states, not in a free democracy." "In the event of a government victory," said the *New York Daily News*, "the press services of the United States will be under the thumb of the White House."

These were not extremist positions. They represented a fair sample of the opinion handed down by the press, sitting as a supreme court, long before the government brought its case to trial and won the first round in the United States District Court of New York. The Associated Press proudly published a volume of the collected editorial judgments for the instruction of the country.

The country rode out the storm with equanimity. Dimly or otherwise, the people perceived that the newspapers, once again, had proved unable to separate their commercial privileges from their civil rights. The AP suit did not suppress one newspaper. It threatened none with any form of censorship or restraint. It was a civil action, initiated under universally respected statutes of long standing, against the members of a newsgathering organization, on the charge that they had used the association for the purpose of discouraging or limiting commercial competition among themselves. . . .

II

There is much talk of freedom, but not enough of what freedom is *for*. The value of personal liberty rests not upon any putative divinity, nor upon the naturalness of "natural rights," but upon the plain fact of its social usefulness and, indeed, its indispensability in a democracy.

Freedom was not won by a newspaper lobby, though the proprietary interest claimed therein might make one think so. Like other civil liberties, this one arose from a slowly developed conviction among the people that when self-government was desired, freedom was a good thing. The press became free, therefore, not as a favor to those who happened to own it, but because men hoped by means of a free press to attain a desirable social end.

The end was unmistakable. It was to promote the widest possible freedom of expression. It was to insure the people unrestrained access to the means of expression. It was to set up an institution, separate from government itself, that would represent the people directly in public affairs.

Milton stated the faith: "And though all the winds of doctrine were let loose to play upon the earth, so Truth be in the field, we do injuriously by licensing and prohibiting to misdoubt her strength. Let her and Falsehood grapple; who ever knew Truth put to the worse in a free and open encounter?"

The purpose of a free press was to insure that Truth did grapple fairly with Falsehood. Give government power to license or prohibit, and force became party to the struggle—force that might be exerted on the side of Truth, to be sure, but that might just as easily sustain the opposite side. What the people wanted was a free and open encounter. Assured of that, they were willing to take their chances on Truth's winning out in the end.

It is precisely this foundation of a free press that the modern economic development of journalism in America has undermined.

Once liberated from government restraint, the press burgeoned and proliferated alongside democracy itself. Newspapers sprang up, flourished, died, and were replaced. Two and sometimes five grew where one had grown before. The tramp printer and ambitious editor marched in the van of westward migration. During the expansive period of the nineteenth century every party, every faction, had its own newspaper. A shoestring and the gift of gab were almost all a man needed to launch one. The press was free, enterprise was free, the land was free.

When the last frontier had been conquered, however, maturity wrought quick changes in the press as in the entire economy. Personal journalism gave way to the corporation and the chain. Consolidation and concentration supplanted individualist expansion.

Simultaneously, Bennett, Pulitzer, and Hearst uncovered the mighty secret of "popular" (sometimes called "yellow") journalism—a talisman that shifted emphasis from information to entertainment, from opinion to titillation, from enlightenment to something like a daily variety show.

The resulting mass circulations not only enriched the owners, but estranged them from their readers. For the allegiance of readers could now be secured by manifold entertainment values, rather than exclusively by the paper's quality as a medium of news and opinion. Little Orphan Annie took over some of the functions of Horace Greeley. If the reader did not like the editorials, he could be held with the sports page or the sex stories. If he grew restive in the half-knowledge that his news was being poisoned with bias, he could be soothed with a comic strip.

In one sense the attainment of commercial independence brought the press a new freedom. At least it was now possible to escape the toils of party and factional obligations. No longer need a certain section of political opinion be placated in order to hold circulation. Newspapers ceased to be party organs. "Independent Republican," or "Independent Democrat," or just plain "Independent" displaced on the masthead the once proud proclamation of party faith. Many an editor of a *Blankville Democrat-Times* had to explain to his readers that now this was just a name.

On balance, freedom from parties was net gain, an appropriate parallel to the growth of independent voting. Yet something deeper was involved. What had happened was that the press had driven the piers of its support down through the soil of politics to the bedrock of the economic structure. It had, indeed, become an integral part of the economic structure. Instead of reflecting a variety of opinions thrown out by underlying forces, it turned to throwing out opinions of its own, as one of those forces. Business had run politics and politics had run the press. Now the newspapers, as part of business, helped to run politics. They were in the big time.

The new position accentuated a natural drift toward the elimination of competition. Where on the old basis there might be ample room in one city for a Republican, a Democratic, and perhaps two or three other papers, the acquisition of economic power created urgent impulses toward monopoly. Why have two "independent" papers, when one might serve as well?

Other forces were working in the same direction. Competition for new comics, new features, new reader-lures, steadily increased the cost of publication and wiped out the marginal competitors. The emergence of radio as a heavy bidder for the advertiser's dollar set up the final strain that drove newspaper after newspaper into oblivion. From 2042 in 1920, the number of dailies declined to 1787 in 1942. Today more than a thousand cities are one-paper towns.

So extragovernmental forces accomplished, to a substantial extent, what government had been enjoined from attempting. The press was cut off from intimate contact with its readers, not by a royal licenser, but by bigness. No official censor, but the disappearance of newspapers from the field, came to diminish unrestrained access to the means of expression.

Not only did the number of newspapers in each community decline. The surviving owners took on more and more the monolithic character of a class. As businessmen, they reflected the prejudices and attitudes of businessmen. The newspaper in Topeka tended to share the political and economic philosophy of its counterpart in Providence, and both found more in common with the shoe manufacturer and the steelmaker than with the majority of their readers. The era of the great editors passed, and the publishers took over: publishers who desired, above all, to make money, and whose social outlook could not escape domination by that purpose.

III

. . . The effects are most serious in the smaller cities. Metropolitan populations can and do support some degree of competition, but the people of a thousand cities do not. In many a community the biggest single political fact may be the existence of a certain newspaper and a certain publisher. In a real sense this man is an arm of government, and a peculiarly irresponsible arm. Politicians of both parties crave his favor. Mayors, governors, legislators, and Congressmen drink at the well of his wisdom. Civic movements start or stop according as he nods or shakes his head.

Generally this man is not a sinister character. He often has a hazy notion of public service somewhere in the back of his mind, and convinces himself, at least, that he's doing the best he can. The point is that he exercises power. And with few exceptions he exercises it as the representative of a small but nevertheless potent group within the community. His cronies are the bankers, the manufacturers, the utility operators, the department store tycoons. The habitat is the Chamber of Commerce, the well-stocked clubs, and the suburban estates of the rich. The ideas he absorbs and the attitudes he reflects are those of the well-heeled upper crust.

Advertiser influence, as such, has probably been overemphasized. In real life industrialists and department store managers do not pound on the publisher's desk and demand favorable treatment. They do not have to. An owner who lunches weekly with the president of the local power company will always grasp the sanctity of private enterprise in this field more readily than the public-ownership ideas of a few crackpots. With the best of will, he may tell himself that his mind is open. Yet as a businessman whose concerns are intimately bound up with those of other businessmen, he has a vested interest in maintaining the status quo.

This attitude filters down, by well-defined channels, to his staff. In extreme cases it colors the news, and in others controls the selection and emphasis of news. Almost any newspaper will live up to the finest traditions of the press by campaigning for local tax reduction, but few fight with equal ardor for improved public services when the consequence is *higher* taxes for the publisher and his friends. Fewer still find themselves stirred, say, by the civil rights of workers in a labor dispute.

Without orders, without crude directives, city editors fall easily into the habit of saving their big type for safe topics like rape and burglary, and burying the "hot" (the ideologically dangerous) news in the back pages. Reporters learn not to scrutinize too closely the sacred cows of the community, and editorial writers husband their mightiest blasts for the remotest wrongs.

So the problem of a free press has changed with the times. Its chief antagonist is no longer government,—though indeed assaults from that quarter must constantly be fended off,—but ownership as conditioned by modern economic circumstances. Because they are big, newspapers overawe local and sometimes other governments. Because they are monopolistic, they do not restrain one another. Because they are organs of entertainment which thousands find interesting if not indispensable, they need recognize but a token *noblesse oblige.* Their principal function remains what it was,—to inform about and conduct a continuing inquisition upon public affairs,—but the discharge of this responsibility has gradually shifted from the people as a whole, adequately represented by many competitive journals, to a narrow and narrowing class of publishers who share the same ideas to an astonishing degree.

IV

In candor, redress cannot be expected from a revival of competition. The clock does not turn back. Having survived one era of jungle warfare, and facing now a new kind of rivalry in radio, the newspapers will not tolerate a further division of the spoils. And save for a few venturesome souls, the prospective rewards are unlikely to attract new enterprisers. Except as it occasionally shrinks, the present structure of the business is likely to endure.

Nor can one look with much confidence to other forms of ownership. A national newspaper regionally published by the government would certainly sicken publishers everywhere with dread, and might for a spell delight readers who love nothing better than a fight; but the corruptions it would invite foreshadow more evil than good. Coöperative ownership, whether by staff or readers, offers some attractions, but the prospect of widespread development along this line in competition with the giants already in possession is not encouraging. Labor newspapers, farm newspapers, and their like offer little general appeal and no guarantee of genuine devotion to the general welfare.

The new birth of freedom, if any, must come from within. It must emerge, not from dreams of the press as it might be, but from the premeditated acts of those who have a stake in the press as it is: the owners, the staffs, and the readers.

Upon the public, it must be confessed, rests the smallest share of the responsibility. For, though the readers are the ultimate jury, and though they can create or not the climate in which a truly free press may flourish, they exercise but a negative and tenuous control. It may be true that people get the kind of newspapers they deserve, but what they deserve, in the sense of what they demand, is largely determined by what they get.

That holds true particularly where one paper dominates or monopolizes the field. A steady diet of a monopoly paper blunts the critical sense and dulls discrimination. One forgets, reading the same paper every day, what kind of paper it might be. One tends to absorb, even while protesting against them, the attitudes and prejudices that shape the lineaments of the news to which he is exposed. We may rightly expect of readers, in time, a more articulate demand for decent journalism, but for the most part the initiative necessarily lies with those inside the business.

There are so many people (and so many kinds) inside the business that it is easy to shift responsibility from one to another. Leaving the front office out of account for purposes of this discussion, the responsibility borne by the men and women who make the newspaper is clear. The reporter, the copyreader, the news editors—all who have a hand in filling the news and editorial columns—owe to themselves and to the country a higher regard for the professional demands of their job.

No working newspaperman, I suppose, can honestly deny having at some time written something that at least bruised his conscience. There are skeletons in every closet: instances in which, from good motives or bad, stupidity or design, the great power momentarily vested in a (usually underpaid) newspaperman has been misused. Nor is the perfectibility of newspapermen any closer than that of human nature. And yet we of the working press have a duty to keep professional conscience alive.

I should define professional conscience as love of truth combined with zeal for the people's cause. To dispose of quibbling at once, I hasten to affirm, as an article of faith, that truth exists, even though apprehension of it varies; and to add that disagreement on what the general interest may be does not prejudice the fact that there *is* a general interest of all the people, as opposed to special interests of special groups.

This brings us to the perennial question of "objectivity." Both love of truth and zeal for the people's cause are essential to a satisfied professional conscience, and a proper balance between them equally so. One can respect facts, yet, lacking devotion to an ideal, fall into a quite barren and spurious "objectivity" that is impaired by the very absence of a point of view. To report with deadpan detachment a Congressional debate composed of lies violates honest journalism as much as direct falsification. On the other hand, a point of view can achieve such dominance as to destroy fair reporting at the roots. In that case it does not matter whether news is distorted to the left or distorted to the right.

The newspaperman's problem is to reconcile heart and head: to discipline the impulses with an intellectual regard for truth, and at the same time to inflame curiosity with a social purpose. This marriage takes place when he sincerely represents, in judgment, in selection, in emphasis, in the responses of his news sense, the whole people and not any one section or class; and when he devotes the whole of his technical competence to the pursuit of truth as best he can perceive it.

Given such a union, differences of approach can be tolerated. Two copyreaders sitting side by side may differ violently on the manner in which a story is handled, but their disagreement becomes significant only when it involves literary prostitution—that is to say, only when professional judgment gives way to emotional prejudice, or to unseemly attachment to a set of preconceived ideas, or to an overweening desire to make good with the front office. One does not ask that the control of news content be divorced from human nature; only that it be free and pledged, in the broadest sense, to the public welfare.

True professional freedom combined with high professional competence constitutes the definition of a great newspaper. All great newspapers have had them both—the *New York Times* under Ochs, the *St. Louis Post-Dispatch* under Bovard, the *New York World* under Frank Cobb, and so on down the honor roll. These papers had objectivity, in the sense of fair and responsible reporting, and they had behind and above that technique an unflagging will to see justice done.

We cannot all be great. But we can preserve professional standards from corruption. We can attain the dignity (even though underpaid) of a good job well done. We can put aside the cynicism which slants the news to a dominant group in the community. We can justify our right to wield the mighty power of the printed word by proving our ability to use it in behalf of the people. So used, it becomes a free press.

V

In the last analysis the question of freedom limps home and settles down on the doorstep of ownership. The readers can boil with discontent, but their immediate influence upon the newspaper of today is bound to be tentative. The working staff can glow with good resolutions, but in the end fulfillment depends not only upon the limitations of human frailty, but on the intangible atmosphere whose chief ingredient is the attitude of ownership.

What is required of ownership is the abandonment of its claim to the perquisites of absolute monarchy. If the request seems absurd, so to the possessors of power a challenge of their right to exercise it has always seemed unreasonable.

Under modern conditions the irresponsible control of newspapers in behalf of a narrow economic interest is incompatible with the social purpose of their freedom. That purpose is now, as it was in the beginning, to give the people at large genuine representation, not only "against" their government, but against the special interests that seek to gain their own ends through government. When newspapers become a confederate of those interests, the people are denied that free access to the means of expression which permits Truth and Falsehood to grapple in "free and open encounter."

Conditions that might have safeguarded this purpose in an earlier and simpler day have vanished. New enterprises no longer spring up overnight. One newspaper may no longer check and offset another. Competitive restraints upon the abuse of power have been diluted by the monopolistic consequences of competition.

Having taken on the character of semi-monopolies, the newspapers are affected with a public interest exactly as are the utilities, the railroads, the milk supply. Socialization or regulation, the appropriate remedies in the case of other monopolies, do not recommend themselves because the peculiar function of the press demands real separation from government. This we have achieved at the cost of a growing separation from the people. To close the gap, we now need a recognition by ownership that it is a trustee and not a dictator.

In practical terms such a constitutional revolution calls for a new kind of newspaper owner, and new methods by which he exercises his power. I do not hope for the voluntary reform of Colonel Robert R. McCormick, but it is obvious that his type of autocracy (somebody once called him the best mind of the thirteenth century) is ill-suited to the times. As the older generation of publishers dies off, as new men assume their responsibilities, as a few working newspapermen worm their way into property, the opportunity arises for a change of outlook.

What a free press needs is an owner who recognizes that he is selling circulation and prestige, not an economic point of view or service to special interests; and who, above all, recognizes that selling something is not his first obligation at all, but is subordinate to his responsibility to represent the unrepresented. A man who can divorce himself from the associations and outlook that normally go with wealth; a man who can sacrifice even his own short-range interest as a business entrepreneur in favor of his long-run interest as the champion of a greater cause; a man whose passion for the general welfare overcomes his desire to impose his own ideas upon the community; a man of wisdom and humility, character and devotion, courage and modesty—here is the kind of newspaper owner who can make the press free.

Such ownership would develop new methods of management. It would exploit, and thereby stimulate, the professional instincts of the working staff. There is a streak of the actor in nearly every newspaperman. Nothing drives him like approval from men he respects, and nothing disillusions him like doing nasty chores for men he does not respect. Good management would operate the newspaper as the great coöperative endeavor it must be. It would temper hierarchical authority with democratic participation, instilling in the newest reporter a sense of active contribution, and granting real power to the responsible editorial workers. In short, it would function as a constitutional monarchy.

Is it possible? Can newspaper owners so far subordinate their property stake as to serve the people rather than a class? Whether the press survives as a vital instrument of democracy will depend upon the wisdom and temper of its owners. Theirs it is to decide whether they shall rise above selfishness or remain representatives of wealth and economic power; whether they shall fight the people's battles against special interests or fight the people for the interests; whether they shall administer a trusteeship or exploit a privilege.

The press will become free when its owners permit it to become free.

PROBLEMS

1. What for Tourtellot are the two prerequisites of a democratic society? How closely does this approximate Dewey's definition of democracy "as a way of life"?

   What for Tourtellot are the two primary functions of a free press? (Hayakawa's distinction between *fact* and *opinion* may help you see what Tourtellot has in mind.)

   What two criteria of conscientious journalism does Tourtellot develop from his analysis of the functions of the press in a democracy?

2. In urging that the press must not be "a weathervane of public opinion," Tourtellot is giving one answer to the critical question: In a democracy should the press *reflect* or *help to form* public opinion? What main potential dangers to a democratic way of life do you see in each tendency?

3. In answering the criticism that the social attitudes of newspaper owners today are too much influenced by powerful economic interests, Tourtellot tries to show that the influence of advertisers is negligible. Are there any other aspects of present-day newspaper-publishing which would need to be examined before reaching a conclusion as to the influence of business interests upon editorial policies? Does Lasch raise one of them?

   What economic changes, in Lasch's opinion, have made Milton's "free and open encounter" unrealistic and meaningless in today's press?

4. In what ways would domination by certain editorial personalities constitute a threat to democracy? Cite specific examples of this domination in the American press today. Can domination by personalities be a threat to democratic processes in other fields (e.g., political parties, corporate management, labor unions, educational policies, scientific research, entertainment)? Cite specific examples of this kind of domination.

5. Does Tourtellot's generalization that a newspaper is now "a composite personality reflecting the minds of many editorial forces" hold true of the newspaper or newspapers which you read? Is the fact that a large *number* of people express their opinions in today's press a proof that there is a wide *diversity* of opinion expressed? Is the presence of one writer with views different from those of the editors sufficient proof of real "balance"?

   How many daily and weekly papers are published in your city

or rural community? Make a representative collection of issues of these papers covering a span of at least one week for dailies, one month for weeklies. Do the papers definitely and consistently differ in any ways (Democratic and Republican? pro- and anti-union? pro- and anti-Fair Deal? for and against the present policies of the city council, school board, and so forth)? Do your findings support Lasch's contention that newspapers have become the spokesmen for *one* force in the community, reflecting that one group's attitudes most of the time?

6. In what respects, according to Tourtellot, has "the commercial growth of the press" made it easier for the press to fulfill its obligations to the people in a democracy? What evidence does Tourtellot give of the press's *having used* these improvements to fulfill its moral responsibility to the people? Can you find any specific evidence of this from a careful reading of the papers you have collected?

7. Tourtellot is impressed by the good record of the press in warning Americans in the 1930's of the fallacies of isolationism. But in what major areas of American life does he believe the press has *not* done a good job of presenting all the available facts? What evidence from your own newspaper reading (again, you may draw on your already available collection, but you should keep adding to it) do you have that it has failed to do so in these fields? In your opinion, are there any other kinds of social issues concerning which the press has not been sufficiently objective?

8. Does Tourtellot develop any specific ways in which the people can become more critical of the press while continuing to get information and opinion from the press as it exists today? And does he suggest any ways in which people, *if* more critical than they have been in the past, could bring about this improvement?

9. Lasch finds, in the reading public, little possibility of a "new birth of freedom" in the press. Compare this point of view with Tourtellot's. Do you, as a newspaper reader, feel as helpless to improve your city's newspapers as Lasch believes you are? Why, or why not? Is there any single answer to this one? Any evidence that either Tourtellot or Lasch, or both, are reaching oversimplified answers?

10. Lasch turns hopefully, but with reservations, to a second group, the newspaper staffs, in whom he wants to keep "professional conscience" alive. He defines "professional conscience" as "love of truth combined with zeal for the people's cause." Are there parallels today between the problem of maintaining "professional conscience" in the members of newspaper staffs and preserving and strengthening it in the four traditional professions of law, medicine, clergy, and teaching?

As a news reporter, you cover a campaign for a city bond issue to raise more money for the city's schools, a project to which your paper's ownership is opposed on the grounds that property taxes are already too high. You have no views either way on the subject. What specific problems will you have to face in maintaining both "an intellectual regard for truth" and "social purpose"?

If you are a reporter believing in the desirability of such a bond issue and also working for a newspaper that favors it, what will be your problems of "professional conscience"?

11. When Lasch turns to a third group, the owners, he finds their newspapers to be "semi-monopolies" and, so, "affected with a public interest exactly as are the utilities, the railroads, the milk supply." What could you, as the owner of a paper, do to influence other people's opinions that you could not do as a mechanic, storekeeper, carpenter, doctor, teacher, or politician?

But what consideration makes Lasch feel that socialization or forms of partial government regulation are not practical in the newspaper field? Do you agree with him or not? Why?

12. Do you consider Lasch's final and main recommendation, that newspaper owners develop a new conception of their role in society and new, more democratic methods of management, merely a pious, impractical hope, or do you believe it *is* a practical recommendation? What specific factors make it practical or impractical? Support your answers with specific evidence drawn from your reading of a representative sampling of the American press. (Here, of course, you will need to avail yourself of the resources of a good college or city library as well as those of your local newsstand.)

Joseph T. Klapper and Charles Y. Glock

"Trial by Newspaper" presents one aspect of present-day journalism that has particularly worried thoughtful newspaper readers—the ability of a powerful press in a free country to try individuals and groups and to pass judgment on them through their "reporting" of the news. This article is of special interest because it illustrates the increasingly frequent endeavors of social scientists to study the press objectively and to gather data on the actual operations of today's press. The authors are neither newspaper men nor politicians but social analysts. This study is one of a series of researches on the role of mass media of communication in United States society by the staff of the Columbia University Bureau of Applied Social Research.

TRIAL BY NEWSPAPER *

On March 2, 1948, a subcommittee of the House Committee on Un-American Activities denounced Edward U. Condon, Director of the National Bureau of Standards, through the medium of the U. S. press. The subcommittee asserted that Dr. Condon "appears" to be "one of the weakest links in our atomic security." Its report, quoted in part by various newspapers, presented 27 paragraphs of "information . . . in substantiation of this statement." Part of this information consisted of excerpts from a letter written by FBI chief J. Edgar Hoover to Secretary of Commerce W. Averell Harriman.

Simultaneously the Department of Commerce, under which the Bureau of Standards operates, announced that Dr. Condon had been unanimously cleared by the Department Loyalty Board five days previously. Dr. Condon himself at once denied the subcommittee's allegations, asserted his loyalty and reliability, and shortly thereafter expressed his eagerness for a public hearing by the Committee—an eagerness which he had expressed several times previously in response to similar accusations made by its chairman, Representative J. Parnell Thomas, in magazine articles published a year before.

During the succeeding four and one-half months the "Condon case" became a *cause célèbre*. At least three Congressional committees, the Federal Bureau of Investigation, the Atomic Energy Commission, two executive departments and President Truman himself played speaking roles in the drama. Numerous learned, scientific and juristic societies, as well as various individuals, eminent and otherwise, issued statements. In the course of the controversy, the Administration's refusal to surrender the FBI letter to Congress led to extraordinary Congressional repercussions, including an attempt to write into law certain provisions regarding the retention and release of data to Congressional bodies. The Condon case itself for a time became only an incident in this argument. It was revived on various occasions, however, by additional attacks on Dr.

* From Joseph T. Klapper and Charles Y. Glock, "Trial by Newspaper," *Scientific American*, February 1949.

Condon and by statements in his support. From time to time the Committee promised to grant Dr. Condon a public hearing, but the hearing never took place. The case continued to be argued in the press, albeit less frequently, even after the Atomic Energy Commission announced on July 15 that "on the basis of the voluminous record before it, the members of the Commission" were fully satisfied as to "Dr. Condon's loyalty to the United States" and considered his clearance for access to restricted data to be "in the best interest of the atomic energy program."

The Committee on Un-American Activities itself has made no formal determination of its charges against Condon. The case has been conducted largely in the press. Many citizens have become concerned about the affair as a striking example of what has sometimes been called trial by newspaper. They believe that the Condon case poses the question of the responsibilities of modern organs of mass communication toward the liberties and reputations of individuals.

As a result of this interest, the Bureau of Applied Social Research of Columbia University was asked by *Scientific American* and six eminent scientists to conduct a study of the press treatment of the Condon case. The scientists were: Harrison Brown and Harold C. Urey of the University of Chicago; Philip M. Morse of the Massachusetts Institute of Technology; George B. Pegram, Dean of the Columbia University Graduate faculties; Charles Lauritsen of the California Institute of Technology, and John C. Warner of the Carnegie Institute of Technology.

The study that was undertaken is known in communications research as a "content analysis." In general terms this means a detailed examination of verbal or pictorial material for the purpose of providing an objective description of the material. For example, a literary critic who analyzes the novels of a given century to determine their political tenor is, in a sense, performing a content analysis. Students of mass communications, however, use the term in a narrower sense. They mean by it a study in which the material is classified according to objective criteria and thus rendered susceptible of statistical description.

The term itself, and the conscious practice of this discipline, are relatively new in social science, as is the whole field of communications research. It is only during the last 30 years that such giants of communications as the modern press, the radio and the screen have come to address and to influence whole populations at once. And it is only in the last decade or two that social psychologists have taken systematic note of these forces of opinion. Content analysis is one of several techniques they have developed for the objective study of the media of communication.

Content analysis has already been successfully employed in a number of complex inquiries. The treatment of minority groups in popular fiction, for example, has been examined through a content analysis of magazine stories. During the war content analysis was used with some success by Government agencies to predict enemy actions. Certain characteristic modes of speech were observed to have increased in frequency during enemy propaganda campaigns preceding surprise invasions. By observing the frequency of such modes of speech in current propaganda, U. S. analysts were able to note when a new invasion move appeared to be imminent.

THE METHOD

The Bureau of Applied Social Research and the sponsors of the analysis agreed at the outset that the study would be directed entirely to the press treatment of the Condon case, as distinguished from the case itself. Neither the Bureau nor the sponsors considered themselves qualified to evaluate or analyze the activities and statements of the various agencies and individuals involved. No attempt has been made, for example, to assess the truth or falsity of the charges brought against Dr. Condon. We have been content with noting in detail what charges against Dr. Condon were reported in the press, what support for these charges was there offered, and the like.

It was soon found that to analyze the material on the Condon case in a representative cross section of the whole U. S. press would be a huge task; even to determine what papers would constitute such a cross section would involve a research project of no mean dimensions. It was therefore decided to focus the study on the press of a single large city. Because of the number and variety of its dailies, the New York City press was selected. Material was drawn from all of the nine general daily papers of that city, *viz.,* the *Times,* the *Herald Tribune,* the *Daily News,* the *Daily Mirror,*

PM and its successor the *Star*, all morning papers; and the *Sun*, the *World-Telegram*, the *Post Home News* and the *Journal-American*, all evening papers, some of them with week-end editions. The period studied was from March 1, 1948, to October 31, 1948, inclusive, *i.e.*, from the issuance of the subcommittee report to a date three and a half months after the Atomic Energy Commission had cleared Dr. Condon.

The Bureau set out to approximate as closely as possible a complete coverage of all news articles on the Condon case in all issues of the nine New York newspapers during the given period. This coverage was sought by two independent means. All the papers were asked for a list of the dates on which articles mentioning Dr. Condon were published (replies were received from every paper except the *Mirror*). Library editions of all papers were then searched for the articles published on those dates. In addition, a press clipping service was retained to make an independent search of all available editions of the nine papers for the entire period covered. Despite the precautions taken, it is quite possible that some articles or references to the case may have been missed. There may be variations in completeness of coverage from paper to paper. Any misses that occurred may be considered random, however; the missing material, if any, would not significantly affect the findings, which are almost always stated in terms of ratios or percentages.

All the relevant material in each news article was divided into "statements," each statement consisting of a single complete idea, *e.g.*, "Dr. Condon was denounced by the Thomas Committee." A statement might be a sentence or a single word; for example, "The martyred Dr. Condon will be called to testify" contains two statements: one that Dr. Condon will be called to testify, the other that he is martyred. The total number of statements in the 306 news articles examined was 4,589. Of these, 680 neutral statements of identification (*e.g.*, "Dr. Condon is director of the National Bureau of Standards") were eliminated, since analysis of them seemed purposeless. This left 3,909 for analysis.

The statements were then classified in various categories known as "dimensions," such as the identity of the person or group to whom the statement referred (called the "referent dimension"), the paper in which it appeared, the theme of the statement, the person or group who made it, the basis offered for the statement, and so on. There were 23 such dimensions. The crucial part of this process was the classification of the theme of the statement. To make this as objective as possible, the themes were subdivided at the outset into numerous specific categories, so that the classifiers or coders were not asked to decide whether a given statement was "favorable" or "unfavorable" to the referent (*e.g.*, Dr. Condon), but to describe it in terms of what it actually said. For example, a statement such as, "Dr. Condon is alleged to have associated with a Soviet spy" was classified under the theme: "Association with person in Soviet or Soviet-satellite circles who is allegedly subversive or an espionage agent." These various specific categories were later grouped under more general classifications to furnish the basis for analysis. Thus the statement quoted above became part of a group headed: "Association with allegedly questionable persons." This group of statements in turn eventually was placed in the general category of statements unfavorable to Dr. Condon.

The statements were all coded on the basis of the original specific criteria. As a check on objectivity, each statement was coded by at least two different individuals, and discrepancies were submitted to several independent checks by supervisors. Thus every coded statement was the end product of a process involving the detailed breakdown of an article, the isolation of the statement, its classification by two different coders in 23 dimensions, comparison of the two codings, and final approval for the next operation.

After they were coded, the statements were recorded on International Business Machine (Hollerith) cards. It thus became possible to determine quickly, by means of IBM sorters, precisely what "dimension combinations" existed, and in what degree. If it seemed desirable to know, for example, how many times the *Sun* reported a demand upon President Truman for release of the FBI letter, the machine was merely set to pick out the cards punched $\frac{1}{8}$ (column 1–hole 8: *Sun*), $1\frac{8}{5}$ (referent: Truman), $3\frac{3}{7}$ (demand for release of FBI letter). The results of the various machine "runs," taken individually or compared with one another, comprise the findings.

Despite the pains taken to ensure the highest possible degree of consistency, accuracy and objectivity, it must be remembered that we are here dealing not with the relatively stable phenomena of the physics laboratory but with the subjective phenomenon of language, which is as variable as human thought. Some degree of flexibility and interpretive inconsistency is therefore inevitable. While this margin of error is believed by the Bureau to be at the very minimum consistent with the nature of the task, one must lean backward in the interpretation of the findings. A very small percentage difference in two contrasted types of press treatment may not be significant in some cases; a notable percentage difference, however, can safely be regarded as significant.

The problem of the present study was to determine the nature of the "trial by newspaper" that Dr. Condon had received in the New York press. This involved a statistical measurement of the extent to which the newspapers treated him favorably or unfavorably. To that end the objective description of the press content on the case was analyzed as to the number of statements critical of Dr. Condon and those sympathetic to him; the number reporting demands for the FBI letter and those reporting refusals, and a miscellaneous category of statements that may be classified as neutral to Dr. Condon.

A statement was classed as unfavorable to Dr. Condon if it criticized him directly or reflected on him indirectly by supporting the Un-American Activities Committee's treatment of the case. An example of the first type of statement is: "Dr. Edward U. Condon . . . accused by a Thomas subcommittee . . . of associations with Soviet spies." An example of the second type: "McDowell insisted that the Committee's previous labeling of Condon stands as an 'almost perfect description.' " Similarly, a statement was classed as favorable to Dr. Condon if it supported him directly (*e.g.*, "Dr. Condon . . . whose integrity and patriotism have been fully recognized by his scientific peers"), or criticized the Committee (*e.g.*, "The . . . Committee's attack on Dr. Edward U. Condon was condemned today as 'irresponsible' by 200 leading scientists").

Thus the statements on each side could be broken down into two categories: (1) anti-Condon and pro-Committee, (2) pro-Condon and anti-Committee. As will be seen, such a breakdown produced some interesting findings.

Analyses were made of the emphasis given to the respective statements and of the way in which they were presented. It must be kept in mind that this is not a study of the editorial statements

made by the papers themselves but of their news coverage of the
story; that is, of the statements made in the news columns by reporters and their sources. Obviously what a newspaper reports
about an event is shaped to a large extent by the event itself. When
a paper reported an event unfavorable to Dr. Condon it was under
no obligation to create an event sympathetic to him to furnish a
balance. Thus the fact that a paper may have reported more unfavorable than favorable events is not in itself necessarily a sign
of bias. Bias may be shown, however, in the manner in which a
paper reports an event and in its selection of which events to report
and which to omit. An outside observer, lacking the newspapers'
access to the events on which they based their reporting, can only
judge their treatment of the Condon case by comparing the way in
which the various newspapers dealt with the same events.

WHAT WAS SAID

The first general finding is that in the New York press taken as
a whole there was a preponderance of statements favorable to Dr.
Condon. Of the 3,909 analyzed statements, 745 or 19 per cent were
unsympathetic to Condon, and 971 or 25 per cent were sympathetic.
These proportions, applying as they do to the total coverage by
the entire New York press, are not particularly meaningful: few
persons would consistently have read all nine papers and been
exposed to this comprehensive coverage. More significant are the
differences among the papers. The range of these differences is indicated in the percentages of pro-Condon and anti-Condon statements in the individual newspapers:

	Pro	*Con*
Times	65	35
Herald Tribune	64	36
Star	63	37
Post	57	43
World-Telegram	50	50
News	49	51
Mirror	47	53
Sun	43	57
Journal-American	18	82

(Because the *Journal-American* published relatively little on the Condon case, the findings for this paper may be less meaningful than for the others.)

Most of the pro-Condon statements were contributed by the first four papers—*Times, Tribune, Star* and *Post*—which accounted for nearly two thirds of the total New York coverage of the story in terms of number of statements. In the four papers taken as a group, statements sympathetic to Dr. Condon outnumbered unsympathetic ones in a ratio of 17 to 10. In the other five papers, which have a much larger total circulation than the first group, statements unsympathetic to Dr. Condon predominated in the ratio of 13 to 10 for the group as a whole.

Analysis of the two categories of statements on each side of the case—*i.e.,* those relating directly to Dr. Condon and those relating to the Committee—revealed another interesting difference in the handling of the case by the two groups of papers. There were few statements in praise of the Committee's treatment of the case: of the total of the anti-Condon statements in all the papers fewer than one in 13 supported the Committee itself. When it came to the pro-Condon statements, however, there were contrasting results in the amount of criticism of the Committee in the two newspaper groups. In the *Times, Tribune, Star* and *Post,* more than one third of the statements on Dr. Condon's side consisted of criticisms of the Committee's procedure. In the other five papers, this proportion was nearer one fourth. In other words, the second group published a substantially smaller proportion of statements criticizing the Committee than did the first group.

The statements favorable and unfavorable to Dr. Condon taken together accounted for 44 per cent of the 3,909 on the case. Of the rest, a surprisingly large group—some 15 per cent of all statements—concerned the struggle between Republican Congressmen and the Administration over the release of the FBI letter. The remaining 41 per cent of the statements in the case were classified as descriptive background of a neutral character.

A further breakdown showing how the treatment of Dr. Condon fluctuated during the progress of the case also yields significant information. In April, when the battle over the FBI letter reached its peak, the reflections of this event were markedly different in the two groups of newspapers. The *Times, Tribune, Star* and *Post* continued to give greater attention to the Condon case itself and to publish more pro-Condon than anti-Condon statements, although the ratio for the group fell to 12 to 10. In the other five papers, however, statements about the letter actually outnumbered statements about the Condon case proper, and the ratio of statements unsympathetic to Condon rose to 23 to 10. When the Atomic Energy Commission cleared him in July, the *Times, Tribune, Star* and *Post* presented a 14-to-10 ratio of statements favorable to him, but the other five papers, in spite of his clearance, remained on the other side of the fence; in that month they printed an average of 11 anti-Condon statements for every 10 pro-Condon. Thereafter there was relatively little press activity on the Condon case, but in September, when the Un-American Activities Committee promised new "shocking revelations," the statements published in the group of five papers were 26 to 10 anti-Condon. In other words, two months after his AEC exoneration, the five papers were still presenting a predominantly unsympathetic picture.

These are simply objective data revealed by the analysis. Whether they show that the New York press was fair or unfair in its coverage of the case is a matter of interpretation, which is beyond the scope of this analysis. The interpretation will depend on the standards applied by the observer. Some may consider that justice would have been served by a perfect balance of pro- and anti-Condon statements in a paper's reporting. On this point, however, the analysis developed certain other pertinent data.

The data had to do with the sources, character and repetition of statements on the case. Because this analysis dealt with statements concerning Dr. Condon himself, the findings from this point will include only statements directly pro- and anti-Condon; *i.e.,* they exclude the statements for and against the Committee. Of the statements against Dr. Condon, 88 per cent were made by members of the Un-American Activities Committee directly or in excerpts that they quoted from the FBI letter. The accusations against Dr. Condon were virtually a monopoly product of the Committee, for some of the remaining 12 per cent of anti-Condon statements were made by Dr. Condon himself or by his defenders in reviewing what the Committee had said about him.

On the other hand, the sources of the pro-Condon statements were legion. They included two departments of the executive branch of the government, the Commerce Department Loyalty Board, the Atomic Energy Commission, entire departments of leading universities, and dozens of scientists and scientific societies. Analysis of the weight given by the various papers to the sources of these statements yielded significant differences. The *Times, Tribune, Star* and *Post* gave considerably more attention to the width of Dr. Condon's support than did the other papers; 21 per cent of their pro-Condon statements were attributed to scientists and scientific societies, while in the other five papers only 4 per cent of the statements favoring Condon came from these sources. Indeed, it appears that those five dailies all but ignored the multitude of meetings, letters and statements in defense of Condon by reputable scientists and institutions. As a result, 77 per cent of the case for Dr. Condon as presented to the readers of those papers came from Dr. Condon himself, from representatives of the Administration, or from unnamed sources.

A similar analysis was made of the bases of the anti-Condon and pro-Condon statements and the relative weight given to them. The case against Dr. Condon was made up almost entirely of three charges: 1) that he associated with suspected persons, 2) that he was lax in regard to U. S. security, 3) that he was unfit in some other unspecified way.

Of the statements making the first charge, 89 per cent identified Dr. Condon's associates only in vague terms or did not identify them at all. His associates were generally described as persons "alleged" or "known" to be espionage agents, or as Soviet or Soviet-satellite diplomats, or as persons suspected of being subversive, without any specification as to why they were under suspicion or any evidence that Condon knew that his associates were under this vague cloud. Only eight per cent of the statements regarding association actually named his associates, and in most of these cases the charges were equally vague. With regard to Dr. Condon's "laxity," nearly all of the statements were simply assertions, most of them being repetitions of the phrase "the weakest link"; there was little or no specific indication as to how he may actually have endangered national security. In the third category, the allegations were even more vague. Indeed, whatever impression may have been produced on casual readers, the content analysis indicates that the case against Dr. Condon as presented in the newspapers may well

have raised a question in careful readers' minds as to whether there
was any case at all.

The case *for* Dr. Condon contains a substantial amount of specific
material. About a quarter of the pro-Condon statements rest on the
fact that he was cleared by official investigations. Other favorable
statements are based on "two exhaustive FBI investigations" and
several documents, still others on testimonials to Dr. Condon's
loyalty and competence from a variety of sources. Yet in comparison
with the case against Condon these facts were lightly treated by
a majority of the New York papers, which throughout the case
gave far heavier emphasis to the allegations by the Un-American
Activities Committee than to the support of Dr. Condon from various sources.

HOW IT WAS SAID

A description of what the press said and what it omitted can
give only a relatively superficial picture of its coverage. Equally
important is the nature of the treatment, and the manner in which
newspaper techniques affected the picture presented to the reader.
These factors are difficult to analyze in any objective fashion, but
the Bureau approached the problem from several new angles and
obtained some fruitful results.

One approach was a test of the material by the criterion of the
repetition of statements. In any continuing news story, it is to be
expected that a newspaper will frequently find it necessary to review past events as background. In making the selection of what
background information to print, the newspaper obviously exercises
more selective judgment than it can with respect to the new material, for the background provides many more items from which to
choose. If, for example, the Un-American Activities Committee announced that it intended to hold a hearing on the Condon case,
the "news" was pretty well restricted to that fact, but in injecting
background into the report a paper could choose from among a
number of statements, such as that Dr. Condon had been accused
of associating with spies, that he had been cleared by the Loyalty
Board, and so on. Thus it is of considerable interest to see what the
papers chose to include as background in their reports as the news
developed.

In the analysis of this phase of the newspapers' coverage, all statements printed within two days after an occurrence were classified as "new" and all others as "old." The general finding that resulted from this analysis was that in eight of the nine dailies the "old" or repeated statements built up the case against Dr. Condon more than the case for him. About 57 per cent of the case against him in the papers consisted of revivals of the original charges. On the other hand, criticisms of the Un-American Activities Committee were seldom repeated; only 11 per cent of the statements in this category were revivals.

In every category of statements on the case except the one that covered criticisms of Condon, new statements out-numbered the old. The newspapers repeated general denunciations of him six times as often as they repeated general statements in his support. If they had published no "old" statements at all, the score for statements directly naming Condon would have been 416 pro to 301 anti, instead of 695 to 631 the other way.

There is no reason to believe that this result was deliberate. But the fact remains that the reporting techniques employed by the papers served to inflate the case against Condon far beyond its native size.

Another significant finding concerns the newspapers' handling of the Committee's promises of a hearing to Dr. Condon, and of the breach of that promise. All the papers reported the promises much more often than the breach. Here again, however, there were substantial differences between the two groups of papers. The *Times, Tribune, Star* and *Post* published 14 statements on the Committee's promises for every 10 statements on its failure to keep the promises. In the other five papers as a group the ratio was about eight to one.

SUMMARY

Thus the content analysis produced these principal findings: the nine New York papers showed wide variations in their news treatment of the case, although all were reporting the same story. Some presented a picture predominantly favorable to Dr. Condon, some predominantly unfavorable. As reported in all the papers, the charges against Dr. Condon were vague. The width of the support of Dr. Condon received substantial attention in the *Times, Tribune, Star* and *Post* but very little attention in the other five papers. The background material revived for use in the running news stories had the effect of building up the case against Dr. Condon but did not build up his defense to anywhere near the same degree. All the papers reported the Committee's promise to give Dr. Condon a hearing far more often than they reported its failure to do so.

Such are the objective findings. The writers have attempted to avoid judgments, or have labeled them clearly when they seemed unavoidable. How or why the press treatments here described took the form they did, and whether the papers should be commended or condemned are questions to be considered by interested students of the press.

PROBLEMS

1. In what specific ways did the researchers of the Bureau of Applied Social Research of Columbia University seek to assure *objectivity* in their study of the Condon "trial by newspaper"? Do you see any other ways in which they could have achieved even greater objectivity?

2. In what ways do their investigation and their evaluation of findings meet, or fail to meet, the criteria of the scientific method evolved in your reading and discussion of the section "Reasoning Inductively"? Does the appearance of this article originally in *Scientific American,* a journal devoted to reports of interest to scientists, necessarily constitute evidence of its scientific character?

3. Review the ways suggested in "Distinguishing Fact from Opinion" in which a picture "predominantly favorable" or a picture "predominantly unfavorable" of the same man or program may be presented. Which of these ways were evidently used by the various papers investigated in this survey?

4. Why should vague charges be *suspect?* Why are such charges frequently very effective?

5. The investigators found that in five New York papers the "width" of Dr. Condon's support received "very little attention." Why would the width or distribution of a government scientist's support be a matter of particular interest to anyone interested in determining the scientist's fitness for his post? In any attempt to understand a controversial

public figure, why would it be important to note the number and variety of sources of praise and criticism?

6. The investigators noted the cumulative effect of mere repetition of the original charges against Condon. Why is counting the same thing twice a fatal error in scientific thinking? From your own personal experience or reading illustrate the various forms this type of error in observation may take. For example, a venerable means used by charlatans to hoodwink the public is to have a small number of people go in and out of a store or office to give the impression of great numbers of patrons. Similar devices have been used in battle when a small number of men has wished to frighten off a much larger force. Have you ever noted that *one* piece of gossip, whether true or not, may be repeated in many forms, going through all sorts of changes, and create the effect of many scandalous incidents? or how *one* instance of a "cure," frequently referred to, can come to be "many cures"?

7. The investigators discovered that the press reported the Committee's *promise* of a hearing far more often than they reported its *failure* to grant the hearing. What factors, besides the conscious desire of a newspaper to give an incomplete picture, might make such "unfinished business" common in newspaper reporting? in our own accounts of a series of events? How is this related to the experience we have all had of reading headlines for weeks about a scandal involving a man who is cleared, on an inner page, five weeks later?

John Bainbridge

Today most of us can read. Such literacy, a relatively recent development in man's history, has meant, among other things, a tremendous increase in the number of magazines designed to meet the demand for reading material. Many magazine readers, however, have run into two obstacles: first, their inability, under the pressures of work, play, and just plain laziness, to read more than a fraction of that total output, and, second, their difficulty in understanding the writing of specialists. Now, what could seem a more sensible way of getting over these two obstacles than to have somebody go through the monthly mass of magazine-writing, pick out the best-written, most comprehensible, and most representative articles, boil these down (tossing out time-wasting irrelevancies and technicalities), and offer them to the hurried, tired general public in one neat package?

This kind of answer has seemed to millions of readers to settle both the problems of amount and of difficulty quite adequately.

In the following selection from his witty, fact-packed book, *Little Wonder,* John Bainbridge suggests that the "digest" sort of answer may not be so adequate as many of us have imagined. Indeed, he indicates that the "digest" method may have created new difficulties for the reader who wants to know what is happening and what people are thinking about it.

This selection is included here for two reasons: (1) most students, once they have become aware of the problems in the way of getting sound information and thinking logically about it, want to know what they are getting in their favorite magazines; and (2) their discovery of facts about one of their main sources of facts and ideas (the *Reader's Digest* is read by more Americans than is any other magazine) usually leads them to examine thoughtfully other sources of their facts and ideas—newspapers, advertisements, radio broadcasts, and motion pictures.

DIGESTING A DIGEST *

When DeWitt Wallace established *The Reader's Digest,* he summed up the aim of his magazine in a slogan: "An article a day from leading magazines, in condensed, permanent booklet form." This slogan, reminiscent of Dr. Eliot's Five Foot Shelf and other short cuts to culture, was printed on the first page of every issue of *The Reader's Digest* from August, 1923, through May, 1939. In the issue of June, 1939, the motto was quietly altered. Wallace deleted the phrase "from leading magazines" and substituted the less reassuring phrase "of enduring significance." To many people in the publishing business, this change was more amusing than surprising; it seemed to them long overdue. For years, the fact that *The Reader's Digest* had ceased to be solely a reprint magazine had, to its devoted students, been as obvious as the falseness of Groucho Marx's mustache. By millions of less analytical readers, however, the *Digest's* metamorphosis has as yet apparently never been noticed. It is evidently as hard for a *Digest* fan to think of his favorite magazine as anything but a regurgitative journal as it would be for a

* Part III of a Profile in *The New Yorker.* Copyright, 1945, John Bainbridge.

clean-shaven Groucho to stalk Mrs. Rittenhouse. The *Digest* has not exerted itself immoderately to shatter the illusion. A year after acknowledging, by implication, the changed character of his magazine, Wallace printed a warm testimonial to it by John Kieran, the amiable permanent expert of "Information, Please!" Kieran, paraphrasing the chant of millions of other *Digest* devotees—"I don't have time to read *all* the magazines, so I just read the *best* from all of them in the little magazine that fits right into my pocket"—said that the *Digest* performed a great service for him by sifting the best articles from the "vast flood of contemporary letters. It is the one periodical I read regularly, knowing that in it I will get the best sum and substance of today's literary output." Kieran ended, not unexpectedly, with a quotation from *Hamlet:* "For this relief, much thanks." Alas, poor Kieran! He did not know the *Digest* well.

The transformation of *The Reader's Digest* into something other than a digest began in the early thirties. Among other things, it was a maneuver of self-defense. A small rebellion against the *Digest* had broken out among a group of strong-minded publishers and editors, who considered denying the *Digest* the privilege of reprinting articles from their magazines. Threatened with the possible loss of his sources of supply, Wallace countered by hiring a few men to write articles directly for the *Digest*. The rebellion petered out, but Wallace, perhaps expecting another one later on, continued to build up his defenses by having his writers turn out more and more material. In June, 1930, he began publishing occasional articles that were on the borderline between reprints and originals. These, it was announced in the *Digest,* were based on articles that had appeared in other publications. The magazines were not identified and the articles, written by Wallace's staff authors, were anonymous. These articles, presented under a rather evasive editorial note reading, "It was felt that on this subject, the interest of our readers is best served by this summary, specially prepared by one of our editors," bore such arresting titles as "Music and Animals" and "Why Be Bald?" Wallace continued to serve the best interests of his readers with similar summaries until February, 1933, when he at last decided to publish the first admittedly original article. This historic contribution was written, and signed, by Henry Morton Robinson, at present a Roving Editor of the *Digest,* and was entitled "Insanity—The Modern Menace." There were fourteen other original articles in the *Digest* that year, none of which seemed to charm its readers more than a piece called "The Burning Question," an article about cremation.

Until 1935, Wallace may reasonably have wondered whether he hadn't made a mistake in going into the intricate business of manufacturing articles instead of simply reprocessing old ones. As far as anyone could tell, the customers seemed to like the reused goods as well as the new. He nevertheless kept offering more samples, and of the forty originals he printed that year, one turned out to be a startling success. This was a sanguinary piece about automobile accidents called "—And Sudden Death," written by J. C. Furnas. It turned out to be the most widely read magazine article ever published anywhere. . . . What effect the extensive distribution of this gruesome work of art had on reckless driving is hard to say with certainty, but it may be significant that in 1936, the year after it came out, 1,720 more persons were killed in automobile accidents in this country than the year before, and the figure rose even higher the next year.

Whatever the practical results of the Furnas article, the effect on Wallace was exhilarating. It bolstered his confidence in his editorial judgment, and it provided an excellent retort to the editors of other magazines who had got into the habit of patronizingly calling him "the world's greatest second-guess editor." In thirteen years as a publisher, Wallace had reprinted hundreds of articles published by other editors and not one had been half as sensational as a piece he thought up by himself. . . . Since it seemed clear that his hunches about what people want to read were as good as or better than those of any of his colleagues, and since he was also suffering from a combined creative and evangelical itch, Wallace determined to become a permanent first-guess editor. To do this overtly, he was aware, would bring up a perplexing publishing problem, for if the *Digest* began appearing with large numbers of frankly original articles, many readers like John Kieran might get the impression that their favorite periodical was no longer providing them with an accurate cross-section of the best sum and substance of the current literary output. Wallace solved the problem by inventing the "planted" article—perhaps the most important journalistic innovation since the invention of the digest magazine itself. A *Digest* "plant" is the same as a *Digest* original, with one exception. Both plants and originals are planned, assigned to authors, and paid for by the *Digest*. The original articles are published in the *Digest* without being ascribed to any other magazine. Before a plant appears in the *Digest*, however, it is sent to some other periodical; say, the *Rotarian*. The *Rotarian* publishes the article. The *Digest* then "reprints" it, under a line saying "Condensed from the *Rotarian*." The advantages of the planting system to Wallace are obvious; it allows him to have the fun of being a first-guess editor and at the same time to observe the letter, if not the precise spirit, of what is expected of a reprint magazine.

For some reason, Wallace has always been something less than garrulous about the extent of the *Digest's* planting activities. People who have been interested enough to ask the *Digest* how much of the magazine's content is supplied by other periodicals and how much is originated by the *Digest* have received responses in straight-from-the-shoulder double talk. However, an irrepressible statistician named George W. Bennett recently knocked himself out getting up some figures and arrived at a reasonably accurate answer to this question. During the five years from 1939 through 1943, the *Digest* printed 1,908 articles of one page or more in length, not including the book section or such filler items as "Picturesque Speech and Patter." Of the 1,908 articles, Mr. Bennett was able to identify 1,718, or ninety per cent, either as articles the *Digest* actually reprinted or as articles the *Digest* actually produced itself. Mr. Bennett was unable to get scientific data on the other ten per cent because of unanswered letters, unanswered telephones, slammed doors, and blank memories. Of the 1,718 identifiable articles, 720 were merely reprinted, in the old-fashioned meaning of the word, by the *Digest* from other periodicals. Bennett calls these genuine reprints. An additional 316 articles were written solely for the *Digest* and printed there only. Bennett calls these bona-fide originals. The remaining 682 articles were written for the *Digest*, planted in other periodicals, and then "reprinted" by the *Digest*. Bennett calls these plants, or disguised originals. In other figures, 720 articles, or forty-two per cent, were genuine reprints, and 998, or fifty-eight per cent, were either bona-fide or disguised originals. Later samplings made by Bennett show about the same percentages for 1944 and 1945. Thus, approximately three out of every five *Digest* articles now originate in the *Digest's* offices. Or, in fewer words, considerably less than half of its content is reaped from other periodicals. Or, in still fewer words, *The Reader's Digest* is no longer primarily a digest.

This entertaining state of affairs is not so obvious to ordinary magazine-readers, because the *Digest's* planting operations are so scattered. In the five years from 1939 through 1943, the *Digest* planted articles in more than sixty publications. During this period, the *American Mercury* was credited as being its largest source of reprinted articles. Of the seventy-four pieces taken from the *Mercury,* the majority were planted by the *Digest.* More than half the articles credited to the *Rotarian, Hygeia,* the *Kiwanis Magazine, Survey Graphic,* and the *American Legion Magazine* were also originated by the *Digest.* Of forty-seven articles reprinted from *Harper's,* eight were *Digest* plants; of thirty-nine furnished by the *Atlantic Monthly,* eight were plants; of four credited to the *Yale Review,* three are known to be plants; of eight taken from the *Nation,* five were plants; of twenty-six credited to the *New Republic,* eight were plants and thirteen others were on the *Digest's* presses before the *New Republic* appeared on the stands with them. This is a plain indication that they were prepared under what a *New Republic* official has called "a special arrangement." Two, and perhaps more, of the four articles credited to the *North American Review* were placed there by the *Digest,* and of four winnowed from *Asia,* two were planted. The *Digest* gave *Commonweal* credit for nine reprinted articles; all were plants. In the same period, twenty-one articles were credited to the Baltimore *Sunday Sun;* all were plants. During these five years, the *Digest* reprinted one or more articles from *Harper's Bazaar, Free World, Saturday Night, Parents' Magazine, Woman's Press, National Safety News, Stage, Yankee, Progressive Education, South Atlantic Quarterly, Family Circle Magazine,* and the *Virginia Quarterly Review;* all were plants.

Not every magazine and newspaper that has had relations with the *Digest* has participated in its planting system. Between 1939 and 1943, there were six periodicals which, though they took no articles from the *Digest,* supplied it with two dozen or more articles apiece. These were *Life,* the *American Magazine, Collier's,* the *New Yorker,* the New York *Times,* and *Fortune,* in the order of the number of articles reprinted. Among the other non-collaborating periodicals that furnished only genuine reprints, though fewer than two dozen, were the *Saturday Evening Post, Time, Good Housekeeping, McCall's, Newsweek, Woman's Home Companion,* and the New York *Herald Tribune.* Recently, the *New Republic,* the *Nation, Free World,* and *Commonweal* have announced that they will be sown no more. Their reasons range from disagreement with the *Digest's* editorial bias to a lack of interest in the kind of article offered. "We just got fed up with printing their buncombe," the editor of one of the reconstructed journals has explained.

The reasons given by editors who support the planting system are varied, too. Probably the most enticing ones are that it is a handy way to get articles and that the articles don't cost anything. Some substantial publications, such as the *Atlantic Monthly* and the Baltimore *Sun,* however, refuse to accept the pieces as charity; when editors of these periodicals take an article submitted by the *Digest,* they pay the author of the piece at their regular rates. The author has, of course, already been paid by the *Digest.* . . .

The Reader's Digest feels that its planting operations are completely misunderstood. For example, it is inaccurate, the *Digest* explains to its critics, to say that a piece it sends to another magazine is a planted article; it should be called a coöperatively planned article. Since the *Digest* believes that it is misunderstood, it seems only fair to present the publication's position, and perhaps such a presentation can best be accomplished by adopting the "Mr. Pro and Mr. Con" running-debate technique that the *Digest* itself has often used in dealing with such controversial questions as "Should Post-Mortem Examinations Become Common Procedure?" That form will be followed here in considering the question "Is It Is or Is It Ain't a Digest?" All the statements made by Mr. Pro are quoted verbatim from a report submitted by *The Reader's Digest* to the Board of Education of Passaic, New Jersey, which had expressed to the management of the *Digest* an interest in certain aspects of its procedure, including the operation of the planting system. Mr. Pro's remarks can therefore be assumed to represent the official *Digest* view. He begins:

MR. PRO: The next charge leveled against the *Digest* had to do with the practice of "planting articles in other magazines." Here the critics of the *Digest* took a very simple routine process in the production of the magazine and distorted it, misrepresented it, and unblushingly lied about it, with the result that there is created in the mind of the uninformed the image of a conspiracy—

MR. CON: Get to the point, Mr. Pro.

MR. PRO: Let us look at the facts. It is true that the *Digest* does not confine itself to publishing articles and stories previously and independently published by other magazines. In large part it does just that.

MR. CON: On the contrary, it does just the opposite, if by "in large part" you mean a major portion—which, I grant you, you wouldn't necessarily have to mean. Over half the articles published in the *Digest* in a five-year period studied by George W. Bennett were not previously and independently published by other magazines. They originated in the office of the *Digest*.

MR. PRO: But it also published original articles which have appeared nowhere else and it furthermore obtains material which it offers to other magazines prior to publication in the *Digest*. In none of these procedures is there anything secret or sinister.

MR. CON: Would you mind, then, stating just how many original articles the *Digest* prints and how many it plants, or, as you say, offers to other magazines before publication in the *Digest?*

MR. PRO: (*No answer.*)

MR. CON: Proceed.

MR. PRO: It is true that the *Digest* sometimes offers to other magazines complete articles, condensed versions of which subsequently appear in the *Digest.* Often these articles are worked out in collaboration with the editors of other magazines.

MR. CON: And more often they are not. As a rule, the editor of a magazine has never seen or heard of a *Digest* plant before it turns up in his office. If the articles were, as you say, worked out in collaboration with the editors of other magazines, how do you explain the fact that editors reject so many of these pieces? The rate of return of articles sent out for planting is, as you know, high. Many editors remark with pride that for every *Digest* plant they accept, they reject from two to four more. But go ahead.

MR. PRO: A fee is paid to various publications which guarantees to the *Digest* the right to republish their available material. This is simple business practice, and in no sense implies any editorial control of these publications. The core of criticisms of this procedure consists in the accusation that articles politically slanted are farmed out in this way. The balance of facts is all on the other side. How much does *The Reader's Digest* influence the policies of other publications on political or economic matters? Or how much—

MR. CON: Sorry to interrupt, Mr. Pro, but you're getting off the subject again. What you were going to say is that only a small percentage of *Digest* plants are concerned with such controversial issues as economics, government, politics, and industrial and international relations. That may well be, but perhaps the reason is that not all other magazines want to be sown with *Digest* articles concerned with these issues, or with your point of view on them. Can you think, offhand, for example, of a half-dozen magazines that would have been glad to take the responsibility for printing that curious *Digest* piece called "Our Deep Dark Secrets in Latin America"? Many people, you recall, considered the article so mischievous and full of misinformation that they agreed with Senator Joseph Guffey, who said in Congress that the *Digest* owed an apology and an explanation to the people of the United States for publishing it. Anyway, the question isn't how many articles on controversial topics the *Digest* plants. The question is how many articles on *all* topics it plants. The fact that it plants so many is the real core of the criticisms.

MR. PRO: (*Serenely*): Certainly there is no reason to attribute any possible "influencing of other editors, or periodicals, or public opinion itself" to the practice of offering an article on the habits of animals to a nature magazine, or a report on dental progress to a dentists' journal. This is not a public disservice but a public service.

MR. CON: Oh, come now, Mr. Pro. You're talking as if *The Reader's Digest* were the Rockefeller Foundation. The *Digest* is a commercial enterprise, like any other magazine, not a philanthropy. It gives planted articles to nature magazines and dentists' journals and other publications so it can use the names of these periodicals on its cover and over the articles and thus keep up the pretense that it is a reprint magazine. If it isn't solely for this reason that the *Digest* plants these pieces, why does it go to all the trouble of planting them? Why doesn't the *Digest* simply print them as original articles? Furthermore, Mr. Pro, you refer to the planting business as "a very simple routine process," giving the impression that it is common practice in the trade. Of course it isn't. The planting system is unique with the *Digest,* and it doesn't seem so very routine even to the *Digest.* For one thing, the job takes the full time of a senior editor of the *Digest,* Mr. Howard Florance, and his staff, who are kept busy peddling these so-called "coöperatively planned" articles. And don't forget that time the *Digest* condensed an article from the *Nation* so ingeniously that it ran four hundred and sixty-eight words longer than the article it was condensed from. Apparently the *Digest* occasionally neglects to get the coöperation of other editors very far in advance. Many letters accompanying articles sent out for planting are dated only two or three days before the *Digest* goes to press. "We are hoping," one of these letters reads, as you may recall, "to print the story in our July *Reader's Digest*, out about June twenty-fifth, and would be happy to credit it to your periodical." The letter is dated May 21st, one day after the normal date for closing your July issue. Other letters give the impression of even greater hurry. "If you don't want it," one reads, "will you let us know promptly? Or, rather, will you forgive me if I call up Monday afternoon to ask if you are at all interested?" Another: "Would you be very kind and read it as soon as possible, as we are making up the next issue? Perhaps you would be able to telephone some time today?" Some have a pleading note. One, scribbled in pencil, says, "Can you use this? Before Jan. 25. In haste." In haste indeed. The letter was written two days after the usual *Digest* press time.

Since the rate of rejections is high, Mr. Pro, many articles have to be peddled from one magazine office to another before they are finally planted. Even then, trouble sometimes occurs. For example, there was an article about a South American newspaper that the *Digest* planted, or thought it had planted, in a periodical that I will call *Good Neighbor*. In checking the piece, the editors of *Good Neighbor* discovered some errors, decided not to print it after all, and notified the *Digest*. But the *Digest* had already gone to press with the article, confidently crediting *Good Neighbor* as the source. So the *Digest* appeared with the article which it said it had "Condensed from *Good Neighbor*." This was a rare feat; the article from which the condensation was presumably made had never been published by any periodical on earth.

No, planting articles is not very simple, Mr. Pro. It is a tricky business. Do you remember a magazine called the *Living Age?* It was, as you know, once an old and respected periodical, but it fell on hard times and was bought for fifteen thousand dollars in June, 1938, by three men, Joseph Hilton Smyth, Walter Grey Matheson, and Irvine Harvey Williams. The money to buy the magazine was furnished by the Japanese government through the local Japanese vice-consul, Sintaro Fukushima, who also helped underwrite the magazine's overhead by contributing about twenty-five hundred dollars a month. In September of 1942, Smyth and his colleagues were arrested by the F.B.I. and later pleaded guilty to having run the *Living Age* in behalf of the Japanese government between June, 1938, and December, 1941. During this time they had accepted approximately a hundred and fifty thousand dollars from the Japs. Smyth and his colleagues were sentenced to seven years in a federal penitentiary. While the *Living Age* was being run for the benefit of the Japanese, the *Digest* reprinted thirteen articles from it. Actually, the majority were plants, or, to use the *Digest's* phrase, articles cooperatively planned by the editors of the *Digest* and the editors of the *Living Age*. Three of the pieces were written by *Digest* editors. Of all the articles furnished by the *Digest*, possibly the one that caused Sintaro Fukushima the most amusement was the piece the *Digest* planted in the May, 1940, issue of the *Living Age* and "reprinted" in the *Digest* in June. This was entitled "How Smart Are the Japanese?" Of course, the editors of the *Digest* had no way of knowing that the *Living Age* was a Japanese propaganda organ, so there was nothing treasonable about dealing with it. But the case does illustrate that planting is not at all a routine procedure. It is an involved technique, and sometimes even perilous. Since you said earlier, Mr. Pro, that there is nothing secret about the planting system, do you feel that to describe its operation constitutes what the *Digest* has called a smear?

MR. PRO: In view of these facts, it clearly appears that the so-called "planting" of articles has to deal with a variety of subjects, very few of which are controversial in character; that, in fact, what is a simple magazine procedure has been misrepresented and made into a smear. It has been alleged that the *Digest* has changed. In a sense this is true. . . . The *Digest* has outgrown the limitations of selecting its material from magazines alone, and now includes selections from newspapers, books, and professional and trade journals; from public speeches, from radio programs, motion-picture scripts, and from any other source, including any original source, that provides material which, in the judgment of its editors, will be of interest to its readers. . . . So the *Digest* remains the true digest of American literature today.

MR. CON: *Caveat emptor.*

PROBLEMS

1. Before reading this article, what was your conception of the way in which *The Reader's Digest* is written and put together? On what evidence had you based your conclusion? If your picture of the magazine has changed, can you now see clues in the *Digest* itself that you had overlooked?

2. If you were a teacher aware of Bainbridge's article, what would you ask yourself and try to answer before deciding to use, or not to use, *The Reader's Digest* in your classroom?

3. Can you see any similarities between the "digest" practice of printing "planted" articles and the following: (a) a magazine that calls itself a "news magazine" or "news survey" and in various ways (statements of opinion, emphasis, omission) expresses its editors' own views; (b) a newspaper or magazine that does not publish the names of its owners and editors or sponsoring groups; (c) a small newspaper that depends on "boiler plate" (news and views "all ready to go") sent out by central news agencies to which it pays a set subscription fee; and (d) editorializing under the guise of advertising?

4. In reading a variety of periodicals presenting a variety of viewpoints, how would one protect himself from being taken in by any one of them? How would such reading enable him to spot any slant behind the apparently impartial system used by *The Reader's Digest?* For instance, would a reader who read liberal *and* conservative journals be able to see in what direction a journal that purported to have no bias might actually lean? To test this method, read through at least three issues of *Newsweek, Harper's Magazine,* and *The Nation.* Pick issues which cover the same time span so that you may compare the treatment of the same events by these three quite different periodicals. (Other magazines worth comparing in similar fashion are *Time, The Atlantic Monthly,* and *The New Republic.* And, for those having access to well-equipped libraries, *The Wall Street Journal,* the London *Economist,* and the London *New Statesman and Nation* are well worth exploring. For some brief and stimulating estimates of leading American newspapers and magazines, written from the viewpoint of one who is rather sharply critical of most of them, see pages 615-679 of Harold Laski's *The American Democracy.*)

Alexander Klein

Alexander Klein, who has written and produced motion pictures for commercial firms and educational organizations, here surveys three popular mass media—movies, radio, and television. He clearly sees their present shortcomings and proposes some specific means by which he believes they can realize their vast potentialities for social good.

THE CHALLENGE OF MASS MEDIA: MOVIES, RADIO, TELEVISION *

"Here is the most wonderful medium for communicating ideas the world has ever dreamed of, yet at present the magic toy is used in the main to convey outrageous rubbish. . . . The real danger is . . . that its uses will fail to measure up to the magnificent opportunity it offers."

This quotation, curiously enough, does not come from one of our latter-day critics of television. It comes from a lament over the misuse of radio published back in 1924 in the old *Century* magazine. But the applicability of these words to television, radio, and motion pictures today is a measure of our continuing failure to develop these technically superb means of mass communication along the lines of their artistic, cultural, and educational potentialities. It has become a truism that in fifty years of motion pictures and thirty years of radio, neither has made more than a start towards realizing its possibilities as a force for intelligence and social awareness, although attacks on the controllers of both and suggestions for improvement have been appearing continually for many years.

Today we face the most acute need for mass intelligence in the history of the world, yet there is no plan in effect to bring the media of mass communication in line with this vital social need. Now is a strategic time for tackling the problem. A new medium—television—has invaded the field. Radio and the motion picture

* Alexander Klein, "The Challenge of Mass Media," from *The Yale Review,* Summer, 1950, copyright, Yale University Press.

are no longer entrenched, smug dictators, and television is still in the developmental stage. Concerted action *now* might bring about fundamental changes in the whole program and establish a pattern for the future that would be closer to the best interests of our society.

In order to understand the present state of mass media, we need to know something about how they arrived there. We shall find that their shortcomings are largely outgrowths of our culture as a whole, as well as of the special factors obtaining in each medium, rather than of the special failings in the men who operate them. Let us begin by looking at the motion pictures.

The businessmen who first invested capital in motion pictures—"pioneers of the industry," as they are now known—were quickly rewarded by profits far beyond their original expectations. The consequence was that film-making, which was approached in France as an art, was considered almost wholly as a commercial venture in this country. Edison saw the film as revolutionizing education; it "can stir up sluggish brain cells as all the printing presses in the world cannot," he declared. But, in spite of the impetus given educational films by their widespread use among the armed forces during the last war, not much more than a beginning has been made in using them for civilian education, either in school or out. . . .

Hollywood's artistic ineptness and thematic shoddiness have become bywords, just as its glamour, extravagance, and technical excellence have. But until recently at least, criticism of motion pictures has been almost completely cancelled out by other considerations: the success of Hollywood's big-business tactics, the fact that motion pictures are accessible to most people and relatively inexpensive to see, and the function performed by the stars in satisfying an emotional need in many of their admirers for a life less humdrum than that of factory or home. All too often, Hollywood has capitalized on these conditions in such a way as to merit its reputation for maintaining the lowest common denominator in taste and values.

In spite of many (though not nearly enough) fine films, motion pictures have, in general, spread only the veneer of culture: sophistication in cosmetics, clothes, rackets, repartee; superficial, distorted history and biography. Yet the power of the motion picture is unquestioned. The amount of print devoted to stars and performances in books, newspapers, and magazines, year after year, is one tribute to its influence. The impact of movies on adolescents, as reported by Leo Rosten, the Lynds, and others, is another. Not only do children find in pictures the outward trappings of behavior—speech and gesture and costume; they find there, too, the values they attach to behavior.

The Hollywoodian view of America prevalent abroad is still another cause of widespread concern. The recent articles by Norman Cousins, Eric Johnston, and Samuel Goldwyn in the *Saturday Review of Literature* point up the special strategic and policy problems posed, in this era of the cold war, by the picture of American life and values created abroad by our motion pictures. Some readers of these articles may have felt that the controversy (understandably narrowed by considerations of the cold war) missed the heart of the matter; by concentrating on the overt subject matter of our films and on their surface representation of American life, the articles seemed to ignore both the artistic merit of films and the underlying values implied in their form and content. Those who followed the controversy and the resulting correspondence may have been left with the impression that Hollywood's virtue could be measured by the number of pictures dealing with the "right" subjects produced. Such a yardstick is ridiculous, of course. A good picture can deal with any subject under the sun; it is what is done with the subject that counts. Shoddy values and lack of artistic merit can, in the long run, have a more pernicious effect on our standing abroad, and on our own development, than failure to choose the "right" subjects.

But today the film companies are in trouble, not only artistically but commercially. With admission prices the highest ever and ability to buy tickets estimated at 50 percent higher than before the war, the Johnston office admits an 8.5 percent loss on film rentals between 1946 and 1948, and "The Film Daily Yearbook" reports a drop in box-office grosses of nearly 13 percent from 1948. Back in 1930, the "Yearbook" reported that 90 million tickets were being sold weekly, but its estimate for 1949 is only 70 million, or a loss of 22 percent during a period when the population increased by 20 percent or more. Audience Research, Incorporated, whose estimates of motion-picture attendance are consistently lower than those of the "Yearbook," places current weekly admissions at 62 million, a drop of almost 7 percent since 1948, and of almost 23 percent since 1946. It is estimated that 65 percent of the motion-picture audience is under 30 years of age, with attendance beginning to decline at 19. Some 65 million potential adult customers attend rarely or not at all. The Johnston office reports that motion pictures' share of every dollar spent for recreation by the American public has declined by one-third in the last twenty years.

In his public speeches, Mr. Johnston has been urging that more adult pictures be produced, while some intelligent producers, like Dorê Schary, continue to reiterate, with some justice, that since studios are in business to make a profit, not to improve the taste of the public, they cannot afford to make too many "good" pictures. Of course, studios have to show a profit, but there are still at least two replies to Mr. Schary's argument: (1) There have been many films which were both distinguished and profitable—"Hamlet," "Henry V," "The Life of Émile Zola," "The Snake Pit," "The Search," "The Story of Louis Pasteur," to name only a few—and the list of undistinguished films which failed to make a profit is a long one. (2) The motion-picture companies have used their booking monopoly to force their inferior productions on the exhibitors, but they have not applied the same power to place superior films on the market. Only rarely have they "taken a chance" and made superior pictures (usually based on a book or play which had already achieved unusual success), and then they have awarded themselves that popular Hollywoodian honorary degree—they are "pioneers." Today, there are several hopeful signs on the horizon—the end of block booking; the popularity of foreign films; Dorê Schary's advent as production chief at Metro-Goldwyn-Mayer; the possible passing of the double feature under pressure of television. But the industry, by and large, is still "playing it safe" by making so-called mass-appeal (synonymous with unintelligent) pictures. Only recently, for example, it was reported that Frank Capra and William Wyler, whose records as makers of profitable pictures are well above the average, have suggested several projects in a row to their studios, only to have them rejected as poor financial risks.

Anyone interested in understanding why we lack better films should read the articles by important Hollywood figures in *Variety's* recent anniversary issues. They are more illuminating than edifying. One contributor regards pictures as "products," in the same sense as automobiles, at the same time claiming that Hollywood movies are helping to make a better world. Another boasts loudly that Hollywood has the world's best creative brains. All, of course, write of the need for "quality," though there is little internal evidence that the word has a very precise definition. Usually it means more of the same financially successful productions that previous years have seen. Those who hope for change must look elsewhere.

Looking elsewhere, they will find that some excellent suggestions have been made. Recent recommendations have called on Hollywood film-makers to—

(1) Set aside some of their profits for experimentation and for prestige items, as many publishing houses and most large corporations do. ("Research laboratories" might prove unexpectedly profitable.)

(2) Organize a self-regulatory body to see to it that studios produce a certain percentage of pictures in the "public service" category, in the same way that radio stations devote a certain amount of time to such programs.

(3) Make low-budget adult films and see to it either that they are shown to the audience that wants them—perhaps by assigning two days a week to such films—or that they are exhibited with features of wide appeal, to attract a combined audience.

(4) Develop the talents of their own workers, by giving them a freer hand and by placing more emphasis on the creative aspects of film-making, less on the technological.

(5) Overcome their fears of pressure-groups, so that films will no longer have to run through a mill that reduces them to syrup before they reach the screen.

(6) Develop saner, more imaginative advertising and publicity.

To date, Hollywood seems to be turning a deaf ear to these suggestions.

There are two other courses of action to bring better films to our screens which might be taken within the present pattern of production and distribution:

(1) Group sponsorship of motion pictures. Plays backed by as many as eighty people have been produced, and these plays have included musicals with budgets of $300,000. Since many more pictures than plays make a profit, it ought to be much easier to find this kind of financing for films. It has already been done successfully

in France. With famous stars or directors taking the lead, it should be feasible to finance pictures on a profit-sharing basis, by means of stock-floating or subscription. Art film groups (to which, *Variety* reports, some 100,000 people belong) might serve as a nucleus for subscription campaigns. And wouldn't many thousands invest $5, $25, or more to be partners with a distinguished actor or director or writer in a film venture? A "serious" picture financed by thousands of people would have that many press agents publicizing it for months. Distributors would be foolish not to handle such a film.

(2) Film transcriptions of plays. The camera can make current theatrical offerings available to wide audiences, never reached by touring companies. By use of several cameras a certain amount of motion-picture technique could even be incorporated in these transcriptions. The production cost would be low, and audiences would receive more adult entertainment on the screen than they now get. Such a project would, of course, also mean additional revenue for the theatre.

Turning from the motion picture to the radio, we see that though the details of the situation are very different, the central problem remains the same: how to achieve better use of a technically magnificent instrument of mass communication.

According to a recent survey sponsored by the Radio Manufacturers' Association and the National Association of Radio Broadcasters, the American public owns more than 70 million radio sets. The Broadcast Management Bureau estimates that 94.2 percent of American families have at least one radio in working order. This is a very impressive percentage—far higher than the percentage of eligible voters participating in a national election, for example. The recent Lazarsfeld-Kendall survey ("Radio Listening in America") showed that 49 percent of the radio audience listens one to three hours an evening; 24 percent tune in four or more hours a night—all this in addition to daytime listening. Today radio is (and tomorrow television will be) the most pervasive means of mass communication. What do the American people hear over these millions of radio sets?

The programs available were recently surveyed by the Hutchins Commission on Freedom and Responsibility of the Press, Radio, and Movies. The results are far from reassuring: news analyses are available to only 40 percent of set-owners, and 90 percent of these analyses are by poorly qualified commentators; forums are within reach of only 15 percent for about one hour a week, and 50 percent of all forums are aired at poor listening times. The Hutchins Commission report agrees that the sum of radio drama is piddling, as is the educational value of radio, despite several University of the Air courses, a number of other worthwhile programs, and the work of such men as Sterling Fisher and Lyman Bryson. The National Association of Broadcasters admits that regular radio stations give no more than four percent of their time to educational or cultural programs, including forums and the like, while commercials occupy 14 percent of their time. And there can be little doubt that the commercials come at better listening hours.

Is the radio audience satisfied with the programs it is receiving? According to the Lazarsfeld-Kendall report already mentioned, 20 percent want more serious programs—and 20 percent of 70 million sets is 14 million. An audience of 14 million listeners is not inconsiderable. Some of the other findings of this report are illuminating. When people were asked to check the kinds of programs they liked, 30 percent checked classical music; 50 percent checked comedy; 40 percent, discussion of public issues; 70 percent, news. Although 26 percent said that they listened "for entertainment only," 52 percent—twice as many—said that they listened to entertainment *and* serious programs. These figures assume greater significance when we remind ourselves that program preferences depend on availability and that taste is conditioned. If "serious" programs were more numerous, more interesting, and scheduled more regularly and at better listening hours, they would probably find a much larger audience. But as long as "serious" or "public service" programs are considered the reverse of entertainment, they will be scheduled irregularly and at bad listening hours.

Recent recommendations for improving radio have included the following suggestions:

(1) Broadcasters should break the sponsor-agency grip on programs. As everyone knows, broadcasting in America is supported by advertising. But does that in itself mean that the programs must be poor? Do not nearly all newspapers and magazines carry advertising, too, and (in spite of some abuses) maintain a lively press? There is a significant difference. The newspapers and magazines are planned by editors and publishers to include advertising. Broad-

casts are planned by advertisers and their cohorts, the advertising agencies, to include entertainment. If broadcasters could plan their programs as a whole, and sell space to advertisers, as a newspaper does, it would mean much better-balanced programs.

(2) More and better forums, news commentary, and educational and documentary programs should be broadcast at regular hours when a large audience is available. The Federal Communications Commission could regulate not only the number of hours to be devoted to public service, but could also decide at what hours these programs are to occur. More thoughtful preparation could go into these programs. One sometimes hears a forum in which the speakers seem to have only a vague idea of what is expected of them or where they are going; a good moderator is not enough to make a good forum. Skilled planning and good hours might attract sponsors for such programs.

(3) Multiple programs should be broadcast from one station, where this is feasible and necessary to please listeners of different tastes.

(4) Minorities should be allocated more time at better hours.

(5) A clearinghouse should be set up for reporting good programs so that all stations can benefit from the advances of one.

Subscription radio—broadcasts to which a listener subscribes, as to a magazine—was briefly discussed a few years ago, but it did not develop. Now there are proposals to have radio stations sponsored by one or more of the great Foundations; perhaps something will come of this. At one time there were between 176 and 202 educational radio stations operating in the United States (estimates vary), but during the depression the number dropped to between 30 and 35. Since the end of World War II there has been a minor renaissance; and there are now well over 100 in operation, though many have inadequate frequencies or power assignments, or operate only a few hours a day. There is no available estimate of the size of their combined audience, but, in terms of the total listening public, it cannot be very large. Educational radio stations represent slightly more than three percent of the total number. Their influence on the industry exceeds their numbers, however, because of the stimulus they offer to commercial stations.

The Allerton House Report (the report of a conference sponsored last summer by the Rockefeller Foundation in conjunction with the Institute of Communications at the University of Illinois) urges educational institutions to enter into mass education by means of radio and television, with Foundation, commercial, or governmental aid.

A new medium that promises to have an even greater mass appeal than either radio or motion pictures and that even now presents the same kind of problems they have presented is television.

Already there are 103 stations and half a dozen more under construction. New sets are being bought at the rate of four or five hundred thousand a month; the nearly six million sets already purchased are used by many times that number of people; more than 60 percent of the nation is already within range of television signals. It is expected that within five years—some think within three years—more than half the families in America will own television receivers. As soon as the FCC lifts the "freeze" on allocation of licenses (which it imposed in 1948 to permit planning of allocations in order to avoid interference among stations) the building of new stations will go into high gear. The twelve Very High Frequency channels can accommodate 499 stations, and the 42 Ultra High Frequency channels theoretically can make room for 1682 more. But the number that come into being will be sharply limited by the fact that it requires a fairly large population to support a television station. Many that are built will be so-called satellite stations, which will not originate programs but will simply reproduce signals from other stations.

Television will almost certainly be even more centralized than radio, because fewer stations will be operating and greater expense will be involved in creating original programs. Television will, in time, replace radio as the mammoth of the mass media, and as a visual medium it will wield more power, displacing, in part at least, the motion-picture theatre, at the same time perhaps invading the motion-picture screen itself. Subscription television, or "phonevision," now being experimented with in the Chicago area, may eventually bring unsponsored film programs into the home on a box-office basis. But even these may be sandwiched between commercials. Meanwhile, the new medium has been following closely the sponsor-agency pattern of radio. Although the National Broadcasting Company recently announced plans for regular educational telecasts, and some adult programs are already being presented, apparently the values of television will, in general, parallel those of radio. A recent article on television in *Fortune* touched not at all on such minutiae as taste, culture, and education.

Last April, Mr. Edward Lamb, who owns television stations in Erie, Pennsylvania, and Columbus, Ohio, contributed an article to the Sunday *Times* on the state of television. "What control does an aroused nation have over this rapidly growing enterprise?" he asked, and answered his own question: "Actually, very little."

Mr. Lamb continues:

The Federal Communications Commission is barred by Congress and by court decisions from regulating the program content of radio and television stations. To be sure, the F.C.C. does have authority to refuse to renew licenses where the broadcaster has not programmed "in the public interest," but few, if any, licenses ever have been canceled on that ground alone. The United States District Court at Philadelphia recently ruled that a state is also without authority to control programs traveling in interstate commerce by coaxial cable or by micro-relay.

Since state and national regulatory bodies are impotent to force programming in the public interest, the TV broadcasters have practically no accountability to anyone. There are TV stations in the United States, especially in the areas where there is only a single station, which simply "sit on the coaxial cable" and have no local or public service programming whatsoever.

In the last analysis the only control over the programs sent into the homes of millions of Americans rests pretty largely in the "consciences" of the private owners of these video stations. In them alone rests a power of thought control, possibly a power of influencing people greater than that ever before vested in any other medium.

Mr. Lamb suggests in conclusion that we "safeguard the cultural standards of our economy" by improved programming and by making available to non-profit organizations facilities for programs in the public interest. "Indeed," he declares, "such a program might well preserve the private system of broadcasting in the United States."

In any discussion of the shortcomings of mass communication, there is one myth which is certain to appear. This is the notion that the motion pictures and the radio offer "what the public wants." "After all," apologists ask, "the public casts its votes at the box-office and in the Hooper survey, doesn't it?" The answer is yes—but a severely qualified yes. In the first place, as facts mentioned earlier in this article indicate, many people refrain from voting. Not all the people who rarely or never go to the motion pictures are invalids, blind, or indigent. Some of them—perhaps a great many of them, perhaps millions—stay away because they do not want what the motion-picture theatre has to offer them. So it is with radio. Though half the potential audience listens one to three hours a night, and though 24 percent listen four hours or more, that still leaves slightly over a quarter who own radios but listen less than an hour or not at all. Clearly, there must be millions of people who sit next to a radio every night and do not bother to turn it on. That it offers nothing they want to hear suggests itself as an explanation. When the sponsors of mass entertainment fail to take into account these millions who refrain from voting at the box-office or at the dial, they are not only misrepresenting to themselves what the public wants; they are losing money.

Furthermore, those who express preferences cannot go very far beyond what they are already receiving. A listener who wants *more* symphonic music must already have heard *some* symphonic music. Nor is it likely that he will ask for more if he has heard only a little bit. The good as well as the not-so-good requires more than one exposure to catch on; if the radio must reiterate the virtues of a toothpaste or a cigarette hundreds of times in the course of a year in order to make people remember it, perhaps it could repeat something worth remembering a few times before declaring that the public is unresponsive.

My proposal for a method of improving these means of mass communication is a group of projects sponsored by the government. Before the reader cries out in despair at the prospect of more government enterprises, let me remind him once more that responsible sources tell us that nearly 95 percent of all Americans have radios available. Do 95 percent go to high school? Yet we have long believed that public support of formal education is desirable and necessary. Do 95 percent use public libraries, or even have public libraries available? Yet we pay taxes for libraries. In essence, what I suggest is a kind of cultural TVA, for mass communication and entertainment are a "public utility," perhaps of even more far-reaching consequences than electric power. The development of a nation's taste and intelligence, its cultural, spiritual, emotional, and social nourishment is a matter of public concern.

I do not in any way suggest that the government take over these means of mass communication. We do not want the radio to give us only the voice of George Orwell's Big Brother, or the motion-picture screen to give us only his face. The question is: do we dare leave radio to the Big Brother of the advertising agencies? do we dare leave the screen to the Big Brother of the producers? The program I propose is a program designed to introduce a new and much-needed element into these means of mass communication—to prevent, rather than to create, monopoly, and to help private enterprise to do a better job.

For the motion pictures, what is needed, in my opinion, is a National Film Commission to promote and, if necessary, to produce films of greater artistic merit and richer social content. This Commission would consist of the best creative Hollywood craftsmen (such as John Ford, John Huston, Elia Kazan, Dudley Nichols, Dorê Schary), documentary film-makers (such as Flaherty and Lorentz), film critics (such as Bosley Crowther and James Agee), and representatives from the other arts (such men, say, as Robert Penn Warren, Lionel Trilling, Arthur Miller, Kermit Bloomgarden, Brooks Atkinson, William Faulkner, Edmund Wilson), as well as men from the fields of education, psychology, the social and physical sciences, and philosophy. (Does this sound too conglomerate a group to function effectively? It is no more heterogeneous than the personnel of a major studio.)

This Commission would invite submissions of film stories, scenarios, novels, plays, much as a major production company does. It would then recommend projects for production and offer them to commercial producers on a competitive bidding basis, as authors' agents do now, with the proviso that the spirit of the work must be adhered to. (At present, a few writers of great prestige are able to make such demands. In suitable circumstances, the Commission could protect other writers in the same way.) If no commercial company wished to produce a recommended film, the Commission would arrange to have the film produced with government funds, hiring personnel and leasing studio facilities in Hollywood and arranging for distribution through a regular commercial distributor. The Commission would own no studios; it would produce pictures with leased equipment, and that only as a last resort; nor would it be in direct competition with private industry, since it would produce only those pictures which private industry could not or would not produce.

What would such a Commission accomplish? First, it would bring to bear on Hollywood an outside cultural influence badly needed. Second, it would undoubtedly increase the number of superior films produced by Hollywood itself. If 25 to 50 superior films were produced each year, some through the work of the Commission, others by Hollywood working independently, the effect on the audience would be appreciable. Children would develop slightly higher standards, more mature values, and greater social awareness. The entire process of improving taste (which Dorê Schary, in a recent interview, said the studios could afford only on a limited scale) would be accelerated. In short, Mr. Schary and other intelligent movie-makers would be aided in their desire to make more good films. Third, through the medium of some of these feature films we would be enabled to achieve important educational and informational goals, creating mass awareness and understanding of specific problems. In essence, what this amounts to is a national film bill to parallel Representative Javits' national theatre bill.

To obviate the possibility of the Commission's controlling the movies or setting up in permanent competition with Hollywood, a ceiling would be placed on the number of films it could finance, in part or whole, limiting it to a small proportion of the total product. Precautions should be taken, by putting membership in the Commission on a rotating basis, to prevent the domination of one taste or bias year after year and, by carefully designed legislation, to prevent political control of the motion-picture industry. This plan would not be expensive. An annual allotment of as little as fifty cents per capita would provide enough money to produce 50 to 60 feature films. The returns from the exhibition of the films might cover most of this. Indeed, the Commission might actually make a cash profit, and the profit to the nation as a whole is certain. (The Commission might also serve as a central clearinghouse for all educational films being produced, so as to avoid current duplication, except when it is desired in order to develop better presentation methods. A basic plan for the production of films to be used in education could be set up and Hollywood companies encouraged to enter the field.)

When it comes to television, I would suggest that one channel be set aside for non-commercial entertainment, educational and documentary purposes, with programs to be supplied by a combination of private groups and government, and an administrator and advisory commission managing this national network. Financing of both programs and stations might well be on a multiple basis, with state and local governments, private foundations, universities, and other non-commercial groups all participating, and the federal government subsidizing the entire affair through a "grant-in-aid" or similar system.

The production of programs by United Nations Radio and their broadcasting by the National Broadcasting Company and other networks (as well as local stations, using transcriptions) is an interesting example of government sponsorship with commercial collaboration. The programs are an outstanding example of the fine material which should reach the airwaves more often.

Through a national pool of programming, the network I propose would be able to attract fine creative talent and first-rate technical and administrative personnel, such as no isolated non-commercial station could afford. Only programs which commercial networks refused to telecast regularly at good viewing hours would be used. And, should a sponsor wish to underwrite a program for telecasting on a commercial network, his offer would naturally be welcomed, provided he did not change the format or subject matter, and control of the program remained in the hands of its creators. Thus commercial telecasters would profit by having better programs and by reaching a more selective audience.

Such a national television network would gradually educate and improve public taste by exposing it to superior programs, just as manufacturers "upgrade" their customers to buy and demand a better product by exposing them repeatedly to it. Craftsmen would be encouraged to experiment and work on ideas and programs in which they strongly believed, so that we might see a true development of the potentialities of the medium.

In each local area there might well be initiated a pooling of governmental and private funds and effort to erect a non-commercial television station, eventually to be part of this network. The cost of this entire program would be negligible in relation to its values. Fifty cents per capita would provide enough money to run 150 to 200 television stations.

Meanwhile, the FCC should immediately reserve one channel until a decision is made on possible governmental entry into the field, or until private groups can raise funds to build and operate stations. Already the channels on the Very High Frequency band are exhausted in the major cities. The FCC must not let all the Ultra High Frequencies fall into commercial hands. (Should Ultra High Frequencies prove impracticable, current licensees could be reimbursed and the airwaves reclaimed for public use. Naturally, if radio remains a potent force, a parallel national radio network should also be established.)

A National Film Commission and a National Television and Radio Network are not panaceas, nor need they be idealistic dreams. They cannot be brought into being nor operate effectively unless an organized, intelligent, discriminating audience takes the lead in pressing for improvement (*not* censorship) of our mass media. To date, the audience has defaulted. But we must realize that the owners of the mass media, for all their talk of "pure entertainment," desire the approval of the vocal, well-educated minority. Organized audience action can achieve results both within the existing pattern and in reshaping that pattern. To help assure an aware, appreciative, critical audience for the future, one might well add a third point to this program: the introduction of a basic course on mass media into the school curriculum.

Most of us are, as usual, involved in the daily round and in the burning issues of the moment, to the exclusion of more fundamental and far-reaching problems. The problem of mass media is both crucial and central. The time for action is now. And there is much to be done. Given sufficient public reaction, the governmental measures suggested here could in time become a reality, an integral part of our democratic system. But silence and inaction mean tacit acquiescence, defeat by default. And unless we act soon to reform our mass media, they will almost certainly succeed in wholly deforming us.

PROBLEMS

1. Analyze *your own radio listening or television seeing for one day* by making the following breakdown (possibly using the newspaper radio-television log as a memory aid):

   a. How many programs were of local origin? How many were network hours?

   b. How many programs were sponsored by advertisers? By big "national" advertisers? By local advertisers? How many hours were not sponsored by advertisers?

   c. How many hours were devoted to entertainment? How many hours were not primarily intended to entertain, e.g., news, commentaries, forums, educational programs, events in the public interest?

   d. At what times was "high quality" material offered (e.g., symphonic music, United Nations broadcasts, forums, mature drama)? At what times was "low quality" material offered (e.g., "soap operas," crime serials, popular music, comic shows, vaudeville, "give-away" quiz shows)? [Note: the editors are here following the widely accepted meanings of "high quality" and "low quality" without necessarily subscribing or asking you to subscribe to these definitions.]

2. There are many reasons for going to movies. They include:

   a. To see a particular star

   b. To get away from a humdrum task

   c. To see a particular type of movie: Western, crime, mystery, comedy, musical, war picture, historical romance

   d. To see a picture of special interest to you because you have lived in a certain area that is the locale of the film, because you know someone in the picture, because you are interested in animals, or because it portrays an experience you have lived through

   e. To see the dramatization of a book you have read

   f. To see evidence of technical skills, e.g., photography, musical effects, dancing, acting, direction, set-design, costume-design

   g. To see the treatment of some important controversial issue, e.g., race, migratory workers, postwar problems and adjustments

   h. To familiarize yourself with a different set of mores, i.e., attitudes toward sex, crime, family, the United States, as reflected in foreign films

   i. To see bold, imaginative, unconventional treatment of seemingly commonplace ideas, as in, e.g., "The Bicycle Thief," "The Baker's

Wife," "The Informer," "The Long Voyage Home," "The Lonely One," "The Search," "Monsieur Verdoux," "The Fallen Idol"

When your motive in going was item *a*, *b*, or *c*, did you usually find that you got what you went for? When your motive was *d*, *e*, or *f*? When your motive was *g*, *h*, or *i*?

Do your answers to these questions support Klein's contention that Hollywood's offerings are shoddy, meeting "the lowest common denominator in taste and values"?

3. How do Klein's figures on the number of people who "stay away from" movies and radio indicate a failure of *inductive* thinking on the part of those movie and radio producers who say, "We give the public what it wants"?

4. What error in *deduction* is made by those who say, "People who listen to this stuff must not want 'better things' or they'd ask for it"?

5. Advertising men recognize the power of repetition in selling their merchandise. How might one apply the same principle to the problem of elevating the taste of the general public? What error does any one of us make by concluding after a few attempts—a handful of symphonies and forums, a low-budget picture without advertising "hoopla"—that you can't raise the public's taste?

6. How do the present upset conditions in radio and the movies, brought on by television, create possible opportunities for improving all three media?

7. What do you think of Klein's proposals to improve radio, television, and movie fare? What possible dangers lie in these suggestions? What are the dangers in "doing nothing about it" and ignoring these or other suggestions for improvement?

GENERAL PROBLEMS: *Evaluating the Mass Media of Communication*

1. Assume that you are publicity chairman of an organization that wishes to persuade non-members in your community to attend your Little Theater production, support the Community Chest, vote bonds for a certain civic undertaking, support a local initiative measure on the ballot, vote for a certain candidate for office, or some such thing. On the basis of your knowledge of the community and what you have learned about present-day mass media, plan your publicity campaign. In your planning consider the following specific questions, as well as any others that need to be answered in solving your general problem:

a. What kinds of people is each medium most likely to reach in your community? (People with what economic and social status? political, moral, and religious attitudes? vocations? national backgrounds? special interests? group prejudices, "blind spots"?) What will be the size of the groups?

b. What groups do you need to reach in order to gain your objective?

c. What does each of the groups you wish to reach *expect* from the medium it most frequently uses? (Broad or more sophisticated humor? sentimental entertainment? sensationalism? experimental or orthodox handling? information? serious argument?)

d. In the light of the main characteristics of each group you have decided to reach, what grounds for appealing for the group's support seem most practical?

e. Are there special factors which may require consideration in your mapping of a campaign, e.g., distraction of group's attention by other events? expense? possible opposition that might make it difficult for your side to get a hearing?

In handling this problem realistically you will need to think in terms of a specific organization, a definite belief or action which you will promote, and a particular community. Also, you will get most out of this problem if, after putting yourself in the position of the publicity man, that is, the propagandist, you shift your attitude and consider your data in the light of what you are likely to be most of your life: part of the potential audience that the propagandist, no matter what his program is, will want to reach and influence.

2. Bainbridge has described what he believes to be the formula used by the most widely distributed magazine in the world today. Now, can you find the basic formula which *your* favorite magazine, or your second choice if your favorite happens to be *The Reader's Digest,* follows? You can find this formula if you investigate at least four issues and look systematically for evidence of repetition in subject-matter, in kinds of group-appeal, in methods of presenting material, in ideas and attitudes given a warm or cool reception, in the mixture of entertainment and information, in the mixture of fact and opinion, and so forth. You can find it if, while avoiding a mechanical listing of details, you also do not overlook details which, taken along with other details, may point to an important element in the magazine's formula; for instance, rather obvious jokes in a joke column may not be significant alone but *may* be a further clue if you also find the cartoons simple, the treatment of scientific subjects "popular" or sensational, and the fiction uncomplicated. To be more specific still, one criticism of one prominent Democrat or of one Democratic Party idea

is no proof that the magazine is regularly anti-Democratic, but if you also find other unfriendly portraits of Democratic leaders, articles that attack parts of the Democratic Party's program and more frequently support Republican Party stands, then you have probably discovered *one* of the magazine's formulas, namely, opposition to the Democratic Party and the ideas it represents.

Do not worry about the possibility of your magazine's not having a formula. The chances against its lacking a formula are tremendous, for a magazine, if it is to survive, *must* have a policy, that is, it must have decided what groups of readers it will aim for and what sorts of ammunition it will use. Magazines may differ in the number of different reader-types they try to reach and in their ingenuity in varying the offerings within the formula, but they will certainly try to decide who their readers will be and what is needed to satisfy them. In this connection, do not be misled by the example provided above into ignoring appeals and formulas other than the purely political. Some magazines, for instance, base their formulas on being "nonpolitical."

3. Compare today's issues of two newspapers in their presentation of *a single news event* involving a controversial issue of local, state, national, or international importance, e.g., American foreign policy, bills in Congress, taxes, wage demands, cost of living, government expenditures, loyalty probes, Communism, military policy, government economic controls, socialized medicine, or any local community problem on which there are opposed points of view. The following questions may provide a practical basis for the comparison:

a. Do you find any significant difference in the *headlines* as to size, aspect of story presented in them, and their use of the language of report and opinion?

b. Do you find that the papers *in their news columns* cover the same facts relating to this controversy, or do they tend to give different sets of facts? If you find such a difference, how do you account for it? Is there any difference in the amount of attention given to the various groups of facts? Do you find any difference in the order of presentation?

c. Do you find that the papers differ appreciably as to the amount of space and position given to the news stories connected with the controversy? Are there any signs of "burying" or "playing up" any particular news stories because they might hurt or help one side?

d. Is there any use of "colored" or "loaded" language in these news reports in each paper? If you find it, what difference in opinion does it suggest?

e. Do your answers to these questions indicate that one or both of the papers are using news events as propaganda for a point of view?

Does a further examination of the two papers, their handling of other news stories, their headlines, their placement of news, their editorials and syndicated columns, suggest possible reasons for any variation you noted in the news accounts?

4. You have probably noticed that in these last two sections of *Think Before You Write* the propaganda-channels of facts and ideas given most attention are the newspapers, magazines, movies, and radio. This would seem, by implication, to give *books* a minor role in influencing men's ideas and conduct, instead of the major role traditionally attributed to them, especially by educators. Hummel and Huntress, however, suggest several very important points that must not be forgotten, namely, the *nature* of the book-reading part of the public, the strength of the influence of books on book-readers, and the relative importance of the effects of these people's ideas and actions upon other men. But, before allowing ourselves to be swung over to the view that the special nature of books and book-readers cancels out the advantage of numbers on the side of the mass media, we might also note that the mass media are of very recent origin, that until the last 100 years books were almost the only vehicle for transmitting facts and ideas. It might be that they are rapidly losing importance with the development of other means of communication.

If you are interested in thinking through this question of the relative significance of books as a means of influencing human behavior, the most practical place to start would be with your own book-reading. A simple, introspective survey will not give sufficient grounds for a *final* answer to this question of book influence versus influence of other media, but it may lead you to change some of your assumptions about your own reading and thinking.

First, list *all* the books (not regular class textbooks) you can remember reading during the past six months, or longer, if you can go further back. Then, on the basis of this list, set down the following factual data:

a. Number of books whose contents you remember clearly? less clearly? not at all?

b. Number of books that were light, quickly-read fiction ("hammock reading")? more complex, serious fiction of ideas? non-fiction on controversial subjects? biographies and autobiographies? travel writing? humor? mainly pictures (photography, cartoons)? technical writing (physics, welding, zoology, dietetics, psychology)? history? plays? poetry? philosophy?

c. Number of books which effectively changed your mind on some point? Number of such books which were primarily factual? more emotional in their appeal? Number of books which changed your mind just a little? Number of such books which were mainly factual? more emotional in their appeal?

On the basis of this limited survey, answer the following questions: How big an influence on *your* judgment do books seem to have in comparison to the influence of the daily newspapers, magazines, radio broadcasts, television shows, and motion pictures? Does the influence of books seem to be mainly in certain fields? Does it seem to be as strong or deep as the influence of the mass media? stronger? In your case, do books appear to be losing out to the mass media?

5. Perhaps, like many another student of propaganda and the present media of communication, you have thought, "Yes, I can now see how the propagandist operates, especially how he depends on my not analyzing his statements and so swallowing all he says. But, even though I know I'm being fooled (and even *how* I'm being fooled!), what can I do about it, on the positive side, if I do not have the *time* to check on the facts in other sources and to investigate other points of view? I can't read *everything*, keep up with all the movies, listen to many different broadcasts. It's all just too hard to do!" Possibly your despondency was caused, not by pressure of time, but by other limiting conditions, such as your not having enough money to buy several papers, lack of public library facilities, your town's having only one daily paper (or two papers owned by one man), or the obvious difficulty of tuning in on more than one radio network at a time.

You have real reason for concern over any of these obstacles, but are you acting wisely if you go on to conclude, without further investigation of ways to get over them, that they are insurmountable?

Survey all the things you might do to get more facts and varying points of view under one of the following conditions: (a) if your problem seems to be mainly one of "not enough time"; (b) if the main difficulty lies in your not having enough money for papers, magazines, books; (c) if you have neither library facilities nor your own ways of getting papers; (d) if your principal difficulty stems from such limitations as a local news monopoly, lack of variety in motion picture offerings, and narrow reception on your radio set.

6. In an unemotional way outline the specific features of the mass media in two hypothetical communities: (1) an ideal situation in which the main means of communication are used to the fullest extent as democratic channels for public information and argument, and (2) a deplorable situation in which the mass media are used undemo-

cratically to contribute to public misinformation and ignorance of more than just one set of facts and opinions. Such a summary may help you to see more clearly the *potentialities* of our present mass media for both social and antisocial ends. In setting down these two lists, you have all of the articles and problems in the last two sections of the book to draw from for ideas, so it is not nearly so formidable a task as it may at first appear. Moreover, this problem will test both your *understanding of* and your *skill in applying* the ideas of these last two sections. It's the proof of the pudding!

Now, find where your own community lies, probably between these extremes, these two ends of the scale. In taking this final step be careful to apply to the existing situation the same specific, stable criteria you used in creating your hypothetical desirable and undesirable situations.